School Reform
The Critical Issues

*The Hoover Institution
gratefully acknowledges generous support from*

KORET FOUNDATION

in the publication of this volume.

School Reform
The Critical Issues

Edited by
**Williamson M. Evers, Lance T. Izumi,
and Pamela A. Riley**

HOOVER INSTITUTION PRESS
Stanford University
Stanford, California

PACIFIC RESEARCH INSTITUTE
San Francisco, California

Hoover Institution Press Publication No. 499

Copyright ©2001 by the Board of Trustees of the
    Leland Stanford Junior University
All rights reserved. No part of this publication may be reproduced, stored in a retrieval system, or transmitted in any form or by any means, electronic, mechanical, photocopying, recording, or otherwise, without written permission of the publisher.

Pages 431–435 constitute an extension of this copyright page.

First printing, 2001
07 06 05 04 03 02 01 00   9 8 7 6 5 4 3 1

Manufactured in the United States of America

The paper used in this publication meets the minimum requirements of the American National Standard for Information Sciences—Permanence of Paper for Printed Library Materials, ANSI Z39.48–1984.

Library of Congress Cataloging-in-Publication Data

School reform: the critical issues / edited by Williamson M. Evers, Lance T. Izumi, and Pamela A. Riley
        p. cm.—(Hoover Institution Press publication; no. 499)
    ISBN 0-8179-2872-3 (alk. paper)
    1. School improvement programs—United States. 2. Educational change—United States.
I. Evers, Williamson M., 1948– II. Izumi, Lance T., 1958– III. Riley, Pam. IV. Hoover Institution on War, Revolution, and Peace. V. Hoover Institution Press publication; 499.
LB2822.82 .S372 2001
371.2'07—dc21
                                              2001039650

Contents

Acknowledgments

The editors wish to thank the Hoover Institution and the Pacific Research Institute for backing this joint project. Without the collaborative spirit fostered by John Raisian, the director of the Hoover Institution, and Sally Pipes, the director of the Pacific Research Institute, this undertaking would not have been possible. The editors gratefully acknowledge the generous support this publication received from the Koret Foundation and its board of directors and staff. Tad Taube, president of the Koret Foundation, was instrumental in proposing this collaborative effort. For copyediting and supervising the physical production of the book, we must thank staff at the Hoover Institution Press and its executive editor, Patricia Baker, together with Publication Services of Champaign, Illinois, and cover designer Andrew Ogus.

We also thank Barbara Schatz and Kate Feinstein for providing assistance on this project, and, in particular, we thank K. Gwynne Coburn of the Pacific Research Institute for coordinating the production of the manuscript.

Introduction

Although an increasing number of states and school districts are adopting a variety of education reform programs, too many of these so-called reforms are based on political palatability rather than on whether they will actually increase student achievement. Increased per-pupil spending, smaller class sizes, more technology in the classroom, and national certification of teachers may be relatively easy for political and education decisionmakers to propose and enact, but there is little evidence that such measures have more than a minor impact on improving the ability of students to read, write, or do math.

In order to effect real and long-lasting change, it is necessary to understand the basic nature of our education problems and the remedies that address them. This anthology seeks to accomplish these important objectives.

A joint undertaking of the Hoover Institution and the Pacific Research Institute for Public Policy, *School Reform: The Critical Issues* assembles some of the most insightful and provocative articles on education reform in recent years. The subjects covered touch such critical areas as teaching and classroom methodology, testing, special education, school choice, and many others. The articles state the problems realistically and then propose reasonable and effective alternatives.

For example, in the first selection on progressive education, two articles by *Los Angeles Times* reporter Richard Lee Colvin discuss the nature and pitfalls of the education philosophy that is so popular in university schools of education. In the first, Colvin describes the views of Alfie Kohn, one of the most visible proponents of progressive education, whose anti-testing, anti-grading, pro-student-self-esteem message is popular among many educators. In the second, Colvin describes a Berkeley, California elementary school that has implemented many of the progressive ideas supported by Kohn and others, with disastrous results. In the same section, renowned education author E.D. Hirsch, Jr., outlines a more traditional and empirically supportable alternative teaching strategy.

The section on teachers reveals some of the shortcomings surrounding the profession, with Sol Stern on the stifling effect of teacher unions, Maribeth Vander Weele on the difficulty in firing bad teachers, and Heather Mac Donald on why teachers are ineffective. These are followed by articles about real change, such as Siobahan Gorman's piece on teacher evaluation and Diane Ravitch's article on testing teachers. In another section, Chester Finn, Jr., and Michael Petrilli analyze the downsides of reducing class size, while William Capps and Mary Ellen Maxwell explain why it is better to have smaller schools.

Overall, then, this book will give the reader, whether he or she is a legislator, school board member, teacher, member of the media, or parent, an understanding of why schools and students are underperforming. It will also explain why some reforms are destined to be disappointments whereas others have been proven to work. The editors hope that the lessons contained in the articles in this volume will inform the continuing debate over education reform. It must be emphasized that these are not just academic lessons. The prospects of our students depend heavily on the kind of education policy we adopt. The goal of the book is to guide policymakers and the public in decisions that will not just promise change but actually deliver results that ensure a brighter future for our children.

School Reform
The Critical Issues

TEACHING APPROACHES

PROGRESSIVE EDUCATION

. . . .

School Reforms Hinder Learning, Crusader Argues

Richard Lee Colvin

This selection first appeared in the *Los Angeles Times* on 22 February 2000. Richard Lee Colvin is an education writer for the *Los Angeles Times*.

Conventional wisdom says schools will improve by imposing tough new standards on students.

Nonsense, says author Alfie Kohn, a popular speaker among parent and teacher groups.

How about testing children and holding them back if they don't measure up?

Child abuse, Kohn retorts.

A high school exit exam? Ranking schools by performance? Rewarding schools, teachers, and students who succeed?

Hogwash, hogwash, hogwash, says Kohn.

So, to sum up, Kohn, a former teacher and prolific author, thinks that every major effort to improve California's public schools is, to put it mildly, misguided and will make things worse instead of better.

Kohn's decidedly contrarian views might be dismissed as the ravings of an education radical. But as parents start to see how the education reforms of the last few years change what their children learn and how they are taught, as it becomes apparent that many students may be held back a grade or denied a diploma, objections are surfacing nationwide.

"I'm not alone," Kohn said. "A lot of parents get it. It's the people who have the power who don't."

3

Indeed, with governors and legislatures turning up the heat on schools to get better with a steady press of tougher standards, tests, and school rankings, Kohn's rants are resonating with mainstream audiences at schools, PTA meetings, and education conferences that are troubled by the reforms.

To be sure, polls show strong support for standards among parents. They also detect misgivings.

The American Association of School Administrators polled 750 parents across the country last fall and found that 42% believed that children were spending too much time taking tests and 78% thought that standardized testing was making teachers teach to the test.

Kohn is not the only one to give voice to the growing uneasiness with what reform has wrought. Jerome T. Murphy, dean of the Harvard Graduate School of Education, said states need to slow their march to standards to deal with such issues.

"We're getting closer to the point where there are going to be very, very serious consequences in terms of kids not getting high school diplomas and kids being left back," he said.

But Kohn, with a flair for the provocative, is a highly visible exponent. On his Web site (www.alfiekohn.org), hundreds of parents share their misgivings about reforms that have taken hold across the country. The parent of a fifth-grader from Virginia complains about standards that are "unfair, unreasonable and . . . promote memorization as the only means to survive."

A parent and school board member in Wisconsin bemoans that preparing for and taking tests means that children lose time for "discussing, cooperating, playing, experimenting, creating and enjoying themselves." A school administrator from Irvine writes that, like Kohn, she thinks that standards "demean students and teachers alike."

Recognizing the potential for grass-roots resistance to derail the decade-old standards movement, U.S. Secretary of Education Richard W. Riley on Tuesday will devote his annual "State of American Education" speech to ways to head off a backlash.

Energetic Speeches

Kohn nurtures this nascent backlash by traveling the country to give high-energy—his critics say shrill—speeches and peddle his books. In March, he has nine engagements, including several near his home outside Boston and others in Chicago, Atlanta, San Francisco and, on March 2, Cal State Northridge.

Other authors plow the same ground. But Kohn is taking it a step further, trying to organize a resistance movement. Via the Internet, he's working with allies in thirty-seven states to organize boycotts of standardized tests, which have occurred in Ohio, Michigan, and Colorado, and protest the publishing of scores in newspapers.

"The pressure to raise scores and everything to do with accountability is squeezing the intellectual life out of classrooms," Kohn said during a recent two-day swing through California. "What's being proposed to fix the problems of schools, at best, doesn't address the underlying causes and, at worst, makes them worse."

Such comments infuriate officeholders working to translate Americans' strong dissatisfaction with public schools into policy.

After Kohn spoke to the state school board association of Wisconsin in January, Gov. Tommy G. Thompson, one of the most visible governors in the standards movement, castigated him.

"It's unconscionable to stand before the students of this state and tell them they don't need to be tested, don't need to meet standards of excellence," Thompson said. "We owe them that, because life will not be getting any easier for them once they leave our schools."

Thompson's reforms have met resistance from Kohn and likeminded constituents. In a battle that Kohn touts on his Web site as a triumph for democracy, parents from Whitefish Bay led a successful campaign to persuade the legislature to back down from requiring students beginning in 2003 to pass a rigorous high school exit exam.

At the heart of the reform movement that Kohn and his allies oppose are standards for what students need to know in a given subject. Forty-nine states have adopted standards for at least one subject, most within the last three years. Forty-one test their students' knowledge of those standards, according to a survey by *Education Week*.

In 1997, California adopted standards in math, language arts, science, and social studies that are among the most detailed—and rigorous—in the nation. Starting the next year, all public school students were required to take the SAT 9 standardized test. Those scores will be factored into a number of high-stakes decisions, from promoting a student to the next grade to ranking schools by performance.

One state where politicians are hearing complaints is Virginia. The state's standards call on fifth-graders to know about such early American cultures as the Anasazi and to be able to explain the "motivations, obstacles and accomplishments" of major expeditions from Spain, France, Portugal, and England.

How students perform on tests in the third, fifth, and eighth grades affects whether they are promoted and eventually will determine whether they graduate.

Paul Montgomery, a training executive with an apple processing company in Stephens City, Va., said his daughter got an A in social studies last year. But she failed the state's exam, which he said showed that the test was arbitrary and unconnected to what is being taught.

"You don't know what you missed, all you get is this score and there's no opportunity for follow-up," said Montgomery, who shared his frustration on Kohn's Web site. "It just looks to me like the government had a good idea and then has created a monster, a very ugly monster."

Changes in the Classroom

Marty Guthrie, mother of a kindergartner, a fourth-grader, and a seventh-grader in Arlington, Va., a suburb of Washington, D.C., said she has seen changes in their classrooms since the state's Standards of Learning were introduced.

She bemoans the disappearance of the "writer's workshop," during which her fourth-grade daughter and her peers used to share their poems and essays. Most lessons have become more structured.

"During conferences with the kids' teachers what comes up time and again is that, 'We're doing this because of the standards' or that 'We can't do that because it's not in the standards test,'" she said.

As parents start to fret over the reforms and their consequences, along comes Kohn with his criticisms "and they really resonate," Murphy said.

Philosophically, Kohn, 42, is allied with the "progressive" wing of education.

Intellectual offspring of the philosopher John Dewey, progressives believe that schools should be democratic and shaped primarily by the curiosity of students rather than a static curriculum. In addition, like the Swiss psychologist Jean Piaget, they think of learning as a two-way process in which children "construct" knowledge from their experiences rather than simply absorb what they are told.

"This does not mean we don't teach fractions, but we don't teach fractions or history or grammar except in the context of real questions that kids want to ask," he told parents in San Francisco. "If they're not nested in questions that they ask, and want to answer, they won't remember them."

After teaching briefly in private schools, Kohn began working as a freelance journalist. His books decry competition, grades, praise or incentives of any type to motivate working or learning. His most recent book is *The Schools Our Children Deserve: Moving Beyond Traditional Classrooms and "Tougher Standards"* (Houghton Mifflin Co., 1999).

In that book he complains that standards and tests require schools to adopt what he calls the "bunch 'o facts" philosophy of teaching, to the detriment of thinking and understanding.

Fact-Based Teaching

The main target of Kohn's ire is E.D. Hirsch, Jr., a University of Virginia English professor who in 1996 published a book with a similar title—*The Schools Our Children Need*—that argues the opposite point of view. In a series of books that began with *Cultural Literacy* in 1987, Hirsch asserts that, indeed, there is a body of knowledge that children need to learn to succeed in the world.

"Facts are pretty important, that's what I'm for, definitely," Hirsch said in response to Kohn's "bunch 'o facts" description. The reason, he said, is that there is a high correlation between students' "breadth of knowledge" and achievement. The relationship between knowledge and performance in school as well as after leaving school is twice as strong, according to research quoted by Hirsch, as the relationship between family income and performance.

More affluent students, he argues, pick that knowledge up informally at home. Less affluent students, having fewer opportunities, do not. So, the more information schools can share with students—about the ancient pharaohs, the works of Shakespeare, or the multiplication tables—the better.

"What really bugs me about the progressive tradition is that it has an unequal effect on educational opportunity," Hirsch said. In contrast, he said, academic standards "have a social justice effect and the more established they become the better the rural and inner city disadvantaged students will be served."

In November, Kohn spoke in Monterey to a conference of the California League of High Schools and urged teachers and administrators to "roll back this awful juggernaut before it's too late" by boycotting the state tests.

Kohn's speech was warmly greeted, but the organization's executive director, Peter Murphy, said it wasn't likely that his members would heed the call to fight back.

"The law is the law and they're going to have to deal with standards," he said. "They want to have high standards and help their students meet them."

But some of those who heard the message were inspired.

Pamela Curtiss-Horton, an Oakland first-grade teacher, has distributed Kohn's articles to her fellow teachers. She tells parents they can decide not to have their children tested, and she refuses to use district-mandated test study sheets.

"I take the stand that they can do whatever they want to me, but I'm not going to do something that's harmful to my students," she said. "I teach them what they need to learn."

. . . .

A Unique School or Out of Step?

Berkeley Campus has everything going for it except rising test scores. Students are taught to learn through "discovery." Some wonder whether that is the culprit.

Richard Lee Colvin

This selection first appeared in the *Los Angeles Times* on 2 September 1999. Richard Lee Colvin is an education writer for the *Los Angeles Times*.

BERKELEY—Columbus Elementary School seems to have everything going for it. Everything, that is, except good test scores.

The school spends almost $8,000 per pupil, far more than the national average of $6,300, to pay for extra training for teachers, equipment and books galore. Its campus is new, designed as a cozy village of airy, ochre-colored cottages.

Mental health counseling, social workers, and tutoring before and after school are available. Perhaps most important, the school is richly endowed with an asset considered essential to academic success: involved parents.

Parents helped raise $1.2 million, an unheard-of sum for a public elementary school, to cover "extras" such as a science lab and day-care facilities for the campus that opened in 1997 to replace buildings damaged in the Loma Prieta earthquake.

But the school also stands out for something else: its staunch commitment to "discovery learning," a decade-old philosophy that says students learn more deeply when they figure things out for themselves through trial and error and individual projects.

It is an approach rapidly falling out of favor among school reformers, who argue that highly structured lessons are more likely to turn around a situation in which nearly two-thirds of the state's fourth-graders are poor readers.

If there is any place that so-called progressive methods should work, it is at Columbus, given its extra resources.

However, in the two years since the school reopened, its test scores have dramatically worsened. Columbus Principal Rebecca Wheat and her teachers worry that they are running out of time. If scores don't improve, the state could eventually take over the school and replace them. More immediately, raising money to continue the comprehensive array of services will be difficult if test scores remain low.

Scores for grades two and three range from the 23rd to the 35th percentile in reading, math, language usage, and spelling, as measured against a national norm. That means the average third-grader at the school reads worse than 77% of students nationally.

The scores for grades four and five are somewhat better, but have fallen across the board by as much as 14 percentile points.

"These are very, very high-stakes tests," Wheat said.

She believes that the school's teachers do pay enough attention to teaching basic skills. "Our decisions have been very thoughtfully made," Wheat insisted. "But I do think the pressure for test scores does put pressure on people to do more direct teaching."

At Columbus, the debate over how to teach is complicated by the wide range of students it serves. Located in one of the poorest neighborhoods of west Berkeley's flatlands, Columbus also draws from affluent areas in the hills overlooking the campus of the University of California.

The income gap, which tends to fall along racial lines, shows up in the test scores. Last year, scores for the 18% of students who are white were generally twice those of African American students, who make up 31% of the students. White students also scored far higher than the 40% of the students whose first language is not English. Moreover, that gap grows larger as students get older.

A Safety Net of Support

The school's efforts to make all students and their families feel comfortable—regardless of the language they speak or what they do for a living—are striking.

The school has a language "immersion" program that, deliberately, has half native English speakers and half Spanish speakers and is taught entirely in Spanish. All children first learn to read in Spanish, but the Spanish speakers also pick up English from their classmates. Gradually, teachers introduce more formal English instruction with the goal of all children winding up fully bilingual.

Teachers and office workers speak Spanish. The school has tried to attract poorer families to after-school enrichment activities such as stick drumming and yoga by subsidizing fees. Last year the school hired seven "parent advocates" to help parents obtain a wide range of services: from child care to dental services and even emergency surgeries.

The idea, said Alison T. Jones, the coordinator of services for students at risk of failing academically, is to "provide a safety net of tutoring and family support so that when the kids are together in the classroom, those differences are not so apparent."

But teachers at Columbus are philosophically opposed to separating students by reading level or ability. "If you put all the low kids together, it's deadly. The level of discussion is not high and the motivation is not there," said Mary Burmeister, a teacher who was conducting a reading lesson for a dozen fourth-graders one sunny day in May.

To engage the students, she put the title of the day's story on the board—*The Friends of Kwan Ming*—and told them to write down a prediction of what it was about. "Spelling doesn't count," she told them.

Then she had them share their answers with a partner and then with the whole group. Finally, she read the story to them, because although some of the students were capable of reading novels by the author

Roald Dahl on their own, others were learning-disabled and not reading at all, and still others were not fluent in English.

Columbus uses federal funds to provide tutoring before school for those who are falling behind. But those who need it don't always show up, Jones said.

"Mondays are difficult," she said one morning, observing a remedial session with two students instead of the eight who were scheduled. Sometimes, families are contacted by the parent advocates, who may help arrange transportation.

The school also uses federal funds and a subsidy from the Berkeley Unified School District to pay the salaries of two teachers who are trained in Reading Recovery, a controversial program that has shown mixed results and is very costly.

"Even if Reading Recovery doesn't help their reading that much, they've got this one-on-one attention and it's really helped [students'] self-esteem," Jones said.

What the school does not do is systematically teach the sounds of letters. That is now the approach to reading instruction sanctioned in state law covering textbook purchases and professional development.

Instead, Wheat said, teachers are being trained to address the sounds of letters as the need arises, while students are puzzling through books. That way, she said, teachers can individualize instruction.

Doug Carnine, a professor at the University of Oregon, said that approach might be widening the gap between low- and middle-income children rather than narrowing it.

More affluent or advanced students, he said, might not need the practice and reinforcement characteristic of teacher-directed, phonics-based programs. But weak readers do. "What does it mean for a school . . . to sanction an instructional approach that's probably more suited to the most advantaged?" he asked.

Columbus' teachers are undeterred by such talk.

Ann Gilbert, a fifth-grade teacher, watched as her students worked in pairs measuring the angles of various geometric shapes. The point of the exercise was to discover that the size of the angles in five-sided shapes always add up to the same.

But she wasn't telling her students that. Even when they came up to her with questions, she didn't clue them in. Such a lesson probably won't pay off in higher test scores immediately, she said. "But it will by the end of high school because they'll really know it," she said.

A science lesson that began on the school's oval central courtyard and playground followed a similarly indirect path. Students had spent an earlier session making houses out of cardboard and painting them black, yellow, or white.

On this day, they were supposed to put a thermometer in each house and record the change in temperature. The point was to discover that the black houses got the hottest and the white houses remained the coolest.

But the data recorded by students showed that the yellow paper houses absorbed less heat than the white ones—the wrong conclusion. Rather than correct the mistake, or have them repeat the experiment, teacher Nancy Bynes tried to start a discussion about the results.

"The yellow and white results are a mystery to me. I want to hear your ideas," she said.

When her prompts failed to get a discussion started, Bynes told the students to write about what they had seen. Some produced a few partial sentences. A few filled a page. One girl wandered around the room until Bynes sat her down, wrote out several sentences, and left blanks for her to fill in.

"It shows you we need the services we're getting," Bynes said. "We have a lot of work to do, a lot of work to do."

Alfie Kohn, whose new book, *The Schools Our Children Deserve*, attacks the nationwide movement to raise academic standards through testing, said Columbus should not be judged on its test scores.

"Tests are not intended to look at how much kids understand and how well teachers are helping kids understand," he said. "The tests are designed for the purpose of artificially spreading out scores so they can rank kids against one another."

Parents Stay Committed

State Secretary of Education Gary K. Hart has heard the anti-testing argument many times. He agreed that test scores alone do not provide a full picture of a school. Still, he said, they provide a key element of Gov. Gray Davis' program to make schools accountable for producing results.

He said the state is not trying to dictate how teachers teach. But, he said, "if we're doing all these discovery-learning type things and people are feeling good about what they're doing but they can't show much in the way of . . . basic skills, it's got to raise concern."

So far, parents have not begun to abandon Columbus.

"I'm not even slightly fazed by [dropping test scores]," said Maureen Katz, a psychoanalyst who is a parent of a first-grader at the school. "For me, what's important is the experience my child is having in the school."

Last year, her daughter, Ally, painted portraits imitating Matisse and worked on a mural in the style of Diego Rivera. But she also learned to read in English and Spanish and, over the summer, she has read five books in each language.

Moreover, Katz said, despite its test scores the school remains popular in the district, which has a process by which parents can request where they want their children to go to school. If the state were to try to punish the school for its low test scores, she said, parents would organize in protest.

Still, parents' expectations are high. Jesus Mena, a former parent at the school, said parents will expect to see scores going up by next year. This year, he said, parents want to get a clearer picture of what students are expected to know so they can keep track of whether the school is meeting its goals.

"We are the recipients of these services and we want to be able to say, 'These things are not working,'" he said.

Wheat says the school is working on an improvement plan. It will receive a $75,000 grant this year to add three hours of after-school instruction to reinforce each day's lessons in reading, math, and science and provide a place for children to do homework.

Beyond that, she said, she will convene meetings to ensure that teachers are meeting the state's academic standards for what children should learn.

Finally, the school will apply for a state grant of $50,000 to pay for outside experts to help it figure out a strategy for turning things around.

Like other schools seeking that money, Columbus will have to submit an improvement plan to the state. If the plan is approved, the school could receive an extra $200 per pupil per year. The catch is that test scores must go up by 5% a year or the state can pull the rug from under the school and its leaders and take it over.

Wheat is confident that scores will go up. But, she said, the payoff from the school's comprehensive mix of services won't be seen for many years.

The true test will be how many of her students eventually complete high school, go on to college, and stay out of jail. "Test scores are certainly part of the whole picture," she said. "It's part of it. But it's not the whole thing."

· ·

Opposing Approaches So Johnny Can Read

Finding the Answers in Drills and Rigor

E.D. Hirsch, Jr.

This selection first appeared in the *New York Times* on 11 September 1999. E.D. Hirsch, Jr. is a professor at the University of Virginia and author of *The Schools We Need: And Why We Don't Have Them* (Doubleday, 1996).

The most interesting debate about American education concerns why the United States has not fulfilled the egalitarian aims of schooling as well as other democracies have. The main cause of inequality in American schools, I have argued, has been the dominance of the progressive-education tradition, which has seriously misconceived itself as the guardian of social progress and democratic ideals.

In this regard, I hope Howard Gardner is right that my work poses a threat to the assumptions of the progressivist tradition.

If we are lucky, the end of the 1990s will mark the end of spurious connections between educational ideas and political affiliations.

During the last two decades, when Democrats have controlled a school board, the district has tended to favor the whole-language method of teaching reading, to encourage the use of calculators for "math understanding" (instead of memorizing the multiplication table), and to disparage multiple-choice tests, all positions connected with progressive education but not logically with the platform of the Democratic Party.

By contrast, when a majority of school-board members have been Republican, the district has tended to favor the explicit teaching of phonics, the memorization of the multiplication table, and the use of standardized tests, positions properly associated with educational conservatism but not necessarily with political conservatism.

On the contrary, political conservatism, understood as the preservation of the social status quo, is best achieved by progressive educational methods.

There have been recent signs that the politics of education is belatedly becoming more sophisticated. As long ago as the 1930s, Antonio Gramsci, a brilliant communist opponent of Mussolini, denounced the new "progressive" ideas that were being introduced into Italy from the United States. He argued that social justice required educational conservatism because only if the poor worked hard in school to accumulate the "intellectual baggage" of the rich could they earn money and wield the levers of power. Gramsci, the Communist, serving on a modern American school board, might surprise fellow board members by voting with Republicans.

So might James S. Coleman. Progressive methods failed disadvantaged students, he concluded after a decade of inquiries into the implications of his famous 1966 report, *Equality of Educational Opportunity.* What people remember about his 1966 report is that schools appear to count for little in determining educational achievement, whereas family background matters a great deal. This statistical fact upset many people, including Coleman, because it dashes the democratic hope of giving all students an equal chance by simply putting rich and poor together in the same common school. If the common school does not in fact reduce the advantages of wealth and privilege, then the premises of democratic education must be reexamined.

After the Coleman report, one had a choice of two positions: One could become an advocate of compensatory education to narrow the achievement gap between groups, or one could adopt the determinist view that the schools can do little to rectify the ills of the wider society. The deterministic position, which excuses the schools for failing to reduce the test-score gap between groups, is widely held in the American educational world. But after further research, Coleman adopted the compensatory position.

Published in the '80s, that research showed that most Roman Catholic schools were better at achieving equity than most public schools. Catholic schools followed a rich and demanding curriculum, required a lot of drill and practice, and expected every child to reach minimal goals in each subject during the year. As a result disadvantaged children prospered academically, as did their advantaged peers, and the schools narrowed the gap between races and social classes.

This deeper inquiry of Coleman's started a controversy almost as fierce as the one surrounding his 1966 report. It was seen as an attack on public schools, but, as Coleman unanswerably pointed out, his findings were not limited to Catholic schools; the very same democratic results were being achieved by the few public schools that defied progressivist doctrine. Consistent with that finding is the fact that recent improvements in equity have been achieved only by school reforms that use conservative methods like drill and practice (e.g., the Success for All program at Johns Hopkins) and a demanding curriculum (e.g., the "Core Knowledge" series of books).

After so many practical failures, few educational experts overtly label themselves progressivists, but one can detect de facto progressivists by certain distinctive traits. First, there is their belief that knowledge and skill will be gained incidentally from intensive study of a few subjects. This incidental method claims, against all evidence, to achieve greater depth, as if there were a simple trade-off between depth and breadth. A claim is made under various labels and slogans such as "the project method" and "less is more" that exposure to a few complex experiences will cause understanding to occur naturally, an idea that first gained currency during the Romantic movement.

The persistent attractions of this "natural" method may possibly be explained by the vestigial Romanticism of American culture, but as Lisa Delpit observes in her book *Other People's Children,* the progressivist mode of teaching has consistently failed to benefit African-American children (and many advantaged children as well).

Another mark of progressivism (and another vestige of the Romantic movement) is its criticism of an "overemphasis" on language. Emerson said: "We are shut up in schools and college recitation rooms for 10 or 15 years and come out at last with a bellyful of words and do not know a thing." But as Ms. Delpit points out, these antiverbal ideas have done the most harm to the most disadvantaged students. Their greatest deficits are in vocabulary and the conventions of literate language; they make up math deficits much more readily than language deficits.

Keith Stanovich and his colleagues have shown that a score on a standardized reading test in first grade is the best predictor of 11th-grade academic achievement, a shocking indictment of present-day schools and a powerful illustration of the accuracy of standardized tests and of the centrality of verbal training for determining life chances.

Disparagement of objective tests is a third way to detect progressivists. Their hostility to tests is not surprising, given that progressive methods fail to improve test scores. Yet standardized reading tests are among the most valid and reliable assessments that exist and among the most important instruments for measuring excellence and fairness in education. To take a reading test, a student has to perform the very skill being assessed. These tests, even in their much-maligned multiple-choice forms, are highly correlated with each other and with real-world reading skills.

Competence in reading (that is, in comprehension) is central to academic achievement and to participation in economic and political life. High school graduates who read well enough to get into top colleges know about 100,000 words, which means an average learning rate of more than fifteen new words a day, an astonishing number attainable only by wide reading and by psychological mechanisms that are only beginning to be understood.

A broad vocabulary is an index to broad knowledge, and broad knowledge, extended over time, is the key to depth of knowledge and to a general ability to learn new things.

Since the late '60s it has been known that high literacy entails prior background knowledge over many different domains. Within a given literate culture, the most literacy-enhancing background knowledge can be identified and taught to all students. Theory predicts that teaching such a high-octane curriculum will raise everyone's reading and learning levels and narrow the achievement gap between social groups. This prediction has now been confirmed by independent researchers.

Teaching a curriculum that produces high literacy for all is a potent way of fostering the egalitarian goal of democratic education. But before we can advance toward that goal on a broad front, many progressivist ideas will have to be discarded.

· ·

The Schools They Deserve

Howard Gardner and the Remaking of Elite Education

Mary Eberstadt

This selection first appeared in *Policy Review* in the October/November 1999 edition. Mary Eberstadt is the consulting editor to *Policy Review*.

Our postmodern times, it is often observed, are rough times for orthodox belief. But religious beliefs aren't the only ones being put to the test these days. Certain established secular creeds, too, seem to be taking their lumps.

Consider the ostensible fate of one particularly long-running such orthodoxy, educational progressivism. It is true, of course, that classrooms across the country continue to exhibit progressively inspired practices, from "natural" ways of teaching math to "whole language" rather than phonetic reading methods; true, too, that one of the doctrine's most cherished dicta—its preference for "critical thinking" over what is disdainfully called the "mere" accumulation of facts—is enshrined in the heart of almost every teacher and embedded in textbooks and teaching plans from kindergarten on. All this has long been so, and must bring some consolation to the rank and file.

But it is also true that educational progressivism, in practice and in theory, is fast losing ground. For almost two decades, in fact, that particular set of ideas—grounded in Rousseau, transplanted in America by John Dewey and his followers, and disseminated through the educational establishment by generations of loyal acolytes ever since—has suffered what must only appear to the faithful as one ignominious setback after another.

There was, to begin with, that famous—some would say infamous—1983 report by the National Commission on Excellence in Education, *America at Risk*, documenting the distinct mediocrity of the nation's students and by corollary the impressive failings of its schools. These failings, certain observers were quick to point out, had risen more or less exactly alongside the ascendance of progressive ideas in the public schools. At the same time, and even more annoying to progressives, such critics were turning out to have echoes at the highest levels of politics. After 12 years of Republican governance—including most notably William J. Bennett's tenure as secretary of education—"standards," "testing," "achievement," and other terms regarded by progressives as ideological fighting words were once more in national circulation.

Yet even that much in the way of public criticism, one suspects, could have been comfortably countenanced by the flock; they had, after all, grown accustomed in the course of their long history to challenges from traditionalists of different stripes. But then, as the 1980s wore on into the '90s, came an outpouring of influential books and articles from critics who could not possibly be written off as tools of reaction. Some of these claimed sympathy with progressivism's aims while dissenting from what had been committed in its name. For these critics, what mattered was not the "otherwise unassailable precepts" of progressivism, as the historian Diane Ravitch once put it, but the fact that these precepts had gotten twisted around in practice to become "justification for educational practices that range from the unwise to the bizarre." It was a message that reached an ever-wider audience of the concerned, as the statistics on everything from reading to the SATs piled up worse by the year.

But the harshest blow to progressive ideas, and what ought to have been the most demoralizing, came in the even more unexpected form of the writings of literary scholar E.D. Hirsch, Jr. A Gramsci-quoting, self-described political liberal, Hirsch did more than deplore the excesses of progressivist practice; he attacked the creed itself head-on, and on moral grounds to boot. In 1987, his profoundly influential book *Cultural Literacy* argued that progressive ideas in the schools were depriving all students, particularly those least advantaged, of the knowledge required for citizenship and a decent life. Some years later, in *The Schools We Need and Why We Don't Have Them* (1996), Hirsch went even further, arguing in meticulous detail that "the mistaken ideas" of progressivism had led to "disastrous consequences," and that "since mistaken ideas have been the root cause of America's educational problems, the ideas must be changed before the problems can be solved." Whatever the educational establishment may have made of all this was of little moment next to Hirsch's actual resonance with readers across the country. The ideas in his books—along with his Core Knowledge Foundation and its grade-by-grade, content-laden K–6 curriculum—effectively laid the groundwork for what was, and is, an anti-progressive educational counterculture.

Nor is that all. What must have been even more galling to progressives, priding themselves as they do on the tradition's claim to speak for the common man, is that during the same years in which their creed itself was being thrashed in the middle and higher reaches of public opinion, millions of people who had never even heard of Rousseau or Dewey turned out to be busily repudiating their legacy down below. This is the real meaning of what is often referred to as "the ferment in American schools." For almost two decades now, alarmed by all the same things that alarmed the authors and readers of *America at Risk*, parents and school boards across the country have seized on one educational experiment after another in the hopes of improving the schools—experiments that by their very design send shudders through the enlightened heirs of Dewey.

Many districts and states, for example, have opted for mandatory standardized testing. They have, further, adjusted the curriculum to cover the contents of those exams—in the deploring phrase of progressive educators, "teaching to the test." Other districts are experimenting with financial incentives that these same educators also deplore—merit pay for teachers, school vouchers for disadvantaged families. Some schools have completely reconfigured their courses according to exactly the sort of fact-based learning progressives most heartily oppose; some 400 schools across the country, for example, the vast majority of them public, now claim to be based in whole or in part on Hirsch's Core Knowledge program. Finally, and just as dramatic, is the fact that still other parents have voted for standards and content with their feet by fleeing to the burgeoning rolls of private and parochial schools or—in a phenomenon that progressively inclined educators barely even mention, so much does it affront their first principles—into the also-burgeoning home school movement, now numbering some one and a half million students.

It is all the more curious, then—it is in fact a puzzle begging for solution—that in the elite circles of higher education where the progressivist tradition still burns bright, the public drubbing their doctrine has endured for nearly two decades now has induced little more than the occasional flinch. In these circles, quite unlike those school districts across the country now noisy with democratic experimentation, an altogether different atmosphere reigns. Here, the very innovations for which many in the public clamor—vouchers, school choice, charter schools, standardized tests, and all the rest—continue to be designated, when they are mentioned at all, as reactionary or nostalgic exercises in discontent. Here, the ideas of the progressive tradition's sharpest recent critics, above all those of Hirsch, continue to be dismissed with genteel contempt. Here, as anyone can see, the long-running doctrine of progressivism continues to reign serenely, exactly as if the rising tide of criticism and the mass defections into enemy territory were not shaking the philosophy's throne to its foundations. All of which suggests that this may be a particularly opportune time to examine what form progressivism now survives in, and the source of that form's appeal.

"First among Equals"

Like any other successful academic orthodoxy, including others that have come to be rejected by the ordinary people in whose name they were devised, the tradition of educational progressivism has never lacked for friends in high places. Indeed, it is no exaggeration to say that in the professional world of education itself, the doctrine has a near-perfect monopoly on academic prestige. One highly eminent figure in this world is Theodore Sizer, chairman of the Education Department at Brown, whose Coalition of Essential Schools project includes over 200 high schools organized according to progressive principles—student "exhibitions" rather than tests, an emphasis on "habits of mind" rather than accumulation of knowledge, a passion for relevance (one class recently studied *Othello* for its parallels to the O.J. Simpson trial), and so on. Many other figures less well known bring a similar cast of mind to related experiments and projects. And, of course, given the ideological homogeneity of the field, these like-thinking educators often work together, with the largest and most heavily funded of their projects typically collaborative efforts.

Yet if, in this collegial world, a single figure could be said to be "first among equals," as James Traub put it recently in the *New York Times*, or "the premier American scholar addressing educational reform," in the words of the like-thinking Sizer, it would have to be psychologist and celebrity intellectual Howard Gardner—professor of Cognition and Education and adjunct professor of Psychology at Harvard University; adjunct professor of Neurology at the Boston University School of Medicine; co-director since the early 1970s of Project Zero at the Harvard Graduate School of Education, whose many programs and institutes continue to attract educators from all over; author of some 18 books and hundreds of articles; and recipient of 12 honorary degrees and "many honors," as his latest book jacket copy puts it, including but hardly limited to a 1981 MacArthur fellowship. Gardner's ubiquity both inside the world of education and out almost challenges description. He is a leader in more projects and studies than can be listed here, a steady contributor to tomes from the higher journalism to the specialized literature on down, and a fixture on the lecture circuit (he delivers some 75 talks a year) whose professional interests span everything from classical music to studies of the brain-damaged, political advocacy to developmental psychology, oversubscribed teacher workshops at Harvard to a more recent sideline in corporate consulting.

Daunting though it may be to contemplate, this resume does not even begin to convey Gardner's overriding influence in one particular realm of American education, and that is the world of elite private schools. Today, more than any other single figure, he seems poised to leave his stamp on a generation of students at many of the country's most prestigious schools.

Gardner's influence has a surprising history, as he himself has written and other reports agree. In 1983, the story goes, Gardner published what is still his best-known and most influential book, *Frames of Mind*. There, he challenged the professional convention of dividing intelligence into verbal and mathematical forms, and insisted instead on the existence of seven (he would later say eight, and is now equivocating about a ninth) separate "intelligences" of "equal priority," those being the mathematical-logical, linguistic, spatial, bodily kinesthetic, musical, interpersonal, and intrapersonal. Dense and jargon-ridden, as well as mildly esoteric—its main target, as Gardner has written, was Jean Piaget's conception of intelligence as scientific thinking—*Frames of Mind* was executed, and indeed intended, for a limited scholarly audience. "I believed," as the author himself put it later, "that my work would be of interest chiefly to those trained in my discipline, and particularly those who studied intelligence from a Piagetian perspective."

The professional world, for its part, was unconvinced. As Gardner accurately summarized the book's reception later, "a few psychologists liked the theory; a somewhat larger number did not like it; most ignored it." In the *New York Times Book Review*, psychologist George Miller pronounced the theory "hunch and opinion"; in the *New York Review of Books*, meanwhile—where Gardner's own essays on subjects inside and out of his chosen fields are frequently featured—psychologist Jerome Bruner praised the book for its timeliness, but went on to conclude that Gardner's "intelligences" were "at best useful fictions."

And these were just the friendly critics. In *The Bell Curve* (1994), to no one's surprise, Charles Murray and Richard J. Herrnstein dismissed Gardner as a "radical" whose work "is uniquely devoid of psychometric or other quantitative evidence." Yet others with no visible dog in the fight over intelligence turned out to echo the charge. Robert J. Sternberg of Yale observed that "there is not even one empirical test of the theory"; Australian specialist Michael Anderson complained similarly that "the scaffolding is the theory." Though some put their kindest face forward, praising the author of *Frames of Mind* as "brilliant" and his thesis as "original" or "powerful," few of his professional peers would venture, then or since, that anything Gardner was up to amounted to science. Piaget, at least so far as the professional world was concerned, did not stand corrected.

Nonetheless, there was one audience-in-waiting positively electrified by Gardner's message, and it was moreover enthusiastically indifferent to the book's scholarly critics. That audience, as it turned out, came from the ranks of private school administrators and teachers. As Traub put it last year in the opening of another article on Gardner, this one for the *New Republic*, "Howard Gardner first realized that he had struck a chord in the national psyche when he gave a speech to private-school administrators on his new theory of 'multiple intelligences' and saw the headmasters elbowing each other to get into the hall." Gardner himself recalls the moment with dramatic detail in his 1993 *Multiple Intelligences: The Theory in Practice:*

> Some months after the publication of *Frames*, I was invited to address the annual meeting of the National Association of Independent [i.e., private] Schools. . . . I expected the typical audience of fifty to seventy-five persons, a customary talk of fifty minutes followed by a small number of easily anticipated questions. Instead . . . I encountered a new experience: a much larger hall, entirely filled with people, and humming with excitement. It was almost as if I had walked by mistake into a talk given by someone who was famous. But the audience had in fact come to hear me: it listened attentively, and grew steadily in size until it spilled into the hallways on both sides of the room. . . . [A]fter the session had concluded, I was ringed by interested headmasters, teachers, trustees, and journalists who wanted to hear more and were reluctant to allow me to slip back into anonymity.

The event that proved a turning point in Gardner's personal life would also mark a turning point for his admirers in the tonier schools. Today, as if in vindication of the judgement of those enthusiasts who catapulted his ideas to celebrity heights, Howard Gardner bestrides their world as no other single influence or figure of inspiration. In addition to his omnipresence on the lecture circuit, Gardner's books and videotapes and software are in constant demand (his CD-ROM tour of the intelligences sells for $435 for a set of five); his workshops for teachers and other educators at Harvard are early sell-outs; and hundreds of schools now claim, in varying degrees, to have remade themselves in keeping with multiple-intelligence theory. And though some of those schools are public—there is no shortage of funders or educators interested in trying Gardner's ideas—there can be no doubt that it is the private school world, today as in 1983, that is clamoring for multiple-intelligence products, paying for Gardneriana, and conforming their classrooms to his dicta. Indeed: In what may be the single most telling detail of Gardner's influence in the world of elite education, Traub reports that "when the directorship of one of New York's most prestigious private schools recently came open, almost every candidate for the job mentioned Gardner in his or her one-page educational-philosophy statement." In sum, as one educator put it to Traub, "Howard is the guru, and *Frames of Mind* is the bible."

Progressivism, Properly Understood

If so, the holy writ has now been enlarged once more, and the reader curious as to what the private schools are clamoring for need look no further. For this year Gardner has published yet another book, *The Disciplined Mind: What All Students Should Understand* (Simon & Schuster, $25.00). Unlike *Frames of Mind*, which as we have seen reached the general reader only inadvertently, *The Disciplined Mind* takes no such risk; it is overtly aimed at "individuals"—indeed, "individuals all over the world"—who "care about education." Here, the author promises with typical sweep, he "seek[s] to synthesize over thirty years of research in the cognitive and biological sciences, and over fifteen years of involvement in precollegiate education," to find the features of "good educations . . . everywhere in the world."

Somewhat incongruously, progressivism's most visible public defender opts here for an Olympian tone. He is "weary," he explains, "of debates that array one educational philosophy against another." Though it is true, he elaborates later, that "much of what I write about can be identified with the educational tradition of John Dewey—with what has been called progressive or neo-progressive education,"—it is also true, as he acknowledges, that this tradition has become a code word in the minds of some for low or no standards and poor work. In that sense, Gardner writes, "I reject the baggage that has . . . come to be associated with this label." Contrary to what critics have suggested, "one can be progressive while also espousing traditional educational goals and calling for the highest standards of work, achievement, and behavior." This book, in the author's telling, is a statement of that other progressive philosophy, progressivism properly understood—not the old and tarnished version of yesteryear, but a kind of souped-up version, a muscular version, a kind to which even conservatives and traditionalists, or so the author seems to hope, might warm.

Where does this new progressivism lead? The answer is something of a mystery, at least at first. For Gardner is also "weary," as it turns out, of what he calls the "instrumental or momentary" issues in education today—issues like "vouchers," "charter schools," "teachers unions," "local control," "national standards," "international comparisons," and all the quotidian rest. Such issues, Gardner argues, "skirt the most fundamental question" of the purposes of education itself. These purposes he identifies as a "quartet" across "educational time and space": "to transmit roles; to convey cultural values; to inculcate literacies; and to communicate certain disciplinary content and ways of thinking."

Alongside this quartet of purposes, the author simultaneously outlines a "trio of virtues" that "should animate education"—truth, beauty, and morality—and produces examples of how each of these realms might be approached. To gain an understanding of truth, he suggests, students might study the theory of evolution; of beauty, Mozart's *The Marriage of Figaro*; and of morality, the Holocaust. These choices, the author readily acknowledges, are "time-bound," "place-bound," and even "personal"; they are not intended to signal a "fixed canon," which the author himself ardently opposes. One could easily substitute other instantiations in their place, he goes on to explain—for example, approaching truth through "folk theories about healing or traditional Chinese medicine," beauty through "Japanese ink and brush painting" or "African drum music," and good and evil through "the precepts of Jainism, the stories of Pol Pot and Mao's Cultural Revolution," or "the generosity of bodhisattvas." The point, it appears, is not to "privilege" any particular set of examples; not one is "sacrosanct," and in any event, Gardner writes, "I do not believe in singular or incontrovertible truth, beauty or morality." "No doubt," the author goes on to acknowledge, "there are various routes" to such understanding (later in the book, he will identify six such "pathways"); the one outlined here is merely his own "preferred path."

Anyone reading this far into his argument may long since have started wondering what a curriculum—to say nothing of a lowly classroom—might look like when cut to the specifications of all these purposes, virtues, and pathways. But the reader must be patient; list-wise, we have only just begun. The Six Forces That Will Remake Schools are easy enough to digest (as is the by-now obligatory point that "changes in our world are so rapid and so decisive that it will not be possible for schools to remain as they were or simply to introduce a few superficial adjustments"). Similarly, the six "most prominent ideas ushered in by the cognitive revolution" can be managed without headache. So can the seven "mind and brain findings" that "ought to be kept in mind by anyone concerned with education," off the track of Gardner's main point though they may be.

It is when the author returns to his main subject that the conceptual challenge begins in earnest. For it turns out that there are not only Four Approaches to Understanding ("learning from suggestive institutions," "direct confrontations of erroneous conceptions," "a framework that facilitates understanding," and "multiple entry points"), but that the fourth of these, in keeping with multiple-intelligence theory, is itself subdivided into seven further categories (the entry points in question being narrative, numerical, logical, existential/foundational, aesthetic, hands-on, and interpersonal), *and* that room must be left for metaphor, similes, model languages, and other means of making sense of the con-sequent "multiple representations of the Core Concept."

What all this means for the classroom is anybody's guess, but what Gardner himself says it means looks something like this: A "narrative entry point" into the subject of evolution, for example, might be the story of Darwin's voyage on the Beagle, or the tale of his fellow evolu-tionist and grandfather, or the saga of the Galapagos finches. A "nu-merical entry point" might be a study of the beak size of the same finches. Other entry points might include, say, breeding fruit flies (hands-on), watching a documentary (aesthetic), or recreating the de-bates that followed publication of Darwin's theory. Similarly, the *Marriage of Figaro* might be studied via the human struggles it contains (existential-foundational), comparison of meter and rhythm in two arias (numerical), or performing parts of the score (hands-on). As for the Holocaust, one might, say, study the history of artists persecuted under Hitler (aesthetic), read the literature of survivors (existential-foundational), or focus on a specific event such as the Wannsee confer-ence (narrative). A classroom designed by Gardner, in other words, might do all these things—or it might, even more important, do none of the above; we are reminded repeatedly, as he puts it toward the end, that "these choices are illustrative only."

Well, so be it. Now, if the content of such an education is indeed ad hoc, arbitrary, in permanent flux, then we can only evaluate that edu-cation by means of its methodology. About that methodology Gardner is quite clear—he favors "depth over breadth," (pursuing a small number of topics rather than conveying large amounts of information); "construction over accumulation" of knowledge (an emphasis on personal questioning rather than memorization); "the pursuit of knowledge for its own sake over the obeisance to utility"; "an individualized over a uniform education" (a preference that allows "the natural inclinations of the human individual to unfold and endure"); and "student-centered" rather than "teacher-centered" education (meaning that students join in the process of "assessing" themselves). Personal relevance, student-led classrooms, hands-on, performance-oriented activities—does any of this sound familiar?

> "Learning by doing" was a central element in the . . . curriculum . . . [as were] educational methods that discarded the mere accumulation of knowledge and made learning a part of each student's life, connected to his or her present situation and needs. These were schools of the future. . . because they exhibited "tendencies toward greater freedom and an identification of the child's school life with his environment and outlook."

The description here comes from Diane Ravitch in *The Schools We Deserve,* and she is quoting John Dewey. The year in question is 1915.

The Shock of the Old

In sum, the vision on which Gardner insists so passionately in *The Disciplined Mind* is not exactly new. It is, in fact, older than most people now alive, as was demonstrated most elegantly by the progressives' nemesis, E.D. Hirsch, Jr., three years ago in *The Schools We Need and Why We Don't Have Them.* Gardner, of course, is profoundly aware of Hirsch's opposing perspective, which he describes in his latest book as "a view of learning that is at best superficial and at worst anti-intellectual." (That's when Gardner is minding his literary manners. On the lecture trail, he prefers the jab of "Vanna White knowledge.") Yet it is an interesting fact that Gardner, for all that he describes his own latest book as part of a "sustained dialectic"—read disagreement—with Hirsch himself, in fact mentions his adversary only a few times, while *The Schools We Need and Why We Don't Have Them* appears not at all.

Interesting, but not at all surprising. For that last book of Hirsch's, *predating* Gardner's though it did by three years, uncannily provides the intellectual genealogy of just about every tenet of *The Disciplined Mind,* most of them presented by the author as if they were thought up just yesterday.

"Changes in our world are so rapid and so decisive," Gardner's argument begins, "that it will not be possible for schools to remain as they were." "The claim that specific information is outmoded almost as soon as it has been learned," writes Hirsch in *The Schools We Need and Why We Don't Have Them*, "goes back at least as far as [William Hearst] Kilpatrick's *Foundations of Method* (1925)." Subject matter, Gardner argues, should not be "privileged"; what matters is that education be centered on the child rather than the subject. "Dewey's words, disposing of the polarity between child-centered and subject-matter-centered education," Hirsch observes after quoting them, "were published in 1902." What of the concomitant idea—also part of the "child-centered" curriculum—that testing amounts to "spitting back" material, and that children should instead "construct" answers for themselves? "The campaign against giving students tests," Hirsch explains, "is an integral part of a Romantic progressivism that goes back to the 1920s. . . . [O]rthodox educational doctrine since the 1920s has been consistently opposed to testing and grading."

And so on, and on—and on. The superiority of "hands-on" experimentation versus "drill-and-practice" teaching, the importance of "individual differences," "learning styles," and an "active learning environment"? These buzzwords and all they represent, the nuts and bolts of *The Disciplined Mind*'s imagined classroom, turn out to date to an exceedingly influential document published by the Bureau of Education and called *The Cardinal Principles of Secondary Education*—published in 1918. The main focus of this document, as it happens, was an attack on the idea—one resonating these 80-plus years later in Gardner's arbitrary trio of evolution, Mozart, and the Holocaust—that subject matter per se should anchor a curriculum. "This hostility to academic subject matter," writes Hirsch, "has been the continued focus of educational 'reform' ever since *Cardinal Principles*—a tradition that needs to be kept in mind when current reformers attack 'mere facts' and 'rote learning.'"

Just as what is significant in *The Disciplined Mind* is not new, so its particular novelty—that architectonic of trios, quartets, sextuplets, and septuplets of principle, intelligences, and entry points and all the rest—is not terribly significant. In fact, the most vaunted part of that architectonic— the identification of the multiple intelligences, and the insistence on a curriculum intended to elicit all of them—is, unfortunately for the rest of Gardner's argument, its weakest link.

Consider only what multiple-intelligence theory forces him to say about one of his own chosen subjects, the teaching of the Holocaust. No one could object to the reading of survivor stories, say, or to an in-depth look at Eichmann's trial in Israel in 1961, or to reviewing the literature on the Wannsee conference. But the insistence that these are mere "entry points" for certain kinds of "intelligences," entry points no more or less "privileged" than any other, will not stand up. It is very difficult to accept that the author himself believes it. After all, the Holocaust could also be "entered" through a study of, say, how concentration camps boosted local employment rates. Would Gardner really sanction that approach, rather than appear to "privilege" conventional sources?

Even worse are the tortured passages where the cumbersome re-quirements of his theory force him to invent other "entry points" aligned to the more avant-garde "intelligences." It is hard, for example, to read under "interpersonal points of entry" his assurance that "The Holocaust provides many opportunities for role play" without a twinge of uneasiness. Occasionally, one feels the strain of his material stretch-ing round his theory to the ripping point—as in his admission that "when it comes to the relationship between the Holocaust and artistry, one must tread carefully," or in the howler, "Hands-on involvement with the Holocaust must be approached carefully, especially with chil-dren." To say that the multiple-intelligences approach runs the risk of trivializing serious subjects—a risk Gardner briefly acknowledges here—is one thing. But to advance beyond those claims about entry points to say that it does not even matter *whether* the Holocaust is taught, much less how, is to enter a zone of relativism where few readers would care to follow. Clearly, Gardner expects good taste to govern the class-room. But this preference must go unspoken, since to introduce it is to open the way to objective "standards" and other rigidities he disavows.

What, finally, of the author's promise to deliver progressivism with a difference? For all the reassurances ("I am a demon for high standards and demanding expectations"), for all the talk of "rigor," "high stan-dards," and the rest, no ways and means are introduced here that would translate these terms into accountability—none, that is, beyond the up-holding of "regular assessments," and what that means is anybody's guess. As James Traub put it pointedly in the *New York Times Book Review*, "One would like to ask Gardner, an erudite and wide-ranging thinker, if that was how school equipped his own mind."

Gardner, of course, would protest that such ideas have never really been tried. "Educational experimentation" in this century, he believes, "has occurred chiefly on the margins"; progressive educators "have had relatively little impact on the mainstream of education throughout the contemporary world." The argument that something has never been tried, that last gasp of exhausted ideology, is in this particular case quite wrong; the Everyclass all these educators love to hate—one with "prevalent lecturing, the emphasis on drill, the decontextualized materials and activities ranging from basal readers to weekly spelling tests," as Gardner puts it—has been out of fashion and in many schools stigmatized, apparently without the progressives' ever having noticed it, for decades now. To the extent that it is reviving in American schools today, it is on account not of the establishment educational culture, but of a counterculture that is now declaring, whether overtly like the educational reformers or tacitly through the many experiments now under way in the schools, that a hundred years of progressive experimentation is enough.

To Each, According to His Means?

It appears, then, that progressive educational ideology has come full circle. Born near the turn of the century in hopes of raising the downtrodden up, it survives now as the ideology of choice of, by, and for the educational elite.

Indeed, it is increasingly recognized as such. Consider this comment by Nathan Glazer, writing last year in the *New Republic* of the sharply opposed visions of E.D. Hirsch, Jr., and progressive educator Theodore Sizer: "The question of what's best for the classroom," Glazer concluded, "may simply be a matter of class—social class. In some schools, with some students, one can teach for understanding and depth. . . . For others—frankly and regrettably—there are no such things." Gardner, similarly, for all his talk of an "education for all human beings," notes that "for those disadvantaged children who do not acquire literacy in the dominant culture at home, such a prescribed curriculum [as that recommended by Hirsch and others] helps to provide a level playing field and to ensure that future citizens enjoy a common knowledge base." Progressivism, it appears, is not for the weak—or the backward, or the poor.

So what's in it for the elite—all those headmasters and teachers and parents still elbowing their way into Gardner's lectures? Why the enduring appeal to them of progressive ideas? Three sorts of explanations come to mind.

The first is institutional. The means by which academic ideologies perpetuate themselves have been closely studied elsewhere; the particular case of progressive ideology has probably been explained best, again, by Hirsch in *The Schools We Need and Why We Don't Have Them.* Almost all the leading figures in the field of education—all the most prestigious institutions—are considered, and consider themselves, heirs to Dewey's tradition. This fact is important. It means, for example, that graduate students seeking out the "best" schools and professors will find themselves educated—and, of course, penalized or rewarded in their professional lives—by people imbued with the ideas that overwhelmingly dominate these schools. It also means that teachers, headmasters, and others who pride themselves on staying au courant will likewise gravitate to the same ideological home base.

A second way of explaining progressivism's latest lease on life is more prosaic, and concerns those on the consumer end of private education. In a review of Gardner and his ideas for the *Richmond Times-Dispatch,* Robert Holland recently quipped that multiple-intelligence theory "encourages the egalitarian delusion that we all are utterly brilliant in equally important ways," thus providing "an escape route from accountability." He is, of course, absolutely right; that "delusion" is the main source of the theory's very human appeal.

On any bell curve, after all, half the results will fall below the norm; *somebody* is going to be in that bottom quintile, or two quintiles, and so on. Now, parents everywhere have a natural aversion to thinking their own child is average or worse; from the parental point of view, as the Russian joke has it, every baby is a "normal genius child." Add to that natural aversion the fact that, at the upper reaches of the private school world, some parents are paying $10,000 to $14,000 a year per child; these sums alone are a powerful disincentive against giving parents bad news. Many parents send their children to private school, after all, precisely so that they do not have to worry about their education. Grades and standardized tests are a constant reminder that problems might still surface at any time. Thus, private school parents, possibly more than others, may be susceptible to multiple-intelligence-style ideas that emphasize the talents of their children, while not putting those talents on the line in any way that will rouse parental concern. There is also, of course, no denying the fact that classrooms like these have always had a certain snob appeal. Grades and tests, they imply, are for the ordinary kids; no means of measurement could do justice to ours.

But there is a larger, more sociological explanation for the success of such a vision in the private schools today, an explanation that ought to make progressives themselves uncomfortable if they ever take occasion to reflect on it. For the fact is that in placing their bets on the most advantaged children—those children of the kind of people who have taken multiple-intelligence theory to heart—progressive educators can hardly lose.

How could they? Teach those children Inuit and Swahili all you like; they, unlike their less advantaged counterparts, will pick up the French or Italian or whatever they need when the time comes for traveling abroad. Withhold from them all that distasteful factual information with no fear of penalty—most of them, again unlike their less fortunate fellows, will pick up the facts from their reading and conversation outside the classroom. Deny them, if you like, geography; they will find, say, Madrid or the Euphrates from the airport when they get there. Refuse to administer tests—excepting of course the intelligence tests so tellingly required by almost every private school in the land—again, with impunity; most of them will have individual tutors for the SAT and AP exams when the time comes.

All of which is to say that when the children of today's Gardner- or Sizer-influenced schools go on from strength to strength later in life, that fact will tell us very little about the intrinsic worth of progressive ideas or the merits of the classrooms where those ideas roam free. All success will prove is that the overwhelming advantages with which most of those students are blessed—the homes packed with books, the money that makes travel and other forms of personal enrichment a fact of life, the literate and high-functioning parents and peers, the expectations and, for many, the genetic advantages with which they are born—amount to more human capital than any classroom, including mediocre and worse ones, can reduce by much.

Viewed this way, the revival of progressive ideas among elite schools and students may seem a harmless enough experiment; and so, from the perspective of those particular individuals, it probably is. All the same, this ideological renascence has its dark side. The more the private schools tack to the wind—abolishing grades, eradicating tests, and otherwise disposing of the instruments that have traditionally allowed worse-off students the means by which to elevate themselves—the harder it will become for any child to join those schools except through accident of birth.

After all, they will not be able to join them by dint of hard work; the curriculum is constantly in flux, so there is nothing to prepare for. Nor will their graded schoolwork elsewhere grant them entrée; this merely proves they have been "force-fed" facts. As for more subjective measures, like a teacher's recommendation—well, that teacher was almost certainly not trained according to theory; she probably just was "privileging" certain kinds of performance in the usual suspect way. The school without recognizable assessments and a fixed curriculum—the school of which progressive educators, today or yesterday, continue to dream—is a school stripped of handholds from below.

As for the poor and disadvantaged themselves—well, as enlightened voices are now saying, let them have Hirsch. Come to think of it, the implied contest there has a certain charm. Let the games begin.

What Is an Educrat?

Debra J. Saunders

This selection first appeared in the *San Francisco Chronicle* on 4 January 1998. Debra Saunders is an editorial writer for the *San Francisco Chronicle*.

What is an educrat? The word is a hybrid, combining the Latin part of *educator* with the Greek part of *bureaucrat*, an educrat. I didn't invent the term, although I wish I did.

I use it because it captures a special kind of person in the education world: pinheads who are so process-oriented that they are more excited about the process of learning than the myriad wonders that can be learned.

Simply put, educrats believe in process—as opposed to educators, who believe in results. Educrats focus on how children learn. Educators focus on what they learn.

Can a teacher be an educrat? Yes, although I should think most teachers are educators, not educrats. (Bet that a teacher with a Ph.D. in education is an educrat, one with a Ph.D. in math is an educator.)

Are there any good educrats? Sure. Percentage-wise they probably average out to about the same as reformed ex-cons.

What is the difference between an educator and an educrat?

Educrats care if children feel good about reading. Educators care if children can read.

Educrats believe that children can't enjoy math unless the lessons are all about *them*. They load math classes down with "fun" assignments—drawing favorite foods or writing poems about math. Educators rely on the joy of numbers.

Educrats think students don't need to know where all American states are as long as students know how to read a map.

Educrats say they want children to think for themselves, then make them work in groups.

Educrats are obsessed with achieving racial diversity in lessons, regardless of subject area, and in school statistics. Educators are obsessed with educating.

Educrats have turned science into an ecological jihad. They think cell structure is too boring, so they sex up science class with dire warnings on the evils of global warming, trash, and pesticides.

Educrats believe that the important thing is that children can "communicate mathematically" and scientifically. Educators think kids should know math and science.

Educrats write history standards, such as: "Students should be able to identify and explain how events and changes occurred in significant historical periods." Educators realize the sentence is utterly meaningless.

Educrats believe social studies should make children feel good about themselves. Educators use social studies to move students beyond their parochial lives.

Educrats say public schools should teach "values," then write "values" curricula that preach that values are relative.

Educrats believe public schools should require students to serve as community "volunteers." Educators wish the schools would require that students earn passing grades before they are promoted.

Educrats think a class is doing well if the students are performing at the same level. Educators want better students to do their best.

Educrats care about students knowing how to do things—solve problems, present an argument—"in different ways." Educators care about students doing the above well.

Educrats complain that the schools are asked to do too much, then propose to add new programs to promote social equity—try "gender awareness" sessions—to the school day.

Educrats blame parents when young children can't read. Educators believe it is the job of teachers to make sure that every child can read and comprehend.

An educrat talks up the Internet as the great information equalizer. An educator sees some value in the Internet, as well as its great potential to help kids cheat and play video games.

Educrats believe in knowing how to sizzle different kinds of meats in different ways for diverse peoples; educators want steak.

CURRICULUM AND METHODS

Developmental Appropriateness:
Review—Years of Promise: A Comprehensive Learning Strategy for America's Children

Philip H. Abelson

This selection first appeared in *Science* on 13 December 1996; reprinted with permission from *Science*, copyright 2000, The American Association for the Advancement of Science. Philip Abelson is the former editor of *Science* magazine.

The U.S. educational system was designed a century ago to prepare children to hold jobs and raise families in a world that relied primarily on physical labor. Because of the large role of agriculture and an abundance of natural resources, the nation could prosper even if many young people did not develop their full intellectual capabilities. During the 20th century, the United States depleted major natural resources while incurring a huge trade deficit. Now it faces a future in which it must increasingly turn to high-technology products as a source of economic security. In this area, it will be competing with countries whose young citizens are demonstrating greater academic competence than ours.

Two examples are Taiwan and South Korea. Unlike the United States, these nations have emphasized raising the educational standard of their whole populations rather than that of an elite fraction. As a result, their children achieve better average test scores in science and mathematics than do our children, many of whom fail at school. In an increasingly knowledge-based global economy, unsuccessful students tend to be only marginally employable, and the wages of the unskilled have been steadily falling. Unless changes are made, the social and budgetary costs of educational failures in the United States are likely to increase.

The need to improve the U.S. educational system has been recognized by a number of educators and foundations. The Carnegie Corporation of New York has made long-term determined efforts to enhance the nation's understanding of child and adolescent development and to foster better outcomes for our young people. A recent Carnegie publication, *Years of Promise: A Comprehensive Learning Strategy for America's Children*, provides information about changes needed to achieve better results in the education of children aged 3 to 10. "During these seven years, children make great leaps in cognition, language acquisition, and reasoning, corresponding with dramatic neurological changes," notes the report, and it provides references to substantial bodies of research confirming that the educational attainments of nearly all U.S. children could be greatly increased. Many factors influence children's intellectual development, among which are the skill, warmth, and enthusiasm of teachers. However, as the report states, "Schools may have the primary responsibility for children's formal education, but their educational success is influenced by far more than what happens to them in school. Families, preschools, religious and other community institutions and, beyond these immediate influences, the broader array of institutions that bear on children's lives—the media, employers in all sectors, higher education, and government—have shared responsibility to contribute to children's learning and healthy development."

Parental involvement in the education of children is especially important. From age 3 to 5 in particular, children should be read to frequently. In these years, when brain activity is high, parents have a unique opportunity to foster a love of learning. As children grow older, parents should maintain involvement in their education, including interaction with teachers. Research has shown that these activities have beneficial effects. When children are in primary school, parental influence decreases and is in part replaced by that of peers and TV. Today, most single parents work, as do about 75% of married mothers of children in school. A frequent result is latchkey youngsters who come home to an empty house and a TV set. A few TV programs are suitably educational; others are trash. The Carnegie report states that there are about 20 to 25 violent acts per hour in children's programs. By the time they reach the age of 18, Americans have typically watched 15,000 hours of TV, which is more time than they have spent in classrooms. Studies have shown that children who are heavy TV watchers tend to put little effort into schoolwork, get lower grades, and have weak reading skills. The report strongly recommends improved TV programming. It also points out the value of community after-school activities, but warns that quality standards for such programs need to be established and enforced.

Unless our educational system is substantially improved, the U.S. economy and national security will deteriorate. The education of all children from their early years through adolescence should have a long-term high priority.

. . . .

Science Friction

Steve Olson

This selection first appeared in *Education Week* on 30 September 1998. Steve Olson covers science and science education from Bethesda, Maryland.

Setting education standards for math and science was supposed to be easy. As education scholar Diane Ravitch wrote in a *Washington Post* op-ed piece during the debate over national standards: "Mathematics and science work according to the same principles regardless of the city, state, or nation. The airplane that just flew over my house doesn't care what country it is in; it works the same way in Austria, Nigeria, and Japan as it does in the United States."

But California's recent efforts to set academic standards have turned expectations on their head. The language arts and history/social science standards, which have inspired heated debates elsewhere, emerged from the state standards commission with little controversy. But the quest to arrive at a set of science standards—and math standards before them—has set off a nasty intellectual tussle.

California is certainly not the first state to write science standards; almost 40 have documents that describe what students should know and be able to do in the subject. But California's feud raises a worrisome issue at a time when education is heavily invested in the idea of standards-based reform: Writing science standards is not as easy as most people thought it would be.

And now, with a decision from the state school board due in days, the conflict has flared up again. Scientific societies from across the country are attempting to dissuade state board members from accepting the science document prepared by the standards commission.

What that document says likely will shape science instruction in California for years to come and probably will influence classrooms nationwide. With 5 million school-age children and 10 percent of the nation's textbook market, California's actions can't be ignored. The state has been moving toward high standards in science education—and never quite getting there—for the past 15 years. The process began in 1983, shortly after Bill Honig was elected state superintendent. It was a particularly unsettled time. *A Nation at Risk*, with its dire warnings of educational mediocrity, had just been published. International assessments ranked American students low in academic performance. Predictions of a collapsing education system seemed a telling rebuke to the Reagan administration's "Morning in America" optimism.

A forceful innovator, Honig instituted a number of far-reaching reforms. But his most important innovation focused on shaping what gets taught in the classroom. He created panels of teachers, experts from various academic fields, and members of the business community to rewrite the state's curriculum frameworks to describe a vision of what all students should know.

Honig's blueprint was one of the first clear statements of what has since become a touchstone in education. Other policymakers soon latched on to his idea of high and specific expectations as a driver of education reform. And by the end of the 1980s, at a historic education summit in Charlottesville, Va., convened by President Bush, the nation's governors agreed on the need to set high academic standards for all students.

The frameworks that California constructed under Honig, however, went beyond standards. They were broader and more discursive, encompassing both content and method of instruction. They were meant to determine what and how students should learn, which in turn would shape textbooks, staff development, and especially assessments.

The plan did not fare as well in practice as in theory. One big problem, many observers believe, was the frameworks' tendency to prescribe pedagogy. In science, for example, successive revisions of the frameworks moved progressively toward experiential learning, overarching themes, and a "less is more" philosophy toward content.

When such progressivism, especially in language arts, seeped into the statewide testing system, the public balked. In 1994, shortly before being reelected, Republican Gov. Pete Wilson responded to widespread public criticism of the California Learning Assessment System, or CLAS, by killing the test.

California educators and policymakers decided that one reason for CLAS's failure was a lack of clear, easily measurable content standards. To change that, the legislature in 1995 created the academic standards commission, a group of 21 representatives from the scientific, academic, and parent communities. Wilson appointed 12 people to the commission; the new state superintendent, Delaine Eastin, appointed six and was named a commissioner herself; and the California Assembly and Senate each appointed one member.

From the beginning, the legislature wanted the commission to be as open as possible. "An explicit decision was made that this should be a public process, not one internal to the education community," says Scott Hill, the executive director of the commission. "It was supposed to be a Madisonian experience, where people with widely different philosophies would come together to fight over what the standards should be." As a result, the commission did not turn to task forces of educators to write the standards, as most states have done. Instead, it hired consultants to compile drafts, which the commission would then review and revise.

The legislature directed the commission to write standards in four areas: language arts and mathematics first, followed by history/social science and science. Given California's legendary clash in the 1980s over phonics vs. whole language, everyone geared for a battle over language arts. Surprisingly, mathematics emerged as the flashpoint.

A backlash against the existing math frameworks had been building for several years. Well-organized parent groups in Palo Alto, San Diego, and elsewhere had been protesting the gradual alignment of math instruction with the standards promulgated by the National Council of Teachers of Mathematics. In the views of those critics, the NCTM standards deemphasize basic skills like computation and overemphasize discovery-based learning.

The commission's work on math standards became a lightning rod. Advocates testified at public hearings, packed commission meetings, and aired their arguments in the media. Newspaper articles and opinion pieces descended to the level of pitting "Third World–worshipping, standards-loathing" reformers against "math nazis." Wracked by dissent, the commission struggled toward consensus. Finally, with its deadline looming, it agreed on a document to forward to the state school board, though one commissioner felt compelled to append a minority report.

At the state board, the situation worsened. Made up entirely of Wilson appointees, the board felt that the proposed standards still slighted the basics. Two of its members edited the document to correct the problem, though opinion is still divided over how much the edits changed the standards. For example, the board changed one 3rd grade standard from "build up the multiplication table from 0×0 to 10×10 and commit to memory" to "memorize to automaticity the multiplication table for numbers between 1 and 10." Finally, last December, the board ended the protracted battle and approved the math standards.

Against this backdrop of bitterness and acrimony, the work of the commission's science committee began.

As the math standards staggered toward completion last fall, the commission put out a request for proposals for consultants to draft the science standards. Two groups of science educators and scientists applied for the job.

One, the Science Coalition, was led by Bonnie Brunkhorst, a professor of science education and geology at California State University–San Bernardino and a former president of the National Science Teachers Association. Members of her group generally favored the progressive-style reforms that have swept science in recent years, which made some of them chary about getting involved in standards-setting. Having watched the uproar over math, they knew the political climate did not favor their ideas. But they decided to try to work from the inside rather than from the outside. "We wanted to make the document as good as possible," says Art Sussman, the director of the Eisenhower Regional Consortium at WestEd, a federally funded education laboratory in San Francisco, and a leader of the San Bernardino group.

The other group, known as Associated Scientists, was led by Stan Metzenberg, an assistant professor of biology at California State University–Northridge. This group was stocked with advocates of more traditional teaching approaches. Its roster also featured three Nobel Prize winners—Harvard's Dudley Herschbach, Stanford's Henry Taube, and Glenn Seaborg.

Though Seaborg and the Associated Scientists offered to write the new standards for free, the commission voted in January to award the contract to the San Bernardino group, pointing to its experience producing standards and its more thorough proposal. The decision immediately was protested, and after considerable media coverage, the commission compromised. It hired both groups and asked them to merge their memberships to produce the drafts. The governor named Seaborg as both a member of the commission and the chairman of the panel that would review the consultants' work and then prepare it for a vote before the full commission. Seaborg is an icon of science. Now 86, he is one of the last old-guard scientists who worked on the atomic bomb in World War II. In 1941, he discovered the element plutonium, which contributed to his 1951 Nobel Prize in chemistry. During the war, he headed the group that devised the processes used to produce the plutonium for the bomb dropped on Nagasaki. In 1974, he discovered another unstable element, atomic number 106, which was recently named seaborgium.

Seaborg also has a longtime interest in education. A member of the national commission that produced *A Nation at Risk,* Seaborg and Harvard physics professor and historian Gerald Holton generally are credited with writing the report's most striking passages. And as a professor at the University of California, Berkeley, and the chairman of Berkeley's Lawrence Hall of Science, Seaborg often has decried the sorry state of scientific literacy in America.

The decision to merge the two groups quickly ran into trouble. Though outwardly quite similar, the groups had radically different ideas about science education. Seaborg opened a commission meeting in June, for example, by announcing that he wanted to break the high school standards down by grade level, despite a previous agreement that the standards should cover grades 9–12 as a whole. He went on to fault what was then the current draft of the standards for not introducing astronomy in 1st grade, cells in 2nd grade, and atoms in 3rd grade, as is done in the Core Knowledge Sequence derived from the ideas of E.D. Hirsch, Jr., a professor at the University of Virginia in Charlottesville.

"We've been trying very hard to make these standards rigorous," Seaborg said at the meeting, a tie with the periodic table of elements peeking from beneath his three-piece suit. "We want them to be well-coordinated so that in elementary school students are prepared for middle school, and in middle school they are prepared for high school. I believe that there's a tendency to underestimate what students can learn, and that's something I've been arguing against—people who want to take all of these things out because they say that children can't understand them."

The first major issue to emerge in the committee concerned how much content to include, particularly at the elementary level. From the beginning, Seaborg and his allies adhered to a "more is more" philosophy—both in terms of the amount of material covered and its depth at each grade. "I don't believe you can do harm by introducing material too early," says Metzenberg, the lead consultant for Associated Scientists. "There's a possibility that an idea might go over some students' heads and that they might be frustrated by that. But to say that things are made of objects too small to see and those things are called atoms, I don't think that hurts a child."

Seaborg, and others in the Associated Scientists group, do not reflect the consensus of the larger scientific community, says Ramon Lopez, the director of education for the American Physical Society in College Park, Md. Considering California's vast influence on textbook and curriculum development nationally, the state board should not endorse a document that many scientists disapprove of, he argues.

"Scientists understand that you learn science by doing science," says Lopez, whose group is leading the latest campaign against the proposal. "Simply by the breadth of the content material and the prescriptive level of detail, it is very difficult to imagine that teachers will be able to do much more than have kids memorize things."

Another point of contention among standards commission members involved the structure of science classes. Early drafts of the document combined the standards for grades 6–8. That way, each school could decide when to teach earth science, life science, and physical science and whether to teach the subjects in an integrated or disciplinary fashion.

Such clustering of standards was criticized by Seaborg and others. The original legislation had called for grade-by-grade standards, though standards documents for other subjects already had ignored that edict. What's more, standards that span several grades would make it difficult for test-makers to design the companion assessment system.

The committee almost splintered over the issue. Joining Seaborg among the dissenters was Hoover Institution fellow Bill Evers, the commissioner who had written the minority report on the math standards. Together, they threatened to write another minority report that they would present to the state board. "All of our work was colored by that threat," says Sussman of the Science Coalition. "It weakened the position of [our] group. We knew we could win some battles within the commission that we would lose with the board." Reluctantly, the advocates of clustered standards agreed to have students study earth science in 6th grade, life science in 7th grade, and physical science in 8th grade.

But several on the science committee remained uncomfortable with such a traditional tack. Mike Aiello, an award-winning biology teacher at San Luis Obispo High School, pointed to the recent poor showing of American students on the Third International Mathematics and Science Study as proof of the need for an integrated approach. "The lesson of TIMSS is that we ought to build on these subjects each year," he says. "That way, as kids move through the system, they will retain more knowledge, and we won't have to reteach so much."

Slowly a compromise began to emerge. The standards would continue to focus on a separate discipline in each of the three grades. But each grade would include strands from the other two disciplines. For example, sections titled "Earth and Life History" and "Physical Principles in Living Systems" were added to the 7th grade standards for life science.

The final major controversy revolved around the high school standards. The first draft included an enormous amount of material. A single example from a single discipline, physics: "Students know that the force on a moving particle (with charge q) in a magnetic field is $qvB \sin(a)$ where a is the angle between v and B (v and B are the magnitudes of vectors **v** and **B,** respectively), and students use the right-hand rule to find the direction of this force."

Teachers on the committee said it would be impossible to teach all students all that material. As Aiello puts it, "If you don't give people something that's a reasonable stretch, a lot of people will just say, 'Forget it.'" After lengthy discussion, another compromise was reached. Some of the standards would be marked with asterisks, indicating that those items were optional. Students would be expected to master all the standards without asterisks. In addition, high schools would be expected to offer all the asterisked material for students who planned to go on in science. And in a final twist, the committee recommended that all students master the asterisked standards in at least one scientific discipline.

Seaborg had a problem with the plan. He believed that far too many items remained optional. "The standards would be strengthened by removing the asterisks on some of the 9–12 standards to raise the level of expectations for all students," he told the other commissioners.

During the standards commission's two years of work, the media often characterized the disagreements as a split between scientists and science educators. Outsiders also often blamed the commission's differences on politics. But the lines were not nearly that clear.

Many of the commissioners and consultants caution against dividing the group into two separate camps. "It makes for good arguments," says WestEd's Sussman. "But it doesn't do much to resolve the issues."

Metzenberg agrees. "There are polar extremes on many of these issues, and both extremes are wrong."

Still, the commissioners had profound differences on issues that go to the heart of education—instructional style, the appropriate age at which to introduce material, the best way to assess student learning, and the interpretation of research. Their frequent clashes were rooted in fundamental disagreements over what and how children should learn.

On one side, says Bill Evers of the Hoover Institution, are people who emphasize the content of science instruction. On the other are those who focus on inquiry as a means of learning science. "The content-rich group believes that instruction should be mostly the conveying of objective knowledge," explains Evers, a Seaborg ally on most issues. "That doesn't necessarily mean rote memorization. But memorization doesn't strike them as counterproductive. So the lecture method, while it shouldn't occupy 100 percent of a class, could be used to convey knowledge, and they would be comfortable with that."

In his formulation, the opposing camp focuses on the process of doing science. Members of this group believe that students master content largely from doing projects in which they can rediscover scientific concepts for themselves, Evers says.

Bonnie Brunkhorst, the lead consultant for the Science Coalition, rejects Evers' distinctions. "We're all in favor of students learning content, and it's irresponsible to say that any one group favors content more than any other," she says.

The two also disagree over the issue of age-appropriateness.

Brunkhorst insists that introducing certain scientific ideas to students too early is counterproductive. "When we know from generations of experience that most students cannot learn a particular abstract concept when they are 5 years old, it's not responsible to say that we're going to teach them that concept anyway. You need to focus attention on what students can learn and then leave open opportunities for them to learn more."

For his part, Evers says the notion has been overblown. "Young people have open minds. So students are being cheated by not getting a full range of instruction in the younger grades. Instead of talking about what's age-appropriate," he argues, "we should be talking about what's intellectually appropriate."

Instructional methods and assessments are additional points of difference between the two. Lectures should be just part of the instruction mix, Brunkhorst believes. And assessments should consist of multiple measures, not the straightforward tests of content mastery favored by Evers.

These are not easy issues to resolve. Evers terms the research base favoring inquiry-based learning "a joke." But he admits that research supporting direct instruction is equally deficient.

Counters Brunkhorst: "For the last 100 years, we have practiced a traditional approach to teaching, and we have a rich base of evidence that this approach has not worked. It might have worked for the Glenn Seaborgs of the world, but we haven't succeeded in making science usable for the general population. What more evidence do we need than the millions of students who have come through our educational system without learning science?"

There were times during the standards-writing process in which the differences among the commissioners appeared insurmountable. The process seemed on the verge of breaking down.

But it did not. In the month before the commission's July 1 deadline for turning the standards over to the state school board, members of the science committee held a flurry of telephone conference calls and hurried meetings near airports. They added some content at the elementary school level, smoothed out the disciplinary strands at the middle school level, and agreed on what should carry an asterisk at the high school level.

On the day before the final scheduled meeting of the full commission, the committee decided that the standards were ready to go.

First, though, all the commissioners had to vote on the standards. The tally was 16 in favor, none opposed, and two abstaining. (Three commissioners were not present.) One abstention was from La Tanya Wright, a parent and home-schooler who worked on the history/social science standards. Ms. Wright was concerned about the optional items, given that the standards were meant to apply to all students.

Seaborg also abstained. He continued to contend that too many of the high school standards had asterisks. And he insisted that the high school standards should be broken down by grade and discipline, with biology in 9th grade, chemistry in 10th, physics in 11th, and earth science in 12th.

After the commission's final meeting, the state board told the members that their job was over. Originally, they were to have converted the content standards into performance standards, which would then have been converted into tests. But the governor pressured the commission to relinquish that task to the school board.

Even though their job is completed, the commissioners wonder if their effort will have an impact. Good science classes require well-trained teachers, up-to-date materials, a supportive school system, and time to do the job right. A sheaf of standards sitting on a shelf doesn't magically produce those things. "This commission can write standards, but that doesn't mean anyone's going to do anything," Aiello says.

Nor do standards provide the resources many say are needed to improve California's overall education performance. The state remains in the bottom third of the nation in per-pupil spending, for example. "The educational system is entrusted with achieving high standards but is not given the resources to deal with all the problems it faces," says Hill, the commission's executive director.

Still, the commissioners were generally pleased with their work. Even Seaborg praised the standards as "challenging," despite the reservations that led to his abstention from the final vote.

"It's been a difficult process," concludes Hill, "but this is democracy in action."

. . . .

Dictatorship of Virtue

Multiculturalism in Elementary and Secondary Schools

Richard Bernstein

This selection first appeared in the *American Experiment Quarterly*'s Summer 1998 edition. Journalist Richard Bernstein is a book critic for the *New York Times*, where he has also been United Nations correspondent and national cultural correspondent. Two of his four books are about China; he opened *Time* magazine's first Beijing bureau in 1980.

In his book Dictatorship of Virtue: Multiculturalism and the Battle for America's Future *(1994), Bernstein wrote, "Scratch the surface of a multiculturalist curriculum, and there is this worm gnawing away at any notion of American goodness. What emerges is the passion play of victims and oppressors, colonizers and colonized." A* Boston Globe *reviewer called the book "tart, sometimes eloquent, always graceful and lucid." Bernstein spoke to a Center of the American Experiment audience on this subject in October 1997.*

One of the frustrations of the topic of multiculturalism and the assault on the concept of an American identity is that it takes such a multitude of forms that it is difficult to keep track of it all. Multiculturalism and its closely allied phenomenon of political correctness (PC) show up mostly in small ways, in a statement here, a program there. It is not a centralized movement with a head office and an official newsletter. It is, in short, difficult to keep track of and difficult to define with precision. And when we do define it, we tend to focus attention on certain outrageous episodes that happen to catch the media's attention—like some excess of gender-neutral language, or the book *Politically Correct Bedtime Stories*, or an outrageous sexual harassment charge: a six-year-old boy, for example, accused of harassment for kissing a six-year-old girl on the cheek.

But most often the examples are too small to make it into the newspapers, even though it is this nonspectacular, normative sort of PCness that, in my view, is the real PCness. Let me give you an example, an illustration of the way in which the PC sensibility has become so pervasive as to have become normal, almost unnoticed.

I was in Barnes and Noble, where I had occasion to leaf through a large, reference-sized volume called *Masterpieces of World Literature* published by HarperCollins. It provided short, readable, quite high quality articles on perhaps a couple hundred acknowledged literary masterpieces. I was doing a review for the *New York Times* on a novel that was based on the Oedipus plays by the immortal Sophocles, and I needed a kind of Cliffs Notes fix to remind me of some of the characters' names and their roles. I was reminded, reading the synopsis and the explanatory articles on *Oedipus the King* and *Oedipus at Colonus,* of how staggeringly great the Sophocles plays are and why they have stood the test of time. For me the essential element of those plays was Oedipus's amazing integrity, his courage in accepting the consequences for what was—true—a flaw in his character, but what was also an unmerited tragic fate. I hadn't read or seen or even thought about the Oedipus plays for many years, and so, reading the articles in *Masterpieces of World Literature,* I found myself once again inspired by Sophocles' great vision. This was a writer who dared to imagine the unimaginable and, in so doing, created two works of staggering strangeness, moral illumination, and poetic grandeur.

The other works in *Masterpieces of World Literature* had much the same ring. I won't list all of the books that are included, but I did note down the first work for each letter of the alphabet, beginning with *Absalom, Absalom!* by William Faulkner and ending with *Waiting for Godot* by Samuel Beckett, with such works as Voltaire's *Candide,* Dickens's *David Copperfield,* Steinbeck's *East of Eden,* and Rabelais's *Gargantua and Pantagruel* in between, along with *Hamlet, The Iliad, Das Kapital,* Sappho's "Ode to Aphrodite," *Paradise Lost,* the *Ramayana, The Tale of Genji, The Trial* by Franz Kafka, and *Ulysses* by James Joyce. A good list for lovers of literature.

Then I noticed that there was a whole set of these *Masterpieces* books, and it was the others in the series that bring me to my point. The other volumes were *Masterpieces of Women's Literature, Masterpieces of African-American Literature,* and *Masterpieces of Latino Literature.* I breezed through these other volumes and found what I expected to find. Let me give you a sense of it by going over the list—first work for each letter of the alphabet—for the *Masterpieces of Women's Literature.* There was, first, *Adam Bede* by George Eliot, a book that happens also to be in the *Masterpieces of World Literature* list. The first book under *B* was *Backlash* by Susan Faludi. This book, published in 1991, is a lengthy argument by a journalist for the *Wall Street Journal* to the effect that men were finding ways to rob women of the progress made by the women's movement. You can agree or disagree with Faludi's argument, but even if you agree, would you place her book, not yet a decade old, into the "masterpiece" category? Would you call it "literature"? I happen to know Susan Faludi, and I like her, even if we don't always see eye to eye. I think she would probably agree that putting *Backlash* on a list of literary masterpieces is a bit of a stretch.

It gets worse—or, at least, it does not get better. Next on the women's list is a work called *Calm Down Mother,* a one-act play by Megan Terry. The women's book in its summary categorizes each work according to what it calls "type of plot," and *Calm Down Mother*'s type of plot is "feminist." I had not realized that the word feminist could be used to describe a type of plot. I wonder: Is there a type of plot that is black? Another that is white? Christian? Jewish? Are there Republican plot types and Democratic ones, conservative and liberal? I suspect that an "antifeminist" plot might have a hard time making it onto the masterpieces of women's literature list.

To continue, though I promise not for too much longer. The next work, the first book listed under *D: A Diary from Dixie* by Mary Boykin Chesnut. This book is a Civil War diary that "reveals a keen awareness of the oppression to which women—black and white, slave or free—were subjected during that period." Chesnut, the description of her book continues, was "fond of her husband" (I like that expression, "fond of her husband," which stands in stark contrast to the possibility that Chesnut actually loved her husband), but she saw all women, rich and poor, as "slaves to men."

And so we find another illustration of another characteristic of multiculturalism, and we are only up to the letter *D*. It is what I call the equality of suffering syndrome, and the main idea is that all people who are not white and male have been equally victimized by that vale of tears that is patriarchal history. Mary Chesnut may or may not have actually believed in the antebellum American South that slave women and free women were equal sufferers. If she did believe that, then she was a very foolish woman and her works would almost by definition have to be excluded from any list of "masterpieces." In any case, the little blurb about her illustrates another element in the multiculturalist picture, which is its careful, assiduous, reverential cultivation of the cult of victimhood, by which women, gays and lesbians, Hispanics, Asians, disabled people, and various others are assumed to be just as disadvantaged as blacks were in American history.

Just for your information, some of the other works that are listed are *Fear of Flying* by Erica Jong, *The Female Eunuch* by Germaine Greer, *The Feminine Mystique* by Betty Friedan, *Against Our Will* by Susan Brownmiller, and *Intercourse* by Andrea Dworkin, this last book described as one in which the author "attributes women's societal subordination to their becoming a colonized people through the act which intimately connects them to their oppressors—sexual intercourse."

Politics and Power Grabs

What does the example of *Masterpieces of Women's Literature* tell us about the multiculturalist world that we inhabit? Or, to put this question a different way: What is the connection between the book in Barnes and Noble and an issue that has arisen lately in Minnesota, the issue of the Department of Education's newly published Rules for Educational Diversity? I think there are two connections, two ways in which the ideology behind the book and the ideology behind the rules manifest the same misconceived tendencies.

First, they both show that material is being chosen not because of its intrinsic merit, but because of the requirements of group politics. Secondary works are elevated to the status of "masterpiece" by political decree, in the same way that educational requirements are altered to try to bring about an arithmetic equality of results among every group in the society. Second, they both show the way in which what is presented as a literary or educational program is really a political program, or even a grab for power. *Masterpieces of Women's Literature,* with its inclusion of every feminist tract ever written and its choice of secondary works showing the supposed oppression of women, poses as a literary endeavor; actually, it is pure politics, a politics that pushes us to redefine literary standards—or, what is more common, to eliminate them altogether on the grounds that they are, as Catharine MacKinnon has said, just the things that white males value about themselves anyway. A similar statement can be made about the Rules for Educational Diversity; it is a political program—an effort to purvey a particular, rather left-wing way of looking at the world—that preempts opposition by portraying itself as a way of making educational advances for disadvantaged students.

I happen to have some background information about the situation in Minnesota that might shed some light on what these rules would actually do to the schools if they were adopted. Some years ago, when I was doing research for my book, I was looking for a school that had adopted multiculturalism as its official philosophy. I wanted to visit it, interview teachers and administrators, see classrooms and curriculum materials, and get a sense of what the multiculturalist system of education of the future would look like. I chose the Hans Christian Andersen School of Many Voices in Minneapolis. It was here that I first encountered that not-very-euphonious phrase *MCGFDA pedagogy*, which reappeared in the diversity rules proposed for the entire state. MCGFDA stands for multicultural, gender fair, disability aware. What is it?

Let me be clear about one thing. I spent two days at the Hans Christian Andersen School of Many Voices, and I was impressed with the spirit of the enterprise, the liveliness and attractiveness of the place itself, the dedication of the teachers, their obvious energy and commitment. Like Will Rogers, I didn't meet anybody I didn't like. They clearly believed that they were doing what was best for children, especially the black, Hispanic, and Native American children who made up about three-quarters of the school's population.

But when I looked at the curriculum, at the message conveyed to the pupils there, I did not have a favorable impression. The school was a realm for the practice of the victim cult, with white males set up as the victimizers of all of the nonwhite peoples, who represented the good. The underlying message of the place (actually, it wasn't all that underlying: it was pretty overt) was that we are all different rather than all the same and that we have to stress that difference, to identify with it in almost everything we do.

The most conspicuous part of the school—aside from the banner with the fabled initials MCGFDA on it—was the veritable cult of difference that existed there, the power of the pressure on pupils to think of themselves as members of small groups whose character and identities stemmed from that association. I attended a poetry-reading class for one of the lower elementary grades (the school went from kindergarten to fifth grade). As each poem was recited, the teacher would ask the students to identify its ethnic origins. And so after the poem, the children would shout out "Langston Hughes—African American." They sang in unison "European American" after the name of another poet, "American Indian-Zuni" after a third, "Asian-Chinese" for yet another. The feeling pervaded the school that recognizing the diversity of American life was not just a goal created in the service of tolerance, but that it was the ultimate objective of the entire educational experience, the single-issue campaign to be waged through the six years that children would spend there. A banner displayed in the school saying "I Learn Through Diversity" summed up this idea. But that seemed to me an empty slogan, a phrase utterly without real meaning. How does one learn through diversity? Does it help with addition? Can you master a foreign language with it? Does it teach correct English usage? Could there be another banner reading "I Learn Through Homogeneity"?

On a bulletin board, I saw a display of essays in which the children expressed their ideas on making the world a better place. At the bottom of each little essay, the pupils had written their names and their ethnic identity, along the lines of "My name is John Smith and my culture is European American" or "My name is Elisa Jones and my culture is African American." There was, in other words, no American culture, no common culture at the school. There were just separate cultures, which, upon further scrutiny, were actually divided into two cultures: the hegemonic white male culture and all the oppressed cultures.

My impression of a left-wing and highly politicized curriculum was intensified when I asked several social studies teachers what they actually taught. Their answers suggested that the notion of victims and victimizers was an organizing principle of the school's program. Whom do the students admire after they have finished at the school? I asked one teacher. Her reply: "The sentiment in my room is that they don't like Christians and they don't like white people, because they saw what has been done in the name of Christianity and what the white people did to the Indians and the Africans."

What about George Washington? I asked, wondering if there was at least one admirable white person for American children to admire. What do you teach about him? "That he was the first president, that he was a slave owner, that he was rich—not much," she replied. This teacher (who, it must be stressed, was a dedicated person who gave a strong impression of caring deeply about her pupils), told me that her pupils did learn about Eli Whitney, the cotton gin inventor, in her social studies class. The children learn "that he stole his invention from a woman who didn't patent it," she said, spoiling my illusion that at least some whites could be portrayed in a generous and positive way under the strict rules of MCGFDA pedagogy.

Clichéd Diversity

This brings me to my second observation, about the use of that word *diversity* and its actual meaning, as in a phrase like "educational diversity rules." Actually, of course, multiculturalism has almost nothing to do with culture, and it isn't multi either. *Multiculturalism* is a code word for a left-wing political program that preempts opposition by presenting itself as a call for respect, tolerance, and diversity. The reality is that, as it is practiced, multiculturalism is not respectful or tolerant of difference, and its idea of diversity is an extremely truncated one. Diversity to a multiculturalist means a group of people who look different and who have different sexual practices, but who, when it comes to politics, think pretty much alike.

Put another way, "diversity" in practice is actually a political philosophy lying on a rather narrow band of the political-cultural spectrum that is utterly and exclusively Western in origin and inspiration. As a journalist who has done a fair amount of traveling in the world, I sometimes imagine what a multiculturalist would make of the actual diversity that exists across the globe, as opposed to the comforting, cliché-ridden "diversity" of the American multiculturalist imagination. The truth of the matter is this: If you want real multiculturalism, get on an airplane and go someplace else—out there in that great region of the world called Abroad, where practices like female circumcision abound, along with amputation of the hands of thieves, head-to-foot veils for women, and death sentences for those who write supposedly "blasphemous" books. That place called Abroad, by the way, is not the place where tolerance for homosexuality was invented, or equal rights for women, or where the phrase about all men being born equal and endowed by their creator with certain inalienable rights was struck. Try getting on the bus in China and you will see what multiculturalism is all about.

My point is that multiculturalism is at best a misnomer, a well-intended but inaccurate synonym for a set of values that is Western in origin and that makes up a key part of the American culture to which we all actually belong, even as multiculturalism denies that there is such a thing as a common American culture. The funny thing is that in all of my travels among the multiculturalists, I almost never encountered one who had actually bothered to undertake serious study of another culture. It might have something to do with the fact that it's a lot easier and more emotionally gratifying to learn a few honeyed and heartwarming clichés than to acquire in-depth knowledge.

Except, of course, when our own culture enters the picture and then, suddenly, the same warm feelings about the worth and value of all cultures no longer apply. One of multiculturalism's main features is its denigration of the West. The multiculturalist is a bit like the "idiot" in

The Mikado who sings enthusiastic praises of "all centuries but this and every country but his own." There are more than a few odd things about this, not least of them the fact that nothing could be more Western in origin and in values than multiculturalism itself. Beyond that is the not insignificant fact that our culture happens to have produced a larger number of people living in stable conditions of freedom and prosperity than ever before in human history. We have our problems, true, but we are also better off in the United States of America with our own culture, not with the Chinese culture or the African culture, or what the inventors of those heartwarming clichés like to call the holistic Native American culture. For the members of my subgroup, the Jews, the gradual realization in practice of American values has led to greater prosperity for more people in conditions of the greatest political freedom and the fullest participation than at any time in Jewish history since the destruction of the Second Temple. There is, in other words, something more to this culture than the allegory of unfairness and victimization that the pupils are learning at the Hans Christian Andersen School of Many Voices.

I, for one, prefer to be a member of the culture that we share as Americans. I am glad that, when I went to public school in a little town in southeastern Connecticut in the benighted and nonmulticulturalist 1950s, no well-meaning and virtuous educational bureaucrat had decreed how good it would be for me to have to stand up and say to the others, "My name is Richard Bernstein and my culture is Jewish American." To have done so would have been to reduce the real and ineffable complexity of human life to a few simple concepts that these bureaucrats, in their ignorance, think they understand. I would want my children, in their public institutions, to be treated irrespective of their private identities, not to have those identities hung on their breast like a badge of merit. I am a Jew. I am an American. It is for the public schools to inculcate the knowledge and the awareness that I need in the American part of my identity; the other part of it is my business.

Mastery or Representation?

What multiculturalism does, of course, is make private identities the business of bureaucrats. It also leads citizens to make demands on each other based on their racial or sexual identities, a practice that I believe will prove to be divisive and harmful. And it encourages children to see themselves as defined by their origins rather than as self-fashioning individuals. Multiculturalism is based on the idea that race and ethnicity determine not only your social position but also a great deal about the way you learn and look at the world. One of the multiculturalist leaders I encountered in my research a few years ago was an educational consultant named Peggy McIntosh of the Wellesley Center for Research on Women, who lectures to school systems around the country on such things as white privilege and the different "way of knowing" of black children and white children. This is a little hard to believe, but Ms. McIntosh gets a respectful hearing for the idea that white children engage in something called "pinnacled learning" while black children engage something that she calls the "lateral" part of the psyche. In "pinnacled" learning the stress is on "mastery," on correctness versus wrongness, while lateral learning has to do with "our connections with the world, as we grow and develop as bodies in the body of the world."

The plain fact is that if children are going to do well in life as adults they are going to have to achieve a degree of "mastery," of learning how to get things right rather than wrong. Certainly every child is entitled to sensitive, individual treatment, to a degree of nurturing and encouragement that is appropriate to that child. But the various theories about multiculturalist education—most important, that children's all-important self-esteem hinges on, as the common phrase has it, "seeing themselves reflected in the curriculum"—are more often than not just a lot of silliness masquerading as sensitivity to the spiritual makeup of each child. The truth is that the children who are doing the best in school today, Jews and Asians, are precisely those children most ignored by the multiculturalist imperative. They are the children whose groups are almost not reflected in the curriculum at all. In Milwaukee a few years ago, half of the valedictorians in the city's high schools were the children of Hmong refugees, a group that, you can be sure, had not yet been incorporated into the multiculturalist curriculum.

And yet, the effort to create a curriculum based not on what children need to know but on some principle of racial and ethnic representativeness continues to gain momentum in school systems across the country. It is the rough equivalent of *Masterpieces of Women's Literature,* with its implicit advocacy of the idea that literature has sex or race, that there is something fundamentally different in the idea of women's literature or men's literature. When it comes to literature, I think that one would be far more challenged by Sophocles than by Erica Jong, and I would rather that schools taught the former, even if Sophocles is just another dead white European male and a representative of the white male patriarchal culture.

In the educational sphere, diversity sweeps out of the picture the inescapable fact that there is a body of knowledge that all children must master for success in the future and that this knowledge has no race or sex. To encourage children and their parents in the idea that racial and sexual representativeness is the key to a better educational experience is to defraud them. That is the most painful irony of the multiculturalist-diversity program: It is harmful and fraudulent for the very people it is supposedly aimed at saving. *Masterpieces of Women's Literature* is a political program justifying itself as a literary one. Multiculturalism is, similarly, an effort to advance a debatable political proposition, a debatable vision of American life, as an educational panacea. We shouldn't fall into the honeyed multiculturalist trap. We don't need it and shouldn't want it.

Richard Bernstein's speech was part of American Experiment's Tim Penny–Vin Weber Distinguished Fellows symposium series, which focused in 1997 on the excesses of multiculturalism. Following his speech, Bernstein spoke with members of the audience, including discussion leaders Vin Weber and Tim Penny, former Minnesota representatives to Congress.

Vin Weber: *You've seen the bumper sticker that says "Celebrate Diversity." Doesn't that obscure the fact that, simply put, diversity creates a lot of problems? Not that it is something you necessarily want to resist, not that we haven't overcome those problems in the past, and certainly not that it isn't valuable for people to have broadening experiences, but isn't the hard reality that demographic change in a country does cause friction and tension and problems? Instead of mindlessly saying we should celebrate these things, I would be seriously thinking about how we deal with the problems and the consequences.*

Richard Bernstein: *I agree, but that is a given of American life, and it is not a given that is going away. We do come from different backgrounds: We are a multiracial society, we were multiracial from the very beginning, and we are becoming more multiracial now. Immigration from Asia is very strong.*

Whether you think of immigration as an element of enrichment or as a problem—and I think of it as both—one of the great things about living in America is that we are diverse. But what does that really mean? When the diversity advocates talk about diversity, it is a code word for a political ideology. It has nothing whatsoever to do with the ways in which a society copes with group identities. American society has coped reasonably well, especially in the past half century. It coped very badly with racial diversity for much of our history, but in the past forty or fifty years, it has allowed people to carve out a sphere in their private lives, and to some extent in their public identities, for their particular group identity. It is OK in American life to present yourself—even publicly—as Jewish, Italian, black, Latino, or whatever, but everyone masters a central, public American culture. What multiculturalism does, it seems to me, is to stand that brilliant solution on its head: It declares that your group identity will be the main feature of your public identity rather than a secondary or private element. The idea that in order for students to do well in school they have to be immersed in their culture is an offshoot of that.

Teachers don't really know what those cultures are, nor do they appreciate the extent to which recent immigrants have come to America—like others who came earlier—in order to take advantage of the freedom and opportunity this country offers. And teachers seem to be abysmally unaware of the fact that in many instances the students who do the best in school are not those who have been immersed in their native cultures.

When I was in Milwaukee in 1992 or 1993 as part of the research for my book, I learned that roughly half of the valedictorians in the Milwaukee high school system—there are something like fourteen or fifteen high schools—were the children of Hmong people, people from the mountains of Laos who fought on the American side during the Vietnam War. They are not immersed in Hmong culture in the schools, and they do not see themselves reflected in the curriculum in the Milwaukee public school system, yet they do very well. The whole idea that in order for students to do well they have to be immersed in their culture is silliness. There is no substantiation for that in actual experience.

Tim Penny: *Someone remarked at a dinner the other evening that the debate about the quality of our schools, which ought to be about education, has been distracted by a debate about race. How do we find our way back?*

Richard Bernstein: *We certainly should not ignore the problems that some groups are having in the schools. Why the achievement of black children and Latino children seems to be below that of many other children is a problem that we can't turn away from and expect that we are going to offer an alternative to the diversity initiative. Let's face it, that's where the diversity initiative comes from—from a genuine concern that some segments of the population, on average, are not doing as well as others, and so a requirement comes along that every segment of the population shall do as well as every other segment in graduation rates, in representation in the curriculum, and so on. This is a genuine concern, and it is not one that we can ignore.*

It comes down to more attention to the schools, better basic education, more parent involvement in the schools—not to offering the panacea that if you see yourself reflected in the curriculum or if you are segregated into your own little cultural department of the university or the school, somehow your educational achievement is going to improve. It is a fraud perpetrated on the people who most need help that identifying more with their culture will improve their self-esteem and raise their achievement levels. Achievement levels go up because of good schools, good teachers, a curriculum that is based on what children really need to know, the tools that they need to master in order to get ahead in life.

Peggy McIntosh is the head of something called the SEED program—something about equal educational development—and a member of an organization called the Wellesley Center for Research on Women. It doesn't get more politically correct than that. She gives speeches all around the country on two kinds of learning. She starts out by talking about a little black girl she saw in Roxbury, Massachusetts, who was having difficulty adding up columns of figures. You see, this little black girl couldn't learn how to add up columns of figures because she was being culturally excluded from the school. The school was a white cultural school, and white people believe in what McIntosh calls pinnacled learning, which stresses right answers versus wrong answers.

Black people, McIntosh says, engage in a kind of lateral connectedness, in being "bodies in the body of the world." These are phrases that she uses over and over again. How insulting to say that black people are not concerned about getting it right or getting it wrong, that for them adding up a column of figures is somehow a different experience from a white person's adding up a column of figures. That kind of nonsense is very pervasive. We have to combat that kind of nonsense, but we also have to make sure that all children learn how to add up that column of figures.

Ruth Wollenberg: *My children attended school in the Hopkins district [just west of Minneapolis], which is using the SEED project to educate and inform teachers and parents. I asked about funding and found that it is grant money. How can we stop this project from being so pervasive?*

Richard Bernstein: *The cultural wars are real wars.*

When I did the research for Dictatorship of Virtue, *I got some financial support from the Smith Richardson Foundation and the Bradley Foundation, which are generally associated with conservatives—though I don't think of myself as a conservative. Nobody at either of those foundations ever asked to see a word that I wrote. They just thought the project was a good one.*

There is so much money around for multiculturalism; the foundations in general are extremely left-wing. The Ford Foundation especially has practically invented all of this stuff through financing the education and legal defense funds. Take a look when the MacArthur Foundation publishes its "genius awards" list and see how much more likely you are to be a genius if you study lesbian literature of the nine-teenth century than if you study Sophocles.

There's plenty of money available for this kind of thing. Why? Because it pre-sents itself as virtuous, as concern about the effects of racism and sexism, about the plight of the disadvantaged, and so forth. Certainly we must not ignore the reality of that plight. There are people who need help, and it is incumbent on those of us who don't believe in the Peggy McIntosh way to develop an alternative.

Alternatives are being carried out all over the country in all kinds of places. The program that the Bradley Foundation spends most money on is scholarships for chil-dren from low-income families who get into a parochial or private school. The Bradley Foundation will guarantee that that student will be able to go to that school, irrespective of financial need. It is a school-choice program, a way of subsidizing parents who want to send their children to better schools. The beneficiaries of that program overwhelmingly come from segments of the population that most need help, and they are getting good basic education for a better future. There needs to be more of that kind of thing.

Edward C. Anderson: *I used to be on the Hopkins school board, and I will tell you that in a big Minnesota school district, the middle-level management is very tough on this stuff. They are true believers.*

I would guess that 50 percent of graduating high school seniors don't know who wrote the Declaration of Independence, who George Washington was, who Babe Ruth was. Aren't we already way behind [in educating students about a common culture]?

Richard Bernstein: *I don't share that concern. I do feel that popular culture is very powerful, and that it draws people in and gives them a common culture, and that common culture transcends individuals' backgrounds.*

What I worry about is that in stressing immersion in your own culture and seeing yourself reflected in the curriculum, we are going to lose sight of what is truly great and challenging. Youth is wasted on the young, and that's already a big obstacle to overcome, but it is an especially big obstacle when adults are helping the young to waste their youth by not introducing them to the great works and the challenging ideas.

The educational curriculum in being politicized is also being watered down. If children in elementary school are not really learning about George Washington and the colonial struggle for independence, they are losing out. Most of us don't study George Washington anymore when we are in our twenties and thirties. We learn about him at a certain time, and not to learn about him is not just a matter of los-ing the common culture; it is also a matter of not learning something that is impor-tant and valuable about the creation of the political values that have made America free and prosperous.

In New York state, for example, students studying the creation of the federal Constitution are required to learn that federalism was modeled in part on the Iroquois Confederation. The central governing body and the five Iroquois tribes are now seen as equivalent to the federal government and the state governments. There is a whole mythology in books and papers and all kinds of curriculum materials that show the contribution of the Iroquois in the creation of the American system of government. If it were true that the system was modeled on the Iroquois, then of course we should learn it, because truth ought to be our most important commodity. It happens not to be true. It is a silly educational compensation that takes away from the difficult issue of how you create a government out of nothing. What kind of system do you create? What were the real problems that Thomas Jefferson and others faced as they wrote the Declaration and then moved on to form a government? If we don't learn about that, then we are not being schooled very well in the principles and challenges of political life. That's where I think we are falling down.

One of the elements in this picture is that multiculturalism does not come with a head office; it has numerous manifestations. To some extent, it's a sensibility that flourished among young adults in the 1960s, when, for the first time in American life, we began to see ourselves not as basically good with some faults, but as basically flawed with some good things. It's a vision of America as essentially a bad place characterized overwhelmingly by its vices rather than its virtues. This idea took hold of an entire generation who are now in their forties and fifties and at the height of their careers. They inhabit the important departments in the universities and the editorial boards of newspapers, including my own. This generational attitude is very important.

If I weren't worried about it, I wouldn't have spent three years on my book. People are becoming aware of this point of view and beginning to talk about it and forming groups in opposition to it. If there were a headquarters of academic multiculturalism and political correctness, it would be the Modern Language Association. Now there is a counterorganization, the Association of Literary Scholars. The National Association of Scholars, which has branches in practically every major university in the United States, is fighting against a lot of these trends. Another side has risen and the battle is joined; it is now up to us to win that battle. I think we can do it, but it is not going to be easy.

Vin Weber: *We've talked about academia and the nonprofit world, but it seems to me we're letting one big sector of American life—corporations—off the hook. Otherwise hard-headed, sensible businesses are absolute suckers for any cause that describes itself as multicultural or diversity-oriented. Virtually every major company now has a "diversity officer." Hasn't this permeated the corporate culture, as well as academia and the media and everybody else?*

Richard Bernstein: *Education is really at the root of the question—it's the future success or failure of American life—but, yes, I think that the post-1960s liberal culture dominates American life. Michael Lind, in* The Next American Nation, *divides American history up into different periods and argues that we are now in the multiculturalist phase, in which we arrange American life according to arithmetical formulas in which people are represented not on the basis of their individual merit, but on the basis of their membership in small and easily recognizable groups. Corporations have not suddenly been seized by the Peggy McIntosh philosophy, but are protecting themselves against the litigiousness of American life through diversity officers and sensitivity training sessions.*

The first chapter of my book, titled "Elementary Diversity," is an account of what you learn in sensitivity training these days. People of good sense are becoming aware of what is really going on in the guise of this benign and well-intentioned program. In theory, there's nothing wrong with corporations getting together and talking about how we all get along and what people from different groups think about each other. Healthy discussion would be fine, but it is indoctrination into proper thinking about race, sex, and the oppressiveness of American life. It is a kind of mandatory chapel, and that is why I oppose it.

David Pence: *As we try to find a way to get around diversity, what should our common culture be? I don't understand how we are going to get beyond multiculturalism unless we are able to make these very simple statements: That there is a religious sensibility that unites us, that we are created by God, that we all have souls. That's a darn good way to start a society from nothing; that's what we did, and that's what we are trying to do. You seem to shunt religion off to the side as a way to bring us together. Would you comment on that?*

Richard Bernstein: *Of course, religious freedom and religious tolerance are fundamental to American life, and one of the great achievements of American life has been to create a society in which we have synagogues and churches of all different sorts— and now, increasingly, mosques and Buddhist temples—side by side. I cling to the old-fashioned liberal notion that religion should be separate from publicly enforced action. I don't think that it would be appropriate for the state as embodied in the schools to insist on religion or on religious conviction as a basis for the American identity.*

I recognize, by the way, that these are difficult questions: Exactly what are the elements of the American identity? What should be put in and what should be left out? Whatever it is, I know that it should be decided on the basis of truth and real educational value rather than satisfying the requirements of an interest group or a pressure group, including religious pressure groups. I am opposed to the teaching of creationism in the public schools because it is simply not scientifically verifiable.

Religion for me is a preserve of private life, and the ability of Americans to keep religion in the individual's private sphere and not to have it operate in a very active way in the public sphere is one of the elements of the American genius and one of the elements for domestic tranquility, freedom, and prosperity. I really wouldn't want to tamper very much with that system.

Mary Ann Nelson *[superintendent of schools in Fridley, a Minneapolis suburb]: This is the kind of balanced dialogue we need. When you try to move forward with an idea like the SEED project, there are people of varying degrees of passion and thoughtfulness. I've worked in two districts where the SEED project has worked; there are a lot of people of good common sense who have treated it as merely a way to expand on understanding different cultures, not an ideological war.*

It seems to me that we've gotten on the wrong track with this focus on cultural differences to the point where we have failed to talk about personal values that are core democratic values. When you talk about differences among cultures, the thing that I think people fear is people who aren't like them, who don't have common values about appropriate behavior, whether it is in school or in the community. What we've tried to do in our school is talk about core democratic values and how to use them as a base for standards of behavior for parents as well as staff members. Would you comment on our failure to talk more about core democratic values and fight for them because they are what's right and good?

Richard Bernstein: *I appreciate what you're saying. It's easy for me to talk: I'm not a teacher or a school superintendent. I'm a newspaper reporter, and maybe that's why I don't feel qualified to come up with an alternative. I do think that there is something wrong with the way the multicultural movement approaches these issues, but I'm sure it is extremely difficult in the real world when you have to deal with all these constituencies and all of these passions to iron out a curriculum and a program and an educational philosophy that has support from the public and that also works. I admire people who can do it.*

Norms of behavior are very important, and they cannot be treated as attributes of one culture or another. Like the Peggy McIntosh theory about black children learning through some sort of lateral connections and white children learning through a pinnacle model, there is this notion that black children are somehow more active and a little more unruly than white children and therefore a different standard should apply to them. Treating children differently according to their race is the wrong way to go. We have to have the same expectations of all children, and we have to teach the same core values and the same core curriculum to all children—not as an aesthetic matter, and not to make America unified. I'm not worried about America being disunified; I don't think we're going to fracture like Yugoslavia. What I'm worried about is that certain groups in the population are not going to do well, and the way to help them do well is to teach them the same things we teach the groups that do do well and to make sure that they acquire the culture and the values and the knowledge that will enable them to go to medical school instead of working at Taco Bell. A lot of the educational philosophy that is current today is more likely to send them to Taco Bell.

Vin Weber: *I'm troubled by your answer to the question about religion because this whole topic and religion are all one in my mind. In the book* Modern Times, *Paul Johnson lays out his thesis that moral relativism is the dominant intellectual trend of this century and is responsible for most of its atrocities. It seems to me that what we are talking about is an outgrowth of our society's increasing inability to make definitive statements about virtually anything. The culture we have developed in this country is superior in measurable, quantifiable terms—life expectancy, infant mortality, and so on—to what has been achieved elsewhere. Religious traditions inculcated the values of both the citizenry and the elites in the society that produced that superior culture. The dominant culture is now hostile to those religious traditions. It seems to me that we are declaring war on the religious traditions that gave us this successful culture and trying to replace them with a secular religion.*

Tim Penny: *This reminds me of Richard's earlier comment about multiculturalism being like a religion in the way that it brings a sensibility factor rather than academic discipline into the educational setting. It's easy to get funding for multiculturalism, but you would have a lot of difficulty if you tried to bring into the school setting any sort of discussion about different religions in society and our communities. We can't seem to give true depth to this multiculturalism debate.*

Richard Bernstein: *There are some things we can agree on; maybe it will help to define the area in which we don't seem to agree, although it may be narrower than is apparent.*

I certainly agree that the political left and the identity politics the left has been promoting—the educational philosophy and the vision of American life that we find somehow off the tracks—is antireligious. American life is portrayed in the schools as an unrelieved history of oppression by a privileged white male majority, and religion is portrayed as complicit in that history of oppression. In that sense, bad history and bad values are being taught. There would have been no civil rights movement in America had we not come from a Judeo-Christian tradition, and of course the black civil rights leaders came out of the churches. The black churches were the centers of resistance to segregation and Jim Crow; they created a sense of dignity and worth among black people.

The genius of the civil rights movement was to insist not that "we blacks" are different and demand that our difference be respected, but that "we blacks" are the same and expect our sameness to be acknowledged in behavior and in law—and one of the things that makes us the same is our immersion in Christian society and Christian values and in the way those Christian values have been given secular expression in the Declaration of Independence and in the other principles of American life. Those are important, essential notions in the American experience, and they should be taught. Religious values should be given their proper place in the history of American life. There we agree.

The question that I heard was different, though. I thought I heard that we ought to be having prayer in school, Bible classes in school, that there ought to be instruction in the tenets and beliefs of Christianity, or perhaps Judeo-Christianity.

David Pence: *You assume that when people talk about religious sensibility they mean Bible reading and specific sectarian-type education in the schools, but I didn't say that. I do say this: There is a religious sensibility about what a human person is that lies at the core of the American experiment and at the core of the idea of limited government. You have limited government because you believe man is meant for something other than the state, other than political unity, which is an important idea but not the most important idea.*

The only solution to multiculturalism is to ask what we agree on. How do we teach these kids? Why do we tell them they've got to respect each other? It has to do with the fact that we are created by God in his image. If we don't say that, we can't put together all the people who make up America.

Richard Bernstein: *You are right to correct me: You didn't say anything about prayer in schools and Bible study and that sort of thing. But to make it a part of the curriculum that you must believe we were created in God's image is to me an importation of specific religious belief into a governmental institution; it is the kind of thing that is prohibited by the Constitution and the kind of thing that I* would want *to be prohibited by the Constitution.*

There is an important distinction to be made between studying the role of religion and religious values in American life—most often a role that we would see as progressive and successful—and making religious conviction central to the educational experience in the public schools. I don't know exactly how you would do that, what language you would use, what text you would use, but I don't agree that that is what we should do. Religion is for communities, families, individuals to decide for themselves in their private lives. For government to get involved is to go beyond its legally permissible scope.

COMPUTERS/DISTANCE LEARNING

Should Schools Be Wired to the Internet?

No—Learn First, Surf Later

David Gelernter

This selection first appeared in *Time* on 25 May 1998. David Gelernter is a professor of computer science at Yale University.

Quack medicine comes in two varieties: "irrelevant but harmless" and "toxic." The Administration's plan to wire American classrooms for Internet service is toxic quackery. Four-fifths of U.S. schools have Internet access already; instead of wiring the rest, we ought to lay down a startling new educational directive: First learn reading and writing, history and arithmetic. Then play Frisbee, go fishing, or surf the Internet. Lessons first, fun second.

I've used the Internet nearly every day since September 1982. It's a great way to gather information, communicate, and shop. And in one sense, the Internet is good for the American mind. Up through the early '90s, everyday written communication seemed to be dying out. Thanks to e-mail and fax machines, writing has come back. In this respect, the Internet could be a fine teaching tool—a way to share good, scarce writing teachers. One teacher could manage a whole district of students if they were all connected electronically.

But the push to net-connect every school is an educational disaster in the making. Our schools are in crisis. Statistics prove what I see every day as a parent and a college educator. My wife and I have a constant struggle to get our young boys to master the basic skills they need and our schools hate to teach. As a college teacher, I see the sorry outcome:

students who can't write worth a damn, who lack basic math and language skills. Our schools are scared to tell students to sit down and shut up and learn; drill it, memorize it, because you must master it whether it's fun or not. Children pay the price for our educational cowardice.

I've never met one parent or teacher or student or principal or even computer salesman who claimed that insufficient data is the root of the problem. With an Internet connection, you can gather the latest stuff from all over, but too many American high school students have never read one Mark Twain novel or Shakespeare play or Wordsworth poem, or a serious history of the U.S.; they are bad at science, useless at mathematics, hopeless at writing—but if they could only connect to the latest websites in Passaic and Peru, we'd see improvement? The Internet, said President Clinton in February, "could make it possible for every child with access to a computer to stretch a hand across a keyboard to reach every book ever written, every painting ever painted, every symphony ever composed." Pardon me, Mr. President, but this is demented. Most American children don't know what a symphony is. If we suddenly figured out how to teach each child one movement of one symphony, that would be a miracle.

And our skill-free children are overwhelmed by information even without the Internet. The glossy magazines and hundred-odd cable channels, the videotapes and computer CDs in most libraries and many homes—they need more information? It's as if the Administration were announcing that every child must have the fanciest scuba gear on the market—but these kids don't know how to swim, and fitting them out with scuba gear isn't just useless, it's irresponsible; they'll drown.

And it gets worse. Our children's attention spans are too short already, but the Web is a propaganda machine for short attention spans. The instant you get bored, click the mouse, and you're someplace else. Our children already prefer pictures to words, glitz to substance, fancy packaging to serious content. But the Web propagandizes relentlessly for glitz and pictures, for video and stylish packaging. And while it's full of first-rate information, it's also full of lies, garbage, and pornography so revolting you can't even describe it. There is no quality control on the Internet.

Still, imagine a well-run, serious school with an Internet hookup in the library for occasional use by students under supervision who are working on research projects; would that be so bad? No. Though it ranks around 944th on my list of important school improvements, it's not bad. But in reality, too many schools will use the Internet the same way they use computers themselves: to entertain children at minimal cost to teachers. If children are turned loose to surf, then Internet in the schools won't be a minor educational improvement, it will be a major disaster. Another one. Just what we need.

. . . .

The Learning Revolution

Lewis J. Perelman

This selection is taken from *Market Liberalism: A Paradigm for the 21st Century,* edited by David Boaz and Edward H. Crane, published by the Cato Institute, 1993. Lewis Perelman is author of the best-selling book *School's Out* (Avon Books, 1993) and principal of the Perelman Group, a consulting firm.

The collapse of the Soviet empire is just one of the most dramatic symptoms of the dawn of the new knowledge-age economy. One of the most critical of the many profound impacts of the technological revolution is the global obsolescence of traditional education and training institutions. Prosperity in the new economy depends on a complete replacement of worn-out public policies that are intended to subsidize and "save" those institutions. The new policy paradigm must focus on (1) abolishing the wasteful paper chase for academic credentials and (2) commercializing (not just privatizing) the economy of academia, the biggest and probably the last great empire on earth.

The New Economy

In the new economy being formed by explosive advances in information technologies, knowledge has become the crucial factor of production. Contrary to much of the conventional (and backward-looking) wisdom driving most recently proposed economic strategies, software has displaced manufacturing as the key to national economic strength, and learning has become the crucial form of work required for self-reliance and prosperity.

With learning now the indispensable focus of work, entertainment, and home life, the attempt to keep learning confined in the box of the government-controlled empire of school and college classrooms threatens to be as counterproductive as were political efforts at the beginning of the 20th century to protect the vast horse industry against the threat of the automobile.

National economic leadership, security, and prosperity at the beginning of this century depended on the swift, wholesale *replacement* of the horse-based transportation system by an all-new system based on the automobile (and shortly thereafter, the airplane). In the same way, economic progress in the 21st century will depend on the rapid replacement of schools and colleges—a $445 billion-a-year industry in the United States alone—by a new commercial industry based on the technology I call hyperlearning (HL).

Henry Ford's Model T was not an invention so much as the integration of a set of technical advances in power plants, rubber tires, electrical systems, and other components as well as fuel refining, production engineering, employment policies, and marketing strategies—a total system that changed not just transportation but the entire fabric of Western society. Similarly, HL represents the integration of skyrocketing advances in the so-called artificial intelligence of computers and robotics, broadband multimedia communications, "hyper" software needed to cope with the resulting information explosion, and even "brain technology" that is expanding our understanding of how human and artificial brains work.

"Hypermated" learning loops increasingly form the core of just about every kind of economically productive activity. The London Stock Exchange has replaced legions of shouting floor traders with an automated telecomputing network, following the lead of America's NASDAQ. The most prosperous farmers today spend more time working with computers than combines. Political rhetoric notwithstanding, factory "jobs" are not coming back: They are bound to become as productive, and hence as scarce and knowledge demanding, as farm jobs. General Electric's state-of-the-art light bulb factory in Virginia employs one-third the number of workers employed by the factory it replaced— and none ever touches a light bulb. Each of the few workers employed in Corning Glass's most modern plants is trained to be able to run every operation in the factory, not to do a "job." The work is primarily troubleshooting and managing the software of the automated systems that do the actual manufacturing.

The HL revolution cannot be brought about by any "reform" or "re-structuring" of schools and colleges, any more than the horse could be retrained or even genetically inbred to become a car. "Break-the-mold" schools can't and won't.

Education: A Barrier to Progress

A critical feature of the new world order marked by the collapse of so-cialism is that education, once widely viewed as an engine of prosper-ity, has become the major *barrier* to global economic progress.

The *overeducation* of the workforce is one of the major causes of the economic slump that has plagued the U.S. and other modern national economies for some three years. Roughly three-quarters of the thousands of employees being eliminated by major employers such as IBM, General Motors, and TRW are managerial, professional, and technical workers with extensive college and postgraduate education. In the present reces-sion, corporate middle managers have been 2.5 times more likely to be-come unemployed than the average worker. In past recessions, laid-off factory workers were rehired when sales recovered, but the recent rapid growth of white-collar unemployment represents the permanent elimi-nation of jobs. In the recession of the early 1980s, white-collar employ-ment kept on growing, and 90 percent of white-collar employees who lost their jobs were rehired within a few months. In the latest recession, white-collar employment has declined, and fewer than 25 percent of the dis-placed white-collar workers have been able to find new jobs.

Recent political campaign proposals called for more "investment" in the U.S. workforce in the form of expanded spending on traditional ed-ucation and training programs. The rhetoric masked the reality that the United States currently has the most highly schooled workforce in its history: From 1970 to 1989, workers with four years of high school in-creased from 31 to nearly 39 percent of the workforce, and the propor-tion of the U.S. workforce with at least four years of college nearly doubled from less than 11 to over 21 percent. Fewer than 23 percent, and probably no more than 15 percent, of U.S. jobs will call for college degrees in the 1990s. With over a quarter of the workforce planning to earn college diplomas, it is likely that 10 percent of U.S. college gradu-ates will be unemployed by the end of the decade, and between a quar-ter and a half of the graduates will be underemployed in jobs that do not really require their degrees.

The ongoing deflation of academic credentials will only be accelerated by the end of the Cold War. In the wake of the "brain glut" unleashed by the collapse of the Soviet Union, U.S. companies such as AT&T, Corning, and Sun Microsystems have been hiring top Russian scientists and engineers, among the best educated and most skilled workers in the world, to work in Russia for salaries on the order of *$60 a month*. And some 2 million of America's own most technically schooled and skilled workers are destined to become unemployed over the next two years as a result of defense spending cuts and force reductions.

A prime flaw in the whole educational system is that it was designed in the midst of the Industrial Revolution of the 19th century to prepare people for industrial-era jobs. But the kinds of skills required to work productively in the knowledge age are almost the opposite of the skills demanded for academic success. And the message buried in the statistics is that "jobs" for both the over-schooled and the unschooled are fast disappearing. Entrepreneurial skills are the ones most needed in the new economy, where the majority of the "workforce" will be made up of contractors, consultants, free agents, and traditional business creators and owners. Yet the competencies needed for successful entrepreneurship are almost totally ignored by the existing educational and training system.

Even as the services of the scholastic sector become increasingly irrelevant to the economic aspirations of the great majority of Americans, the cost of the obsolete academic bureaucracy continues to soar. Add the $50-billion-plus that employers spend to educate employees to the $450-billion annual school and college budget, and throw in at least another $100 billion a year spent on "hidden" forms of education (such as conferences and conventions), and the education sector is virtually tied with the health care sector as the biggest industry in the U.S economy.

The upward spiral of costs has been almost as explosive in education as in health care. Real spending per student in U.S. K–12 schools (discounting inflation) has grown some five times since the 1950s. In the 1980s real U.S. spending on K–12 schools grew by nearly a third; spending on colleges grew even more, by about a half.

Productivity, the key issue that has been neglected by education and training policies, needs to be the focal point of the new policy paradigm. Growth in productivity—increasing the amount of wealth produced by each hour of labor—is the essential measure of a nation's standard of living and relative "competitiveness." Weak growth in productivity has been the central symptom of America's economic malaise for some two decades.

Poor and declining productivity is the main reason the education sector has become a barrier and a threat to economic progress in the modern world. Education as an industry is nearly twice as labor intensive as is the average U.S. business, and its relative labor costs are more than twice those of high-tech industries such as telecommunications. Moreover, while the productivity of other information-based industries has been advancing smartly, even explosively, the soaring costs and stagnant output of the education sector have spelled a steady decline in productivity at least since the 1950s.

The sheer size of the education sector, America's first or second biggest industry, thus has been dragging down average growth in productivity. And education is undermining the national standard of living even more because, in addition to being a very large business, it is one that is strategically critical to the growth of a knowledge-age economy. With the learning enterprise playing the central economic role in the knowledge age that steel making played in the industrial age, a weak and declining learning sector is undercutting the development of nearly every other modern business.

The productivity-focused goals of the new paradigm of national learning policy that should replace intrusive and irrelevant "national education goals" can be summarized in four simple words: More, Better, Faster, and Cheaper. That is, policy needs to ensure the rapid development of HL systems that enable citizens of all ages to learn more about everything; to learn better, especially those things that are relevant to productive work; to learn faster, with less waste of time; and to do all that at lower and steadily declining cost.

HL technology already exists and is achieving those productivity goals in the segments of the national learning enterprise that are compelled by competitive forces to seek more and better learning in less time at lower cost—notably, in corporate and military organizations. For instance, U.S. corporate and military educators spend about 300 times more of their instructional budgets than public schools do on systems based on increasingly advanced computer and multimedia technology. The reason is that, in the competitive environments of the marketplace and the battlefield, learning objectives are focused on competency rather than credentials, and there are powerful rewards for productivity and thus for innovation.

The Action Plan

The national action plan needed to replace the worn-out and outdated education establishment with a 21st-century HL industry has four key strategies.

Decredentialize

First, America needs to eliminate the economic value of academic credentials. Credentialism has been the key barrier that has thwarted a half-century of attempts at educational reform and restructuring. As long as the public has reason to believe that elite academic credentials—based on attendance at the "right" institutions—are the essential passports to lucrative employment and other economic opportunities, the public will continue to resist any reform that gives learning and competency priority over testing and sorting. As long as public policy continues to presume that the cognitive needs of the "work-bound" population warrant categorically different, and hence inferior, treatment than those of the "college-bound" population, expenditures on education will continue to undermine rather than strengthen economic progress.

The economically productive alternative to credentialism is certification of competency. In short, people's opportunity to participate in employment or entrepreneurship should be based only on what they know and what they can do. There is simply no job or enterprise in this economy that truly requires an academic diploma or degree for successful performance. As Chief Justice Warren Burger wrote in the landmark civil rights case of *Griggs v. Duke Power,* "History is filled with examples of men and women who rendered highly effective performance without the conventional badges of accomplishment in terms of certificates, diplomas, or degrees."

A broad, even universal, commitment on the part of U.S. employers, as well as financing and other institutions, to eliminate the currency of diplomas would lead necessarily to a huge demand for effective tools to assess the know-how of applicants for jobs, small-business loans, and so forth. Sophisticated assessment tools already exist and are being used by leading employers such as the U.S. Army, Corning, Allstate, and Toyota. Making competency-based employment (and other economic access) a universal practice would spawn the rapid growth of a high-tech, profitable, cost-effective assessment industry. Funding for that new industry would come from some of the hundreds of billions of dollars that would be saved when tax and tuition payers were freed from paying tribute to the diploma mills.

There are several steps the new president should take to help achieve the goal of a diplomaless economy.

Federal Employment and Contracting.   As the nation's biggest employer, the federal government should demonstrate its commitment to decredentialization by reforming its own employment and contracting practices to eliminate all requirements for and references to scholastic diplomas and degrees. Military and other federal agencies already are more advanced than many other employers in relying on competency-based employment and training procedures, so the scope of this reform is not likely to be drastic. Much of it probably can be achieved by executive order, although some new legislation may be required to reconcile competency testing with civil rights law.

"SCANS II."   The Secretary's Commission on Achieving Necessary Skills (SCANS), which was convened by Secretary of Labor Elizabeth Dole and included representatives of a range of American industries, worked productively from 1990 to 1991 to define a set of competencies needed for employment in the modern economy, as well as criteria for assessing those skills. The new administration should help move the SCANS work from theory to practice by inviting U.S. employers, either through trade associations or individually, to join a coalition pledged to implement the kind of competency-based employment practices suggested by SCANS within a reasonable period of time—say, by January 1, 1995. The coalition could establish an oversight committee or council to monitor progress and to target regulatory or legal barriers that the government needs to reduce. The president also might establish, either through an executive agency or the employer coalition, something like the Baldridge Award (for quality management) to acknowledge leaders in competency-based employment.

Civil Rights.   The new president should order the Justice Department to review existing civil rights laws and regulations to determine to what extent employment discrimination based on academic diplomas may be in violation of the law.

Assessment Research and Development.   Through executive directive and whatever enabling legislation may be necessary, the new president should establish a new federal program of research and development on human performance assessment, aimed at advancing the cost-effectiveness of the technology needed to measure what people know and can do in the context of real work requirements. The program might best be centered in the National Institute of Standards and Technology (Commerce Department)—with active collaboration of the Defense Department (e.g., the Defense Advanced Research Projects Agency, the Office of Naval Research, and the Army Research Institute) and the National Science Foundation—or in the new Department of Knowledge Resources suggested below.

Entrepreneurship. The new president should order that, in all the above initiatives and others, preparation for and competency at entrepreneurship should be given priority at least equal to or greater than that given to employment.

Commercialize

In recent years many politicians, business leaders, and families have begun to appreciate the essential importance of breaking up the socialist monopoly of the government-controlled education system. "Privatization" of public education is much needed and should be a national goal of the new president. But "school choice" is an inadequate strategy for achieving the benefits of a market economy in the learning sector or for unleashing the growth of the strategically crucial HL industry.

In a long list of problems, the primary flaws in the school choice (including college choice) strategy are *vouchers* and *nonprofit organizations*. Because classroom teaching is technologically and economically obsolete in the HL era, choice in the form of vouchers for tuition at present-day schools is as irrelevant to hyperlearning as the choice of horses is to modern transportation. Because the commercial profit motive is absolutely indispensable to drive the rapid technological innovation the HL era demands, choice programs that merely redistribute public moneys among nonprofit schools—whether government owned, private, or church affiliated—are bound to be irrelevant and ineffectual.

Instead, the new administration should be committed to *commercial* privatization of the entire education sector, based on a strategy of *microchoice* using the financing mechanism of *microvouchers*.

To illustrate the idea of microchoice: If our choice of television channels worked the way school choice is proposed to, changing channels from HBO to CNN would require unplugging the TV set, taking it back to the store, exchanging it for a different model, and moving to a new neighborhood. In reality, of course, choosing among dozens or hundreds of video options requires no effort more strenuous than pushing a button. Similarly, modern HL technology can offer the individual even more choices of "teachers" and "schools" than of cable TV channels. HL's broadband, intelligent, multimedia systems permit anyone to learn anything, anywhere, anytime with grade-A results by matching learning resources precisely with personal needs and learning styles.

Microvouchers that use modern electronic card–account technology can enable individual families or students to choose specific learning products and services, not just once a year or once a semester, but by the week, day, hour, or even second by second. Unlike vouchers for school or college tuition, microvouchers will create a true, wide-open, location-free, competitive market for learning that has the elasticity to efficiently and quickly match supply and demand.

Over 90 percent of funding for U.S. public education is supplied by state and local governments, which also have the major policy-making role. Nevertheless, there are several steps the new president can take to commercialize the government-controlled education sector and to promote the development of the American HL industry that must replace it.

Federal Microvouchers.   The new president should seek legislation to merge 90 percent of the existing student loan, Pell grant, Job Training Partnership Act, Trade Adjustment and Assistance Act, Job Opportunities and Basic Skills program, Chapters I and II of the Education Consolidation and Improvement Act, and other federal education and training funds into a single, means-tested microvoucher program that eligible families or individuals could draw on to meet the learning and development needs of people of all ages. Funds should be allocated directly to households, in proportion to individual or family need, to be used for the purchase of any service or product that is demonstrably relevant to learning and development needs. The instrument of expenditure would not be paper stamps or vouchers but electronic account cards similar to credit or bank cards. The HL microvoucher program should leave families free to decide how best to distribute the account resources between adults and children and generally among the members of the household. That provision would recognize that the needs of disadvantaged children in many (perhaps even most) cases may be served best by immediately improving the economic opportunities and status of the parents, as well as by developing the parenting skills.

Family Learning Account. As a complement to the means-tested microvoucher program, the new administration should consider adding a tax-exempt saving program. Individuals should be permitted to make contributions to Family Learning Accounts (FLAs). Those contributions, which would be similar to contributions to Individual Retirement Accounts (IRAs), would be deductible from taxable income, up to some reasonable level, during the year the contributions were made. Unlike withdrawals from IRAs, withdrawals from FLAs would be exempt from both penalty and tax as long as they were expended through the microvoucher program. And such microvoucher expenditures could be repaid to FLAs (with interest) without being counted against the annual contribution limit. Beyond some age limit, provision may be made for FLA funds to be transferred to estates or pension accounts, with appropriate treatment of deferred taxes. Another difference from IRAs would be that FLAs would be designed to serve family rather than just individual needs. The general concept of the FLA is to encourage households to gradually replace the direct government grant funds in microvoucher accounts with tax-favored savings contributions.

Leveraging. Federal funds for education and training represent only about one-tenth of total public expenditure on those areas. A federal-only microvoucher program would, therefore, provide significant benefits only to the most disadvantaged portion of the U.S. population, although it would give the poor more of the freedom of choice and access to learning tools that the well-off already enjoy.

Although most of the economic problem caused by an obsolete, overfunded public education bureaucracy lies in the domain of state and local authorities, the president can use the power of the federal government to influence the direction of state policy. Specifically, the new president should consider making part or full eligibility for the consolidated federal microvoucher–FLA program dependent on state and local participation. The precedent for such a policy exists in a variety of federal transportation, welfare, health, and other programs. For instance, federal law required states to raise the legal drinking age to 21 to be eligible for federal highway funding. The new administration should determine whether such a policy may be necessary, in addition to the oft-cited "bully pulpit," to induce states to reconstruct their education budgets and bureaucracies along the lines recommended here.

Capitalize

The nearly total absence of investment in research, development, and implementation of new technology may be the main reason the education sector is a barrier to the growth of the HL industry and a brake on our whole economy. While the average U.S. business spends 2 percent of its annual revenues on research and development (R&D), and leading high-tech companies plow 7 to 20 percent or more of their annual sales receipts into R&D, the education industry invests less than 0.1 percent of its revenues in the research and development of new, improved technology.

The health care sector, which is essentially tied with education as America's biggest industry, spends about $18 billion annually on R&D; roughly half of that amount comes from government, and the other half comes from companies. In contrast, only about $300 million is spent annually in the United States on research and development of advanced learning technology, and virtually all of that amount is spent by the Defense Department. Another $2 billion a year for the development and acquisition of associated training systems may be hidden in DOD weapons budgets. Defense cutbacks threaten to wither that critical national technology asset, and currently there is no plan to preserve, much less expand, it.

Equally dismal is the education sector's record on capital investment—money that pays for the acquisition and application of technology to improve the quality of products and the productivity of operations. The average American business invests about $50,000 in capital for each job. In high-tech industries, such as computers or telecommunications, from $100,000 to $1 million needs to be invested for each worker. In the education sector, total capital investment per employee is less than $50.

The funding needed to close the yawning technology gap is on the order of $8 billion to $20 billion a year and should come entirely from the reallocation of some of the $445 billion now being wasted annually on the nation's obsolete and bloated education system.

Again, the federal government accounts for only a small fraction of the total funds spent on public education and training in the United States. If the technology gap is to be closed by reallocation from existing expenditures, it follows that most of that money will have to come from state and local rather than federal sources. This is an area in which the new president can and should use federal influence to leverage state policies.

National Institutes of Learning. Part of the 10 percent of existing federal education and training program funds not applied to the microchoice program discussed above should be used for challenge grants to reward states that agree to set aside at least 2 percent of their total current state (and local) education and training budgets for HL research and development. The challenge grants might represent a federal supplement of 10 percent or more to state R&D allocations. The R&D funds should be administered by state Institutes of Learning.

As the states implement the new policy, the state institutes should form a consortium, which could be called the National Institutes of Learning, perhaps with the federal government acting as coordinator. Although government organizations cannot and should not duplicate the product-development role of commercial business, the mission of the National Institutes of Learning should be, from the outset, to realize the ultimate goal of commercialization of advanced learning (that is, HL) technology.

Commercialization necessarily implies effective cooperation between government R&D programs and private industry. The U.S. agricultural research system and the federal Small Business Innovation Research program are two rather successful models that might be productively adapted to this new endeavor.

Learning Redevelopment Banks. The remainder of the 10 percent reserved from current federal education and training funds should be used for another matching grant program to induce states to set aside at least another 3 percent of their total current state (and local) education and training program budgets to help finance the reconstruction of the education sector's socialist economy. Education needs the same kind of major capital investment that other ex-socialist economies need to replace obsolete technology and retrain managers and workers who have little experience with or understanding of market operations. Those funds should be administered by redevelopment banks that, like the World Bank or the European Bank for Reconstruction and Development, will provide loans and grants to help replace government-controlled institutions with private, competitive, profit-seeking enterprises. Those funds and financial institutions need not and probably should not be permanent—a "sunset" provision that would shut them down after no more than 10 years should be included in their charters. But they should be given adequate funding and a long enough lifetime to speed the commercial privatization of the education sector.

Bypass

The huge, century-old Bell Telephone monopoly was forced to break up a decade ago largely because it was bypassed by new technologies that enabled consumers to get superior products and services from other suppliers. Today, "distance learning" technology—using telecommunications and other media to deliver instructional services and resources from anyone, anywhere to anyone, anywhere—is well enough established in America to start to topple the public education monopoly in a similar way. Along with the variety of private school options, the expansion of distance learning will increase the ability of learning consumers to bypass the control of the public school and college bureaucracy, thereby shrinking the government system's client base and reducing its ability to resist the kinds of policies called for above.

In general, the new administration should pursue a strategy of expanding the ability of learning consumers—both families and businesses—to bypass and abandon the established education system in favor of budding HL alternatives. That strategy requires acting swiftly to redistribute consumers, finances, and political influence from the scholastic institutions of the past to the HL enterprise of the future.

Break the Telecommunications Logjam. There is an intimate connection between the creation of the broadband, digital, so-called "information superhighways" needed to form the strategic infrastructure of the knowledge-age economy, on the one hand, and replacement of the medieval scholastic establishment by a high-tech HL industry, on the other: The more rapidly high-capacity, multimedia networks are expanded nationally, the sooner they will bypass and replace academia. And the commercial privatization of the education sector represents a multi-hundred-billion-dollar market opportunity for private investment to reap the rewards of the information superhighway system.

Thwarting both developments is an ongoing stalemate among telephone, cable TV, broadcast, newspaper, and other media interests that have been vying for control of the new communications infrastructure. The new president should act aggressively to end that gridlock by convening a national "summit" meeting of the interested parties and pressing them to forge an effective consensus that can be enacted in federal legislation.

End Direct Institutional Aid. Pending the broad restructuring of federal program funds into the microchoice program described above, the new president should take whatever actions may be necessary to end the allocation of federal funds directly to schools and colleges for instruction-related purposes (as opposed to research grants). The tax exemption of supposedly not-for-profit institutions also should be ended. The idea is to direct funds to the greatest extent possible into the hands of consumers rather than to school and college bureaucracies and to eliminate the tax subsidies that favor would-be nonprofits over commercial suppliers.

Federal Reorganization. Finally, the new president should use his authority to reorganize the executive branch to reflect the technological and economic opportunities of the future rather than the special interests of a fading era. Specifically, the president should create a new Department of Knowledge Resources by merging the Education and Labor departments, the National Science Foundation, the Federal Communications Commission, the National Aeronautics and Space Administration, and part or most of the Department of Energy's national laboratories. The administration also should consider including other relevant research- and knowledge-oriented organizations, such as the Commerce Department's National Institute of Standards and Technology, National Oceanic and Atmospheric Administration, and Census Bureau. The president also should encourage Congress to revise its committee structures along similar lines.

Conclusion

America was founded by people who had the vision and audacity to overthrow tradition and to establish an unprecedented political community, grounded in the radical principles of human liberty and equality. We have now entered a new era when the fabric of whole societies is being rewoven around the world. From Berlin to Vladivostok and from Capetown to Buenos Aires, every major social structure is subject to reappraisal, redesign, and replacement.

Inevitably, the challenges of the dawning knowledge age will demand that the most conservative social glue, education, be reinvented as well. The same HL technology that is driving the overthrow of arthritic bureaucracies holds the key to achieving social reformation swiftly and productively. America's political legacy, her technological vitality, and her responsibility as the world's greatest power all demand that she lead the hyperlearning revolution that promises a new birth of freedom, prosperity, and peace.

DIRECT INSTRUCTION, EXPLICIT TEACHING

Effective Education Squelched

Lynne V. Cheney

This selection first appeared in *The Wall Street Journal* on 12 May 1999. Lynne Cheney is a distinguished senior fellow at the American Enterprise Institute.

After principal Eric Mahmoud introduced a new curriculum at Harvest Preparatory, a Minneapolis elementary school that serves many children from poor families, test scores shot up. Kindergartners, whose reading results had been at about the national average, were now in the 89th percentile.

The new curriculum that proved so effective at Harvest Prep was actually a venerable program with a remarkable record of success. It is called Direct Instruction, and if you haven't heard about it, the reason may be that the nation's education schools don't want you to. In their view, Direct Instruction is pedagogically incorrect. Direct Instruction teachers, operating from detailed scripts, tell kids what they need to know, rather than letting them discover it for themselves, as ed schools advise. Direct Instruction teachers drill students on lessons (a method education professors sneeringly call "drill and kill"). They reward right answers and immediately correct wrong ones, flying in the face of ed-school dogma downplaying the importance of accuracy.

How well Direct Instruction works first became evident in 1977, when the results of Project Follow Through, a huge educational experiment undertaken by the federal government, were made public.

Kindergartners through third-graders who were taught by Direct Instruction scored higher in reading and math than children in any other instructional model. The Direct Instruction children not only proved superior at academics, but also scored higher on "affective" measures like self-esteem than did children in most other programs— several of which were specifically directed toward making children feel good about themselves.

The acolytes of John Dewey and Jean Piaget immediately went on the attack. Spurred on by the Ford Foundation, one group declared in the Harvard Educational Review that it simply wasn't fair to judge a program according to how well it taught children to read and calculate. After all, the program might have other goals, such as developing "a repertoire of abilities for building a broad and varied experiential base." An education professor from the University of Illinois weighed in with an essay condemning the Follow Through evaluation as too scientific. "Teachers do not heed the statistical findings of experiments when deciding how best to educate children," he wrote, nor should they be influenced by what "the rationality of science has to say about a given educational approach."

The attacks were effective. Instead of highlighting Direct Instruction's success, the Office of Education (predecessor of the Department of Education) disseminated data on other models as well, including some that had resulted in students having lower scores than control groups. At the University of Oregon, the only education school willing to give Direct Instruction a home, the developer of the program, Siegfried Engelman, and his colleagues continued to refine their approach and gather evidence of how well it worked. But in 1998, there were only 150 Direct Instruction schools in the U.S.

A major hindrance has been that colleges of education do not teach future teachers and administrators about Direct Instruction; they have to learn about it through happenstance. Thaddeus Lott, the principal of Wesley Elementary School in Houston, was searching for a program for the kids at his school, located in one of the city's poorest neighborhoods, when he chanced upon a book by Mr. Engelman. Mr. Lott instituted Direct Instruction at Wesley, and for more than two decades his students have been distinguishing themselves, producing test scores that put Wesley in the top ranks. Mr. Mahmoud happened to hear of Mr. Lott's success at Wesley—to the benefit of hundreds of Minneapolis children.

And still the ed schools continue their not-so-benign neglect. In recently reviewing dozens of textbooks used to teach future teachers, I found exactly one mention of Direct Instruction, a reference a few sentences long that described it as "prescriptive." A teacher at Mr. Lott's school, Brandi Scott, a recent graduate of the University of Houston, told me that her request to practice-teach at Wesley was initially refused by the college of education. Only after her father, a prominent Houston attorney, got involved was a plan worked out that let her do half her practice teaching at the school.

A recent report by the American Institutes for Research offers hope to those who think that ed school silence on Direct Instruction should end. The report found that Direct Instruction was one of only two educational approaches with strong evidence of positive effect, a conclusion hard to ignore. Equally important, one of the report's sponsors was the National Education Association. If an organization as notoriously intransigent as the NEA can help bring recognition to Direct Instruction, perhaps at long last there is the possibility of persuading ed schools to give it the attention it deserves.

ABILITY GROUPING

. . . .

The Concept of Grouping
in Gifted Education

In Search of Reality: Unraveling the Myths about Tracking, Ability Grouping, and the Gifted

Ellen D. Fiedler
Richard E. Lange
Susan Winebrenner

This article first appeared in the *Roeper Review*'s September 1993 issue. Ellen Fiedler is associate professor in the Gifted/Talented Master's Degree Program, Northeastern Illinois University, and author of *Curriculum for the Gifted: A Practical Guide*. Richard Lange is director of gifted education, staff development, and assessment for Prospect Heights Public Schools, Illinois, and adjunct faculty member, College of Education, National-Louis University in Evanston, Illinois. Susan Winebrenner is an independent consultant in staff development and author of *Teaching Gifted Kids in the Regular Classroom*.

The anti-tracking movement has suddenly become anti-ability grouping, resulting in serious side-effects for gifted students who currently are being served effectively in ability-grouped programs that consistently meet their needs. Closer scrutiny of the research frequently cited reveals commonly held misinterpretations and misconceptions. Six commonly held myths are examined and discussed in relationship to educators' efforts to provide the best instructional programs for all students, including those whose abilities place them at the upper end of the spectrum. Practical realities are emphasized in an effort to encourage schools to provide equality of opportunity rather than the same experiences for all. Consideration is given to serving all students more appropriately by overcoming the abuses of past practice and capitalizing on the knowledge that can be gained by careful examination of the literature and its implications for all students, including the gifted.

Educational bandwagons are a dime a dozen. Educators want to be on the cutting edge of educational improvement and are concerned about excellence in education and about providing programs that help their students. The last thing any educator wants to do is to be responsible for educational decisions that are harmful to anyone, least of all to students who already have had too many disadvantages heaped upon them in their lives. Thus, the pendulum swings again, moving from one extreme to another, typically without ample consideration of the impact of the latest trend in education on those students who benefited the most from some of the approaches being abandoned.

One recurring trend that is taking the educational world by storm is the anti-tracking movement. In the '90s, anti-tracking suddenly has become anti–ability grouping. The side effects of this trend are rippling throughout the schools, from widespread efforts to implement the Regular Education Initiative (R.E.I.) for students with learning handicaps to insidious attempts to eliminate programs for highly able or gifted students. In both cases, the motivation has been admirable; the concern is about the negative effects of locking certain students into unchallenging classes and locking them out of educational situations that stretch their minds. Unfortunately, all of the relevant research and its ramifications have not been thoroughly considered. For example, Slavin's research that recommended heterogeneous grouping for all ability groups systematically omitted data from those students in the top five percent of the school population (Allan, 1991). As Robinson (1990) concluded, the omission of gifted students in research studies can lead to dangerous overgeneralizations by those who interpret the results (p. 11).

In our efforts to be democratic, we have forgotten Thomas Jefferson's statement, "nothing is so unequal as the equal treatment of unequal people." Although Oakes (1986) has acknowledged that ability grouping does benefit the highest ability students, she questions whether we can continue to meet their needs at the expense of all others. Can it be that our school systems are actually giving tacit approval to create underachievement in one ability group so that the needs of the other ability groups can be served? This, indeed, is egalitarianism at its worst.

The purpose of this article is to roll away the clouds of misconception about ability grouping and to shine new light on the issues and their impact on efforts to meet the educational needs of gifted students in our schools. Six commonly held myths are examined and discussed in relationship to providing appropriate educational programs for all students, including those whose abilities place them at the upper end of the spectrum.

Myth #1: Tracking and Ability Grouping Are the Same Thing

Reality. Tracking has been defined as a means of dealing with individual differences whereby educators decide "to divide students into class-size groups based on a measure of the students' perceived ability or prior achievement" (George, 1988). In practice, tracking results in students being assigned full-time to instructional groups based on a variety of criteria, including presumed ability derived from achievement test scores and teacher observations of classroom performance. This often translates to a high-ability group assigned to Teacher A, a middle-ability group assigned to Teacher B, and a low-ability group assigned to Teacher C. Once students are in a certain track, there is very little movement between tracks during a school year or from one school year to another. Consistent placement in the low track clearly leads those students to disenfranchisement in a class system where there are clear differences between the "haves" and the "have-nots."

The commonly accepted meaning of ability grouping, on the other hand, relates to regrouping students for the purpose of providing curriculum aimed at a common instructional level. In elementary schools, this often happens when teachers create more homogeneous reading or math groups while teaching heterogeneous groups for most other subjects. At the secondary level, students may be assigned to high-ability groups in the areas of their strengths and to average- or low-ability groups in other subjects. Ability grouping does not imply permanently locking students out of settings that are appropriately challenging for them; it means placing them with others whose learning needs are similar to theirs for whatever length of time works best.

A variation of grouping practices is called cluster grouping whereby small groups of students with similar instructional needs are clustered within a primarily heterogeneous classroom. For example, four to eight identified gifted students at a particular grade level or in a specific subject area may be placed in the classroom of a teacher who has expertise in differentiating curriculum and instruction for them. This practice is in keeping with the need for gifted students to be with their intellectual peers in order to be appropriately challenged and to view their own abilities more realistically (Feldhusen & Saylor, 1990). With cluster grouping, gifted students may be the only ones grouped together on the basis of similar instructional needs. The other students in their class may comprise a heterogeneous mix, and most of the remaining classes in the school may also be heterogeneously grouped.

If all of the teachers at a given grade level are prepared to provide appropriately differentiated curriculum, the principal may decide to rotate faculty who work in classes where there are cluster groups of gifted students. This strategy can reduce the perceived association between a certain teacher and the "smartest" class (McInerney, 1983). Teachers who work in schools that use cluster grouping report that they have found that new academic leadership emerges in the classes without the cluster group of gifted students; i.e., a new cream rises to the top from among the heterogeneous group.

Myth #2: Ability Grouping Is Elitist

Reality. Elitism might well be defined as arbitrarily giving preference to some group based on a misperception of superiority. Often it is related to an offensive attitude of some group that is or purports to be socially, politically, or militarily superior (P. Plowman, personal communication, January 28, 1991).

However, being able to function at an advanced level intellectually does not, automatically, make an individual better than anyone else. It merely implies a difference that requires an educational response which may be erroneously interpreted by some as giving one group an unfair advantage. Gifted students may be better at many academic tasks, but this does not imply that they should be seen as being better than anyone else. The truth is that most educators of the gifted work diligently to help develop an understanding of giftedness in the context of individual differences rather than as an issue of superiority versus inferiority. This is totally consistent with newly emerging approaches, such as the middle school philosophy, that consider cognitive and affective development as equally important (Hornbeck, 1989).

In reality, keeping one or two highly gifted students in a classroom of mixed abilities actually may have the effect of creating snobbery. Scattering gifted students throughout all of the classrooms in the school may lead them to feel far superior to their classmates and promote arrogance. Imagine, if you will, the gifted student repeatedly getting the answers right and being able to offer complex ideas far ahead of the other students in class discussions. After a while, the gifted student may well surmise that he actually does know more than all the others. Unless gifted students are placed in situations where they can be challenged by intellectual peers, the possibilities that they will develop an elitist attitude might well be expected to increase.

However, when gifted students are grouped together for instruction, the experience of studying with intellectual peers may actually lower self-esteem somewhat (Feldhusen & Saylor, 1990). There is nothing quite so humbling to bright individuals as discovering that there are other students in the group who are equally capable or even more knowledgeable about given topics than they are. If one goal of education is to help all students develop a realistic appraisal of their own ability, students need to measure themselves with appropriate yardsticks. Comparisons are more likely to be accurate when made with others of similar abilities. Sicola (1990) pointed out the relationship between the unique affective and academic needs of gifted students, indicating that these are " . . . best met through the provision of homogeneous grouping in the areas of giftedness for this segment of the school population" (p. 41). This is why many school districts have chosen to continue to group high-ability students together via such strategies as cluster grouping while grouping all others heterogeneously.

Interestingly, educators have no qualms about identifying outstanding talent in athletics and providing specialized programs for students who excel in that area. As Tammi (1990) commented, "Not all students have the ability or desire to participate on a varsity sports team, yet I have never heard any school official argue that singling out talented athletes for team membership to the exclusion of others is elitist. In fact, school districts and local community agencies go to great lengths applauding these athletes' efforts and supporting them in their development" (p. 44). A similar (though not quite so well-funded) example exists in relationship to giftedness in music. If support for students who demonstrate extraordinary talents in these areas is not considered elitist, why should intellectual giftedness be given short shrift?

Myth #3: Ability Grouping Inevitably Discriminates against Racial and Ethnic Minority Students

Reality. For too many years, the inequitable use of assessment procedures did result in minority and economically disadvantaged students being under-represented in high-ability classes and programs for the gifted. However, educators of gifted students have made great progress in refining their identification methods. Wide-spread efforts are being made to overcome the inequities of over-reliance on standardized test score data and assumptions that too often have been made about students who, although gifted, may not fit the stereotype of high achievers with positive attitudes toward school. The direction is away from sole reliance on standardized tests and toward improved approaches that include studying the behaviors of students for indicators that gifted potential exists (Richert, Alvino, & McDonnell, 1982). For instance, methods devised by Frasier (1987), Gay (1978), Silverman and Waters (1988), Swenson (1978), Torrance and Ball (1984), and others are being implemented in order to better identify minority children who are gifted and/or talented. Moreover, significant attention is placed on training teachers to identify gifted students by observing their behavior. At the same time, behavioral descriptors are used to identify other underserved populations, who also have not surfaced due to a heavy emphasis on standardized test scores and classroom performance. Preschool and kindergarten children (Rogers & Silverman, 1988), creative thinkers (Davis & Rimm, 1985), nonproductive gifted students (Delisle, 1981), and gifted students with learning disabilities and other handicaps (Whitmore & Maker, 1985) are among those groups who are being screened more accurately using improved methodology.

Eliminating ability grouping because of inequitable identification procedures is tantamount to throwing out the baby with the bath water. Furthermore, singling out racial and ethnic minority students as the only disenfranchised group is misleading. The intent of gifted programs has not been to exclude certain populations. However, the identification procedures used in the past clearly needed revision, and improved methodologies are already being implemented.

Myth #4: Gifted Students Will Make It on Their Own; Grouping Them by Ability Does Not Result in Improved Learning or Achievement for Them

Reality.   Studies by Feldhusen (1989), Kulik and Kulik (1991), and Oakes (1986) confirm what gifted educators have known for years: Gifted students benefit cognitively and affectively from working with other gifted students. Oakes (1986) specifically reported on the beneficial effects of the advantages that many high school students in top tracks receive from their classes. Feldhusen (1989) reviewed data from several studies conducted by himself and his colleagues and concluded that

> . . . grouping of gifted and talented students in special classes with a differentiated curriculum, or as a cluster group in a regular heterogeneous classroom (but again with differentiated curriculum and instruction), leads to higher academic achievement and better academic attitudes for the gifted and leads to no decline in achievement or attitudes for the children who remain in the regular heterogeneous classroom. Gifted and talented youth need accelerated, challenging instruction in core subject areas that parallel their special talents or aptitudes. They need opportunities to work with other gifted and talented youth. And they need . . . teachers who both understand the nature and needs of gifted youth and are deeply knowledgeable in the content they teach (p. 10).

Although some studies have been done (Slavin, 1990) that indicate no increase in achievement test scores for high-ability students who have been grouped together, the omission of gifted students from such studies makes generalizing to this population highly questionable (Featherstone, 1987). Also, ceiling effects make it extremely difficult to determine whether or not students' learning was enhanced by homogeneous grouping unless off-level testing was used to assess achievement. In other words, grade-level achievement tests fail to reveal growth for students who already perform in the top percentile ranks because they have reached the ceiling of the test—the highest scores attainable for that age group. Only by administering instruments designed for older students can the actual achievement gains be determined for students whose performance places them in the extreme upper range.

Another critical issue needs to be considered: the goals of the gifted program and whether its purposes are actually focused on increasing academic achievement. What gifted students learn should be measured by far more comprehensive criteria than increased achievement test scores. Equally important are the development of socialization and leadership skills, experience with complex concepts and challenging learning, and opportunities to pursue topics in great depth. If such a program is more concerned with helping gifted students work together to grapple with global concerns that are complex and substantive, increases in achievement test scores in specific subject areas are not really appropriate for measuring success.

Myth #5: Providing Heterogeneously Grouped Cooperative Learning Experiences Is Most Effective for Serving All Students, Including the Gifted

Reality.   Every student has a right in a democratic society to learn something in school in every class. However, it is possible that the students who may actually learn the least in a given class are the gifted. So much of what they are asked to learn they may have already mastered. When teachers discover this, they may be tempted to use gifted students as classroom helpers or to teach others, thereby robbing the gifted student of consistent opportunities to learn through real struggle. This situation can have a negative impact on them in many ways, including lowering their self-esteem (Rimm, 1986). Without regular encounters with challenging material, gifted students fail to learn how to learn and have problems developing the study skills they need for future academic pursuits.

Cooperative learning is designed to be used with either homogeneous or heterogeneous groups. Johnson and Johnson (1989) noted, "There are times when gifted students should be segregated for fast-paced accelerated work. There are times when gifted students should work alone. There are times when gifted students should compete to see who is best" (p. 1).

Slavin (1990) stated that "Use of cooperative learning does not require dismantling ability group programs. . . . In a situation where acceleration is appropriate, cooperative learning is likely to be effective if used within the accelerated class" (p. 7).

A further point was made by Silverman (1990), who said, "As children veer from the norm in either direction, their educational needs become increasingly more differentiated. A child three standard deviations below the norm (55 IQ) could not profit from placement in a cooperative learning group in the heterogeneous classroom; neither does a child three standard deviations above the norm (145 IQ)" (p. 6). What seems reasonable is to allow teachers the flexibility to determine which lessons lend themselves to heterogeneous cooperative learning groups and which to homogeneous cooperative learning groups and make professional decisions to place students accordingly.

Myth #6: Assuring That There Are Some Gifted Students in All Classrooms Will Provide Positive Role Models for Others and Will Automatically Improve the Classroom Climate

Reality.   Classroom climate is far more dependent on factors other than having gifted students in attendance who supposedly will provide role models of motivated learning for other students. (See Fraser, Anderson, & Walberg, 1982.) The notion that placing gifted students in low-ability classrooms will automatically have a beneficial effect on students who are performing at lower levels rests on several questionable assumptions: that the performance discrepancies will be perceived as alterable by the less capable students; that gifted students are consistently highly-motivated high achievers who will inspire others to similar accomplishments; and that gifted students placed in low-ability or heterogeneous classrooms will continue to perform at their peak even when they lack regular intellectual peers who can stimulate their thinking.

Research indicates that students model their behavior on the behavior of others who are of similar ability and who are coping well in school (France-Kaatrude & Smith, 1985). As Feldhusen (1989) stated, "watching someone of similar ability succeed at a task raises the observers' feeling of efficacy and motivates them to try the task" (p. 10).

Furthermore, heterogeneous grouping may have negative side-effects both on the gifted students and on the others in the classrooms. Gifted students who are a minority of one or who only have, at best, one or two classmates whose ability level approaches their own find themselves either feeling odd or arrogant. If all the other students watch from the sidelines while the smart one provides all the answers, their perceptions of themselves as competent, capable learners suffer. One former student described it this way: "When Bill [the gifted one] was in class, it was like the sun shining on a bright, clear day. But, when he went out to work with other gifted kids, it was like the sun goes over the horizon. The rest of us were like the moon and the stars; that's when we finally got a chance to shine" (Fiedler, 1980).

As Walberg (1989) indicated, "Educators should be realistic about individual differences. Teaching students what they already know or are as yet incapable of knowing wastes effort. . . . Yet our ideal is equality, of opportunity if not results, and we should take each student as far as possible" (p. 5). Equality in education does not require that all students have exactly the same experiences. Rather, education in a democracy promises that everyone will have an equal opportunity to actualize their potential, to learn as much as they can.

Education in a free society should not boil down to a choice between equity and excellence. Providing for formerly disenfranchised groups need not take away appropriate programs from any other group. As the research clearly indicates, gifted students benefit from working together.

Therefore, it is imperative that ability grouping for the gifted be continued. While the educational community moves toward heterogeneity for students who would benefit more from working in mixed ability groups, it should not deny gifted students the right to educational arrangements that maximize their learning. The goal of an appropriate education must be to create optimal learning experiences for all.

References

Allan, S.D. (1991). Ability grouping research reviews: What do they say about grouping and the gifted? *Educational Leadership, 48(6),* 60–65.

Davis, G.A., & Rimm, S. (1985). *Education of the gifted and talented.* Englewood Cliffs, NJ: Prentice-Hall.

Delisle, J.R. (1981). The non-productive gifted child: A contradiction of terms? *Roeper Review, 3(4),* 20–22.

Featherstone, H. (Ed.). (1987). Organizing classes by ability. *Harvard Education Letter, 3(4),* 1–4.

Feldhusen, J. (1989). Synthesis of research on gifted youth. *Educational Leadership, 54(6),* 6–12.

Feldhusen, J., & Saylor, M. (1990). Special classes for academically gifted youth. *Roeper Review, 12(4),* 244–249.

Fiedler, E.D. (1980). *Gifted programs evaluation report—Stevens Point Area Public Schools.* Unpublished manuscript.

Frasier, M. (1987). The identification of gifted black students: Developing new perspectives. *Journal for the Education of the Gifted, 10(3),* 155–180.

Fraser, B.J., Anderson, G.J., & Walberg, H.J. (1982). Assessment of learning environments. *Manual for Learning Environment Inventory (LEI) and My Class Inventory (MCI),* third version. Chicago, IL: University of Illinois at Chicago.

France-Kaatrude, Al, & Smith, W.P. (1985). Social comparison, task motivation, and the development of self-evaluative standards in children. *Developmental Psychology, 21,* 1080–1089.

Gay, J.E. (1978). A proposed play for identifying black gifted children. *Gifted Child Quarterly, 22,* 353–359.

George, P.S. (1988). *What's the truth about tracking and ability grouping really???* Gainesville, FL: University of Florida.

Hornbeck, D. (Chairman). (1989). *Turning points: Preparing American youth for the 21st century.* Washington, D.C.: Carnegie Commission on Adolescent Development.

Johnson, D., & Johnson, R. (1989). What to say to parents of gifted children. *The Cooperative Link, 5(2)*, 1.

Kulik, J.A., & Kulik, C-L.C. (1991). Ability grouping and gifted students. In N. Colangelo & G.A. Davis (Eds.), *Handbook of gifted education* (pp. 178–196). Boston: Allyn and Bacon.

McInerney, C.F. (1983). *The bottom line series: Cluster grouping for the gifted*. St. Paul, MN: Line, Inc.

Oakes, J. (1986). Keeping track: The policy and practice of curriculum inequality, part 1. *Phi Delta Kappan, 68(1)*, 12–17.

Richert, S., Alvino, J., & McDonnell, R. (1982). *National report on identification*. Sewell, NJ: Educational Information and Resource Center.

Rimm, S. (1986). *Underachievement syndrome: Causes and cures*. Watertown, WI: Apple Publishing Co.

Robinson, A. (1990). Cooperation or exploitation? The argument against cooperative learning for talented students. *Journal for the Education of the Gifted, 14(1)*, 9–27.

Rogers, M., & Silverman, L. (1988). Recognizing giftedness in young children. *Understanding Our Gifted, 1(2)*, 5, 16–17, 20.

Sicola, P.K. (1990). Where do gifted students fit? An examination of middle school philosophy as it relates to ability grouping and the gifted learner. *Journal for the Education of the Gifted, 14(1)*, 37–49.

Silverman, L.K. (1990). *Scapegoating the gifted: The new national sport*. Unpublished manuscript.

Silverman, L., & Waters, J. (1988, November). *The Silverman/Waters checklist: A new culture-fair identification instrument*. Paper presented at the Annual Convention of the National Association for Gifted Children. Orlando, FL.

Slavin, R.E. (1990). Ability grouping, cooperative learning, and the gifted. *Journal for the Education of the Gifted, 14(1)*, 3–8.

Swenson, J.E. (1978). Teacher-assessment of creative behavior in disadvantaged children. *Gifted Child Quarterly*, 338–343.

Tammi, L. (1990). Programs for the gifted are not "elitist." *Education Week, 9*, 44.

Torrance, E.P., & Ball, O.E. (1984). *Torrance tests of creative thinking: Streamlined*. Bensenville, IL: Scholastic Testing Service.

Walberg, H. (1989). Issue: The sorting of students into ability groups has come under increasing fire recently. Should schools end the practice of grouping students by ability? *ASCD Update* (Association for Supervision and Curriculum Development Newsletter), *31(1)*, 5.

Whitmore, J.R., & Maker, C.J. (1985). *Intellectual giftedness in disabled persons*. Rockville, MD: Aspen.

WHOLE SCHOOL REFORM

. . . .

Ready, Read!

Nicholas Lemann

This selection first appeared in *The Atlantic Monthly* in November 1998. Nicholas Lemann, the national correspondent of *The Atlantic Monthly*, is the author of *The Promised Land: The Great Black Migration and How It Changed America* (1991).

A new solution to the problem of failing public schools is emerging: takeover by outside authorities, who prescribe a standardized field-tested curriculum. This runs counter to our long-standing tradition of autonomy for local schools and teachers, but it works.

Most discussion of public education in the United States begins with the premise that big, government-run school systems no longer work. The way to provide a good education to all children, especially poor children, is to turn over control of public schools to smaller, more local, and possibly private operators—to decentralize authority. At the center of the debate is a contest between two ideas: vouchers and charter schools. Vouchers are checks from the government that are issued to parents and earmarked for education; they are redeemable at both private and public schools. Charter schools are new public schools operated by independent groups. "We must . . . bring more choice and competition into public education," President Bill Clinton said last year, in calling for the establishment of 3,000 charter schools. Both ideas address the problems in public education by walking away from them.

The rhetoric of failure is simply wrong. There are 87,000 public schools in this country, with 45 million students—a sixth of the U.S. population. Enrollment is increasing rapidly. The best measure of public schools' performance, the National Assessment of Educational Progress, has shown modest but steady overall gains since it was first administered, in 1970. One has to belong to the small but disproportionately influential subculture that interacts only with private education to believe that public education—rather than specific public schools—has failed. The total enrollment in private, nonsectarian schools where the annual tuition is more than $5,000 is about 400,000—less than one percent of public school enrollment. Catholic-school enrollment is 2.5 million. Public education is by far the largest and most important function performed by government in this country. In no way is it in systemic crisis.

In the public schools that can fairly be described as having failed, most of which are in poor urban neighborhoods, what is actually taking place is a great and largely unremarked centralization of authority. The trend is diffuse, and its precise dimensions are difficult to limn. In at least a thousand American public schools, it is safe to say, outside control has replaced local autonomy during the 1990s. This has affected many more schools and students than has the devolution of authority through voucher programs or charter schools.

During the 1980s many states began imposing measurements of performance on their public schools, usually in the form of obligatory standardized tests in reading and math. (Bill Clinton first gained national attention by doing this in Arkansas.) In this decade, when individual schools or entire districts have persistently turned in poor scores on these tests, outside authorities have often moved in. The school systems of Chicago, Hartford, Cleveland, Baltimore, Washington, D.C., and three cities in New Jersey, among other places, are no longer under the control of the municipal school superintendent. The Pennsylvania legislature is threatening to take over Philadelphia's system. In other cities, such as San Francisco and San Antonio, the school superintendent has imposed "reconstitution" on the worst-performing schools, meaning that the entire staff has been required to reapply for employment and the school has been "redesigned."

In many of these cases, after the change in authority the schools have adopted one of about a dozen national school designs that cover such areas as governance, relations with parents and the neighborhood, teaching techniques, and, especially, curriculum. Many schools that have not been taken over or reconstituted (for example, dozens of schools in Memphis and Miami) are also using these "whole school" designs. Of the three most popular—Success for All, Accelerated Schools, and the School Development Program, all designed by university professors—the first two have each been adopted by more than a thousand schools across the country, and the third by 700.

The outline emerges of a future in which schools that aren't doing their job will lose their independence and will have to adopt a standard mode of operation that has demonstrated good results. This is not what most people think of as the direction in which public education is moving. Even Clinton's constant calls for national education standards mean the setting of goals for what all students should know, not dictating the day-to-day operations of schools. If failure in the public schools is resulting not in decentralization but in the imposition of a template, then we should know it—and think about whether this is a good idea.

American public schools have never been as local as politicians claim to want them to be. In a country as big as ours it would be impractical to leave education entirely in the hands of 14,800 school boards that operate independently. So we have a strange hybrid: a system rhetorically committed to decentralization but in fact centralized in a patchwork, undeliberate way. We have national standardized tests, national teachers' unions, national textbook publishers, and national laws, regulations, and funding programs for schools. No school is free of their influence. But they influence most schools in a haphazard fashion.

The great majority of public schools muddle along fairly successfully. It is students at bad public schools who are the main losers in the patchwork system, and a consistent national standard for how to operate bad schools ought to be considered with their interests in mind.

Recentralizing Authority

At the end of the nineteenth century, New York City, cobbled together out of smaller cities and towns, created the country's biggest centralized public school system. In 1969, following a long, famous, resonant battle, New York dropped centralization in favor of a policy of "community control" and created thirty-two local school boards. This was not an unqualified success, and the move back toward centralization began. In 1989 the New York State commissioner of education created a new status, called "registration review," for persistently low-performing schools, most of which were in poor sections of New York City. The schools were under a threat of having their state registration revoked and being shut down. In 1996 the state legislature essentially rescinded community control, by giving the chancellor of New York City's schools the power to fire principals and school-board superintendents. (Chicago's school system went through much the same cycle, but faster: dramatically decentralized in 1988, recentralized in 1995.) The state commissioner kept up the saber-rattling, and in 1996 New York City's new chancellor, Rudy Crew, took direct control of nine of the worst registration-review schools—six elementary and three middle schools—in the hope of turning them around.

Fifteen percent of the registration-review schools in New York State were in a single school district—Community School District Nine, in the Bronx, the most consistently problematic school district in New York City. Its test scores have always been low, its board has twice been disbanded after the discovery of job-selling and kickback schemes, and in the most notorious incident a school principal was arrested for possession of crack cocaine.

If you drive around District Nine, which is in the collection of neighborhoods known to the outside world as the South Bronx (although it is actually in the West Bronx), you can see how the school system could have become so bad. The neighborhoods are, of course, largely poor and nonwhite, and remote from the mainstream of city life. What is really striking about them, though, is that the schools in them are the biggest buildings. Three- and four-story factory-style brick palaces, built before the Second World War, they tower over the landscape like cathedrals in medieval villages. In its heyday District Nine was a white ethnic working-class residential area; in the late 1960s and 1970s it was a burned-out, abandoned, desperately poor, all-minority area. Today it has been substantially rebuilt and repopulated with black and Hispanic immigrants. Public schools are still where the money and jobs are: The driving force of this school district has long been political patronage, not education.

The nine schools Crew took over are collectively referred to as "the Chancellor's District"; they have been operating separately for two full school years. At the beginning of the first year Crew replaced the principals of all nine schools. At the end of that year three of the schools had actually gotten worse on the crucial measure of reading scores, and only three had improved substantially. Crew replaced four of the nine new principals, and he adopted the Success for All reading program. This time the reading scores at all nine schools (and at three other schools that had been added to the district) rose significantly.

Measured by test scores, one of the worst schools in the Chancellor's District is Public School 63, in the Bronx. We'll stop there for a moment before moving on to the dramatically improved Public School 114, a short distance away. It is helpful to have a sense of what a failed school is really like.

One Fad on Top of Another

Two images of bad inner-city schools prevail in the wider culture: the out-of-control violent school, where weapon-toting gang members rule and teachers cower; and the underfunded school with overcrowded classrooms, peeling paint, leaking pipes, and broken heating. P.S. 63 is neither of these. To be sure, it has a lot of disciplinary problems, but it is only an elementary school. It is not overcrowded, because the surrounding neighborhood, Morrisania, hasn't been part of the revival of the Bronx and is still depopulated. Every day 240 students are bused in from other parts of the Bronx, and the average class size is twenty-three. Chancellor's District schools get extra money, so at the moment an insufficient budget is not P.S. 63's No. 1 problem. Overall, P.S. 63 seems more like a child-care facility than a school—a relatively benign and happy place, where an overall program of instruction was somehow never put in place. When I visited, the school was being run by a young woman named Gillian Williams; she was the fourth principal at P.S. 63 in six years. The New York City teachers' union has proposed to take over the school's management, and if it does, there will probably be a fifth principal, because the head of the union has all but promised publicly to fire Williams. Teacher turnover has also been high. Williams brought in eighteen new teachers, out of sixty-eight, for the 1997–1998 school year.

Control over curriculum in New York City schools has traditionally been diffuse: The state and the city set various standards and benchmarks that schools are expected to meet, although it is not clear what happens if they don't. Otherwise, the schools establish their own instructional methods. Sometimes the superintendent selects the textbooks, readers, and worksheets; sometimes the principals do. During P.S. 63's first year in the Chancellor's District it was redesigned and given the name Author's Academy, to demonstrate its commitment to making students literate. The principal bought a new reading curriculum, which teachers were supposed to use to guide their students to basic literacy. The problem, Williams told me, was that the publisher didn't make good on its shipping date. All year long, the curriculum materials arrived in bits and pieces, and the reading program had no structure at all. The school's reading scores dropped drastically.

The following year Williams came in as principal. On orders from the Chancellor's District she adopted the Success for All reading program, which is extremely demanding. The school also adopted a new math curriculum that year and, because Williams considered Success for All to be insufficient, two other new reading programs. As a result, most of the students were taking three separate and quite different reading classes every day. In third grade, for example, a student would learn one technique in the Success for All class for charting the structure of a story, based on Venn diagrams; another technique in the second reading class, based on "story maps"; and another technique in the third reading class, based on "character maps." The rest of the school day consisted of one math class and one period in the afternoon into which everything else was wedged. And this was just for the students in the main instructional program. A fifth of the school population was in special-education classes, and a fourth in "limited-English-proficient" classes. The school was a library of education vogues and special noncurricular functions.

A School That Works

I spent a good deal of time recently in one of the Chancellor's District schools at the opposite (that is, better) end of the spectrum—enough time to move beyond the Potemkin-village phase of marveling at an inner-city school that works. A description of what happens there should convey what this particular way of fixing a broken school means, what the disadvantages are, and what kinds of opposition must be overcome if these schools are to succeed.

Public School 114 is in a neighborhood called Highbridge, which runs along the Hudson River behind Yankee Stadium. In its glory days, the 1920s, it was a lower-middle-class paradise populated mostly by Jews and Irish-Americans. Even Yankees could and did live proudly in the grand Art Deco apartment buildings along Jerome Avenue and the Grand Concourse; the humbler buildings on the cross streets were for cabbies and shopkeepers. P.S. 114, which was built in 1940, was considered a first-class school that put its students firmly on an upward sociological trajectory.

The neighborhood changed in the mid-1960s, when the Freedomland amusement park on the other side of the Bronx was torn down and the enormous Co-Op City apartment complex was built in its place. Whites left Highbridge for Co-Op City, and blacks moved in from Harlem, and then Puerto Ricans; the student population of P.S. 114 changed, first from all white to mostly black, and then to mostly Puerto Rican. The school's official name, which nobody uses, is Luis Llorens Torres Children's Academy, after the national poet of Puerto Rico. Today P.S. 114 is mostly Dominican. The surrounding neighborhood is populated by a polyglot ethnic working poor. It feels crowded and scruffy, but safe; there aren't many empty buildings. Stores are filled with a wide variety of specialty items from the Caribbean, Africa, and Latin America. The elevated train on River Avenue rumbles by every few minutes.

P.S. 114, a large three-story building, has more than a thousand students, which is a third more than its official capacity. When the state's registration-review list was created, P.S. 114 was placed on it. The school's particular problem was that it had turned into a bilingual-education patronage machine. Students with Hispanic last names—which is to say most students—were assigned to "bilingual" classes taught in Spanish, often by non–English-speaking teachers. The school generally didn't test students or seek their parents' consent before putting them on the bilingual track, and it rarely moved anybody out of bilingual education, because that would have meant losing job slots for bilingual teachers. All of this was and is in violation of the state and city regulations governing bilingual education, but administrative supervision of P.S. 114 was so lax that the regulations weren't enforced. From 1989 to the creation of the Chancellor's District, in 1996, the school suffered no negative consequences for its extremely low reading scores—in fact, the consequences were arguably positive, because the low scores qualified it for special funding. The school adopted a popular and well-regarded reading program, Reading Recovery. But the program was only nominally implemented and didn't have much effect.

Eileen Mautschke, the current principal of P.S. 114 and a thirty-year veteran teacher and administrator in District Nine, describes the condition of the district years ago this way: "The district controlled things. There was so much corruption! Money went into the school board's pockets. Decentralization gave people control over a tremendous amount of money, and very little got down to the schools. District Nine was one of the worst offenders in that respect. There were warehouses elsewhere in the city full of supplies that didn't get to the kids."

In the first year of the Chancellor's District all the elementary schools devoted a ninety-minute period every morning—9:00 to 10:30, the meatiest part of the school day for young children—to reading instruction. Rudy Crew had made an arrangement with the teachers' union under which every school in the district would be allowed to replace half the teachers by transferring them to other schools. (The union was cooperative because it feared that if the Chancellor's District didn't work, the state would hire a private company to run the schools—one that didn't use union teachers.) The schools were told to redesign themselves.

Mautschke took over at P.S. 114 in the middle of the 1995–1996 school year, just before the creation of the Chancellor's District. After off-loading a third of the teachers and hiring new ones, most of them very young, she led the staff through a lengthy series of discussions. At the end of these, P.S. 114 was divided into three mini-schools, called the Author's School, the School of Environmental Studies, and the School of World Discoverers. She began cleaning up the bilingual mess. At the end of her first full year, P.S. 114's third-grade reading score—the number that had gotten it into trouble—had risen moderately.

During the first year, Rudy Crew realized that the Chancellor's District, though an experiment in centralizing authority, was not centralized enough. He brought in a new superintendent, Barbara Byrd-Bennett (who, ironically, had begun her career thirty years earlier as a Harlem teacher fighting for community control) and replaced more principals. Most important, at the heavy prodding of the teachers' union, Crew adopted the Success for All reading curriculum.

The Parris Island Approach

The inventor of Success for All is Robert E. Slavin, an education researcher at Johns Hopkins University who gives off the sweet-and-sour, casual-intense air of a perpetual graduate student. Slavin has been studying education in elementary schools for twenty-five years. In 1986, the Baltimore public school system asked him to try to figure out a way to prevent inner-city schoolchildren from falling permanently behind during their first few years in school. Slavin set up a program of tightly controlled reading instruction, which began at one school in Baltimore in the fall of 1987. The idea was to devise a system that could be transported from school to school. Although during the past decade Success for All has lost its contract with the Baltimore school system, it has grown rapidly elsewhere. By the end of this school year, the Success for All organization will have a budget of $30 million and will operate in more than 1,100 schools all over the country. Among its customers are the Edison Project, which is private; the state of New Jersey; and the cities of Houston, Memphis, and Miami.

There are two reasons for Success for All's quick spread. Of all the school curricula, it comes closest to guaranteeing the result that state education commissioners want: higher reading scores. Although it is quite expensive—about $70,000 per school in the first year and $25,000 a year thereafter—the program is usually paid for by Title I, the federal compensatory-education program, so there is no direct cost to school districts. Because Title I targets schools with high percentages of children from poor families, Slavin says, "high-poverty schools can afford us, low-poverty can't." Success for All is used almost exclusively in poor schools. Most school designs offer testimonials and anecdotes to sell prospective customers on their effectiveness.

Slavin has statistical comparisons of reading scores from schools that use Success for All and similar schools that don't. "There's nothing on most of these programs," he told me. "No data! Organized research with control groups and reports every year, no matter what the data show—that just doesn't happen." The prevailing criticism of Success for All is that it is designed to produce higher scores on a couple of tests chosen by Slavin, for which the control-group schools don't train their students; the gains it produces, according to critics, are substantially limited to the first year of the program. Whether or not this is true, Slavin is right when he says that the other leading national programs for elementary schools can furnish almost no data at all on the results they produce.

It's not difficult to see why Success for All is so much quicker than the other programs to generate quantifiable benefits. The next two most popular programs for elementary schools—Accelerated Schools, devised by Henry Levin of Stanford University, and the School Development Program, devised by James Comer of Yale Medical School—are essentially planning and organization tools that give individual schools great latitude in choosing instructional methods. Success for All tells schools precisely what to teach and how to teach it—to the point of scripting, nearly minute by minute, every teacher's activity in every classroom every day of the year.

When a school adopts Success for All, its top administrators go for a week of intensive training at Slavin's headquarters. Then Success for All personnel come to the school to provide all the teachers with three days of training. The school must designate a full-time Success for All "facilitator" and a full-time parent "coordinator." Success for All representatives visit the school three times a year. Each student takes a Success for All reading test every eight weeks. Teachers must use a series of catch phrases and hand signals developed by Success for All. In kindergarten and first grade every piece of classroom material (readers, posters, tapes, videos, lesson plans, books—everything) is provided by the program. Afterward, Success for All's grip on what goes on in the classroom isn't quite as complete, because other companies' textbooks are incorporated. But it's still tight: At every level Slavin's programs greatly reduce teacher autonomy, through control of the curriculum. Slavin has developed curricula in math, science, and social studies. People usually describe Success for All with terms like "prescriptive," "highly structured," and "teacher-proof"; Slavin likes to use the word "relentless." One education researcher I spoke with called it "Taylorism in the classroom," after Frederick Winslow Taylor, the early twentieth-century efficiency expert who routinized every detail of factory work.

The theoretical foundation of Success for All is supposedly cooperative learning, meaning that students are put into small groups or partnerships and help one another. This is true as far as it goes, but it fails to convey the full flavor of a Success for All classroom. The students do work in teams, but they don't work independently. Cooperative-learning sessions are frequent but strictly time-limited and task-defined. One purpose the sessions clearly serve is to keep students from drifting off during the times when the teacher is leading the whole class. A bit less obvious in the Success for All literature is that it teaches reading primarily through phonics (learning a word by decoding it, rather than deducing its meaning from context), which is not as popular as cooperative learning in the liberal education world. Students are tested, put into groups based on their skill levels, drilled in reading skills, tested again, regrouped, and drilled some more. The ones who are furthest behind receive individual tutoring. But everybody is supposed to learn to read.

A few minutes in a Success for All classroom conveys the Parris Island feeling of the program better than any general description could. It is first grade—the pivotal year. The students sit at their desks holding copies of a story called *Woo Zen*. The teacher stands at the blackboard and says, "Okay, let's get ready for our shared story. Ready, read!" The students read the first page of the story loudly, in unison. The teacher says, "Okay, next page. Finger in place, ready, read!" After a few minutes of this the students have finished the story. Not missing a beat, the teacher says, "Close your books, please. Let's get ready for vocabulary." She moves to a posted handwritten sheet of words and points to herself. "My turn. Maze, haze, hazy, lazy. Your turn." She points to the class. The students shout out the words in unison: "Maze! Haze! Hazy! Lazy!"

Then the teacher announces that the students are going to do "red words"—Success for All lingo for words that students can't decode from their phonemic components. "Okay, do your first word," she says. The students call out together, "Only! *O* [clap] *N* [clap] *L* [clap] *Y* [clap]. Only!" After they've done the red words, the teacher says, "Now let's go to our meaningful sentences." The students read from a sheet, loudly and in unison, the definitions of three words, and then three sentences, each of which uses one of the words. The teacher sends the students into their cooperative-learning groups to write three sentences of their own, using each of the words. "If you work right, you'll earn work points for your work team! You clear?" Twenty voices call out, "Yes!"

Rigor and Routine

Success for All can't work unless a school's principal and teachers co-operate. Partly for that reason, and partly to avoid having the program appear to be imposed from without (though in truth it usually is), Slavin will not sign on with a school unless 80 percent of its teachers have voted by secret ballot in favor of his program. At P.S. 114 in the spring of last year, teachers twice voted it down, even though a third of the teachers were brand-new and the Chancellor's District, the union, and Eileen Mautschke were all pushing hard for Success for All. Then the principal arranged for the teachers to go on a field trip to an elementary school in Brooklyn that used Success for All. On the third and final vote the program passed.

The teachers' reluctance is understandable. Success for All takes over a school and substantially limits teachers' freedom. At P.S. 114, the Author's School, the School of Environmental Studies, and the School of World Discoverers are gone—not to mention the previous, teacher-chosen reading curriculum, which involved more student creativity and less drilling. All over the school are exhortatory posters. A veteran teacher who felt that she had accumulated wisdom over the decades about how to reach children would find that Success for All, in its insistently nice way, was now telling her that everything she thought she knew should be jettisoned in favor of lesson plans from Baltimore.

The atmosphere of the school, though, is cheerful and purposeful, not grumpy. Every morning, as the children stream in, Eileen Mautschke stands in the main hallway presiding over a scene that is impressive for not being completely chaotic: More than a thousand children, at least a third of whom don't speak English and every one of whom is poor enough to qualify for the federal free-lunch program, briefly assemble in a foyer that is far too small to hold them. Last year, when I was there, the school was phasing in uniforms; this year all the students have been asked to wear them. Mautschke, a middle-aged woman with an air of genial, slightly weary unflappability, does not have the strutting disciplinarian aspect of effective inner-city principals in the movies. If you told her that a tidal wave was about to hit P.S. 114, she would smile resignedly, say "Okay," and figure out what to do about it. But she plainly has the school under control. As she cruises the hallways during the day, she greets most of the children she passes by name.

After everyone has arrived and settled down, the hour and a half of Success for All begins. All the teachers in the school, even gym and music teachers, have been pressed into service as reading instructors, to bring down the size of the classes—not to the ideal fifteen but at least to twenty-four. Because there are forty-six reading groups and only thirty-two classrooms, groups meet in every nook and cranny: on the stage of the auditorium, in the library and the gym, in an oversized supply closet, even on the floor at the ends of hallways. It's not a scene of squalor, but it's not a scene you would encounter in a school for the children of the prosperous. P.S. 114 has been spruced up a bit since its worst days. It has the utilitarian look of a big, indestructible public facility—clayey coats of paint, clean linoleum, smudged grated windows, fluorescent lights.

P.S. 114 goes only through the fourth grade. For children that young, and for their teachers, an intensive ninety-minute morning class is so consuming that it uses up most of the school's daily energy supply, not to mention its money. P.S. 114 doesn't do anything else nearly so elaborately as it does reading instruction. Administrators and parents (a parent representative helps in the school full-time, without pay) must supervise the overcrowded lunchroom: Teachers are exempted by their contract from that duty, to compensate for the length of the Success for All classes. Subjects such as science and social studies are relegated to shorter, later time slots. Not even math gets nearly so much time. Low reading scores got P.S. 114 into trouble with the state; thus reading instruction gets extra funds, staff, training, and time.

In addition to the hour and a half of Success for All, P.S. 114 devotes half an hour of every school day to preparation for state-required standardized reading exams. These classes are a junior version of a Stanley Kaplan or a Princeton Review course, in which students take old tests for practice, drill on vocabulary words, and learn little tricks—for example, that guessing on a question is better than giving up. The test that originally landed P.S. 114 on the state registration-review list and then in the Chancellor's District is called the DRP, for Degrees of Reading Power; it was until recently given to third-graders annually in May. The DRP is exactly the kind of test that education reformers most dislike. Children read a series of passages in which every seventh word is left blank, and pick from a multiple-choice menu a word to fill in each blank. They are being quizzed more on vocabulary than on understanding. For that reason New York State has since dropped the DRP in favor of another test. But during the time I spent at P.S. 114 enormous energy went into preparing students for the test—a test that teachers felt should not even be used, and that would in fact no longer be used in New York public schools after the end of that school year.

The fate of the entire Chancellor's District was heavily dependent on what these third-grade reading scores, which had not risen sufficiently in the district's first year, would be. The message had been forcefully communicated to the principals. As the date of the DRP approached, Mautschke and her teachers bore down with remarkable concentration. Every week the school's administrators met in a supply depository off the gym. These meetings were substantially devoted to test-prep matters. All the third-graders were given a pre-test in March. The worst performers were parceled out to the administrators, including Mautschke herself, to be given half an hour a day of one-on-one tutoring in addition to the regular test-prep class.

A leitmotif of the administrative meetings was the complaints of the school's consultant on teaching techniques, Deborah Fuhrer, about the overwhelming focus on test prep; Mautschke, without rancor, but firmly, would overrule her. At the final staff meeting before the day of the test Mautschke outlined a program of concentrated memory drills on certain vocabulary words thought likely to appear on the test. Fuhrer said that this was a bad idea: It was imparting a trick, not a skill. One of the words the students would be taught was "anxiety." "This will increase their anxiety, that's all!" Fuhrer said. "What would you suggest?" Mautschke asked her evenly. "What would I suggest? Prayer. Prayer works well."

The third-graders did their vocabulary drills. When the test results came back, in June, 80.5 percent of the third-graders at P.S. 114 had scored at or above the state minimum level on the DRP. The school's scores are now above the average for all New York City public schools.

Of course, the score increase is a product of test prep, but not only that. P.S. 114's scores on the Success for All reading tests and the third-grade reading test that the state will use next year instead of the DRP (which has been given purely for diagnostic purposes for several years) also went up impressively. Last May, the school was taken off the state registration-review list. On the day parents were to register their children to enter kindergarten, people started lining up outside P.S. 114 at 3:30 A.M. Later registrants had to be assigned to another school, because P.S. 114 could not accommodate anywhere near the number of students whose parents wanted them to go there. The Chancellor's District as a whole registered by far the largest rise in scores on the new reading test of any district in the city. At P.S. 114 most of the students are now learning to read. Only a few years ago that was not the case.

Control Where It's Necessary

Drawing lessons from inner-city education successes (and, for that matter, from failures) can be perilous. An improved school has a Rashomon aspect: The moral of the story depends on who's telling it. Whatever supposedly causes a school to turn around is bottled and exported to other schools, where it may or may not work. The successful school may sink back into desuetude in a year or two. Schools are often accumulations of shiny new reform ideas that have been jammed into the same small space and don't fit together particularly well.

Nonetheless, it seems clear that although several factors were at work in the improvement of P.S. 114, including a good new principal, a higher budget, a turnover in the teaching staff, a cooperative union, better staff training, physical improvements to the building, more parental involvement, and smaller class sizes, the key was the imposition of a tightly defined, proven reading curriculum. The most important thing in education is what the teacher does with students in the classroom. To direct that requires control of the curriculum. Structural changes, supposedly the essence of education reform, can have amazingly little effect if they do not alter what teachers actually teach. The importance of Success for All is less the particulars of how the program works than the general idea that if one method can be proved to work better than any other, nonperforming schools should be required to use it exclusively. Given the paramount importance of reading in a student's education and later life as a citizen and worker, shouldn't we try to identify the best method of reading instruction, demonstrate its superiority, and then require it for children who aren't learning to read? This would inescapably require some centralization of authority over public education.

Airline safety offers a good analogy for what I'm suggesting. You can't fly on an airplane that has no radar or oxygen masks, because the federal government won't allow it. But you can get an unacceptable education in your local school, because so far the federal government has been reluctant to challenge local control. Vouchers and charter schools offer students a way out of bad public schools, but neither option assures decent education for all. Children with unmotivated or unsophisticated parents are left behind, in unacceptable conditions. Control of the curriculum from without—not for every public school, only for failed ones—is the way for the country to ensure a good education for every child.

Centralization is actually occurring fairly rapidly, but rhetorically it is still quite unpopular. We are generally in an anti-bureaucratic phase, and within education there is no organized, powerful force for centralization. Most politicians don't want to do the work of persuading voters that they should be taxed more in order to educate other people's children. Local school boards don't want to give up their power. Christian conservatives are afraid that centralization in the public schools will lead to liberal indoctrination. Economic conservatives want to privatize education as much as possible. Unions resist the teacher-evaluation systems that come with centralization.

From a philosophical standpoint the main force working against centralization is a progressive, humanist, anti-utilitarian view of the purpose of education. Most popular books about the education of young children—*Summerhill, Thirty-Six Children, Death at an Early Age*—take this view. Children are inherently creative, curious, and democratic: Inspirational teachers and supportive schools can awaken and nurture these qualities; grim, factory-like traditional schools can extinguish them. Although progressive education rarely involves the kind of crude ideological brainwashing of which it is often accused, it does operate on an implied social critique: Education should counterbalance the commercial, regimented nature of adult working life. A school should be an arena for open discourse about values, not a job-skills training center. Schoolteachers—smart, hardworking people who aren't paid much and are rarely celebrated—are naturally drawn to the progressive view. It gives them creative latitude in the classroom and gives value to what they do.

What I encountered at P.S. 114 would deeply affront the progressive sensibility in education. Success for All turns teachers into drill instructors. The atmosphere is palpably one of preparing children to become workers. When I was there, Mautschke instituted a system of "scholar dollars," given to students for good behavior and redeemable for trinkets at the school store. The connection between what goes on in school and the economic world could hardly be clearer. And then there is the preoccupation with using children to generate test-score statistics that will propitiate state bureaucrats and keep the money flowing.

Probably the most celebrated progressive educator in the country is Deborah Meier. In 1974, Meier started a public school in East Harlem called Central Park East, which for the two decades she ran it was a remarkable success. Meier must be the only public-school principal to hold honorary degrees from Harvard and Yale and to have received a "genius grant" from the MacArthur Foundation. She recently left New York to start a public school in Boston, partly because she didn't like the direction in which the New York City schools were moving. Meier had helped to raise foundation money in order to "create a different kind of Chancellor's District," one that operated a string of schools on a progressive model of teacher and principal autonomy. But it was clear to her that Rudy Crew wasn't interested in that kind of thing.

I went to see Meier and ask what she thought of the district's adoption of Success for All. Of course she was extremely skeptical. She said it was natural that reading scores in the district were going up—the children were being taught how to do better on tests. "If kids are surrounded by grown-ups who don't have authority, who follow orders, how could they learn to question, to discuss ideas?" And, a little later in the conversation: "It's shameful that we've come to the point of test scores as the end of education. It's critical to do more for the intellectual side of the lives of disadvantaged kids, to introduce them to ideas. School's the only place they'll get that."

The hard nub of disagreement is over what the first task of schools should be—to impart intellectual curiosity or to impart a body of skills and knowledge. What would doubtless strike Meier as the worst excesses of the Chancellor's District and P.S. 114 are not, however, by-products of emphasizing skills over curiosity. They are by-products of decentralization.

True, Success for All and programs like it are the enemies of teacher autonomy. But almost every school that uses Success for All previously had a greater degree of teacher autonomy and was failing to teach its students well. Autonomy is hard to defend where it is demonstrably not working. It is also true that Success for All tilts a school toward reading instruction to the exclusion of other subjects—but if there has to be a tilt, it should be toward reading.

The real solution would be to develop a comprehensive curriculum covering all subjects and the entire school day—in other words, more centralization, not less. This is the aim of the whole-school reform movement, the chief promoter of which, a private organization called New American Schools, now has more than a thousand member schools that choose among eight designs, one of them developed by Robert Slavin. New American Schools persuades public school districts to abandon the usual impulsive way of reforming schools and adopt an all-encompassing design that has worked elsewhere. Even without committing themselves to New American Schools, however, many school districts have moved toward whole-school reform on their own.

Testing excesses are another consequence of decentralization. Every school gives tests. The problem lies in tests that are made enormously consequential even though they have nothing to do with what should go on in the classroom and can be prepared for with trick-pony exercises. If there were a nationally agreed-upon curriculum, regular classroom instruction would be the only test prep students would need.

I'm not suggesting that we impose a required curriculum on the great bulk of American public schools, which are functioning just fine on their own. I am suggesting, though, that nonperforming schools be put into the hands of higher authorities—up to and including the federal government—until they start performing. By far the best and most reliable means for turning these schools around would be to institute a prescribed curriculum that has been carefully researched and field-tested and has been proved to work.

Liberals have long dreamed of using the federal government to fix bad schools. The chief means has been the Title I program, passed in 1965, which gives more than $7 billion a year to schools in low-income areas. The money must be spent on instruction, but not on any particular kind of instruction. We are moving toward a better and more directed use of Title I funding, which now pays for nearly every operating Success for All program. Last year Congress passed a bill that sets aside $120 million of Title I funds for a variety of whole-school designs, with the idea of tilting the entire Title I program toward them if the results are promising. Many of the cities and states that have taken over bad schools have put together money from Title I and other federal education programs to pay for new curricula that are both intensive and imposed.

Changes of this kind are punitive to local school boards, principals, and teachers—but they had it coming. Students in taken-over schools aren't being punished; they're getting a genuine education, and hence a chance in life, that they would otherwise be denied. No reform that lets students abandon the public school system, or lets individual public schools redesign themselves in the absence of guidance, can possibly ensure a minimum standard of education for every American child. Only central control of the curriculum can. A decent education should be a guarantee, not an option.

THE STUDENT

STUDENT BELIEFS/ CHARACTER EDUCATION

Failure Outside the Classroom

Laurence Steinberg

This selection first appeared in *The Wall Street Journal* on 11 July 1996. Laurence Steinberg is professor of psychology at Temple University and co-author of *Beyond the Classroom: Why School Reform Has Failed and What Parents Need to Do* (Simon & Schuster, 1996).

President Clinton's proposal last month to widen access to postsecondary education by granting tax credits to help finance the first two years of college may be good politics in this election year. But if we don't do something to improve the quality of the students who will be entering our nation's colleges and universities, the plan will be disastrous policy. The last thing this country needs is a rising tide of mediocre students riding the educational people-mover for 14 rather than 12 years.

What we need instead is an open and candid discussion of why our high school graduates are entering college so ill-prepared for higher education.

By any credible measure, the past two decades of tinkering with America's schools have been an unmitigated failure. Although there are occasional success stories about a school here or a district there that has turned students' performance around, the competence of American students overall has not improved in 25 years. The proportions of high school juniors scoring in the top categories on the math, science, reading, and writing portions of national achievement tests have not changed in any meaningful way in two decades. SAT scores have not risen since the early 1980s, and they even dropped somewhat in recent years; today they remain lower than they were in the early 1970s. A recent study of the California State University system indicated that half of all freshmen needed remedial education in math, and nearly half needed remedial education in English.

My colleagues and I recently released the results of the most extensive study ever conducted on the forces that affect youngsters' interest and performance in school. Over two years of planning and pilot-testing, four years of data collection in the field, and four years of data analysis, we studied more than 20,000 teenagers and their families in nine very different American communities. Our findings suggest that the sorry state of student achievement in America is due more to the conditions of students' lives outside of school than to what takes place within school walls. The failure of our educational policies is due to our obsession with reforming schools and classrooms, and our general disregard of the contributing forces that, while outside the boundaries of the school, are probably more influential.

According to our research, nearly one in three parents in America is seriously disengaged from his or her adolescent's life, and, especially, from the adolescent's education. Only about one-fifth of parents consistently attend school programs. Nearly one-third of students say their parents have no idea how they are doing in school. About one-sixth of all students report that their parents don't care whether they earn good grades in school.

Nor is there support for achievement within adolescent peer groups. To be sure, teen society in America has never been a strong admirer of academic accomplishment. But widespread parental disengagement has left a large proportion of adolescents far more susceptible to the influence of their friends than in past generations, and this influence is taking its toll on school achievement. Fewer than one in five students say their friends think it is important to get good grades in school. Less than one-fourth of all students regularly discuss their schoolwork with their friends. Nearly one-fifth of all students say they do not try as hard as they can in school because they are worried about what their friends might think.

It's not surprising, then, that very little of the typical American student's time—something on the order of 15 to 20 hours weekly, or only about 15% of his or her waking hours—is spent on endeavors likely to contribute to learning or achievement. In terms of how much time is expected of them for school and school-related pursuits, American students are among the least challenged in the industrialized world. Many spend more time flipping hamburgers and roaming malls than they do in school. For too many students, part-time work and after-school socializing have supplanted school-sponsored extracurricular activities—activities that help to strengthen youngsters' attachment to the school as an institution.

President Clinton has called for boosting American student achievement by 2000. But before we rush once again to reinvent the curriculum, retrain our teachers, refurbish our schools' laboratories or expand access to higher education, here are several steps that must be taken:

- Change the focus of the national debate over our achievement problem from reforming schools to changing students' and parents' attitudes and behaviors. No amount of school reform will work unless we recognize the solution as considerably more far-reaching and complicated than simply changing curricular standards, teaching methods, or instructional materials.

- Conduct a serious discussion about the high rate of parental irresponsibility. The widespread disengagement of parents from the business of child-rearing is a public health problem that warrants urgent national attention.

- Recognize that the prevailing and pervasive peer norm of "getting by" is in part a direct consequence of an educational system that neither rewards excellence nor punishes failure. The vast majority of students know all too well that the grades they earn in school will, under the present system, have little or no impact on their future educational or occupational success.

Although schools have played a role in creating this situation, they have been abetted by parents, employers, and institutions of higher education. In our study, more than half of all students said they could bring home grades of "C" or worse without their parents getting upset, and one-quarter said they could bring home grades of "D" or worse without consequence. Few employers ask to see students' high school or college transcripts. With the exception of our country's most selective colleges and universities, our postsecondary educational institutions are willing to accept virtually any applicant with a high school diploma, regardless of his or her scholastic record. The current practice of providing remedial education in such basic academic skills as reading, writing, and mathematics to entering college students has trivialized the significance of the high school diploma, and drained precious resources away from bona fide college-level instruction.

- Reconsider the proposition that after-school employment is inherently beneficial for teenagers. There is very little evidence that widely available after-school jobs teach students the skills and competencies they will need to be successful, highly educated workers. There is considerable proof, however, that extensive after-school employment has more costs—diminished commitment to school, for instance, and increased drug and alcohol use—than benefits.

- Support school-sponsored extracurricular programs and extend them to as many students as possible. Participation in school-based extracurricular activities strengthens youngsters' commitment to school and carries benefits that spill over into the classroom, especially for students who are having difficulty in school.

- Reestablish in the minds of young people and parents that the primary activity of childhood and adolescence is schooling. If we want our children to value education and strive for achievement, adults must behave as if doing well in school—not just graduating, but actually doing well—is more important than socializing, organized sports, after-school jobs, or any other activity.

For far too long, our national debate about education has been dominated by disputes over how schools ought to be changed without examining the other forces that affect students' willingness to learn and their ability to achieve. It is time to leave behind the myopic view that schools determine student achievement, and, most importantly, that school reform is the solution to America's achievement problem.

No curriculum overhaul, no instructional innovation, no change in school organization, no toughening of standards, no rethinking of teacher training or compensation will succeed if students do not come to school interested in, and committed to, learning. Any policy that merely increases the years of schooling, without ensuring that students and their families are committed to the education process, will be far more costly than any tax credit imaginable.

. . . .

Values, Views, or Virtues?

Kevin Ryan
Karen Bohlin

This selection first appeared in *Education Week* on 3 March 1999. Karen Bohlin is the director of the Center for the Advancement of Ethics and Character at Boston University; Kevin Ryan is the Center's director emeritus. They are the authors of *Building Character in Schools: Practical Ways to Bring Moral Instruction To Life* (Jossey–Bass, 1999).

People are making the connection between the nightly news and discouraging reports on American students. We are regularly bombarded both with scandalous news about our public figures' unsavory acts and hypocrisies and with depressing reports of our students' cheating, lack of self-discipline, and lackluster approach to schoolwork. But things are changing, too. People have again begun to talk about the importance of character and personal integrity. Stephen R. Covey, the author of one of the decade's most widely read books, *The Seven Habits of Highly Effective People*, claims that Americans are shifting paradigms—from a concern for our personalities to a concern for our characters and questions of who we are and the kinds of persons we are becoming. We have grown dissatisfied with the mere social savvy of "winning friends and influencing people." We are bringing back into focus the personal need for something deeper and more stable.

Voices from within and beyond our schools are calling for "character education," something that has been missing-in-action from many schools since the late '60s. The reasons for this renewed interest in what has been called the "schools' latest fad and oldest mission" are many, varying from the high levels of youth pathologies (violent crimes and suicides), drug use, and promiscuity, to the inability of many young people to fulfill their responsibilities as students. Teachers complain that, on the one hand, a small percentage of high-achieving students exude a "me-first-at-all-cost" approach to school and life, and that, on the other hand, by high school a much larger percentage come to school with a sense of "life-sucks-and-then-you-die" defeatism.

These social problems and self-destructive student attitudes are making the teaching career and life in classrooms increasingly more difficult.

Nevertheless, they also are driving an awakening of the conviction that the institution of schools, along with family, church, and community, has an important role to play in helping children develop good consciences and ethical behavior. Often, as a result of the prompting of parents, teachers are rediscovering that they, de facto, are moral authorities and role models. However, being told that they are "character educators" does not tell teachers what they ought to do.

As educators reach out to re-engage this age-old mission, they are discovering that three very different approaches to character education are being advocated. These approaches have as their central focus values, views, or virtues. These "three V's" represent different roads, each claiming to lead to good character. Each purports to provide students with a moral compass to make good choices, keep commitments, and live honorable lives. In effect, though, each of the "three V's" represents not only a different approach, but also a different conception of what good character is.

The Values Approach

This is clearly the most popular approach to character education in American schools. It is based on the psychological concept of "value," what an individual wants or desires or ascribes worth to. One's values can be good or bad, and this approach intends to give children opportunities to learn how to value in order to be clear about their desires and, ideally, to make good choices. In subject-matter discussions and in special exercises, students are urged to make their own choices on a range of moral and nonmoral issues and be ready to articulate them.

The popularity of the values approach, unfortunately, rests on its weaknesses. Students like it because they have the opportunity to focus on themselves and what they like and do not like. Many teachers like it because they can deal with fascinating material, from political scandals to the latest trends in pop culture, and *not have to take a stand*. "And how do you feel about bombing civilians in wartime?" One of the primary premises of the values approach is that teachers and schools should not indoctrinate or impose their values on students. Therefore, the best and the appropriate approach of the school is to give children practice at sorting out their own values.

There are many problems with this approach, which grew out of the moral controversies and confusions of the late 1960s. Its advocates have badly distorted an important purpose of schools. That is, to indoctrinate, or "teach into," the young our society's best ideas about what a good life and a good society are and how to build and strengthen both. A school that does not share with students the hard-earned moral principles and ideas that serve as our social glue, and instead leaves children to discover them on their own, is clearly miseducating. Besides the fact that this values approach itself indoctrinates students with value relativity (I'm OK and you're OK, and different strokes for different folks, and that's OK), it has very little to do with character development.

The Views Approach

Views are the intellectual positions we hold on a range of issues, from politics and the economy to religious practice. Views, like values, can be good, bad, or morally indifferent. Acquiring strong views and attitudes on important moral issues is an integral part of becoming a mature person. We must be careful, nevertheless, about the dangers of launching our character education effort from the platform of multiple views.

The views-driven classroom regularly engages students in discussions of controversial issues. The teacher's job is to help the students, subtly or not, identify with and eventually adopt correct views. While stimulating and engaging, the views-driven approach to character education thrives on controversy, which can sometimes spill out of control into anger and contentiousness.

There is nothing wrong with generating controversy in the careful pursuit of truth, but views-driven character education doesn't usually take this tack. Moral values and principles get muddled in fierce debates over such thorny issues as abortion, homosexual marriage, prayer in school, and whether or not school uniforms should be mandated. An overemphasis on controversial points of view often can generate more heat than light. At worst, it can leave students with the impression that some issues are just "too complicated" or "ultimately, just a matter of opinion." Too often, the moral significance of an issue is reduced to claims and counterclaims, and the moral principles that underlie those claims remain unexamined. Dialogue and inquiry are essential to solid character education. Posturing and politicking, however, are not sound character education. What works for Oprah Winfrey and Jerry Springer may be stimulating, but it has little to do with character development.

In the views approach, character is somehow equated with being aligned with approved views, whether they are on race or the environment or how the genders ought to relate to each other. What matters is not one's personal behavior or the way in which one lives his life, but rather the "isms" he is for and against. This leads to character-by-identification rather than true character education.

The Virtues Approach

By focusing on values, we evoke students' emotional responses. By focusing on views, we stir up a variety of positions on controversial issues. But neither values nor views secure an internal commitment to lead a good life or behaviors consistent with that commitment. We are all too familiar with the intellectual moral theorist who can cite Aristotle, Kant, Confucius, and the Bible, chapter and verse, but is too consumed by his own views to console a sobbing three-year-old by reading a bed-time story or notice that a colleague is overworked and needs a hand. We may also have met the bleeding-heart moralist, who sees injustice and victimization at every turn, but is too paralyzed by the dark side of humanity to take the first step to do anything about it.

Then there are those who only mechanically fulfill moral obligations. Some students candidly admit that they do community service to beef up their resumes. Others fulfill a community-service "requirement," yet fail to help a classmate whose illness forced him to miss school. Good character demands more from us than an intellectual commitment, heartfelt desire, or mechanical fulfillment of responsibilities. It requires virtues, those habits of the head, heart, and hand that enable us to know the good, love the good, and do the good.

What distinguishes virtues from views and values, then, is that virtues are habits cultivated from within the individual and actually improve character and intelligence. The word *virtue* itself comes from the Latin *vir*, which has a root meaning of "force" or "agency." In Latin, the expression *virtus moralis* became the established equivalent of the Greek expression *arete ethike*, "moral virtue" or "character excellence." Virtues—habits such as diligence, sincerity, personal accountability, courage, and perseverance—actually enable us to do our work better and to enjoy it more as a consequence. It is our virtues, not our views or our values, that enable us to become better students, better parents, better spouses, better teachers, better friends, better citizens.

Self-esteem and the satisfaction that accompanies achievement are the fruits, not the roots, of virtue. Virtue needs to be cultivated first. Moreover, virtue serves as a means to human happiness. Martha Washington sums up the connection between virtue and happiness nicely: "The greater part of our happiness or misery depends on our dispositions [our virtues], and not on our circumstances. We carry the seeds of one or the other about with us in our minds wherever we go." Teachers and schools have a place in bringing those seeds of virtue to fruition.

Without a conception of what it may mean for a person to live in an honorable or contemptible way, the views one holds, no matter how well they may be defended, are empty. Without a clear sense of the good, personal values and the ability to show empathy remain hollow. Views are simply intellectual positions, and values evoke neither a moral commitment nor the promise of leading a good life. Virtues, on the other hand, enable us to give shape to and lead worthy lives. Education in virtues—those good dispositions of the heart and mind that are regularly put into actions—is the foundation to solid character development. As Heraclitus put it, "Character is destiny."

Our success or failure at instilling in our students those virtues, which are the backbone of good character, will determine their destinies—and that of our nation.

. . . .

Blame the Schools, Not the Parents

Thomas Sowell

This selection first appeared in the *Orange County Register* on 5 May 1999. Thomas Sowell is the Rose and Milton Friedman Senior Fellow in Public Policy at the Hoover Institution.

Of all the irrational ideas that have been thrown around in the wake of the high school shootings in Littleton, Colorado, one of the most reckless is the proposal to hold parents legally responsible for what their children do.

Whether the particular parents of the particular young killers who committed this particular massacre had knowledge in advance that would make them criminally liable is something for a court of law to decide. What is at issue is whether parents in general should be held legally liable for their children's acts.

Responsibility and control go together. For decades now, our laws and our educational system have consistently undermined parental authority. Yet new legal responsibilities for parents are being proposed after parental control has been eroded.

Preschoolers are taught that their parents have no right to spank them. All sorts of propaganda programs in the schools—from so-called "drug prevention" to "sex education"—stress that each individual makes his or her own decisions, independently of parental or societal values.

Most people have no idea how pervasive and unremitting are the efforts to drive a wedge between children and their parents and to replace parental influence with the influence of teachers, counselors and even the children's similarly immature peers. Many of the books, movies, and other materials used in the public schools mock parents as old windbags who are behind the times. "Trust-building" exercises teach students to rely on their classmates.

Handing out condoms in school and giving girls abortions behind their parents' backs are just isolated manifestations of this underlying philosophy, which reaches far beyond sexual matters.

Nor are these just idiosyncrasies of particular teachers or schools. There are nationwide networks—some of them government-sponsored—which have disseminated pre-packaged programs designed to wean schoolchildren away from the values with which they have been raised and mold them to the values of self-anointed agents of "change."

The materials used and the things said in these materials would simply have to be seen to be believed. I certainly would never have imagined such things before doing research for my book "Inside American Education." My assistant said she had trouble sleeping after seeing some of the movies shown to school children.

Invasions of family privacy with diary assignments and other intrusions are all part of the same mindset. So are groups like the so-called Children's Defense Fund, which seek legal powers to impose their notions of how children should be raised. Hillary Clinton's pious hokum that "it takes a village" to raise a child is more of the same.

What all these efforts have in common, aside from an arrogant presumption of superiority, is a drive for power without responsibility. They don't even take responsibility for their own activities, which are hidden, denied or camouflaged. Above all, they are not prepared to be held accountable for the consequences of their playing with children's minds.

Columbine High School was in the news long before the recent tragic shootings there. It was featured in a "20/20" broadcast about "death education" back in 1991. This macabre subject is one of the endless procession of brainwashing programs that are taking up time sorely needed for academic work in schools across the country. One of the Columbine students who is now grown blames the course's morbid preoccupation with death for her own unsuccessful attempt at suicide.

Zealots who are pushing New Age notions of death under the guise of "education" are undeterred by parental protests that their children are having nightmares or depression. The "educators" who have been on a brainwashing ego trip have done their best to cover their own tracks. Manuals accompanying some of these programs show how to evade and mislead parents and the public.

Running through all these programs is the notion that morality is optional: If it feels good to you, do it!

We will never know how good it felt to those young killers to shoot down those around them. Nor can we know how much the school's own reckless experiments with brainwashing contributed to the tragedy. But it is truly galling to have those who have been undermining both morality and parents for years now demand that parents be held legally responsible for the acts of their children.

· ·

Goodbye to Sara and Benjamin?

Thomas Sowell

This selection first appeared in *Jewish World Review Online* on 10 September 1999.
Thomas Sowell is the Rose and Milton Friedman Senior Fellow in Public Policy at the
Hoover Institution.

Recently a couple of dear friends visited us, bringing with them their six-year-old twins, Sara and Benjamin. These are some of the loveliest children you could meet—not just in appearance, but in their behavior.

They are the kinds of kids you can see in Norman Rockwell paintings, but less and less in the real world.

Now Sara and Benjamin are going off to public school and it is painful to imagine what they might be like a year from now. Most people are unaware how much time and effort the public schools—and some private schools—are putting into undermining the values and understanding that children were taught by their parents and re-orienting them toward the avant-garde vision of the world that is fashionable in the educational establishment.

Today's educators believe it is their job to introduce children like Sara and Benjamin to sex when and in whatever manner they see fit, regardless of what the children's parents might think. Raw movies of both heterosexuals and homosexuals in action are shown in elementary schools.

Weaning children away from their parents' influence in general is a high priority in many schools. Children sit in what is called a "magic circle" and talk about all sorts of personal things, with the rule being that they are not to repeat any of these things to anyone outside this magic circle.

Sometimes they are explicitly told not to repeat what is said to their parents.

Some handbooks for teachers warn against letting parents know the specifics of what is being done and provide strategies for side-stepping parental questions and concerns. Glowing generalities and high-sounding names like "gifted and talented" programs conceal what are nothing more than brainwashing operations to convert the children from their parents' values to the values preferred by educational gurus.

Right and wrong are among the earliest targets of these programs. "There is no 'right' way or 'right' age to have life experiences," one widely used textbook says. Another textbook tells children that they may listen to their parents "if you are interested in their ideas." But, if there is a difference of opinion, parent and child alike should see the other's point of view "as different, not wrong."

Sara and Benjamin are only six years old and are going into the first grade. Will any of this apply to them? Yes. There is a textbook designed for children ranging from pre-school to the third grade, which tells children about their rights and about asserting those rights to parents. Whenever "things happen you don't like," you have "the right to be angry without being afraid of being punished" it says.

In other words, don't take any guff off mommy and daddy. Who are they? As another textbook says, parents are just "ordinary people with faults and weaknesses and insecurities and problems just like everyone else." In many of the textbooks, movies and other material used in schools, parents are depicted as old-fashioned people who are out of touch and full of hang-ups.

What these smug underminers of parents fail to understand is that the relationship of a child to his or her parents is the most extraordinary relationship anyone is likely to have with another human being. No one else is likely to sacrifice so much for another person's well-being. If the avant-garde ideas taught to children in schools blow up in their faces, it is the parents who will be left to pick up the pieces, not the glib gurus.

Most of the classroom teachers who carry out such educational fashions and fetishes have no idea where they originated or what their underlying purpose is. In reality, many of the techniques and strategies used to break down the child's values, personality and modesty are straight out of totalitarian brainwashing practices from the days of Stalin and Mao.

That is the origin, for example, of the personal journals that children are required to keep in schools all across the United States. These journals are not educational. Gross mistakes in spelling, grammar and usage are ignored, not corrected. These journals are gateways to the psyche and the first step in manipulating little minds.

As our friends departed and went off to enroll their children in the public schools, I could not help wondering if I had seen Sara and Benjamin for the last time. Would they still be the same sweet children after they have been used as guinea pigs by those who claim to be trying to educate them?

. . . .

Student Customers Being Sold a Bad Product

Susan Estrich

This selection first appeared on the *EducationNews.org* website on 6 December 1999. Susan Estrich is the Robert Kingsley Professor of Law at the University of Southern California.

Ending social promotion has become one of the rallying cries of the movement to improve schools and hold students to standards of achievement.

Politicians campaign on the issue; legislatures across the county have begun passing laws demanding it. There's just one problem.

What happens when almost half the students can't meet the standards?

That is the situation confronting Los Angeles and that city will not be the only one to face it. Last year, the California Legislature passed a law giving local districts two years to retool their systems to promote students based on academic achievement and not age. In response, Los Angeles decided to begin applying standards for promotion in the second through fifth grades, and in the eighth.

The only problem was that by their own estimate, as many as half the students wouldn't pass the standardized test. The system isn't failing these kids in high school. We're failing them in first grade.

But wait. Maybe the tests are wrong. Maybe they're unfair as applied to those who have just come into a system or school, who don't speak English as a native tongue, who may be disadvantaged in taking standardized tests.

So the school board decided to get a second opinion, what they considered a better one. Last week the bad news came in: Based on teacher evaluations, 40 percent or more of the students in the nation's largest school district don't deserve to be promoted to the next grade.

These results raise any number of very troubling questions. Kids who fall behind in first grade never catch up. Why does it take a state law for teachers and schools to focus on near-majority failure when they are, apparently, quite aware of it? Imagine that 40 percent of the kids in any suburban school district were failing in the teacher's own estimation, every year. Wouldn't someone be screaming bloody murder, pointing out that these children would be handicapped for life as a result of what was going on in that very room or what wasn't?

For much of the last year, the Los Angeles School Board has been occupied by the question of what to do with a $200 million half-finished high school, where construction has been halted because of environmental concerns that should have been addressed before construction ever began. The monumental incompetence of the school district in handling the project is one reason for the replacement of the popular, but ineffectual superintendent of schools. Now, before the project can go forward again, it has to go back and comply with the various governmental mandates intended to protect students from even the remotest possibility of environmental hazards.

There are at least a dozen different laws protecting what goes into a student's lungs. But who is protecting what goes into their heads or doesn't? The damage being done right now far exceeds the threat posed by buried methane gas.

. . . .

Why Johnny Can't Fail

How The "Floating Standard" Has Destroyed Public Education

Jerry Jesness

This selection first appeared in *Reason* Magazine in July 1999. Jerry Jesness is a special education teacher in a south Texas elementary school.

I confess. I am a grade-inflating teacher guilty of "social promotion." I have given passing grades to students who failed all of their tests, to students who refused to read their assignments, to students who were absent as often as not, to students who were not even functionally literate. I have turned a blind eye to cheating and outright plagiarism and have given A's and B's to students whose performance was at best mediocre. Like others of my ilk, I have sent students to higher grades, to higher education, and to the workplace unprepared for the demands that would be made of them.

I am, in short, a servant of the force that thwarts nearly every effort to reform American education. I am a servant of the floating standard.

It does not matter what changes we make in curricula. The floating standard shields the status quo and guarantees the reign of mediocrity. If standards are set high but students lack the skills or motivation to meet them, the standards will inevitably drop. If many students in a given class take part-time jobs, homework will be reduced. If drugs sweep through a school, lower standards will compensate for the lack of mental clarity. Americans want quality education, but when lower grades and higher failure rates reach their own children's classes, they rebel and schools relent. Americans hate public education because standards are low but love their local schools because their children perform so well there.

Schools have their own reasons to play along. Flexible standards mean fewer complaints. When parents are happy, there are fewer lawsuits; when students are happy, there are fewer discipline problems. What's more, schools that fail students who have not met the stated standards have the expensive and unpopular obligation to retain them.

In the short term, floating standards make everybody a winner. Students build self-esteem, parents gain peace of mind, and schools save money. When the payback comes, time and distance keep the student and the school well separated. Teachers who are willing to drop standards, especially those who manage to do so while boasting of raising them, win the enthusiastic support of students, parents, and administrators, while those who genuinely attempt to challenge their charges are harassed, proselytized, or purged.

The Initiation

I was introduced to the floating standard in 1979, while teaching for the Bureau of Indian Affairs on a reservation in western South Dakota. My predecessor had been forced to resign after failing nearly half his students. In his absence, the failing grades were changed and his students were promoted to the next grade. His former students and peers considered him a capable, if imprudent, instructor. It was because of him that my students were willing and able to read grade-appropriate novels, a rarity at BIA schools.

Even though I knew my predecessor's fate, I gave some failing grades for the first grading period. After a few warnings, however, I fell into line. There was no point in doing otherwise. The students already knew that failing grades would mysteriously change over the summer and that they would advance to the next grade. I opted for self-preservation.

A few years later I moved to Texas' lower Rio Grande Valley. Since I was now an experienced teacher and was reasonably fluent in Spanish, I felt that my position would be stronger than it had been at my former school. Besides, at my interview my future principal spoke movingly about the need to push our students to their limits. In the first grading period I boldly flunked a number of students, including the daughter of an administrator of a local elementary school and a star fullback who was also the nephew of a school board member.

Shortly thereafter I was called in to meet with my principal and the aggrieved parents. Such was my naiveté that I actually bothered to bring evidence. I showed the elementary administrator her daughter's plagiarized book report and the book from which it had been copied, and I showed the fullback's father homework bearing his son's name but written in another person's handwriting. The parents offered weak apologies but maintained that I had not treated their children fairly.

My principal suddenly discovered a number of problems with my teaching. For the next few weeks he was in my class almost daily. Every spitball, every chattering student, every bit of graffiti was noted. When there were discipline problems, my superiors sided with the offending students. Teaching became impossible.

So I learned to turn a blind eye to cheating and plagiarism and to give students, especially athletes, extra credit for everything from reading orally in class to remembering to bring their pencils. In this way, I gained the co-operation of my students and the respect and support of my superiors. I gritted my teeth, toughed out the year, and sought employment elsewhere.

It wasn't until after my fifth year of teaching that I finally gave up and accepted that my only choices were either to accept the floating standard or to abandon public education. That year my assignment was to teach beginning English as a Second Language (ESL I) and Plan III (low-group) language arts. My principal was particularly adamant about having all the students pass. After issuing the first round of grades, I found myself in his office more often than my worst-behaved students. He informed me that, since our school offered "ability grouping," there was no reason for any student to fail.

He recommended a few grading techniques to help me help my students pass. All ESL students were to receive passing grades. We could promote even those who failed to learn English to the next grade without promoting them out of ESL I. In language arts, no test was to be graded below "50," even one that was turned in blank. Daily assignments were to be graded according to the number of questions answered, even if all of the answers were wrong. If 8 of 10 questions were answered, the grade was to be "80," regardless of the quality of the answers. Those who still were failing at the end of the grading period were to be offered the opportunity to do reports or projects for extra credit. My neighbor, another low-group teacher who was held up to me as a mentor, boasted that he left the week's spelling words on the blackboard during spelling tests and recommended that I do the same.

I pulled in my horns too late to save myself that year. When I sent students to the office for discipline, the referral forms were placed in my file as evidence that I could not handle my classes. Failing grades were taken as proof that I was not motivating my students. Even chronic truants and habitual drug abusers would presumably have been passing had I been doing a better job of teaching. Besides, my neighbor had the same sort of students as I, and their grades were fine.

The principal recommended that my contract not be renewed. My dismissal hearing was a lonely affair attended only by my superintendent, my principal, a stenographer, and me. No champion of high educational standards descended from his ivory tower to speak on my behalf. I pointed out that those students who eschewed drugs and attended class regularly were doing well. Some of my ESL students had learned enough English that year to function in regular academic classes, and many of my language arts students were beginning to write coherent essays. I offered student compositions and tests as proof and suggested that we compare my students' standardized test scores with those of other students in the same track. My arguments fell on deaf ears.

That job and its $17,000 annual salary were hardly worth fighting for, so I left quietly. After a year as a salesperson and graduate student, however, I began to miss the classroom and decided to give teaching one more try. I returned to the district where I had given a failing grade to a star fullback. My superiors correctly assumed that I had learned my lesson and welcomed the return of the prodigal teacher. Just as Orwell's Winston Smith was finally able to win the victory over himself and love Big Brother, I was finally ready to embrace the floating standard.

In the ensuing seven years, only two of my students failed. My evaluations were "above expectations" twice and "clearly outstanding" five times. By my fifth year I had climbed to the top of the Texas teachers' career ladder and earned an annual bonus of $3,300.

I really did become a better teacher after my rebirth, if only because I had gained the cooperation of my students and superiors. My classes became much better behaved after I quit trying to force students to learn more than they cared to. My superiors became more supportive, and I actually met with cooperation, not hostility, when I sent students to the office. I tried to be as honest as possible with my charges. All of my students and any parents who bothered to visit my classroom or return my phone calls understood that grades above 80 honestly reflected performance, while those in the 70 range were fluffed up with extra credit. I explained to the parents of my immigrant students that here in the United States passing grades may be given for attendance and minimal effort and do not necessarily reflect mastery of the course material. Students who needed to be pushed lost out, but that was the price of harmony.

The Effective Schools movement of the early '90s gave the brief illusion that schools were ready for real change. In 1991 I was named head of the campus High Expectations Committee. We recommended that administrators stay out of the grading process and that teachers not be required to give evidence that failing students had been retaught and retested. We also suggested that students who complained that their grades were too low or that they were being unfairly retained should be required to prove that they had done the required work and mastered the required material. Our recommendations disappeared over the summer. In their place was a plan to give high achievers pizza parties and letter jackets.

Why the Floating Standard

Years ago there was a con game called the razzle-dazzle. Players threw marbles onto a numbered grid. The total corresponded to another number on a chart, where the winning numbers were very high or very low. Since there were many marbles, the odds of hitting such a total were infinitesimal. The operator could give the player the illusion that he was winning early in the game by miscounting in the player's favor. When it appeared that the player was close to winning the jackpot, the operator began counting the numbers as they really were.

Like the razzle-dazzle man, schools have fooled their clients by miscounting in what appears to be the clients' favor. By giving high grades and class credit to anyone willing to occupy space in a classroom, schools create the illusion that their players—their students—are winning. Only after leaving school and facing work or college do the students discover that they have lost.

Knowledge is power, but a diploma is just a piece of paper. Our schools have undersold the former and oversold the latter. Most employers would rather hire a tenth-grade dropout with a solid tenth-grade education than a high school graduate with only fifth-grade skills. Likewise, a dropout who later graduates from night school at age 21 will be better prepared for work and life than a student who graduates illiterate at 18. Many students and even parents fail to grasp this simple truth. For too many of them, a diploma is a sort of philosopher's stone, an object that can magically guarantee one an annual income in excess of $25,000—an object that is, furthermore, an entitlement owed to anyone willing to serve sufficient time in school.

Such students do not see teachers as mentors who help them strengthen their knowledge and skills. They see them as obstacles.

It should come as no surprise that grade inflation and course content reduction have become the norm. Grades are educational quality control, and passing grades "prove" that teacher, student, and school are successful; therefore, the "best" teachers are those who give the highest grades, and the "best" administrators are those who can convince their teachers to do so. In this bizarre system, it is better to teach 10 vocabulary words than 100. If a teacher assigns 10 words and the student learns 8, the student scores 80 on the exam and both teacher and student are successful. If the teacher teaches 100 words and the student learns 50, both student and teacher have failed, even though the second student has learned more than six times as much as the first.

Teachers have an abundance of curricular guides provided by textbook publishers, district committees, and state agencies. Although teachers are required to follow these guides, they are also expected to teach students "where they are at," help them compensate for learning disabilities, modify lessons for various learning styles, reteach students who fail to master material in the allotted time, and so on. A teacher's worst nightmare is to be assigned a "regular" class in which most students' skills are several years below par.

Imagine that you are required to teach *Hamlet* to a group of students who are either unwilling or unable to read such a work. If you demand that your charges read and understand the play, most will fail and you will be blamed. If you drop *Hamlet* and convert the class into a remedial reading course, you will be out of compliance with the curriculum. If you complain that your students are not up to the mandated task, you will be labeled insensitive and uncaring.

Fear not: The floating standard will save you. If the students will not or cannot read the play, read it to them. If they will not sit still long enough to hear the whole play, consider an abridged or comic book version, or let them watch a movie. If they cannot pass a multiple-choice test, try true-or-false, or a fill-in-the-blank test that mirrors the previous day's study sheet. If they still have not passed, allow them to do an art project. They could make a model of the Globe Theater with popsicle sticks or draw a picture of a Danish prince, or Prince Charles, or even the artist formerly known as Prince. Those who lack artistic talent could make copies of Shakespearean sonnets with macaroni letters on construction paper. If all else fails, try group projects. That way you can give passing grades to all the students, even if only one in five produces anything.

Keep dropping the standard, and sooner or later everyone will hit it. If anyone asks, you taught *Hamlet* in a nonconventional way, one that took into account your students' individual differences and needs.

Fixing the Floating Standard

For three decades, dismayed Americans have watched their children's test scores slip relative to those of children in other industrialized nations. Our leaders have responded with hollow excuses. *Too many American children live in poverty,* they say. But so do many Koreans. *Many American children are raised in single-parent homes.* But so are many Swedes. *The United States is an ethnically diverse country.* But so is Singapore. The biggest lie is that we are the only nation in the world that seeks to educate children of all socioeconomic classes. That has not been true for decades.

The reality is simpler than that. Those other nations have fixed standards.

American schools offer fixed standards for their best and worst students, but not for the largest group, those in the middle. Advanced Placement tests are the same throughout the country. International Baccalaureate offers uniform curricula and standards to top-notch students in the United States and in English-language schools throughout the world. Like the Advanced Placement exams, SAT II exams test knowledge in certain subjects. A teacher who prepares students for these tests must teach the intended content of the course or face the embarrassment of having most of his students fail the final test. Likewise, students must learn the material or fail the test and forego course credit. No student, not even a star athlete, can negotiate a higher grade on an A.P. exam.

In my early teaching years, there were no fixed standards at the bottom. We had the Iowa Basic Test, the California Achievement Test, and the Comprehensive Test of Basic Skills, but the low-group classes did not take them very seriously. The Zeitgeist forgave disadvantaged students and those who taught them for poor scores.

That has changed in the past decade. Ever-increasing numbers of states have mandated that their students pass a basic skills test before graduating. In Texas, the euphemistically named Texas Assessment of Academic Skills (TAAS) is the standard. In order to prevent schools from ignoring any class of students, Texas wisely chose to monitor separately the test scores of all racial and economic groups. The state has demanded basic skills for all students, and the schools are delivering.

For those who seek to learn more than basics, however, the effect has been negative. Like other state-mandated minimum skills tests, the TAAS is helping to solve one problem while creating another: Basic skills are now so strongly stressed that academics suffer. Some conscientious English and reading teachers complain that they have had to cut back on literature in order to cover TAAS skills. Teachers who once taught from novels now assign reams of single-page reading passages followed by multiple-choice questions. It should be obvious that a student who has read and analyzed the works of Charles Dickens or Mark Twain would be better able to determine the sequence of events or select the main idea of a paragraph than would a student who spent his academic year reading sample test passages. Unfortunately, not all educational leaders agree, so abundant skills practice, not serious study of literature, has become the norm in too many classes.

Here's how the system works at my school. Our fourth-graders have two 70-minute reading sessions daily. In one session, the children read short selections from books, but in the other they read sample TAAS passages; they are given the entire period to digest a one- or two-page passage and then answer the five to eight questions that follow. They are encouraged to read the passage, highlight key words, write a brief summary of each paragraph, read the answer choices, eliminate unreasonable answers, reread the answers, check for words in the answer choices that match words in the passages, answer the questions, reread, and recheck. One doubts that children taught to read in this excruciatingly slow manner are likely to become avid readers, but, then again, that's not the point of the class.

Similar problems exist in other disciplines. Some science and social studies teachers complain of being told to teach their lessons in the same format, with single-page passages followed by multiple-choice questions. Many Texas elementary math teachers complain that they are encouraged to take advantage of the TAAS' lack of a time limit by having children draw and count sticks rather than memorize math facts.

And the TAAS, of course, is not the only measure of student performance, although it has a monopoly on Texas educators' attention. My district's TAAS scores have risen steadily, but our SAT and ACT scores have remained abysmal. Across the state, SAT verbal scores are exactly the same as they were a decade ago. Our SAT math scores have risen a bit in that time, but are still in the bottom quintile. In some of the state's colleges, more incoming freshmen are put in remedial classes than not.

There's another problem with the notion of national standards. In a nation as large and diverse as ours, it's simply a mistake to require everyone to learn the exact same things. While there is a certain body of history that all Americans should know, it is reasonable for schools to dedicate time to state and local history as well. On literature we cannot agree at all. Perhaps it would be good for black students to have the opportunity to read Wright, Ellison, Hughes, and Hurston before reading Steinbeck and Dickens, as it might it be for students in New Mexico to read Anaya and Cather before Hemingway.

The French can agree that each of their graduates should be familiar with Proust and Moliére. We Americans have no such consensus, so we either test basic skills or leave the choice of what to test up to the schools. The result is standards that are minimal, variable, or both.

The Voluntary Standard

Those who take Advanced Placement or International Baccalaureate tests submit to a voluntary outside standard. There is no reason that we cannot extend this option to other students as well. Textbook publishers, educators, and others could produce competing tests to be given at the end of certain courses. Schools could submit lists of works of literature read and historical eras studied to private testing companies and receive a test compiled from computer databases. These tests would free teachers from the pressure to adjust the content of their courses and would assure students and their parents that the standard for each course is fixed, not floating. If *Hamlet* is tested, then *Hamlet,* not popsicle-stick or macaroni art, will be taught.

Since the tests would be privately produced and their use voluntary, we would not see the public resistance that we have had to national exams. Universities could decide which testing services were most reliable. Admissions preference would likely be given to students who have scored well on reputable tests, allowing the market to choose the survivors.

Parents who trust their schools should be free to place their children in classes without standardized final tests. Those who want an assurance that the course's material is actually being taught should be offered the guarantee that such tests would provide. Those who prefer a fixed standard to a floating one should have that option.

PARENTS AND TEACHERS

....

The Parent Trap

Tom Loveless

This selection first appeared in the *Wilson Quarterly*'s Autumn 1999 edition. Tom Loveless is a senior fellow and director of Brown Center on Education Policy at the Brookings Institution.

A new kind of revolution of rising expectations is sweeping the United States. It is a revolution fomented by reformers who believe that setting higher expectations in the schools is the key to improving academic performance. There is bipartisan political enthusiasm for the creation of tough new learning standards. Just about everyone wants to end social promotion, the practice of passing a student on to the next grade regardless of whether he or she has learned anything. Reformers poke, prod, cajole, and coax schools to embrace lofty academic expectations which, they believe, schools would not adopt on their own. They are confident that such heightened expectations will yield dramatic increases in student achievement.

In focusing on the schools, however, reformers are taking for granted one of the most powerful influences on the quality of American education: the American parent. They assume that parents will do whatever is necessary to raise children's levels of achievement. But will they? Do parents really consider classroom learning the most important aspect of their children's education? What are they willing to give up so that their children will learn more? Will family life change as academic achievement assumes a more prominent role in education? Will political support for reform stay firm if parents recoil from the everyday costs?

There are indications that many parents may have trouble accepting the fact that improving education is not a pain-free exercise. In Virginia, when tough new statewide tests revealed earlier this year that only 6.5 percent of the schools met state standards, many parents (and others) responded with cries of anger and disbelief. Their anger was directed not at the schools but at the standards. There are other signs that parents' commitment to academic excellence is not very deep. A 1996 Gallup Poll asked: "Which one of the following would you prefer of an oldest child—that the child get A grades or that he or she make average grades and be active in extracurricular activities?" Only 33 percent of public school parents answered that they would prefer A grades, while 56 percent preferred average grades combined with extracurricular activities. (Among private school parents, the breakdown was almost the same, 34 percent to 55 percent.)

If the wording of the question is somewhat ambiguous, the importance of nonacademic activities in teenagers' lives is thoroughly documented in *Beyond the Classroom* (1996), a study of how American teens spend their out-of-school time, the portion of their weekly schedule (in theory at least) that parents directly control. Three nonacademic categories dominate, according to Temple University psychologist Laurence Steinberg: extracurricular activities, primarily sports, consuming 10 to 15 hours; part-time employment, 15 to 20 hours; and a host of social activities, including dating, going to the movies, partying, and just hanging out with friends, 20 to 25 hours. The national average for time spent on homework is four hours per week, not surprising given the few waking hours that remain after the whirlwind of nonacademic pursuits.

This distribution of teens' time represents a huge drag on academic learning. More than one-third of the teens with part-time jobs told Steinberg they take easier classes to keep up their grades. Nearly 40 percent of students who participate in school-sponsored activities, usually sports, reported that they are frequently too tired to study. More than one-third of students said they get through the school day by "goofing off with friends," and an equal number reported spending five or more hours a week "partying." And these self-reports probably underestimate the problem.

The big story here is that teenagers' time is structured around the pursuit of a "well-rounded" life. American families might value academic achievement, but not if it intrudes on the rituals of teen existence, especially part-time employment, sports, and a busy social calendar.

This stands in stark contrast to the situation in other nations. In Europe and most Asian countries, it is assumed that the central purpose of childhood is to learn. Part-time employment of teenagers is rare, sports are noticeably subordinate to a student's academic responsibilities, and although there is plenty of socializing, it is usually in conjunction with studying or working with others on academic projects. The American student's four hours per week of homework is equal to what students in the rest of the industrialized world complete every day.

Significant cultural differences also appear in how parents judge their children's academic performance. A study by James Stigler of the University of California, Los Angeles, and Harold Stevenson of the University of Michigan, Ann Arbor, asked several hundred mothers from the United States, Japan, and China about the school performance of their fifth-grade children. More than 50 percent of the American mothers pronounced themselves very satisfied with their children's schoolwork, as opposed to only 5 percent of the Asian mothers. On tests measuring what these same children actually knew, however, the American students scored far below their Chinese and Japanese counterparts. When asked to explain their children's poor performance, the American mothers cited a lack of inborn ability. When the Japanese and Chinese children failed, their parents blamed the kids for not working hard enough.

American parents see academic achievement as a product of intrinsic ability rather than hard work, as just one of many attributes they want children to possess, and as something their own kids are accomplishing anyway. These beliefs, along with widespread peer pressure against academic excellence (who wants to be a "geek"?), an unrelenting strain of anti-intellectualism in American culture, and the weak academic demands of schools, combine to dampen the importance of academics for American youth and their parents.

We need not let educators off the hook, but parents bear some responsibility both for the lax standards in today's schools and for students' mediocre achievement. Parents appear more willing to embrace academic excellence in the abstract than to organize their family's daily life in order to achieve it. They enthusiastically support attempts to change schools in the abstract but are ambivalent when it comes to schools they actually know.

Polls show that parents believe their children's schools have higher standards and are of significantly better quality than the nation's schools in general. This phenomenon—the idea that "I'm OK, but you're not"—

also shows up in surveys on health care (my doctor is great, but the nation's health care stinks), Congress (my representative is terrific, but Congress is terrible), and the status of the American family (mine is in fine shape, but families in general are going to hell in a hand basket).

Such complacency undermines meaningful school reform. Raising the level of achievement is hard work. Unless children can actually learn more math, science, literature, and history without breaking a sweat, then the prospects for reforms that ask children and parents for more—more time, more homework, more effort—are not very good. We don't hear much about what today's educational reforms may require of families. Indeed, when it comes to the subject of parents, the rhetoric seldom gets beyond calls for more "parent involvement" or for "empowering" parents. Reforms that grant parents control over where their children go to school, a favorite of the Right, or that offer parents a stake in governing local school affairs, a favorite of the Left, may prove to be valuable public policies for other reasons, but they have not yet convinced skeptics that they will significantly increase student achievement.

In Chicago, an experiment that involved creating parent-dominated school "site councils" to oversee individual schools produced a few renaissance stories, but also tales of schools engulfed in petty squabbling. As vouchers and charter schools become more widespread, will parents actually take advantage of the opportunities to improve the education of their children? Buried in the national comparisons of private and public schools is an interesting anomaly. Despite well-publicized research showing that private schools outperform public schools on achievement tests, more students transfer from private to public school than vice versa at the beginning of high school, precisely the time when one's academic accomplishments really start to matter in terms of college and employment. Where other kids in the neighborhood are going to school and the desire to keep extracurricular activities close to home appear to weigh heavily in parents' choices.

Another reason to doubt that empowered parents will wholeheartedly insist on higher achievement can be found in the history of American schooling. Schools have always attended to the convenience of parents, and, as a result, cultivating the mind has simply occupied one place among many on a long list of purposes for the school. At the beginning of the 19th century, education came within the province of the family. Children learned reading at home, along with basic arithmetic and minimal geography, science, and history. Farming dictated the tempo of family life.

Older students only attended school during the winter months, when their labor wasn't needed in the fields. At other times, even toddlers were sent to school, crowding classrooms with students from 3 to 20 years of age.

Later in the century, as fathers and mothers abandoned the farm for the factory and intermittently relocated in search of work, the modern public school began to evolve. One of its functions was custodial, providing a place for children to spend the day while busy parents earned a living. The magnitude of the change is staggering. As late as 1870, American students attended school only an average of 78 of 132 scheduled days; today's students spend more than 160 days in the classroom, and the modern school calendar runs to 180 days. More than 90 percent of school-age children now attend high school. At the beginning of the century, less than 10 percent did.

But the school's power is limited. Its monopoly over children's daylight hours never led to the recognition of intellectual activities as the most important pursuits of adolescents, either outside or inside school. Why do parents allow two-thirds of today's teenagers to work? After-school jobs are considered good for young people, teaching them a sense of responsibility and the value of a dollar. Most Americans think it's fine if teenagers spend 20 hours a week flipping hamburgers instead of studying calculus or the history of ancient Rome.

The development of young minds also finds competition in the school curriculum itself. For example, the federal government has funded vocational education since 1917. Americans have always expected schools to teach students the difference between right and wrong and the fundamental elements of citizenship. In the last three decades, schools have also taken on therapeutic tasks, spending untold time and resources on sex education, psychological counseling, drug and alcohol programs, diversity training, guidance on topics such as teen parenting, sexual harassment, and a host of other initiatives that have little to do with sharpening the intellect.

Some analysts maintain that parents don't support such diversions from academic learning, that these programs are nothing more than the faddish whims of professional educators. If so, parents have been awfully quiet about it. A more reasonable explanation is that, with parents busily working at two or more jobs, with many of these topics awkward for parents to discuss, and with parental authority showing its own signs of weakening throughout society, parents now look to schools to provide instruction that they once delivered themselves.

Schools are acting more like parents, and implementing real academic standards will probably force parents to act more like schools. They will need to stay informed about tests scores and closely monitor their children's progress. Parents of students who fall short of standards must be prepared for drastic changes in family life. Summers will be for summer school, afternoons and weekends for tutoring. This will cost money and impinge upon family time. Struggling high school students will be forced to spend less time on sports, to forgo part-time jobs, and to keep socializing to a minimum.

No one knows how parents will react to such changes. Higher standards are overwhelmingly supported in public opinion polls, but what will happen when they begin to pinch? In 1997, hundreds of parents in an affluent suburb of Detroit refused to let their children take a high school proficiency test, arguing that the nine hour exam was too long and that it would unfairly label children who performed poorly. In Portland, Oregon, the school district invited the parents of 3,500 youngsters who had failed statewide proficiency exams to send the children to a summer school session set up at great expense and amid much hoopla; only 1,359 kids were enrolled. Every state has its share of stories. The elimination of social promotion presents the biggest test. Will the parents of children who are compelled to repeat, say, third or fourth grade, continue to support high standards? Or will they dedicate themselves to the defeat and removal of standards? In districts that see huge numbers of students facing mandatory summer school or failing to win promotion to the next grade, will parents push to water down tests and lower passing scores?

Some years ago, I came face to face with some of these implications when I taught sixth grade in a special program for exceptionally gifted, high-achieving youngsters, students approximately two years above grade level in all subjects. The curriculum was accelerated to the eighth- and ninth-grade levels, and I taught all academic subjects. Students applied for admission to the program, and my fellow teachers and I stressed that it wasn't for everyone. Parents seeking an education emphasizing creativity or the arts were advised to look elsewhere. An extremely bright student who hated doing homework would also have had a difficult time.

Getting to know the parents of my students was one of the most satisfying aspects of my job. They were actively involved in the school and indispensable in organizing field trips, raising money for computers, putting on plays, and doing anything else that enhanced their children's education. If ever a group supported lofty standards, this was it. But dealing with parents was not all sweetness and light. Grading policies drew the most complaints. One upset parent threatened a lawsuit because I gave a zero to a student who cheated on a test. In the midst of a three hour, late-night phone call, a mother repeatedly told me that I would suffer eternal damnation because her son had received grades disqualifying him for admission to an honors program.

Complaints were also voiced because I didn't accept late homework—"We had friends over last night and Johnny simply didn't have time to do his history," one father explained in a note—or because I wouldn't excuse absences for family ski trips or a student's "R&R day" of TV soap operas and game shows. And these complaints came despite the fact that enrollment in the program was by choice, the school's reputation for academic rigor well known, and the policies on these issues crystal clear.

Such conflicts go with the territory. Anyone who teaches—and sticks to the principles making the career a serious undertaking in the first place—will experience occasional problems with parents. The usual conflicts stem from the different yet overlapping roles that parents and teachers play in a child's life. Both are concerned with the same individual's welfare, but their roles are not interchangeable. Parents are infinitely more important to a child's upbringing, but the teacher is usually the most significant non-family adult presence in the child's life and, ideally, is more objective about the child's interactions with the larger world. Teachers pursue goals established by society rather than the family. They must be warm and understanding, but they must also make decisions balancing the interests of 30 or more people who have work to accomplish every day in the same small space.

The differentiation of parent and teacher roles, which strengthened schools and families in the 19th century, may be at the bottom of many parents' unrealistic perceptions of their children's school experiences. Just as reformers are probably right that the demand for high educational standards must come from outside the schools, the imposition of academic burdens on children probably must come from outside families.

There is some evidence that parents intuitively understand this. In a recent study by the Public Agenda Foundation that examined how parents view their role in education, parents said that the most significant contribution they can make is to send children to school who are respectful, hard working, and well behaved. They do not want a bigger say in how schools are run. Nor do they want to decide curricular content or methods of instruction. They trust educators who have earned their trust, and they want schools to do their job as schools so that parents can do their job as parents.

These seem like reasonable sentiments. But in the same study, parents also admit that they absolutely hate fighting kids to get them to do their homework. They gauge how things are going at school primarily by how happy their children seem and nearly 90 percent believe that as long as children try hard, they should never feel bad about themselves because of poor grades. These attitudes are potentially in conflict with more rigorous learning standards. If social promotion ends, many children will be held back in a grade despite their having tried hard. And these children will be unhappy. Other children will not get the acceptable grades they once did. A lot of people are going to be very unhappy.

Higher standards and the end of social promotion now enjoy tremendous popular support. But the true test will come when words become deeds. Until now, raising expectations in education has been portrayed as cost-free. It isn't. Schools and students and parents will bear the costs. If parents are not willing to do so, few of the ambitious changes American reformers are now so eagerly pursuing will make much difference.

TEACHERS

Who Teaches the Teachers?

Lynne V. Cheney

This selection first appeared in *The Weekly Standard* on 9 August 1999; copyright News America Incorporated. Lynne V. Cheney is a distinguished senior fellow at the American Enterprise Institute.

With its pictures of earnest schoolchildren busily learning, Regie Routman's book doesn't look dangerous. But like many textbooks used in colleges of education, *Invitations: Changing as Teachers and Learners K–12* (Heinemann, 1994) may be keeping thousands of children from mastering basic academic skills. Future teachers learn from Routman, for example, that entirely too much attention has been paid to phonics, with the result that "some children have difficulty learning to read." In fact, research has repeatedly shown almost the opposite: Attending to phonics is important to *preventing* reading difficulties.

Invitations, one of the most widely used textbooks in ed schools (it's at Vanderbilt, Michigan State, and the University of Arizona, to name a few), illustrates why efforts to improve American education are so often frustrated. Even when evidence about effective teaching abounds, education colleges tend to ignore it, and future teachers don't learn about it. This is true even in states committed to methods shown by research to be effective. Since 1997, for example, Massachusetts has had reading standards that call for the formal teaching of letter-sound relationships. Yet at Lesley College, which prepares more teachers than any other institution in the commonwealth, education students are still learning from *Invitations* that phonics instruction is useless or even a "handicap." Since 1996, California has had a law requiring that future teachers be instructed in "systematic, explicit phonics." Yet education professors at many California institutions (including California State University campuses) are still assigning Routman.

Short on evidence, Routman's book is long on anecdotes—which ed schools have lately been claiming constitute a special qualitative "research," far more useful to teachers than the old-fashioned quantitative kind. Routman presents the case of Maria, a teacher so frustrated that "she often ended the day in tears." The problem is that Maria, who herself had a traditional education, feels obliged to pass on to her students information about such matters as grammar and punctuation. "But," Routman reports, "no matter how hard she tried, things didn't seem to come together for her." Fortunately, Maria attends a summer workshop that shows her the error of her ways and the wisdom of "whole language," an approach based on the idea that children will naturally evolve into readers (and spellers and punctuators) if only adults will get out of the way. With this enlightenment, Maria becomes a teacher who "can offer children choices in decision making about their own learning." Her classroom, freed from focusing on dull matters like capitalization, is a "joyful, collaborative community."

Lest any reader miss the message, Routman also reports on Loretta, a second-grade teacher who has a similar conversion. Her eyes are opened to what she really wants to do (which includes "abandoning spelling workbooks and phonics pages") by a week-long conference called "Creating the Whole Language Classroom." As a result of her enlightenment, Loretta now presides over "a child-centered room in which children are productively in charge of their own learning." Once struggling and frustrated, she is now "a relaxed teacher clearly enjoying herself."

For all the psychic rewards it brings, the conversion that Routman is urging on teachers can apparently be wrenching. Routman quotes a kindergarten teacher who decided to let her students discover phonics for themselves. "I felt real guilty for a long time," she says. A first-grade teacher reports feeling pressured by second-grade teachers who expect kids to arrive in their classrooms knowing phonics: "Also, I feel guilty for not giving spelling tests." Routman, an elementary school teacher in Ohio, notes that she herself has had difficulties abandoning the explicit teaching of phonics. "It has taken me well over ten years to feel completely comfortable with this approach."

A sensible reaction to all this guilt would be to explore whether there's some justification for it. Are whole-language teachers perhaps aware, at least at a subliminal level, of the extensive research showing that a knowledge of spelling-sound correspondences and common spelling conventions is important to becoming a proficient reader? Indeed, this finding has been so well publicized, most recently in a report from the National Research Council entitled *Preventing Reading Difficulties in Young Children,* that it would be hard for them to miss. The American Federation of Teachers has highlighted the research supporting explicit, systematic phonics instruction. The National Education Association recently helped sponsor a project that looked for programs of proven effectiveness and found two for elementary schools—Direct Instruction and Success for All—both strongly based in phonics.

But rather than exploring the sources of whole-language teachers' anxiety, Routman recommends support groups to diminish it. In these groups, like-minded souls offer encouragement to one another and discuss such matters as how to handle parental discontent. One of the support groups she attends, Routman reports, also lobbies against standardized tests in early grades, a campaign that if successful will allow teachers to decide for themselves whether their methods are working. Such a process would be more "meaningful," Routman claims, though it would, of course, leave parents without a clue about how their children are doing in comparison with others.

Routman maintains that her purpose in writing is to help other teachers develop their personal philosophies of teaching. But her book, although it is 758 pages long, doesn't contain information that teachers need to develop a truly informed view. Routman repeatedly mentions whole-language gurus like Kenneth Goodman (who says that phonics-based reading instruction represents a "flat-earth view of the world") and Frank Smith (who says that the ability to read and write is overvalued: "Literacy doesn't make anyone a better person"), but she entirely neglects both Jeanne Chall and Marilyn Adams, authors of landmark studies synthesizing decades of research and making it perfectly clear that reading programs should include systematic and explicit phonics instruction.

Routman is hardly alone in advocating independence for teachers while effectively restricting their choices. *Creating Classrooms for Authors and Inquirers* by Kathy G. Short and Jerome C. Harste with Carolyn Burke (Heinemann, 1996) begins by approvingly describing teachers who "develop their own personal theories of reading and writing" but by page nine has made clear that the only valid theories anyone could possibly develop are whole-language ones.

Similarly, although Short and Harste repeatedly state that children's agendas should drive the classroom, they are also adamant that students sometimes profess goals—such as wanting to spell correctly—of which teachers must be wary. When one of their students, third-grader Maria, writes that she wants to "learn how to spell," she is carefully observed until the authors are sure she does not suffer from "an overconcern with spelling." Even then she gets not a spelling book, but "lessons on strategies," such as "discussing possible spellings with peers." Short and Harste refer future teachers who want more information to J. Richard Gentry's *Spel . . . Is a Four-Letter Word* (Heinemann, 1987), a book that views "good spelling" as "merely a convenience." Writes Gentry, "There are some people like secretaries, who need to be accurate, but usually even they can use a word processor with a good spelling check." Confessing to being a bad speller himself, Gentry helpfully advises students to "make an honest attempt to spell werds wright."

The Short and Harste book dominates elementary education instruction at Indiana University's School of Education, the third largest ed school in the country and the place where Harste teaches. The fact that Harste is president-elect of the National Council of Teachers of English lends added significance to *Creating Classrooms*. The ideas in it are those that the council, an organization some 90,000 strong, promotes through its publications, conferences, and conventions. Future teachers who learn from Creating Classrooms that it is a mistake for the curriculum to be "mandated by 'experts' outside the classroom" are getting something close to the official doctrine of their profession—as well as a rationale for ignoring standards set by states to establish what students should know and be able to do at various stages in their education.

The very idea that there are certain facts that kids should know is, according to *Creating Classrooms*, symptomatic of an antiquated way of thinking. In the updated, postmodern world, people (or at least professors) know that there are no such things as facts. There are only "perspectives," and the proper job of a teacher is to help students develop them. One way to do this, Short and Harste advise, is to ask students "to find a 'fact' that is not true from the perspective of another knowledge system." This is, of course, postmodern nonsense. A fact is not a fact if it is not true. It is an error, no matter one's perspective.

Short and Harste sow further confusion when they write about research. They inform their readers:

> Recently, there has been a new shift. Instead of seeing research as objective and language as value free, researchers are now realizing how subjective the whole process is. . . . The only thing research can do is help a learner or a community of learners interrogate their values.

The fact that total objectivity is impossible does not mean that we are condemned to explaining everything subjectively. Striving for objectivity, as scientists around the world can testify, yields important results. While research in the social sciences is often less exact than research in the hard sciences, it still produces important information, particularly when data converge, as they do in the case of reading.

But how are future teachers to know any of this? They leave Short and Harste and head for elementary classrooms uninformed about the findings of several decades of scientific research on reading instruction and, in any case, encouraged to regard such research as meaningless.

Lest future teachers ever be tempted to think reliable, replicable research has significance, Western Michigan University professor Constance Weaver in *Reading Process and Practice* (Heinemann, 1994) paints a picture of the distasteful types they would be aligning themselves with: members of the Far Right, driven not by the wish to teach children to read, but by "the desire to promote a religious agenda and/or to maintain the socioeconomic status quo." According to Weaver, who directed the Commission on Reading for the National Council of Teachers of English in the late 1980s, right-wing extremists believe that kids who study phonics will get "the words 'right'" and thus read what the Bible actually says rather than approximate its meaning. Moreover, she writes, "Teaching intensive phonics . . . is also a way of keeping children's attention on doing what they're told and keeping them from reading or thinking for themselves."

Nor, in Weaver's view, is it just their own children that phonics-obsessed right-wingers want to oppress. "The political Far Right's agenda is well-served," she writes, "by promoting docility and obedience—on the part of the lower classes." Ultraconservatives advocate phonics teaching because it is authoritarian, she says, and serves to socialize "nonmainstream students, especially those in so-called lower ability groups or tracks . . . into subordinate roles."

Weaver neglects to mention that the phonics cause has advocates who are not Republicans, much less conservatives. One of the standard-bearers in California, for example, is Marion Joseph, a longtime Democrat, who took up the battle against whole language when one of her grandchildren was expected to figure out reading for himself. In the California legislature, Democrats as well as Republicans have enthusiastically backed pro-phonics bills.

But facts haven't stood in the way of ed school professors claiming a political plot of the very worst kind is afoot. A recent president of the National Council of Teachers of English, infuriated with policymakers who insist that government ought to fund only "reliable, scientific" educational research, linked his opponents not only to the red-baiters of the fifties but to advocates of "slavery, racism, genocide, the incarceration of dissidents in mental hospitals, and a host of other injustices."

California State University, which prepares more than half that state's teachers, is one of the institutions at which Weaver's *Reading Process and Practice* is used. Last year, the academic senate there condemned the state's requirement that ed schools teach phonics as a threat to academic freedom. Apparently convinced that he and his colleagues have a right to fill future teachers with anti-scientific claptrap, one Cal State professor told the *Los Angeles Times*, "What we have in the state right now is McCarthyism."

But, as the textbooks used in many ed schools clearly show, what we really have all across the county is a situation inimical to making classrooms function more effectively. Colleges of education, long criticized for teaching trivia, are now doing something much worse: sabotaging the best efforts of reformers to get schools to use methods that work.

Why Johnny's Teacher Can't Teach

Heather Mac Donald

This selection first appeared in *City Journal*'s Spring 1998 edition. Heather Mac Donald is a senior fellow at the Manhattan Institute and a contributing editor of the Institute's *City Journal* (www.city-journal.org).

Americans' nearly last-place finish in the Third International Mathematics and Sciences Study of student achievement caused widespread consternation this February, except in the one place it should have mattered most: the nation's teacher education schools. Those schools have far more important things to do than worrying about test scores— things like stamping out racism in aspiring teachers. "Let's be honest," darkly commanded Professor Valerie Henning-Piedmont to a lecture hall of education students at Columbia University's Teachers College last February. "What labels do you place on young people based on your biases?" It would be difficult to imagine a less likely group of bigots than these idealistic young people, happily toting around their Handbooks of Multicultural Education and their exposés of sexism in the classroom. But Teachers College knows better. It knows that most of its students, by virtue of being white, are complicitous in an unjust power structure.

The crusade against racism is just the latest irrelevancy to seize the nation's teacher education schools. For over 80 years, teacher education in America has been in the grip of an immutable dogma, responsible for endless educational nonsense. That dogma may be summed up in the phrase: Anything But Knowledge. Schools are about many things, teacher educators say (depending on the decade)—self-actualization, following one's joy, social adjustment, or multicultural sensitivity—but the one thing they are not about is knowledge. Oh sure, educators will occasionally allow the word to pass their lips, but it is always in a compromised position, as in "constructing one's own knowledge," or "contextualized knowledge." Plain old knowledge, the kind passed down in books, the kind for which Faust sold his soul, that is out.

The education profession currently stands ready to tighten its already vise-like grip on teacher credentialing, persuading both the federal government and the states to "professionalize" teaching further. In New

York, as elsewhere, that means closing off any routes to the classroom that do not pass through an education school. But before caving in to the educrats' pressure, we had better take a hard look at what education schools actually teach.

The course in "Curriculum and Teaching in Elementary Education" that Professor Anne Nelson (a pseudonym) teaches at the City College of New York is a good place to start. Dressed in a tailored brown suit with close-cropped hair, Nelson is a charismatic teacher, with a commanding repertoire of voices and personae. And yet, for all her obvious experience and common sense, her course is a remarkable exercise in vacuousness.

As with most education classes, the title of Professor Nelson's course doesn't give a clear sense of what it is about. Unfortunately, Professor Nelson doesn't, either. The semester began, she said in a pre-class interview, by "building a community, rich of talk, in which students look at what they themselves are doing by in-class writing." On this, the third meeting of the semester, Professor Nelson said that she would be "getting the students to develop the subtext of what they're doing." I would soon discover why Professor Nelson was so vague.

"Developing the subtext" turns out to involve a chain reaction of solipsistic moments. After taking attendance and—most admirably— quickly checking the students' weekly handwriting practice, Professor Nelson begins the main work of the day: generating feather-light "texts," both written and oral, for immediate group analysis. She asks the students to write for seven minutes on each of three questions: "What excites me about teaching?" "What concerns me about teaching?" and then, the moment that brands this class as hopelessly steeped in the Anything But Knowledge credo: "What was it like to do this writing?"

This last question triggers a quickening volley of self-reflexive turns. After the students read aloud their predictable reflections on teaching, Professor Nelson asks: "What are you hearing?" A young man states the obvious: "Everyone seems to be reflecting on what their anxieties are." This is too straightforward an answer. Professor Nelson translates into ed-speak: "So writing gave you permission to think on paper about what's there." Ed-speak dresses up the most mundane processes in dramatic terminology—one doesn't just write, one is "given permission to think on the paper"; one doesn't converse, one "negotiates meaning." Then, like a champion tennis player finishing off a set, Nelson reaches for the ultimate level of self-reflexivity and drives it home: "What was it like to listen to each other's responses?"

The self-reflection isn't over yet, however. The class next moves into small groups—along with in-class writing, the most pervasive gimmick in progressive classrooms today—to discuss a set of student-teaching guidelines. After ten minutes, Nelson interrupts the by-now lively and largely off-topic conversations, and asks: "Let's talk about how you felt in these small groups." The students are picking up ed-speak. "It shifted the comfort zone," reveals one. "It was just acceptance; I felt the vibe going through the group." Another adds: "I felt really comfortable; I had trust there." Nelson senses a "teachable moment." "Let's talk about that," she interjects. "We are building trust in this class; we are learning how to work with each other."

Now, let us note what this class was not: It was not about how to keep the attention of eight-year-olds or plan a lesson or make the Pilgrims real to first-graders. It did not, in other words, contain any material (with the exception of the student-teacher guidelines) from the outside world. Instead, it continuously spun its own subject matter out of itself. Like a relationship that consists of obsessively analyzing the relationship, the only content of the course was the course itself.

How did such navel gazing come to be central to teacher education? It is the almost inevitable consequence of the Anything But Knowledge doctrine, born in a burst of quintessentially American anti-intellectual fervor in the wake of World War I. Educators within the federal government and at Columbia's Teachers College issued a clarion call to schools: Cast off the traditional academic curriculum and start preparing young people for the demands of modern life. America is a forward-looking country, they boasted; what need have we for such impractical disciplines as Greek, Latin, and higher math? Instead, let the students then flooding the schools take such useful courses as family membership, hygiene, and the worthy use of leisure time. "Life adjustment," not wisdom or learning, was to be the goal of education.

The early decades of this century forged the central educational fallacy of our time: that one can think without having anything to think about. Knowledge is changing too fast to be transmitted usefully to students, argued William Heard Kilpatrick of Teachers College, the most influential American educator of the century; instead of teaching children dead facts and figures, schools should teach them "critical thinking," he wrote in 1925. What matters is not what you know, but whether you know how to look it up, so that you can be a "lifelong learner."

Two final doctrines rounded out the indelible legacy of progressivism. First, Harold Rugg's *The Child-Centered School* (1928) shifted the locus of power in the classroom from the teacher to the student. In a child-centered class, the child determines what he wants to learn. Forcing children into an existing curriculum inhibits their self-actualization, Rugg argued, just as forcing them into neat rows of chairs and desks inhibits their creativity. The teacher becomes an enabler, an advisor; not, heaven forbid, the transmitter of a preexisting body of ideas, texts, or, worst of all, facts. In today's jargon, the child should "construct" his own knowledge rather than passively receive it. By the late 1920s, students were moving their chairs around to form groups of "active learners" pursuing their own individual interests, and, instead of a curriculum, the student-centered classroom followed just one principle: "activity leading to further activity without badness," in Kilpatrick's words. Today's educators still present these seven-decade-old practices as cutting-edge.

As E.D. Hirsch, Jr., observes, the child-centered doctrine grew out of the romantic idealization of children. If the child was, in Wordsworth's words, a "Mighty Prophet! Seer Blest!" then who needs teachers? But the Mighty Prophet emerged from student-centered schools ever more ignorant and incurious as the schools became more vacuous. By the 1940s and 1950s, schools were offering classes in how to put on nail polish and how to act on a date. The notion that learning should push students out of their narrow world had been lost.

The final cornerstone of progressive theory was the disdain for report cards and objective tests of knowledge. These inhibit authentic learning, Kilpatrick argued; and he carried the day, to the eternal joy of students everywhere.

The foregoing doctrines are complete bunk, but bunk that has survived virtually unchanged to the present. The notion that one can teach "metacognitive" thinking in the abstract is senseless. Students need to learn something to learn how to learn at all. The claim that prior knowledge is superfluous because one can always look it up, preferably on the Internet, is equally senseless. Effective research depends on preexisting knowledge. Moreover, if you don't know in what century the atomic bomb was dropped without rushing to an encyclopedia, you cannot fully participate in society. Lastly, Kilpatrick's influential assertion that knowledge was changing too fast to be taught presupposes a blinkered definition of knowledge that excludes the great works and enterprises of the past.

The rejection of testing rests on premises as flawed as the push for "critical thinking skills." Progressives argue that if tests exist, then teachers will "teach to the test"—a bad thing, in their view. But why would "teaching to a test" that asked for, say, the causes of the Civil War be bad for students? Additionally, progressives complain that testing provokes rote memorization—again, a bad thing. One of the most tragically influential education professors today, Columbia's Linda Darling-Hammond, director of the National Commission on Teaching and America's Future, an advocacy group for increased teacher "professionalization," gives a telling example of what she considers a criminally bad test in her hackneyed 1997 brief for progressive education, *The Right to Learn*. She points disdainfully to the following question from the 1995 New York State Regents Exam in biology (required for high school graduation) as "a rote recall of isolated facts and vocabulary terms": "The tissue which conducts organic food through a vascular plant is composed of: (1) Cambium cells; (2) Xylem cells; (3) Phloem cells; (4) Epidermal cells."

Only a know-nothing could be offended by so innocent a question. It never occurs to Darling-Hammond that there may be a joy in mastering the parts of a plant or the organelles of a cell, and that such memorization constitutes learning. Moreover, when, in the progressives' view, will a student ever be held accountable for such knowledge? Does Darling-Hammond believe that a student can pursue a career in, say, molecular biology or in medicine without it? And how else will that learning be demonstrated, if not in a test? But of course such testing will produce unequal results, and that is the real target of Darling-Hammond's animus.

Once you dismiss real knowledge as the goal of education, you have to find something else to do. That's why the Anything But Knowledge doctrine leads directly to Professor Nelson's odd course. In thousands of education schools across the country, teachers are generating little moments of meaning, which they then subject to instant replay. Educators call this "constructing knowledge," a fatuous label for something that is neither construction nor knowledge but mere game playing. Teacher educators, though, possess a primitive relationship to words. They believe that if they just label something "critical thinking" or "community-building," these activities will magically occur.

For all the ed school talk of freedom from the past, teacher education in this century has been more unchanging than Miss Havisham. Like aging vestal virgins, today's schools lovingly guard the ancient flame of progressivism. Since the 1920s they have not had a single new idea; they have merely gussied up old concepts in new rhetoric, most recently in the jargon of minority empowerment. To enter an education classroom, therefore, is to witness a timeless ritual, embedded in an authority structure of unions and state education departments as rigid as the Vatican.

It is a didactic ritual as well. The education professor's credo is: As I do unto you, so shall you do unto your students. The education professor "models" how she wants her students to teach by her own classroom methods. Such a practice is based on a glaring fallacy—that methods that work passably well with committed 22-year-olds, paying $1,800 a course for your wisdom, will translate seamlessly to a class of seven- or twelve-year-olds.

The Anything But Knowledge credo leaves education professors and their acolytes free to concentrate on far more pressing matters than how to teach the facts of history or the rules of sentence construction. "Community-building" is one of their most urgent concerns. Teacher educators conceive of their classes as sites of profound political engagement, out of which the new egalitarian order will emerge. A case in point is Columbia's required class, "Teaching English in Diverse Social and Cultural Contexts," taught by Professor Barbara Tenney (a pseudonym). "I want to work at a very conscious level with you to build community in this class," Tenney tells her attentive students on the first day of the semester this spring. "You can do it consciously, and you ought to do it in your own classes." Community-building starts by making nameplates for our desks. Then we all find a partner to interview about each other's "identity." Over the course of the semester, each student will conduct two more "identity" interviews with different partners. After the interview, the inevitable self-reflexive moment arrives, when Tenney asks: "How did it work?" This is a sign that we are on our way to "constructing knowledge."

A hallmark of community-building is its overheated rhetoric. The education professor acts as if she were facing a pack of snarling Serbs and Croats, rather than a bunch of well-mannered young ladies (the vast majority of education students), hoping for a good grade. So the community-building assignments attack nonexistent problems of conflict. Tenney, sporting a black leather miniskirt and a cascade of blond curls, hands out a sheet of paper and asks us to respond to the questions: "What climate would allow you to do your best work? How should a class act to encourage open and honest and critical dialogue?" We write for a while, then read our response to our interview partner.

Now is this question really necessary, especially for a group of college graduates? Good classroom etiquette is hardly a mystery. In the evil traditional classroom, and probably also at Teachers College, if a student calls another a fathead, thus discouraging "open and honest and critical dialogue," the teacher would simply reprimand him, and everyone would understand perfectly well what just happened and why. Consensus already exists on civil behavior. But the education classroom, lacking a pressing agenda in concrete knowledge, has to "problematize" the most automatic social routines.

Of course, no amount of writing about the conditions for "open dialogue" can change the fact that discussion is not open on many issues at Teachers College and other progressive bastions. "If you don't demonstrate the correct point of view," says a student, "people are hostile. There's a herd mentality here." A former student of Tenney's describes the difficulties of dissent from the party line on racism: "There's nothing to be gained from challenging it. If you deny that the system inherently privileges whites, you're 'not taking responsibility for your position in racism.'" Doubtless, it would never occur to Professor Tenney that the problem this student describes impedes community-building.

All this artificial "community-building," however gratifying to the professors, has nothing to do with learning. Learning is ultimately a solitary activity: We have only one brain, and at some point we must exercise it in private. One could learn an immense amount about Schubert's lieder or calculus without ever knowing the name of one's seatmate. Such a view is heresy to the education establishment, determined, as Rita Kramer has noted, to eradicate any opportunity for individual accomplishment, with its sinister risk of superior achievement. For the educrats, the group is the irreducible unit of learning. Fueling this principle is the gap in achievement between whites and Asians, on the one hand, and other minorities on the other. Unwilling to adopt the discipline and teaching practices that would help reduce that gap, the education establishment tries to conceal it under group projects.

And so the ultimate community-building mechanism is the ubiquitous "collaborative group." No activity is too solitary to escape assignment to a group: writing, reading, researching, thinking—all are better done with many partners, according to educational dogma. If you see an ed school class sitting up in straight rows, call a doctor, because it means the professor has had a heart attack and couldn't arrange the class into groups.

For all their "progressive" sympathies, not all ed students like this regime. "I'm a socialist at heart," says one of Tenney's students, establishing her bona fides, "but some tasks, like writing, are not collaborative. It's hard when someone loses their voice." Another Columbia student in the Education Administration program complains that "teachers here let the group projects run wild." At $1,800 a course, it's frustrating "when the last four sessions of a class are group projects that are all garbage." Lastly, small group discussions have a habit of careening off the assigned topic. The professors rarely intervene, however, says a Teachers College student, "because they don't want to interfere with the interaction."

The elevation of the group entails the demotion of teachers—yet another plank in the Anything But Knowledge platform. To accord teachers any superior role in the classroom would be to acknowledge an elite hierarchy of knowledge, possessed by some but not all, at least without effort. Teachers traditionally represent elitism, learning, authority—everything that progressivism scorns—and so they must be relegated to the role of mere facilitators for the all-important group.

Linda Darling-Hammond's description of collaborative learning perfectly captures how inextricable the political is from the educational in progressive theory. "Whereas traditional classrooms tend to be still but for the sound of teacher talking, learning-centered classrooms feature student talk and collective action." (The "learning-centered classroom" is Darling-Hammond's jargon for a student-centered classroom.) "Collective action"—how exciting! But though lots of undirected "student talk" hardly seems conducive to learning, progressives abhor quiet. David Schaafsma, one of Columbia's more politicized teachers, told his English Methods class of visiting a quiet third-grade class in the Bronx, explaining: "It terrifies me when kids are really really still. They've got to move." It never occurs to these apostles of the Free Self that for many inner-city children, reaching a state of calm attention is a wonderful achievement.

Collaborative learning leads naturally to another tic of the progressive classroom: "brainstorming." Rather than lecture to a class, the teacher asks the class its opinion about something and lists the responses on the blackboard. Nothing much happens after that; brainstorming, like various forms of community-building, appears to be an end in itself. Hunter College professor Faith DiCaprio (a pseudonym) recently used two levels of brainstorming—whole group and small group—with her "Language and Literacy in Early Childhood" class. The class had just read *Wally's Stories* by Vivian Paley, essentially a transcript of free-wheeling discussions among kindergartners in a progressive classroom. First, DiCaprio asked her students what they liked about the book. As students called out their responses—"I liked how she didn't correct the students," "She reminded us why a child-centered room is so necessary: she didn't intrude on their conversation"—DiCaprio writes their responses in abbreviated ed-speak on big posted sheets of paper: "Tolerance: they negotiated meaning" and "Created safe arena."

After DiCaprio fills up the posted pages, nothing happens. Nothing needs to happen, for the lists of responses are visible proof of how much the class already knows. We have just "constructed knowledge." On to the next brainstorming exercise. This time, it's a twofer—brainstorming plus collaborative learning. DiCaprio breaks the class into small groups. Their assignment: List and categorize the topics discussed by the kindergartners in *Wally's Stories*. So the students dutifully make lists of fairies, food, plants, witches, and other meaty matters. One outspoken girl enthuses to her group: "And the kids were smart, they were like, 'The turnips push up with the roots,' and I was like, 'How'd they know that?'" After the groups complete their lists, they read them to the rest of the class. Learning tally? Almost zero.

The consequences of the Anything But Knowledge credo for intellectual standards have been dire. Education professors are remarkably casual when it comes to determining whether their students actually know anything, rarely asking them, for example, what can you tell us about the American Revolution? The ed schools incorrectly presume that the students will have learned everything they need to know in their other or previous college courses, and that the teacher certification exams will screen out people who didn't.

Even if college education were reliably rigorous and comprehensive, education majors aren't the students most likely to profit from it. Nationally, undergraduate education majors have lower SAT and ACT scores than students in any other program of study. Only 16 percent of education majors scored in the top quartile of 1992–93 graduates, compared with 33 percent of humanities majors. Education majors were overrepresented in the bottom quartile, at 30 percent. In New York City, many education majors have an uncertain command of

English—I saw one education student at City College repeatedly write "choce" for "choice"—and appear altogether ill at ease in a classroom. To presume anything about this population without a rigorous content exit exam is unwarranted.

The laissez-faire attitude toward student knowledge rests on "principled" grounds, as well as on see-no-evil inertia. Many education professors embrace the facile poststructuralist view that knowledge is always political. "An education program can't have content [knowledge] specifics," explains Migdalia Romero, chair of Hunter College's Department of Curriculum and Teaching, "because then you have a point of view. Once you define exactly what finite knowledge is, it becomes a perspective." The notion that a culture could possess a prepolitical common store of texts and ideas is anathema to the modern academic.

The most powerful dodge regurgitates William Heard Kilpatrick's classic "critical thinking" scam. Asked whether a future teacher should know the date of the 1812 war, Professor Romero replied: "Teaching and learning is not about dates, facts, and figures, but about developing critical thinking." When pressed if there were not some core facts that a teacher or student should know, she valiantly held her ground. "There are two ways of looking at teaching and learning," she replied. "Either you are imparting knowledge, giving an absolute knowledge base, or teaching and learning is about dialogue, a dialogue that helps to internalize and to raise questions." Though she offered the disclaimer "of course you need both," Romero added that teachers don't have to know everything, because they can always look things up.

Romero's tolerance of potential teacher ignorance perfectly reflects New York State's official policy on learning, a sellout to progressivism in its preference for "concepts" and "critical thinking" over measurable knowledge. The Regents' much-vaunted 1996 "student learning standards" are vacuous evasions of facts and knowledge, containing not a single book or document or historical fact that students should know. Literature? The word isn't mentioned. Instead, proclaim the standards in classic educationese, "students will listen, speak, read, and write for literary response and expression"—literally a meaningless statement, matched in its meaninglessness only by the next "English Language Arts" standard: "Students will listen, speak, read, and write for social interaction." Teachers need to get hold of the third level of documentation accompanying the standards to find any specific historical figures or events or books, but there, excessive detail and gaseous generalization will overwhelm them.

But what New York State expects of its students is a model of rigor compared to what it formally expects of its teachers. The State Teacher Certification Exams are a complete abdication of the state's responsibility for ensuring an educated teaching force. If any teachers in the state know anything about American history, English literature, or chemistry, it is a complete accident, for the state's highest education authorities have not the slightest interest in finding out. The Liberal Arts and Sciences Test, the ticket to a teacher's first five years in a classroom, contains absolutely no substance; at most, it tests reading skills. The test preparation booklet is a classic of educationese. The exam section on "Historical and Social Scientific Awareness" (note: not "knowledge"), for example, tests teachers' "understanding [of] the interrelatedness of historical, geographic, cultural, economic, political and social issues and factors."

Now, by loading on the different types of "issues and factors" that prospective teachers are supposed to understand, the exam ensures that they need know nothing in particular. The only thing that test takers do have to know is the multicultural dogma that there is no history, only "multiple perspectives" on history. The certification exam asks prospective teachers to "analyze multiple perspectives within U.S. society regarding major historical and contemporary issues"—not history, but "historical issues," and not even "historical issues," but "multiple perspectives" on "historical issues." Such a demand is ripe for spouting off, say, on the "Native American perspective" on the Western expansion, without having the slightest idea what fueled that expansion, when and where it occurred, who peopled it, and what its consequences were. In fairness, the Content Specialty Tests teachers must take for permanent certification are much more substantive, especially in science and math, but only one-third of the teachers seeking provisional certification ever make it that far.

The pedagogy portion of the Liberal Arts and Sciences certification exam resembles a catechism more than an exam. "Multiple perspectives" are clearly not acceptable in answering such loaded questions as: "Analyze how classroom environments that respect diversity foster positive student experiences," or, "Analyze how schoolwide structures (i.e., tracking) and classroom factors (e.g., homogeneous versus heterogeneous grouping [presumably by ability], student-teacher interactions) may affect students' self-concepts and learning." Will a would-be teacher who answers that classrooms should stress a common culture or that ability grouping promotes excellence remain just a would-be teacher? One hopes not.

The exams echo with characteristic ed school verbiage. The student doesn't learn, he achieves "learning processes and outcomes"; the teacher doesn't teach, she "applies strategies for facilitating learning in instructional situations." Disregard for language runs deep in the teacher education profession, so much so that ed school professors tolerate glaring language deficiencies in schoolchildren. Last January, Manhattan's Park West High School shut down for a day, so that its faculty could bone up on progressive pedagogy. One of the more popular staff development seminars was "Using Journals and Learning Logs." The presenters—two Park West teachers and a representative from the New York City Writing Project, an anti-grammar initiative run by Lehman College's Education School—proudly passed around their students' journal writing, including the following representative entry on "Matriarchys v. pratiarchys [sic]": "The different between Matriarchys and patriarchys is that when the mother is in charge of the house. sometime the children do whatever they want. But sometimes the mother can do both roll as a mother and as a father too and they can do it very good." A more personal entry described how the author met her boyfriend: "He said you are so kind I said you noticed and then he hit me on my head. I made-believe I was crying and when he came naire me I slaped him right in his head and than I ran . . . to my grandparients home and he was right behind me. Thats when he asked did I have a boyfriend."

The ubiquitous journal-writing cult holds that such writing should go uncorrected. Fortunately, some Park West teachers bridled at the notion. "At some point, the students go into the job market, and they're not being judged 'holistically,'" protested a black teacher, responding to the invocation of the state's "holistic" model for grading writing. Another teacher bemoaned the Board of Ed's failure to provide guidance on teaching grammar. "My kids are graduating without skills," he lamented.

Such views, however, were decidedly in the minority. "Grammar is related to purpose," soothed the Lehman College representative, educrat code for the proposition that asking students to write grammatically on topics they are not personally "invested in" is unrealistic. A Park West presenter burst out with a more direct explanation for his chilling indifference to student incompetence: "I'm not going to spend my life doing error diagnosis! I'm not going to spend my weekend on that!" Correcting papers used to be part of the necessary drudgery of a teacher's job. No more, with the advent of enlightened views about "self-expression" and "writing with intentionality."

However easygoing the education establishment is regarding future teachers' knowledge of history, literature, and science, there is one topic that it assiduously monitors: their awareness of racism. To many teacher educators, such an awareness is the most important tool a young teacher can bring to the classroom. It cannot be developed too early. Rosa, a bouncy and enthusiastic junior at Hunter College, has completed only her first semester of education courses, but already she has mastered the most important lesson: America is a racist, imperialist country, most like, say, Nazi Germany. "We are lied to by the very institutions we have come to trust," she recalls from her first-semester reading. "It's all government that's inventing these lies, such as Western heritage."

The source of Rosa's newfound wisdom, Donaldo Macedo's *Literacies of Power: What Americans Are Not Allowed to Know*, is an execrable book by any measure. But given its target audience—impressionable education students—it comes close to being a crime. Widely assigned at Hunter, and in use in approximately 150 education schools nationally, it is an illiterate, barbarically ignorant Marxist-inspired screed against America. Macedo opens his first chapter, "Literacy for Stupidification: The Pedagogy of Big Lies," with a quote from Hitler and quickly segues to Ronald Reagan: "While busily calling out slogans from their patriotic vocabulary memory warehouse, these same Americans dutifully vote . . . for Ronald Reagan, giving him a landslide victory . . . . These same voters ascended [sic] to Bush's morally high-minded call to apply international laws against Saddam Hussein's tyranny and his invasion of Kuwait." Standing against this wave of ignorance and imperialism is a lone 12-year-old from Boston, whom Macedo celebrates for his courageous refusal to recite the Pledge of Allegiance.

What does any of this have to do with teaching? Everything, it turns out. In the 1960s, educational progressivism took on an explicitly political cast: Schools were to fight institutional racism and redistribute power. Today, Columbia's Teachers College holds workshops on cultural and political "oppression," in which students role-play ways to "usurp the existing power structure," and the New York State Regents happily call teachers the "ultimate change agents." To be a change agent, one must first learn to "critique" the existing social structure. Hence, the assignment of such propaganda as Macedo's book.

But however bad the influence of Macedo's puerile politics on future teachers, it pales compared to the model set by his writing style. A typical sentence: "This inability to link the reading of the word with the world, if not combated, will further exacerbate already feeble democratic institutions [sic] and the unjust, asymmetrical power relations that characterize the hypocritical nature of contemporary democracies." Anyone who dares criticize Macedo for his prose is merely trying to "suffocate discourses," he says, with the "blind and facile call for clarity." That Hunter College could assign this gross betrayal of the English language to future teachers is a sufficient reason for closing its education program down. Rosa's control of English is shaky enough as it is; to fill her ears with such subliterate writing represents professional malpractice.

But Macedo is just one of the political tracts that Hunter force-fed the innocent Rosa in her first semester. She also learned about the evils of traditional children's stories from education radical Herbert Kohl. In *Should We Burn Babar?* Kohl weighs the case for and against the dearly beloved children's classic, *Babar the Elephant,* noting in passing that it prevented him from "question[ing] the patriarchy earlier." He decides—but let Rosa expound the message of Kohl's book: "[*Babar*]'s like a children's book, right? [But] there's an underlying meaning about colonialism, about like colonialism, and is it OK, it's really like it's OK, but it's like really offensive to these people." Better burn *Babar* now!

In New York, as in almost every state, the focus on diversity and anti-racism indoctrination comes with the highest imprimatur. The State Board of Regents requires all prospective teachers to have at least one course in "diversity"; many local ed schools pride themselves on weaving "diversity" into all their courses. The nation's most influential education school, Teachers College, promotes the most extreme race consciousness in its mandated diversity program. In her large lecture course, Professor Valerie Henning-Piedmont sneered at "liberal correctness," which she defined as "I don't see the color of my students." Such misguided color blindness, she said, equals: "I don't see the students."

Expect the folly only to grow worse. A draft report from the Regents Task Force on Teaching, grousing that future teachers lack sufficient grounding in diversity, calls for special training in such challenges as "teaching both sexes," thus further legitimizing the ludicrous proposition that schools mistreat girls. The Regents also make recruiting a more "diverse" teaching force a top priority, based on the assumption that minority students learn best from minority teachers. Currently, 34 percent of teachers in New York City, and 15 percent state-wide, are minorities, compared to a student population that is 83 percent minority in New York City and 43 percent statewide. Asked what evidence the Regents have for the proposition that the color of the teaching force correlates with achievement, Doris T. Garner, staff coordinator for the Task Force, admitted, "I don't think hard evidence exists that would say that." If black students should be taught by black teachers, should white students be taught by white teachers? "I would not recommend that," replied Garner, fearless of illogic.

Since the Regents are making teacher diversity a top priority, something is going to have to give. Currently, blacks fail the content-free Liberal Arts and Sciences Test of provisional certification at a rate five times that of whites. But that's just a temporary obstacle, because the test-bias hounds may be already closing in for the kill: the discovery that the exam discriminates against minorities. The Regents' most recent paper on teacher training warned that the certification exam "must exclude language that would jeopardize candidates, and include language and content that reflects diversity." Now, the only candidates who would be jeopardized by the exam's language are those, of any color, who are deeply troubled by hot air. As for "cultural bias," at present the exam is a rainbow of multicultural examples and propaganda—one sample question, for example, features a fawning review of a "multicultural dance work that is truly representative of the diversity of New York." Don't be surprised if the complete absence of any "bias" in the exam, however, fails to prevent a concerted, taxpayer-funded effort to redraft it so as to guarantee an equal pass rate among all groups of takers.

Though the current diversity battle cry is "All students can learn," the educationists continually lower expectations of what they should learn. No longer are students expected to learn all their multiplication tables in the third grade, as has been traditional. But while American educators come up with various theories about fixed cognitive phases to explain why our children should go slow, other nationalities trounce us. Sometimes, we're trounced in our own backyards, causing cognitive dissonance in local teachers.

A young student at Teachers College named Susan describes incredulously a Korean-run preschool in Queens. To her horror, the school, the Holy Mountain School, violates every progressive tenet: Rather than being "student-centered" and allowing each child to do whatever he chooses, the school imposes a curriculum on the children, based on the alphabet. "Each week, the children got a different letter," Susan recalls grimly. Such an approach violates "whole language" doctrine, which holds that students can't "grasp the [alphabetic] symbols without the whole word or the meaning or any context in their lives," in Susan's words. Holy Mountain's further infractions include teaching its wildly international students only in English and failing to provide an "antibias multicultural curriculum." The result? By the end of preschool the students learn English and are writing words. Here is true belief in the ability of all children to learn, for it is backed up by action.

Across the city, young teachers are dumping progressive theories faster than Indonesian currency. For all the unctuous talk of diversity, many progressive tenets are dangerously ill-adapted to inner-city classrooms. "They don't say 'boo' about this population," scoffs Samantha, a recent Hunter graduate now teaching in Brooklyn's Bedford-Stuyvesant section. "My course in multiculturalism had zero to do with the classroom."

A former dancer, Samantha was an open receptacle for progressive ideas. But her early efforts to follow the model have left her stranded. Her fourth-grade class is out of control. "I didn't set it up in a strict manner at the beginning," she laments. "I gave them too many choices; I did a lot of things wrong." Collaborative learning? Forget about it. "My kids resort to fighting immediately if I put them in groups." Samantha tried to use groups to make a poster on electricity. "It was mayhem; they couldn't stay quiet," she recalls.

The student-centered classroom is equally a fraud. "You can't give them choices," Samantha asserts flatly. Next year, with a new class, she will do things differently. "I will have everything set up to the last detail—their names on the desks, which notebooks to buy, how to label them. They need to know what hook to hang their coat on and where to go from there. Every minute of the day has to be scripted. You can't just say: 'Line up!' because they'll fight. Instead, you have to say: 'Boys, stand up, push in your chairs, and here are your line spots.'"

As for "metacognition," that is out as well. "My kids need the rote; they can't do half of six or four divided by two." Samantha is using the most unholy of unholies to teach her children to read—a basal reader, derided by the education establishment as spirit killing. But the reader gives her specific skill sets to work on, above all, phonics and grammar. "My kids don't hear the correct sound of words at home, such as 'th' or the ending of words, so teaching reading is harder."

Journals, whole language, and "portfolio assessment" became more casualties of the real world at the Holy Cross School in the Bronx. The school recently hired a Teachers College graduate who arrived fired up with those student-centered methods. No more. Now she is working very hard on grammar, according to assistant principal William Kurtz. "Those [progressive] tools don't necessarily work for kids who can't read or tell you what a noun or a verb is," he says. In his own history class, Kurtz has discovered that he needs to be as explicit about study habits and research methods as Samantha is about classroom behavior. "When I give an essay question, I have to be very structured about going to the library and what resources to use. If you don't do that, they look up nothing."

The education establishment would be unfazed by these stories. Samantha and William, it would say, are still prisoners of the "deficit model." All these two benighted teachers can see is what their kids don't know, instead of building on their strengths. If those strengths are hip-hop music, for example, focus on that. But for heaven's sake, don't deny the children the benefits of a child-centered classroom.

In fact, the strict environment that Samantha plans is the best thing that could happen to her pupils. It is perhaps the only place they will meet order and civility. Samantha's children are "surrounded by violence," she says. Many are not interested in learning, because at home, "everyone is dissing everybody, or staying up late to get high. My kids are so emotionally beat up, they don't even know when they're out of their seats." A structured classroom is their only hope to learn the rules that the rest of society lives by. To eliminate structure for kids who have none in their lives is to guarantee failure.

Given progressive education's dismal record, all New Yorkers should tremble at what the Regents have in store for the state. The state's teacher education establishment, led by Columbia's Linda Darling-Hammond, has persuaded the Regents to make its monopoly on teacher credentialing total. Starting in 2003, according to a Regents plan steaming inexorably toward adoption, all teacher candidates must pass through an education school to be admitted to a classroom. We know, alas, what will happen to them there.

This power grab will be a disaster for children. By making ed school inescapable, the Regents will drive away every last educated adult who may not be willing to sit still for its foolishness but who could bring to the classroom unusual knowledge or experience. The nation's elite private schools are full of such people, and parents eagerly proffer tens of thousands of dollars to give their children the benefit of such skill and wisdom.

Amazingly, even the Regents, among the nation's most addled education bodies, sporadically acknowledge what works in the classroom. A Task Force on Teaching paper cites some of the factors that allow other countries to wallop us routinely in international tests: a high amount of lesson content (in other words, teacher-centered, not student-centered, learning), individual tracking of students, and a coherent curriculum. The state should cling steadfastly to its momentary insight, at odds with its usual policies, and discard its foolhardy plan to enshrine Anything But Knowledge as its sole education dogma. Instead of permanently establishing the teacher education status quo, it should search tirelessly for alternatives and for potential teachers with a firm grasp of subject matter and basic skills. Otherwise ed school claptrap will continue to stunt the intellectual growth of the Empire State's children.

· ·

The Truth About Teacher Salaries and Student Achievement

Eric A. Hanushek

This selection first appeared as an advertisement in *The Weekly Standard,* placed by the Hoover Institution, in 2000. Eric Hanushek is the Paul and Jean Hanna Senior Fellow on Education Policy at the Hoover Institution, and a member of Hoover's Koret Task Force on K–12 Education.

The season of teacher contract negotiations tends to bring forth a series of comparisons of teacher salaries with average salaries in other professions. These comparisons, which invariably show teachers trailing others, are frequently linked to arguments about the necessity of having quality teachers. Increasing teacher shortages simply amplify the need to improve teacher wages. What should we make of these arguments?

Research confirms what all parents know: **The teacher is the key ingredient to quality schooling.** A quality teacher is much more important than, say, a small class size.

Similarly, nobody doubts that increasing teacher salaries—for an individual district or for the nation as a whole—will increase the number of people interested in teaching. Thus, improving quality and dealing with shortages would seem directly related to improvements in salaries.

Unfortunately, the argument on salaries, like many others on educational policy, does not hold up because the validity rests on a number of unstated and unproven assumptions.

Let's consider the left-out components: First, when school people discuss salaries, they regularly have in mind raising everybody's salary. This includes the salary of all current teachers, regardless of quality, specialization, or anything else. There exists no overall shortage of people willing to teach or even of people certified to teach. Shortage arguments rest on ideas of specific skills, such as math or science training, but few people arguing for increased salaries would contemplate paying math and science teachers more than elementary English teachers. Second, poor teachers almost certainly value improved salaries at least as much as good teachers. An increase in salaries induces all current teachers to stay in teaching, regardless of how good they are. Third, **quality is not a determinant of salaries.** Teachers' salaries are determined by experience, degree level, and coaching abilities but not by their impact on student learning. Fourth, nobody doubts that increasing teacher salaries will expand the pool of potential teachers from which a district can choose. But the influence on students depends directly on the ability of districts to choose the best teachers from the expanded pool. Research shows that the typical school district does poorly in these choices.

The combination of these factors implies that **there is virtually no relationship between teacher salaries and student achievement.**

Imagine a world where good teachers were paid large salaries and poor teachers were helped to find alternative jobs. Imagine a world where schools could compete for skilled specialists without having to pay the same to everybody, regardless of scarcity. This world would be very different from our current world, and the discussions of pay comparisons with other professions would be more meaningful.

· ·

Why It's Too Hard to Fire Bad Teachers

Think your child's school has teachers that deserve the heave-ho? Good luck. In Chicago and in many other cities, it almost takes a felony conviction to get a teacher fired. And sometimes, even that isn't enough.

Maribeth Vander Weele

This selection first appeared in *The Washington Monthly's* November 1994 issue. Maribeth Vader Weele is inspector general of the Board of Education of the City of Chicago. This article was adapted from her book, *Reclaiming Our Schools: The Struggle for Chicago School Reform.*

At one Chicago school, a teacher locked a special education kindergartner in a closet for hours for defecating in his pants. Another teacher repeatedly used emergencies as excuses for being late, arriving minutes before 10 A.M.—the magic hour before which, under union contract, she could not be marked absent and be docked pay.

The principal of these teachers' school got rid of them the best way he knew how: He transferred them to other schools.

The alternative to such transfers is dismissal hearings that can take years to complete, soaking up a principal's critically needed time and tens of thousands of dollars in legal fees from the school system. And even then, success is not guaranteed.

Public school officials throughout the nation complain about a shared problem: the Byzantine process required to fire inadequate teachers. Although good teachers are the single most essential ingredient in improving education, union power and legislatures have all but completely protected the tenures of the teachers who fail at their jobs.

The catch is that even small numbers of ineffective—and downright dangerous—teachers harm thousands of children for life. "Even if only five percent of the teachers in public elementary and secondary schools are incompetent, the number of students being taught by these teachers exceeds the combined public school enrollments of the five smallest states," Stanford Professor Edwin M. Bridges wrote in *Education Week.*

In one New York City case, the issue went beyond competence and into criminality. In 1990, Jay Dubner, a special education teacher, was convicted of selling $7,000 worth of cocaine and was sent to prison. But it was another two years before the New York City Board of Education finally fired the teacher after a year-long hearing that cost $185,000. The teacher argued that he should retain his job because he was rehabilitated, and a civil court decision overturned his dismissal. Even after years in jail, Dubner continued to collect pay checks. At one point, he worked a school job during the day while spending weekend nights in jail on a work-release program.

School districts across New York spend on average nearly $200,000 and 476 days on each teacher dismissal hearing—more, in some cases, than it takes to convict someone of a crime in the courts, according to a 1994 survey by the New York State School Board Association. "You have to provide documentation on top of documentation on top of documentation," said Erica Zurer, vice president of New York City's Community School Board 13, which oversees one of 32 subdistricts in the nation's largest school system. As a result of publicity and a few flagrant cases involving drug and sex crimes, the New York State Legislature streamlined the process this year. As of September 1, school districts are permitted to suspend without pay any employee convicted of drug crimes or of abusing a minor, either physically or sexually.

In Illinois, the legislature set up an unwieldy process that in 1992 resulted in dismissals of seven (out of 26,000) tenured Chicago public school teachers. Far more should have been fired. According to a study by the Consortium on Chicago School Research, an astounding number of principals—more than two-thirds—said they would fire 6 to 20 percent of their teachers if they could bypass the hearings.

The criteria for firing a teacher, however, depend on more than the judgment of the principal. Chicago teachers cannot be dismissed unless they have failed to improve after a remediation period of 45 days, or are deemed "irremediable." In such a situation, the school system has to prove that a teacher's conduct caused damage to the students, the faculty, or the school, that could not have been prevented had the teacher been forewarned.

But even that understates the obstacles placed in the way of ensuring that students have good, or at least not dangerous, teachers. At Truth Elementary School on the West Side of Chicago, Principal Pernecie Pugh and school board lawyers worked unsuccessfully for more than two years to dismiss Sheila Golub, a 21-year veteran of the

Chicago system whose alleged abuse of a third-grader sent the young-ster to seek medical attention for a head injury in September 1990.

Although Golub claimed she was trying to prevent the child from spinning out of control, the Illinois Department of Children and Family Services investigated the incident and found the charge of abuse legitimate. Meanwhile, parents petitioned to remove the teacher, who they charged had hit students before and had on occasion come to class with urine and feces stains on her clothing. Pugh testified she also con-fronted Golub about menstrual stains and accused the teacher of ex-cessive absenteeism, tardiness, and smoking in school.

The school board issued a formal warning to Golub in December 1990, saying that if she did not correct her behavior, she would be dis-missed. Five months after the first incident, however, Golub was ac-cused of pushing, grabbing, and hitting five more children and slamming another child's hand in a book. The school board dismissed her the following March. In her dismissal hearing, Golub denied abuse allegations made by the seven children, two parents, and Pugh. She also denied that Pugh warned her against using corporal punish-ment. In January 1992, hearing officer Julius Manacker upheld the board action.

But it didn't end there. Golub appealed to the Circuit Court and, in April 1993, was reinstated with two years' back pay. Judge Mary Jane Theis ruled her actions were not "irremediable" because the second set of injuries was not especially severe, despite a system-wide policy against the use of corporal punishment. Theis wrote: "The incidents in the third-grade classroom of Miss Golub could not be termed severe or premeditated. The principal observed no injuries to any of the children and no medical treatment was sought."

It didn't help that previous principals had rated the teacher satisfac-tory or excellent. And what's more, Theis sympathized with the teacher: "The children's testimony before the hearing officer reveals a classroom totally out of control. Maintaining discipline in that setting would have been difficult for the most able teacher."

The community was so outraged that Pugh feared for Golub's safety and successfully won her a transfer to a non-teaching job in a subdis-trict office, where she waited for an assignment for another position. After the nearly four-year process was finally over, Pugh was indignant, and more discouraged than ever. "It is hard to get rid of a teacher—even when they are hurting children. It is hard."

And with all the protections for teachers and extensive appeal opportunities, firing sometimes isn't enough. Laura Ward Elementary School teacher Eli Johnson, who was fired in 1986 for allegedly pushing a fourth-grader into a wall and throwing him onto the floor, was reinstated with back pay in 1988. Hospital x-rays revealed the child suffered a bruised rib. Hearing officer George Edward Larney agreed that the evidence, including testimony from the boy's classmates, indicated that the teacher had physically shoved the child. But while the hearing officer said he deplored the physical force used on the boy, he found insufficient evidence to prove the student's injuries that day were the result of the teacher's abuse. "For all anyone knows, the child could have fallen down the stairs or had been hit by the door as he left the classroom," Larney wrote. "Besides, although the boy had above average reading scores, he had an explosive temper and frequently disrupted class."

Johnson had an otherwise unblemished record and, Larney wrote, had already "endured a certain amount of anguish" in connection with the case. Larney continued to state that there was no evidence that Johnson was unable to correct his behavior, a criteria required by law.

Johnson returned to his school in 1990 only to receive another unsatisfactory work notice in 1991 for improper classroom behavior and for verbally abusing students, after which he took a year's leave of absence. He returned once more and received yet another notice, again for verbally abusing students. In March 1991, the school board issued a formal warning stemming from a report charging that Johnson pushed four children. And in June 1991, he was accused of grabbing yet another student by the throat and pushing her across the classroom.

The teacher's seventh-grade classroom was out of control. Fights erupted regularly, including one in which a child hit another with a window shade. Moreover, Johnson, who had taught in the public school system for 29 years, apparently had no concept of how to teach and assigned little, if any, homework. He conceded in his testimony that he "did not make a teaching program, nor keep a record of attendance or grades of his students," but he blamed the principal for never telling him to do so. His dismissal was upheld by hearing officer Thomas R. McMillan in December 1992, more than six years after the first recorded incident.

Problem teachers influence the entire system. It is not only their ghastly effect on children, who may forever miss out on the multiplication tables or key grammar lessons, or who may learn to detest school so fiercely that they drop out. But their behavior also casts a pall on good teachers, true heroes who because of their commitment to city children refuse to leave for better-managed and amply supplied suburban schools.

A 1993 survey of Chicago Teachers Union delegates shows that teachers understand the injury caused by incompetent colleagues as well as anyone. Seventy-nine percent of the union's own delegates consider the obstacles to removing poor teachers a problem, according to the Chicago magazine *Catalyst*. The only problem teachers consider more serious than dismissing poorly performing teachers was insufficient teaching materials.

To be sure, the protections for teachers do have some positive aspects, notably protection for whistle blowers. Take the case of Marsha Niazmund, a counselor who was transferred from her school for reporting sexual advances her principal, James G. Moffat, had made on students. Moffat at one time was the deputy superintendent of school management services, the second-highest position in the system. He was demoted to the position of principal of Kelvyn Park High School on the Northwest Side during a change of administrations in 1980.

Niazmund was counseling a Kelvyn Park student one day when the girl complained that Moffat had propositioned her. Weeks later, the girl again complained, alleging that the principal had kissed her and removed her bra. Niazmund complained, but the administration apparently did nothing, assuming the charges could not be proven.

When Niazmund persisted, Moffat transferred her out of Kelvyn Park High School in January 1985 to shut her up. Niazmund hired an attorney and tracked down other victims, taking affidavits that led to Moffat's conviction years later.

Meanwhile, the board instituted dismissal hearings—which apply to principals as well—but was unsuccessful when state hearing officer John W. Schelthoff overruled the board: "The hearing officer does not feel that a 30-year distinguished career devoted to education of the community's young should be destroyed on the basis of uncorroborated statements of self-acknowledged sexual miscreants, drug abusers or a few disaffected teachers with obvious personal motives."

In 1987, Moffat was sentenced to 15 years in prison for pressuring five male and female students into having sex with him in his office at Kelvyn Park High School.

Besides defending the dismissal process on behalf of the whistle blowers, the Chicago Teachers Union—whose attorneys were provided with a summary of the findings in this article and declined to comment on the specific cases they handled—argues that the job of every union is to protect its members. And, it correctly notes, it is not the one hiring incompetents. The impossible-to-fire syndrome is only true for "administrators who are either too arrogant or too incompetent to follow a simple due-process procedure," says Whitney Young Magnet School union delegate Robert Mijou. "In my 23 years as a teacher in the Chicago school system, one thing has remained constant: poor management. Education in Chicago is provided in spite of, not because of, management policy. The bureaucracy is more concerned with politics and self-serving image building than with education."

Clearly, school systems need to make sure poor teachers (not to mention convicted felons) do not enter the classroom. Meanwhile, administrators must reserve the right to remove inadequate teachers who slip through the cracks. Here are some suggestions that would immediately improve the quality of teachers and give schools the ability to get rid of the bad apples.

Require teachers to take a competency exam or undergo classroom evaluation periodically. That would assure the public that teachers who received their own educations decades ago keep abreast of changes in the fields they teach.

Require police departments to notify school districts when they learn that they have arrested a school employee for offenses involving sex, violence, or narcotics. State law should provide for automatic dismissal or unpaid suspension of any public school employee convicted of such a crime.

Deprive fired teachers and principals of their state teaching certificates, either permanently or temporarily, so they may not be employed by other districts.

Allow school boards and unions to negotiate their own dismissal process. For example, one principal suggested placing teachers who do not receive "excellent" or "superior" ratings on probation. After three years with such a status, they would lose seniority rights and tenure.

Provide avenues—such as strong inspector general offices—to address corruption. This is necessary to assure whistle blowers and other staff that corrupt administrators, not whistle blowers, will be penalized under streamlined dismissal procedures.

The strength of the public school system depends on the quality of its teachers. But by admitting and maintaining poor or even dangerous teachers, the students, the schools, and the teaching profession itself is put in harm's way.

· ·

How Teachers' Unions Handcuff Schools

Sol Stern

This selection first appeared in *City Journal*'s Spring 1997 edition. Sol Stern is a contributing editor of the Manhattan Institute's *City Journal* (www.city-journal.org).

When Tracey Bailey received the National Teacher of the Year Award from President Clinton in a festive Rose Garden ceremony in 1993, American Federation of Teachers chief Albert Shanker called to say how pleased he was that a union member had won this prestigious honor. But Bailey, a high school science teacher from Florida, is an AFT member no more. Today he believes that the big teachers' unions are a key reason for the failure of American public education, part of the problem rather than the solution. The unions, he thinks, are just "special interests protecting the status quo," pillars of "a system that too often rewards mediocrity and incompetence." Such a system, he says, "can't succeed."

Bailey is right. In the final analysis, no school reform can accomplish much if it does not focus on the quality of the basic unit of education—that human interaction between an adult and a group of children that we call teaching. The big teachers' unions, through the straitjacket of work rules that their contracts impose, inexorably subvert that fundamental encounter. These contracts structure the individual teacher's job in ways that offer him or her no incentives for excellence in the classroom—indeed, that perversely reward failure.

So as Tracey Bailey and many other dedicated teachers have learned, schools can't improve until reformers confront the deadly consequences of the power that teachers' unions wield over a monopolistic industry, not only through contracts but also through the unions' influence on the elected officials who regulate the education industry. Until then, any reform—whether more money for the schools or smaller classes or high national standards or charter schools—will get short-circuited from the very outset.

Trade unionism is a recent development in public education. During the first 100 years of taxpayer-funded public schools, teachers had no collective bargaining rights, though many enjoyed civil-service protection. While the public schools made steady progress during those years, it's indisputable that teachers were underpaid and often were moved around like interchangeable parts in a one-size-fits-all system. Many teachers, along with principals and other administrators, belonged to a staid professional organization called the National Education Association, to which the words "unionism" and "strike" were anathema. Inevitably, teachers working in a factory-style system figured they might as well organize themselves into factory-style unions. The big breakthrough came in New York City in 1961, when the United Federation of Teachers (UFT), led by a charismatic high school math teacher named Albert Shanker—whose recent death deprived the teachers' unions of one of the towering figures in the American labor movement—went on strike and won the right to bargain for all city teachers. Though Shanker insisted that the struggle was about more than mere bread-and-butter issues—that it was also about improving the quality of public education and strengthening democracy—the contract the UFT signed with the New York City Board of Education nevertheless reflected the traditional industrial model. It set up uniform pay scales and seniority rights for teachers, limited their classroom hours, and required new teachers to be automatically enrolled in the union and have their dues deducted from their paychecks.

Following this example, the once conservative NEA also veered toward militant trade unionism. By the mid-seventies it had a majority of the nation's teachers covered by collective bargaining agreements. Now the NEA and the AFT, the national parent body of New York's UFT, together represent more than 3 million school employees, including 80 percent of the nation's 3 million public school teachers. The two unions and their state and local affiliates take in $1.3 billion each year from dues and employ 6,000 full-time staff members.

Today the two national unions cast a giant shadow over not just American public education but also Democratic Party politics. As a California judge recently found, that state's NEA affiliate spent only half of its dues income on activities related to collective bargaining and used the other half for electoral politics, lobbying, and general advocacy for social, educational, and political causes. Nationally, in the 1996 election, the teachers' unions contributed more than $9 million directly to Bill Clinton and other Democratic candidates through political action committees. But the PACs were just the visible tip of a vast iceberg of soft money, independent media buys, thousands of full-time campaign workers paid with union dues, and in-kind services such as phone banks and direct mail advertising. Myron Lieberman, author of a forthcoming book on teachers' unions, estimates that the NEA and AFT together spent at least $50 million for the campaign compared to the $35 million that the AFL-CIO spent. And at last summer's Democratic convention, the teachers' union caucus constituted 11 percent of all delegates—a bigger share than the delegation from California.

These political investments have paid off. In the Clinton Department of Education, former NEA issues director Sharon Robinson is assistant secretary for research and educational improvement, shaping the national education debate with her office's research reports and assessments of student performance. And when the Republican Congress was on the verge of passing legislation last year to rescue a few thousand poor students from Washington, D.C.'s hopelessly broken public school system by offering them private school scholarships, the NEA, fearful that these vouchers might encourage similar legislation in the states, furiously lobbied the White House. President Clinton, who had first indicated that he would sign the bill, backtracked and said he would veto it.

The teachers' unions spend millions each year on advertising to convince the American people that when they flex their political muscle in cases like this, more often on the state than on the national level, they are working for the benefit of the nation's schoolchildren. Their pitch goes something like this: In driving up wages and improving working conditions, the unions have made the teaching profession far more attractive to qualified young people. PAC activities and political lobbying help pressure elected officials to finance education adequately, so that school boards can pay teachers the salaries they deserve, hire more teachers and reduce class size, provide staff development, and purchase books. Result: better schools and improved student performance.

There's some truth in these claims. The rise in the sixties and seventies of powerful teachers' unions with exclusive bargaining rights did lead to a huge jump in public school funding: Between 1965 and 1990, average spending per pupil nationwide increased from $2,402 to $5,582 in inflation-adjusted dollars. The average pupil-teacher ratio dropped from 24.1 to 17.3. The percentage of teachers with master's degrees increased from 23.2 to 52.6. The median years of experience for teachers went from 8 to 15. Between 1979 and 1989 average teacher salaries rose 20 percent in real dollars. Salaries for new public school teachers during that period rose 13 percent, compared to a mere 3.5 percent increase for all other college graduates taking entry-level positions.

Unfortunately for America's children, the rest of the unions' argument doesn't stand up. The extra money didn't improve student performance. To the contrary, during that same period average SAT scores for public school students declined by 10 percent, dropout rates in urban school systems increased, and American students scored at or near the bottom in comparisons with other industrialized nations. After years of examining the data, the nation's leading education economist, Eric Hanushek of the University of Rochester, concluded: "There appears to be no strong or systematic relationship between school expenditures and student performance."

So why did the bottom drop out of American public education just as per-pupil spending soared? Basic economics provides a compelling answer, though countless blue-ribbon commissions, and indeed much of the present national dialogue about school reform, have failed to acknowledge it: The $250 billion public education industry behaves precisely like any other publicly protected monopoly. Union negotiators in the private sector know that if they insist on protecting incompetent workers and cling to outdated work rules, especially in the global economy of the nineties, the company will begin losing market share, and union members will lose their jobs. In public education, by contrast, collective bargaining takes place without the constraining discipline of the market. When school board representatives sit down with union officials to negotiate a labor contract, neither party is under pressure to pay attention to worker productivity or the system's overall competitiveness: If the contract allows some teachers to be paid for hardly working at all, and others to perform incompetently without penalty, there is no real economic danger for either side. After all, most of the monopoly's customers, the schoolchildren, have nowhere else to go. Historically, tax revenues have continued to flow into the schools no matter how poorly they perform. Newark's public schools, for instance, have performed worse and worse in recent years, but per-pupil annual expenditure there is now almost $10,000, 50 percent above the U.S. average.

"Let's roll up our sleeves . . . and work together to give our children the schools they deserve," read the full-page *New York Times* ad taken out by New York City's United Federation of Teachers early this year. "We've tried everything else; now let's try what works," said a second

UFT ad a few days later. These were the opening salvos of a major media blitz laying out the UFT's program for "turning our schools around." The nearly $1 million print, radio, and TV ad campaign was needed, UFT president Sandra Feldman told her members, because "often the union is erroneously looked at as an impediment to school reform, and it's time to set the record straight."

The UFT has good reason to be concerned. In a colossal understatement, one of the ads acknowledged that "recent school report cards show that students in our city are losing ground." Actually, what the State Education Department's recently released school performance reports show is a near meltdown of what was once the nation's premier urban school system.

Third-grade reading scores are among the most useful benchmarks for judging any school system's performance. Children who can't read in third grade are likely to fall even further behind in the later grades. And schools that can't manage to get children reading after nearly four years in the classroom are not likely to do very well in other areas. So it is stunning to discover that only 30.2 percent of New York City's third-graders are reading at grade level, compared to 62.2 percent in the rest of the state, and that the reading scores are dismal not only in schools with high numbers of poor, minority children but in many middle-class schools, in districts that have "choice" programs and districts that have resisted reform, in schools that favor "progressive" teaching styles and more traditional schools. For example, at predominantly middle-class P.S. 87, one of the city's "hot" schools and a bastion of progressive "child-centered" teaching methods, close to half the school's third-graders read below grade level. At the Mohegan school in District 12 in the Bronx, which has a very poor, all-minority student population and follows the more traditional "core knowledge" philosophy of scholar E.D. Hirsch, Jr., only 19 percent of the third-graders read at grade level.

In the 35 years since Albert Shanker and his followers took to the streets, the UFT has become the richest and most powerful teachers' union local in the country. It represents 95,000 school employees, including 60,000 classroom teachers, from whom it collects $60 million in annual dues. School chancellors come and go, but the UFT endures—a perennial power at the Board of Education and in the State Legislature, which regulates the city's schools. It has played a pivotal role in electing (and defeating) mayors and governors and has often exercised virtual veto power over the selection of school chancellors. In 1993 the UFT punished Mayor David Dinkins for not giving in to its contract demands by running a $1 million ad campaign against him at the beginning of the mayoral campaign and withholding the phone banks that were an essential part of Dinkins's successful campaign in 1989.

The UFT, together with New York State United Teachers, the state AFT affiliate, is easily the most powerful special-interest lobby in Albany. In the first six months of 1996 alone, the New York teachers' unions' PAC reported $900,000 in lobbying expenses and political contributions to legislators—three times as much as the next highest group, the state medical societies. The teachers' unions make their contributions to those legislators who are most likely to help them, regardless of party—to the majority Democrats in the Assembly and the majority Republicans in the Senate.

In return, the teachers' unions get to set the limits of permissible education debate in the Legislature. Debra Mazzarelli, the mother of two public school children and a parent activist, learned that lesson after she was elected to the State Assembly from Patchogue, Long Island, two years ago on a platform calling for ending automatic tenure protection for public school teachers. "I was just fed up that we were paying teachers $80,000 a year but couldn't hold them accountable and certainly couldn't fire them if they were incompetent," she said. Her bill to end teacher tenure won support from the New York State School Boards Association, which held hearings around the state. But in typical Albany fashion, the Assembly education committee, led by Steven Sanders, a leading recipient of teachers' union PAC money, won't even schedule a discussion in committee on the proposed legislation. Meanwhile, New York continues to have one of the most restrictive state laws for initiating disciplinary proceedings against incompetent teachers. Largely the work of the teachers' unions, it passed without public hearings and almost guarantees that no tenured teachers are ever fired.

After a recent public conference on the prospects of getting charter school legislation passed in Albany (26 states now have such laws, but not New York), Beth Lief, executive director of a reform organization called New Visions for Public Schools and one of the conference conveners, told a *New York Times* reporter that one group would ultimately decide the fate of the proposal. "There is no piece of education legislation in this state that passes without the UFT," the *Times* quoted her as saying. UFT president Sandra Feldman, standing next to Lief, didn't blink when she heard this assessment of her union's power. Indeed, the UFT leadership seems to enjoy reminding its members of its political clout. The union newspaper recently excerpted without comment an item from *Crain's New York Business* describing Feldman as someone who "wields more control over the education of New York City children than any mayor."

Several former Board of Education officials have told me that the chancellors they worked for would never make a high-level management appointment over the objection of the UFT. Chancellors accommodate the union for two very important reasons: They know that the UFT could have blocked their own appointments, and they realize that they need the union's lobbying power to help wring needed measures and funds from the State Legislature and City Council. As a result of this political alliance of necessity, the UFT has become part of the permanent government at 110 Livingston Street. The same former Board officials told me that UFT vice president David Sherman has had the run of Board headquarters for years and frequently participates in high-level policy meetings.

New teachers quickly learn how central the union is to the system's governance. A senior union official always directs the orientation at 110 Livingston Street for their first assignments. And when new teachers get their first paychecks, they discover that $630 of their yearly wages of $29,000 will be deducted for union dues.

The current contract between the Board of Education and the UFT can best be described as a "we-don't-do-windows" document. Among the tasks that principals are forbidden to require of teachers under the contract: attending more than one staff meeting per month after school hours, walking the children to a school bus, patrolling the hallways or the lunchroom or the schoolyard, covering an extra class in an emergency, attending a lunchtime staff meeting, or coming in a few days prior to the opening of school each September to do some planning.

The contract undermines teacher professionalism, excellence, and hard work in other ways. In all but a handful of the city's schools, principals must fill many of their teacher vacancies according to seniority rather than merit. J. Cozzi Perullo, principal of the elite Stuyvesant High School, has complained that she has no control over who is hired for half of the school's posted vacancies. And when a teacher does transfer from one city school to another, the principal of the new school can't even get the previous principal's written comments on the transferring teacher's personnel file.

The contract makes it almost insurmountably difficult for a principal even to begin the process of charging a teacher with incompetence under the union-written state education law. Every time the principal wants to record a negative evaluation in the teacher's personnel file, the teacher can contest that single entry through three separate grievance procedures, leading all the way up to the Board of Education. Even after the Board has upheld the principal, the teacher, with the help of the union, can go to arbitration to contest the single negative entry. The process is so tortuous that most principals don't even bother trying; they accept it as a fact of school life that a certain number of incompetent teachers must be carried on the payroll.

Jorge Izquierdo of P.S. 163 in Manhattan is one of the rare principals who have not only tried to purge incompetent teachers but are willing to speak publicly about the issue. He told me that in the case of one totally dysfunctional teacher, he has spent close to 100 hours out of the building over the past two years in grievance sessions at the district office, at the Board of Education, and at arbitration sessions. Although every one of his negative evaluations has eventually been upheld, he still must go through the process for another year before this one employee might have to face formal disciplinary charges—a process that could take several more years. "I am like the CEO of a little corporation," says Izquierdo. "I am judged by whether or not I achieve the equivalent of a profit—how much the children gain in learning. But unlike any other CEO, I can't hire the people who work here or fire them when they're incompetent."

What is most revealing about the UFT contract, however, is what it does not say. In its 200 pages of text, this labor agreement breathes not a word about how many hours teachers must work. Article six stipulates only that "the school day . . . shall be 6 hours and 20 minutes" and that the school year lasts from the Tuesday after Labor Day until June 26. School principals may not require teachers to be in the building one day before that Tuesday, one minute before the students arrive each day, or one minute after the students leave.

The number of hours teachers work is not a trivial issue. Teaching is a labor-intensive occupation. At the elementary and secondary school level, teachers get results not necessarily because they are brilliant or attended elite education schools but because of the hours they spend with students in and after school, the hours they devote to reviewing students' work, and the hours they spend speaking with parents.

So how many hours do union teachers really work? According to a survey by the U.S. Department of Education, public school teachers put in an average of 45 hours per week, including time in the class-room, work with students outside the classroom, preparation time in the school building, and work done at home. But since the survey is based wholly on teacher self-reporting, any bias is likely to be in favor of re-porting too many hours worked rather than too few.

Doubtless, many public school teachers in New York do work 45 hours a week or more-at least during the 36 weeks that school is in session. One of the dirty little secrets of the system, however, is that there are many others who work close to, or exactly at, the contractual minimum. In the three different schools my children have attended, they have had several teachers who took the words in the contract about the length of the school day as gospel. Arriving in school just a few minutes before the chil-dren every morning, these teachers were usually out the door exactly at dismissal time. They rarely took any work home, grading at school the homework that they sporadically assigned. Assuming the teachers worked during all ten of the preparation periods provided for in the contract, and if we deduct their 50-minute "duty-free" lunch periods, I estimate that they worked a maximum of 28 hours per week, or about 1,000 hours per year. Some had enough seniority and graduate-school credits to put them at the top of the salary scale (presently $60,000, soon to be $70,000), so that they were earning a wage, not including benefits, of somewhere be-tween $60 and $70 per hour. That's higher than the rate earned by em-ployees with the city's top civil-service titles.

I don't know if 5 percent or 50 percent of the city's teachers work to the contractual minimum. And—scandalously—the Board of Education and city hall are also in the dark about the productivity of the system's teachers. In the past, the Board's labor negotiators tried to raise the issue of monitoring the number of hours teachers work. "The union never wanted to discuss it," one former Board official recalls. "They said their teachers were professionals, and it would be an insult."

It's unthinkable that managers of the city's police, fire, sanitation, or transportation agencies could do their job of trying to improve services without data on worker productivity. In public education, however, the city has agreed to ignore such basic management information. Worse, it doesn't matter, since all teachers get the same base salary, no matter how many hours they work or how effective they are in the classroom. Teachers get raises merely for showing up for another school year or for accumulating more education course credits, not for working hard and doing well.

This pervasive culture of mediocrity and time-serving takes a devastating toll on more ambitious teachers. Five years ago, journalist Samuel Freedman published *Small Victories*, a book about an extraordinary New York City teacher named Jessica Siegel. Following Siegel around for an entire year at Seward Park High School on the Lower East Side, Freedman was able to demonstrate just how much one teacher can accomplish with disadvantaged minority students through sheer hard work and determination. Freedman's reporting suggests that Siegel probably worked more than 60 hours per week, despite being at the low end of the salary scale. The book also makes clear that the system's bureaucracy and the UFT not only did not encourage Siegel but were obstacles she had to struggle to overcome. The union chapter chairperson at the school had a cushy assignment that put her in a classroom for no more than 90 minutes a day—after which she did everything she could to stifle Siegel's creative proposals to improve the school's performance. "The UFT did not exactly run the city school system," Freedman wrote, "but the system could not function without the union's assent."

By the time Freedman's book came out, Jessica Siegel had bailed out of teaching, having lasted ten years. The UFT, of course, is still present in every school, making sure that the city is never allowed to distinguish between teachers like her and my children's work-to-the-contract teachers. Instead of allowing a system of incentives that would encourage more Jessica Siegels to enter the classroom and stay in teaching, the union has been investing its energies in building its political power to ensure that won't happen.

Last July over 10,000 public school employees from every state in the union descended on Washington for the NEA's 75th annual representative assembly. I spent hours in the cafeterias and lounges speaking with delegates from places like Cedar Rapids, Iowa; Birmingham, Alabama; Billings, Montana; Honolulu, Hawaii; Denver, Colorado; and Storrs, Connecticut. Many were longtime union activists who had been coming to the conventions for years, with their very wealthy union paying their expenses.

All believed passionately that public education was under siege by the political right and profit-hungry corporations. One morning over coffee, a delegate from Connecticut told me that his school board was considering contracting with a private vendor to provide food services for the district's schools. His NEA local was mobilizing to fight this proposal, the delegate approvingly reported, because it was a step on the road toward privatizing all the school district's education services.

The NEA wants public education preserved as an enterprise-free zone. Jersey City is a case in point. Last year, Mayor Brett Schundler came up with a plan to give some poor students trapped in failing public schools tax-funded scholarships. When the state blocked Schundler's initiative, a local Pepsico distributor offered to pay for some of the scholarships. The New Jersey NEA affiliate immediately organized a boycott of Pepsi products, and the company quickly backed down. Speakers at the NEA convention threatened similar dire consequences, including more boycotts, for any company that dared to poach on the union's preserve.

It was hardly surprising that the delegates would be preoccupied with the specter of privatization and vouchers. But what was astonishing is that this once conservative organization now favors a political and cultural agenda not only to the left of the national political mainstream but also far to the left of the Democratic Party. It was as if the veterans of the Berkeley Free Speech Movement had taken off their tie-dyed T-shirts, cut their hair, put on 30 pounds, and taken over the Rotary Club.

Besides electing new officers and listening to a lot of speeches, the delegates spent their days at the convention passing resolutions on almost every issue under the sun—from federal housing and immigration policy to nuclear testing and the World Court to support for the special rights of every aggrieved racial, ethnic, gender, sexual-preference, and "otherwise-abled" group, subgroup, and tribe in America. The NEA believes that America faces no Social Security crisis and wants to lower the retirement age and repeal all taxes on Social Security payments. It also doesn't believe Medicare is in trouble and opposes any premium increases. It favors a national single-payer health plan supported entirely by tax revenues, full funding for Head Start programs, and a huge increase in federal spending on education—especially for "disadvantaged students," immigrant and American Indian students, and students with disabilities.

It would be an understatement to say that the NEA favors an expansion of the welfare state. Its economic program more closely resembles the most radical of the European socialist parties. John Berthoud, a senior fellow of the Alexis de Tocqueville Institution, has calculated that if Congress passed all the NEA's legislative proposals, the annual additional charge to the federal treasury would be $800 billion, requiring an average tax increase of $10,000 for a family of four.

The debate on education policy during last year's presidential election made much of the potential fragmenting effects on our civic culture of proposals like school choice or vouchers. Opponents of these experiments argued they would undermine the public schools, society's only means for inculcating children in our common civic heritage. They conjured up all sorts of imaginary horribles, including the specter that families would use vouchers to enroll their children in "David Duke schools," black nationalist schools, even schools that taught witchcraft. As *New Republic* editor Michael Kelly has summed up the case: "Public money is shared money, and it is to be used for the furtherance of shared values, in the interests of e pluribus unum. Charter schools and their like . . . take from the pluribus to destroy the unum."

Welcome to the NEA convention, Mr. Kelly. No charter schools or vouchers allowed, but not much unum either. This assembly of 10,000 public school employees celebrated not our common heritage but rather the disuniting of America. A standing convention resolution requires a set-aside of 20 percent of the convention seats for certain designated minorities. The NEA also officially recognizes numerous caucuses of the fragmented and oppressed and encourages delegates to join one or another, from the African American caucus, Hispanic caucus, American Indian and Alaska Native caucus, or Asian and Pacific Islander caucus, to the women's caucus or the gay and lesbian caucus. Each of these splinter groups proposes resolutions (almost never opposed by any other group) demanding special consideration in education and other domains for their particular ethnic, racial, or gender group. The resolutions add up to a massive assault on precisely those common ideals that the unions always insist are transmitted exclusively by the public schools.

For example, the NEA supports the "movement toward self-determination by American Indians/Alaska Natives" and believes these designated victim groups should control their own education. It supports "the infusion of Black studies and/or Afrocentric curricula into the curriculum." It strongly supports bilingual education for Hispanic students and opposes efforts to legislate English as the nation's official language. It believes that all schools should designate separate months to celebrate Black History, Hispanic Heritage, Native American Indian/Alaska Native Heritage, Asian/Pacific Heritage, Women's History, Lesbian and Gay History—which pretty well takes up the entire school calendar, leaving scant time for plain old American history.

It would be wrong to dismiss NEA convention debates as the adult equivalent of a high school model congress. The NEA's permanent bureaucracy takes the resolutions very seriously. Through its 1,300 field representatives assigned to state and local affiliates and through its permanent Capitol Hill lobbying staff, it works hard to get the convention agenda implemented by Congress and state legislatures and infused into the culture of the schools. The results include everything from distributing a classroom guidebook on sexual harassment by militant feminist Nan Stein of the Wellesley College Woman's Center, to "urg[ing] the appropriate government agencies to provide all materials and instruments necessary for left-handed students to achieve on an equal basis with their right-handed counterparts."

No matter that the voters don't support NEA's diversity and affirmative action agenda: This is America, where you can go straight to the courts. The NEA budgets $23 million a year for its legal arm, headed by a brilliant Washington lawyer named Robert Chanin. Chanin's primary mission, naturally, is to throw up legal challenges to every piece of legislation passed by democratically elected bodies that might free some children from the monopolistic public education system. But in addition, he intervenes in major court battles involving the pet issues of the Left. At the convention, Chanin spoke to the delegates about the NEA's amicus briefs on behalf of gay rights in Colorado, sexual integration of the all-male Citadel, and racial preferences in admissions at the University of Texas Law School. The NEA position had prevailed only in the first two cases, he reported, but racial quotas in the Lone Star State might fare better on appeal.

After the presidential election and the 1997 State of the Union address, with all its emoting about education, the two national teachers' unions may seem more powerful than ever. And with the NEA and the AFT seriously pursuing merger negotiations, a single national union might soon represent 3 million public school employees. It would be the biggest union not just in America but in the world.

Nevertheless, the teachers' unions may not be quite as unassailable as they appear. Despite the millions of dollars they spend on public relations every year, they have been unable to convince the American people that their children's schools and classrooms are in good hands. In a recent book, *Is There a Public for Public Schools?*, former Ford administration secretary of HEW David Mathews underlines the unions' dilemma when he writes that "Americans today seem to be halfway out the schoolhouse door."

Not only are the NEA and AFT clearly out of touch politically with the majority of the American people, but they have also positioned themselves far to the left of their own members. A 1995 NEA convention resolution calling for programs to train teachers to give "accurate portrayals of the roles and contributions of gay, lesbian, and bi-sexual people throughout history," for example, produced a ferocious backlash within the NEA's own membership, particularly in the South. When union teachers began turning in their membership cards and NEA locals faced losing their designation as exclusive bargaining agent, union leaders had to retreat.

The last reliable measures of the voting behavior and political allegiances of the nation's teachers were the CBS/*New York Times* exit polls during the 1980 and 1984 presidential elections. They showed that teachers, far from being way out on the left with their union leaders, were right in the American mainstream. In 1980, 46 percent of them voted for Ronald Reagan, 41 percent for Jimmy Carter, and 10 percent for John Anderson. By comparison, non-teachers went 51 percent for Reagan, 40 percent for Carter, and 6 percent for Anderson. Some 45 percent of teachers identified themselves as Democrats, 28 percent as Republicans, and 26 percent as independents—almost exactly mirroring the rest of the voting population. The 1984 exit polling produced very similar numbers.

The difference in political outlook between the teachers themselves and their union leaders has given rise to some upstart organizations that, though still small, represent a serious enough challenge to the big unions' monopoly to make them uneasy. National Teacher of the Year Award winner Tracey Bailey is now on the board of one such alternative group, the Association of American Educators. When he speaks to teachers, he tells them that they don't actually have to pay dues to a union that seems more interested in gay rights than in getting children to read, that instead they can be members of professional teacher organizations that focus on educating children and still provide such necessities as insurance.

In "right-to-work" states such as Georgia and Texas, where teachers are not coerced into joining unions, independent teachers' groups now have more members than either the NEA or AFT. Even in "union shop" states, many teachers chafe at the unions' political monopoly. In California last year, the Individual Rights Foundation used federal labor law to represent 700 teachers who resigned from the union and were able to get 50 percent of their dues refunded (approximately $300 per teacher) because it was spent on political and social advocacy rather than collective bargaining. And now many of those same teachers have formed their own independent professional organization, the Professional Educators Group of California. The foundation expects the number of teachers defecting from the NEA to climb into the thousands next year.

Altogether the various independent teachers' organizations around the country now have close to 200,000 members. This ferment may lead the way to thoroughgoing teachers' union reform. What this budding movement needs in order to flower is a massive public information campaign. Teachers presently forced to pay dues to the NEA or AFT need to know what the unions are saying in their name and what rights they have to opt out. Parents and taxpayers need to learn more about teachers' union contracts and political lobbying, teacher productivity and credentialing, and even the $100,000-plus salaries of legions of teachers' union employees. It seems safe to say that if the American people merely knew about the resolutions passed at NEA conventions, the exodus "out the schoolhouse door" would accelerate.

The simple act of getting accurate information to the public about teachers' unions can greatly help the cause of school reform. Last year a good-government group called the Philadelphia Campaign for Public Education decided to butt into a nasty battle between the reform-minded superintendent of schools, David Hornbeck, and the Philadelphia Federation of Teachers over the next labor contract. Hornbeck had demanded that, in exchange for a wage increase, teachers should have to report to the schools a half hour earlier than the students and stay in the buildings a little after dismissal time. He also proposed that teachers who receive an unsatisfactory rating from their principals be denied automatic longevity raises. For Hornbeck's effrontery in suggesting that pay be tied to performance, the teachers' union (an AFT affiliate) launched a massive advertising campaign against him, calling him—what else—a "teacher basher."

That's when the Campaign for Public Education decided that the public needed some accurate information about Philadelphia's unionized teachers. The foundation-funded group began publishing a series of colorful newsletters with charts and graphs containing some amazing data about the existing union contract. One of these "School Updates" carried a headline that said "[Philadelphia] teachers enjoy one of the shortest school days in the nation—and Philadelphia's schoolchildren lose." Next to the text was a bar graph showing the number of minutes spent at school by high school teachers in the 21 largest urban school districts in the country. Philadelphia had the shortest bar (followed by New York City). Another newsletter highlighted some of the contract's work rules, including the fact that "open positions in schools are filled according to a pecking order that favors [seniority] over all other factors."

The union's response was first outrage (including an attempt to prevent the newsletters from being printed), then embarrassment, and finally a more accommodating position in the negotiations. The new labor agreement signed last fall contained the provision that teachers who receive an unsatisfactory rating will lose their automatic pay increase—a provision that seems utterly unexceptionable to a normal person but is revolutionary in the context of teacher unionism.

Imagine that there were similar citizen groups in other large city school districts, continuously channeling information to the public about the myriad ways that teachers' union contracts affect the operation and performance of the schools and how teachers' union politics subvert the common culture that the public schools are supposed to transmit. Imagine further that the same citizen groups communicated with teachers over the heads of their NEA and AFT leaders, informing them that they are entitled to resign from the union and receive a refund of that portion of their dues used for purposes other than collective bargaining. Suppose that in New York City, every time the UFT ran one of its full-page ads boasting that it was working to improve the schools, it was followed by another ad by a citizen group describing in simple, factual terms how many hours teachers work under the union contract, how difficult it is to fire incompetent union teachers, how principals are forced to hire teachers on the basis of seniority.

What I have described is not fanciful. It is occurring in fits and starts all over the country and is bound to grow. The only thing that can prevent the teachers' union reform movement from expanding is the one thing the teachers' unions can't seem to deliver—a public school system that works.

. . . .

How Teachers Should Be Evaluated

Siobahan Gorman

This selection first appeared in the *National Journal* (www.nationaljournal.com) on 4 December 1999, and is reprinted with permission; copyright 1999 by National Journal Group, Inc. (all rights reserved). Siobahan Gorman is a regular contributor to *National Journal*.

As the daughter of two public school teachers, Jeanne Slavin Kaplan had always considered herself a "complete teacher advocate." That is, until she had two children of her own in Denver public schools. "I have seen a number of things over the years that have made me re-evaluate my position," Kaplan says.

For example, when her daughter was in the third grade, Kaplan was unhappy with her teacher. So were some other parents. Kaplan tried to get her daughter out of that teacher's class and into another one. When she was unsuccessful, she and other parents persuaded the principal to get the teacher out instead. And the teacher was passed off to another Denver public school.

With pressure building from parents and others, education's accountability movement may soon catch up with teachers. As student test scores come under greater scrutiny from state and school officials, policy-makers and parents are beginning to ask how teachers are measuring up, too. "A lot of districts are now talking about a parallel theme: We've got accountability for students, and maybe we should have accountability for teachers," said Allan R. Odden, a professor of education administration at the University of Wisconsin (Madison). In other words: If children can't be socially promoted, why should teachers?

This year's National Education Summit endorsed a 10-state pilot project to examine performance pay for teachers. At the summit, National Urban League President Hugh Price elicited strong applause with his pitch to free teacher hiring and firing from union collective bargaining. Sen. John McCain of Arizona, a Republican presidential hopeful, has endorsed merit pay, teacher tests, and ways to send potentially bad teachers down another career path. Denver is launching a pilot program to test the link between teacher pay and student achievement.

Although there is a growing consensus among lawmakers and educators that some form of teacher evaluation is necessary to infuse public education with more credibility, the "how" of doing that is tricky. Designing a system that requires accountability without alienating good teachers will be a challenge. Just about everyone agrees that teachers must be on board for accountability to work.

Those who have studied effective schools, especially ones in low-income areas, say that weeding out bad teachers is an important factor in improving student achievement. Robert L. Mendro, chief evaluation officer for the Dallas Independent School District, who studied successful schools in that city, describes the practices of the effective principals he has seen in the schools: "They set this tone—that we expect our kids to learn. The thing they did was to be far less tolerant of bad teachers."

The question of teacher accountability sets up a new debate on measuring teacher success. Subjectivity has always been a sticking point for such measurements, but many researchers say that the availability of data will let them objectively determine teachers' effectiveness. At the forefront of this research is William L. Sanders, a statistician at the University of Tennessee. Sanders has developed a complex statistical model that measures the "value" a teacher adds to his or her students based on their change in test scores over a given year and that factors out such variables as socioeconomic status. The problem, he says, is that "without measurement, [evaluating teachers] is totally a political process."

Sanders has been racking up thousands of frequent flier miles to spread the word, including some for a recent trip to Denver, and other researchers are starting to examine his idea. Sanders has found, for example, that children who have weak teachers for two consecutive years never overcome that setback. In Dallas, Mendro found that students who had excellent teachers for three years in a row scored 40 percentile points to 50 percentile points higher on standardized math tests than students who had sub-par teachers for three straight years. Researchers in Massachusetts and Alabama have come to similar conclusions.

Drawing on the "value-added" research, William A. Galston, a professor in the School of Public Affairs at the University of Maryland, says that schools should give teachers the option of a lower salary with the potential for large bonuses if they can accelerate student performance. This bonus-based approach to teaching, he says, will encourage good teachers to take classes of low-achieving students because they offer a high potential for improvement.

And policy variations on Sanders' theme of measuring teacher ability by student improvement are being discussed and tested in states such as Tennessee and cities such as Denver. In Tennessee, the state's assessment system allows Sanders' "value-added" numbers to be incorporated into formal teacher evaluations. But parents never see the teachers' scores, and the system does not link those evaluations to rewards or sanctions.

In Denver last month, the school board and teachers' union forged a compromise setting up the first plan in the country to tie teachers' bonuses to their own students' achievement. The two-year pilot program offers teachers an annual bonus of up to $1,500 if, with their classes, they meet two specified achievement goals by the end of the year. That compromise exemplifies the pressure unions are feeling to recognize individual teacher performance. "We were bashed for wanting to keep really crappy teachers," said Andrea Giunta, the president of the Denver Classroom Teachers Association.

In North Carolina, schools have been rewarded and punished based on their test scores; individual teachers have not. But detailed measurement is on the way, said John Dornan, the executive director of the Public School Forum of North Carolina, a nonpartisan policy center. "All of the objections about using one test for evaluations—as we get more sophisticated with management of information, those arguments go out the window," he said. "We're suddenly getting into far more sophisticated territory than someone sitting at the back of the room with a checklist."

Proponents of judging teachers based on their students' scores argue that such an approach will further professionalize teaching. "There are very few types of pure output productions in the world. There are subjective judgments made of almost every job and every occupation in this world," said Sue Edwards, the president of the Denver school board. "I'm not afraid of moving in this direction, because I think it will strengthen public education and I think it will strengthen the support for public education."

But some education researchers, such as David Grissmer, who is a senior management scientist at RAND, a Santa Monica, Calif.–based public policy research organization, caution that many factors affect student scores. "In the typical American fashion, we usually go too far in this stuff," Grissmer said. "It's such an appealing concept that they're going to try to move in that direction . . . . We've got to be a little careful about creating a set of bad measures. I think we're on a slippery slope here." And Linda Darling-Hammond, the executive director of the National Commission on Teaching & America's Future, raised concerns about the incentives created by a student achievement–based evaluation. "When you reward teachers for student achievement, nobody wants to teach certain kids in certain communities," she said.

Feeling the pressure, some local teachers' unions are promoting their own answer to the accountability question—teachers judging teachers. They are slowly beginning to support "peer review," a system in which experienced teachers make extensive evaluations of new teachers and veteran teachers who are struggling in the classroom. They then make recommendations to help or, in extreme cases, to dismiss these teachers.

Tom Mooney, the president of the Cincinnati Federation of Teachers, cites his district's record over the 14-year history of the peer-review program. Of the 90 teachers sent to an "intervention" for a big professional development boost, one-third improved and two-thirds were removed from the classroom. Until this year, only a handful of local districts employed peer evaluation, but interest is growing. California this year launched the first statewide version. And New Jersey Gov. Christine Todd Whitman said that a chat with Mooney at the National Education Summit piqued her interest in the program.

"It seems to be reaching critical mass in the last few years," Mooney said of peer review. "I think it's partly the search for effective approaches to accountability that are not just crude and stupid, but are based in professional standards. . . . You need to have a standard, and you need to have a way of enforcing that standard that is credible." But Amy Wilkins, a principal partner at the Education Trust, an education research group, says that peer review fails to "take the obvious next step," to base evaluations on student achievement.

Kaplan, the Denver parent, said that the best way to restore parents' confidence in teachers is to have teachers evaluate one another. The evaluating teacher would factor in several assessment tools, including student achievement, the context within which the teacher is teaching, the background of the students, and the quality of the school administration. The catch, she says, is that the evaluators would have to be willing to expel the bad teachers from the system. "I do think there are a number of teachers who really shouldn't be teaching anymore," she said. "A lot of them are biding their time until retirement."

There may be ground for political compromise in Kaplan's value-added–peer-review hybrid. The National Education Association, which advocates peer review, is willing to listen. Sanders' research "contributes to the debate and the dialogue, and could contribute to the substance," said Chuck Williams, the NEA's director of teacher quality initiatives. "But it could not and should not be the silver bullet."

And some union leaders concede that measurement is inevitable. "When we get to the point, and we will, where we can disaggregate to isolate the impact of a teacher on students learning vis-à-vis other factors, then we can raise this question of rewards and consequences, but until then, it's irresponsible," said Adam Urbanski, a vice president of the American Federation of Teachers and an advocate of peer review.

The real pressure to find a compromise is likely to come from such parents as Kaplan, who will be better armed with information as states start issuing report cards and ending social promotion, the practice of passing children from one grade to the next even when they're not academically prepared. As states move to end social promotion, parental pressure to differentiate between good and bad teachers will grow, Dornan said. And these evaluations will be easier to do. "You're going to open up a whole other layer of scrutiny," Dornan said. "But this time, it will be focused on classrooms, not buildings, and classrooms will be a proxy for teachers."

And, as Kaplan and Sanders pointed out, public schools have plenty of dynamic teachers, but the problem is that teacher quality is so uneven. "All professions have bad eggs," Kaplan said. "This one just happens to affect our society more than most."

. . . .

Put Teachers to the Test

Diane Ravitch

This selection first appeared in *The Washington Post* on 25 February 1998. Diane Ravitch, a senior fellow at the Brookings Institution, is the author of *Left Back: A Century of Failed School Reforms* (Simon & Schuster, 2000).

Last summer, a suburban school district in New York advertised for 35 new teachers and received nearly 800 applications. District officials decided to narrow the pool by requiring applicants to take the

11th-grade state examination in English. Only about one-quarter of the would-be teachers answered 40 of the 50 multiple-choice questions correctly.

As Congress considers reauthorization of the Higher Education Act, teacher education has emerged as a major issue. Many states—and now President Clinton—are clamoring to reduce class size, but few are grappling with the most important questions: If we are raising standards for students, don't we also need to raise standards for teachers? Shouldn't state and local officials make sure that teachers know whatever they are supposed to teach students?

Almost every state claims that it is strengthening standards for students, but the states have been strangely silent when it comes to ensuring that teachers know what they are supposed to teach. Most instead certify anyone with the right combination of education courses, regardless of their command of the subject they expect to teach, and many states require future teachers to pass only a basic skills test.

Today, in some states it may be harder to graduate from high school than to become a certified teacher. Something is wrong with this picture.

Last summer the U.S. Department of Education reported that approximately one-third of the nation's public school teachers of academic subjects in middle school and high school were teaching "out of field," which means that they had earned neither an undergraduate major nor a minor in their main teaching field.

Fully 39.5 percent of science teachers had not studied science as a major or minor; 34 percent of mathematics teachers and 25 percent of English teachers were similarly teaching "out of field." The problem of unqualified teachers was particularly acute in schools where 40 percent or more of the students were from low-income homes; in these schools, nearly half the teaching staff was teaching "out of field."

Many states now routinely certify people who do not know what they are supposed to teach. No one should get a license to teach science, reading, mathematics, or anything else unless he or she has demonstrated a knowledge of what students are expected to learn.

A majority of the nation's teachers majored in education rather than an academic subject. This is troubling, even though most of those who majored in education are elementary teachers. There is a widely accepted notion that people who teach little children don't need to know much other than pedagogical methods and child psychology; that is wrong. Teachers of little children need to be well educated and should love learning as much as they love children. Yes, even elementary school teachers should have an academic major.

The field of history has the largest percentage of unqualified teachers. The Department of Education found that 55 percent of history teachers are "out of field," and that 43 percent of high school students are studying history with a teacher who did not earn either a major or minor in history. This may explain why nearly 60 percent of our 17-year-olds scored "below basic" (the lowest possible rating) on the most recent test of U.S. history administered by the federally funded National Assessment of Educational Progress. Only one out of every five teachers of social studies has either a major or minor in history. Is it any wonder that today's children have no idea when the Civil War occurred, what Reconstruction was, what happened during the progressive era, who F.D.R. was, what the Brown decision decided, or what Stalin did? Many of their teachers don't know those things either.

There are many conditions over which school officials have no control, but they have complete control over who is allowed to teach. Why should anyone be certified to teach science or history who doesn't know what he or she is expected to teach the children?

Many state officials say that they have an abundance of people who want to teach and that this is actually an excellent time to raise standards. For career-changers with a wealth of experience in business or the military, however, obsolete certification requirements get in the way. Instead of requiring irrelevant education courses, states should examine prospective teachers for their knowledge of their academic field and then give them a chance to work in the schools as apprentice teachers.

As Congress ponders ways to improve the teaching profession, it should consider incentives for colleges of liberal arts to collaborate with schools of education in preparing future teachers. Representatives from both parts of the same campus should sit down together, study state academic standards, and figure out how to prepare teachers who know both their subject and how to teach it well. Teachers need a strong academic preparation as well as practical classroom experience to qualify for one of the toughest jobs in America.

Every classroom should have a well-educated, knowledgeable teacher. We are far from that goal today. Congress can address this problem by focusing on the quality, not quantity, of the nation's teaching corps.

Top-Notch Teachers Are Key to Better Schools

Joanne Jacobs

This selection first appeared in the *San Jose Mercury News* on 3 December 1998. Joanne Jacobs, formerly a columnist for the *San Jose Mercury News*, is currently working on a book about a Palo Alto charter school.

The student came from a low-income Mexican immigrant family. She grew up in a Los Angeles barrio.

"How did you get to UC–Santa Barbara?" her roommate asked.

"It was my third-grade teacher, Mrs. Menzer," she replied. Then she wrote a letter of thanks to Diana Menzer.

The student will graduate in June with a degree in Spanish. She's not sure about a career, except that teaching is out. She doesn't have it in her to be a teacher, the letter said.

Menzer will retire at the end of the year. Who will replace her?

California schools already can't find enough qualified people to teach reading in elementary classrooms of 20 students, or to teach math, chemistry, and physics to middle and high school students. With rising enrollments and retirements, we'll need 250,000 new teachers in the next 10 years.

Furthermore, teachers will need to know more and do more than ever before to help students meet the state's demanding new academic standards. So we need smart, educated teachers.

"The largest predictor of student achievement is teacher expertise and qualifications," says Stanford Education Professor Linda Darling-Hammond, who chairs the National Commission on Teaching and America's Future. "It's not rocket science. What the teacher knows and can do has an effect on what the student will be able to learn."

Researchers have looked at scores on licensing exams, units of teacher training completed, and whether the teacher has a bachelor's or master's degree in the field taught. Consistently, teachers with more education in their subject, and in how to teach, have students with higher achievement scores.

In short, teachers can't teach what they don't know. And they can't teach what they do know until they've learned how to manage a classroom, motivate students, and break down concepts so students with limited English, learning problems, and poor preparation can understand.

Educating teachers—both in subject matter and in teaching strategies—is "the single most effective use of an additional dollar," Darling-Hammond says, citing research results. It's far more effective than reducing class size.

So what are California's leaders doing? To lengthen the school year by a few days, the Legislature cut time for teacher training.

At the same time, California is pouring money into reducing class sizes in kindergarten through third grade, increasing the demand for elementary teachers, and making it even harder for urban schools to find qualified teachers.

Enthusiasts for class-size reduction point to Tennessee, where lowering class size to 15 raised achievement. But there was no teacher shortage in Tennessee, no need to compromise on teacher quality to put an adult in every classroom.

"Good teachers produce good students" is the motto of the newly created San Francisco–based Endowment for Excellence in Education (e-mail: gates2excellence@hotmail.com).

Director Shoumen Datta envisions offering stipends to math and science graduates to raise entry-level teaching pay to $36,000 for a bachelor's degree, $40,000 for a master's. The endowment also would pay to send teachers who never studied what they're teaching back to college to strengthen their understanding of the subject matter.

But, so far, the corporate donations aren't flowing in.

Datta was a university scientist and teacher before working in San Francisco Unified as special assistant to the superintendent. He chaired the task force on math and science education for the National Information Technology Workforce Convocation, and formed Associated Scientists, with Nobel laureate Glenn Seaborg, to develop state science standards.

Knowing how challenging the new standards are, Datta is especially worried about elementary teachers' science mastery. Teaching the parts of a flower and the life cycle of the butterfly won't cut it anymore.

Half of California's math and physical science teachers didn't major or minor in the subject. How can schools hire college graduates with math and science degrees when the booming high-tech economy is offering more money, more recognition, more control over their work? After all, schools don't give stock options.

Money isn't the primary issue, says Datta. He lured talented young scientists into teaching in San Francisco. But frustration with bureaucracy drove them out of the classroom and into high-tech industry.

More important than raising teacher pay is raising teachers' ability to be effective, says Darling-Hammond. "The challenge is to create school environments where teachers can do the job well."

The good news is that Gray Davis, who longs to be California's education governor, has named a former teacher, Gary Hart, as his chief education adviser. After serving in the Legislature, where he chaired the Senate Education Committee, Hart became co-director of the California State University Institute for Education Reform, which has focused on ways to recruit, train, retain, and retrain good teachers.

Hart understands that teacher quality is job one for California schools. He will back credentialing reforms, funding for on-the-job help for new teachers, intensive training for experienced teachers.

The hardest challenge will be to make public schools places where the best and brightest can put their talents to use.

School Unions Shortchange Students

La Rae G. Munk

This selection first appeared in the *Michigan Education Report*'s Spring 1999 edition. La Rae Munk is director of legal services for the Association of American Educators. As an attorney, she has represented both teacher unions and private sector management in collective bargaining negotiations. She is author of the study *Collective Bargaining: Bringing Education to the Table*, published by the Mackinac Center for Public Policy.

"When school children start paying union dues, that's when I'll start representing the interests of school children." These candid words attributed to the late Al Shanker, longtime president of the American Federation of Teachers, remind us of an important but often-forgotten fact: School employee unions exist first and foremost to bargain wages, hours, and terms and conditions of employment for their members, and there is nothing wrong with that. But the education of children is, by definition, a secondary consideration for union officials.

It is teachers and school boards, not unions, who are responsible for students' educations. Unfortunately, too many collective bargaining agreements between school districts and unions allow union interests to ignore, or even conflict with, what's best for students. Let's look at just three examples that illustrate the point.

Most union contracts discourage teachers from excelling in the classroom by paying all teachers according to a single salary "schedule." The single pay schedule does not distinguish between mediocre or ineffective teaching and the extra effort put in by the many dedicated educators who often sacrifice their personal time to help struggling students. Teachers are paid the same regardless of their performance, so there is no financial incentive for them to work to be their best. As one former school administrator recently wrote in *Education Week*, "Only the altruism of the best teachers prevents the public school system from collapsing."

Though most teachers do not rank salary as their highest priority, the single pay schedule does hurt morale, makes teachers feel unappreciated, and prevents districts from attracting and retaining the best educators, which in turn hurts the quality of students' education. Unions should drop their opposition to the many school boards who want to reward their best teachers with performance-based salaries but are prevented from doing so by shortsighted mandatory collective bargaining agreements.

At the same time that good teachers are being slighted, bad teachers' jobs and benefits are being protected by unions and union contracts even to the point of absurdity. One of the most outrageous examples of this involved a tenured gym teacher from Ann Arbor, who taught until 1980, when five of his female students testified that he had sexually molested them. The teacher was fired, challenged his dismissal, and his union, the Michigan Education Association (MEA), took up the case. In 1984, while the case was still pending, the former teacher got into a violent argument with his wife and murdered her on their front lawn with an axe. The MEA continued to press the case and in 1993, after 13 years of litigation, won $200,000 in back pay for the convicted murderer (for more information on this and other cases, see www.mackinac.org/mea/).

School districts fearing such costly and unreasonable legal action from unions are often reluctant to dismiss unqualified teachers from the classroom, jeopardizing students' educations and even their safety. Unions should end practices that interfere with administrators who seek to discharge clearly unqualified employees and instead make their top priorities teacher training and development.

Finally, unions often propose contract language to reduce the number of students in each classroom as a way to improve educational performance. They argue that smaller classes will allow teachers to give each student more personal attention, helping to boost learning and test scores. While studies comparing larger and smaller classes are inconclusive about the efficacy of this approach, one thing is clear: The class size issue is easily exploited by some unions to gain greater pay for their members, or even to gain more dues-paying members.

Smaller class sizes are more expensive because districts must hire and pay more teachers to reduce student-to-teacher ratios. But unions do not mind if teachers handle larger classes provided they can bargain for more money for the teachers. For example, the Caro school district's collective bargaining agreement requires that a teacher be paid $4 extra per day for every student above the contractually set maximum class size. So a class with two students over the union-negotiated maximum would net its teacher an additional $176 during the typical month.

How does this hurt education? Professor Caroline Hoxby explained it this way in her 1996 study of compulsory unionism and public school employees: "Teachers unions increase school inputs [costs] but reduce productivity sufficiently to have a negative overall effect on student performance." In other words, the more money that is spent on union demands (in the form of either employee benefits or bureaucratic work rules), the less there is available for scholastic and educational materials for students.

A union's primary duty is to its members (as it should be), but a school district's obligation is to voters, taxpayers, parents, and students. When school employee unions' interests outweigh the responsibilities of school boards during the bargaining process, it is local schoolchildren who often get shortchanged.

EDUCATIONALLY DISADVANTAGED

A Taboo Erodes

Abigail Thernstrom

This selection first appeared in the *National Review* on 20 December 1999. Abigail Thernstrom is a senior fellow at the Manhattan Institute and co-author, with Stephan Thernstrom, of *America in Black and White: One Nation, Indivisible* (1999).

Perk up, everyone. It's true that Jesse Jackson is doing his usual number in Decatur, Illinois. And the Justice Department is threatening to sue Massachusetts over its rigorous and carefully designed statewide tests because many black and Hispanic students do poorly on them. And yes, Al Gore and Bill Bradley both have had kissy-face meetings with the Rev. Al Sharpton. But in fact, it's not just the same old racial scene anymore. Not only is the status of blacks steadily improving; the winds of freedom are now blowing through public discourse on race-related questions.

The shift is subtle, and easy to miss. But think about a phrase George W. Bush has used in two education speeches: "the soft bigotry of low expectations." The cruel (and racially indifferent) dumbing down of American educational standards in the name of racial sensitivity is an issue a handful of conservatives have long raised, and they paid a heavy price for doing so. But times have changed. The word is now out: Black and Hispanic kids do not know enough when they graduate from high school. They have been passed along from grade to grade by schools that pursue a callous, softly bigoted self-esteem strategy.

In its 1978 Bakke decision, the Supreme Court ruled that colleges and universities may consider race only as one of many factors in admissions decisions. No selective institution of higher education paid the slightest attention. Behind soundproof doors, race-driven admissions became the norm. The subterfuge worked for a while, but it couldn't last. Once the facts were exposed, the talk began, and it focused on the core problem: the tiny pool of black and Hispanic high school seniors with strong SAT scores and high grades who could meet the regular admissions criteria at selective schools.

Frank talk, once started, is hard to stifle. It takes on a life of its own. The new intellectual freedom is evident in *The Black-White Test Score Gap*, an important Brookings Institution volume edited by Christopher Jencks and Meredith Phillips. The liberal credentials of Jencks and Phillips are in perfect order, but their voices (and those of their contributors) break with traditional liberal orthodoxy.

For instance, they assert unequivocally that it is lack of knowledge—not white racism—that makes for unequal earnings. They report that among 31- to 36-year-old men with cognitive skills above the 50th percentile on the well-respected Armed Services Vocational Aptitude Battery test, the difference between black and white earnings is a mere 4 percentage points. College graduation rates tell a similar story: Blacks are more likely to earn a college diploma than whites with the same 12th-grade test scores.

Black poverty, racial segregation, and inadequate funding for predominantly black schools are standard items on the list of liberal explanations for black underachievement. Jencks and Phillips dismiss them all. Income inequality, they say, plays a very small role in black test performance; in fact, eliminating black-white income disparities would make almost no difference in the scores of young black children on a basic vocabulary test. Nor does a school's racial mix matter after the sixth grade; it seems to affect reading scores only in the early years, and math scores not at all.

The racial identity of the children in a district does not affect funding, the number of teachers per student, the teachers' credentials, or their pay. Schools that are mostly black, however, have teachers with lower test scores—in part, Jencks and Phillips forthrightly acknowledge, because black schools have more black teachers.

On the other hand, schools are less important than we sometimes think. According to Jencks and Phillips, parents count more:

> Changes in parenting practices might do more to reduce the black-white test score gap than changes in parents' educational attainment or income. . . . Cognitive disparities between black and white preschool children are currently so large that it is hard to imagine how schools alone could eliminate them. . . . Changing the way parents deal with their children may be the single most important thing we can do to improve children's cognitive skills.

This is a tough and startling message. More than three decades after the publication of *The Negro Family: The Case for National Action*, the Moynihan report that was so terribly distorted by civil-rights spokesmen, it is finally okay to raise the subject of black family culture. Jencks and Phillips suggest social scientists take a close look at: "the way family members and friends interact with one another and the outside world"; "how much parents talk to their children, deal with their children's questions, how they react when their child learns or fails to learn something"; and "cultural and psychological differences." In other words, focus on what's going on in African-American homes. Economic and educational resources are far less important.

Jencks and Phillips might be dismissed as members of a tiny sect called "scholars with integrity." But they have unexpected—and important—company: the ever-cautious College Board. In January 1997, it convened a "National Task Force on Minority High Achievement." Among its members were Raul Yzaguirre, president of the National Council of La Raza, and Edmund W. Gordon, the principal author of the dreadful New York State 1991 curriculum guide, *One Nation, Many Peoples: A Declaration of Cultural Interdependence*, which prompted a ringing dissent from Arthur Schlesinger, Jr.

The group contained no conservative voices at all, so its recently released report, not surprisingly, contains much predictable stuff. For example, it says that the end of racial preferences in some states has harmed the efforts of colleges "to promote the academic development" of minorities; that we're not spending enough on urban schools; and that racial and ethnic discrimination is holding back minority students academically. It indulges in the usual psychobabble about low black self-esteem and feelings of alienation from school.

But the task force also breaks important new ground. The report links black and Hispanic wage levels to poor academic performance, and uses National Assessment of Educational Progress (NAEP) statistics to make clear just how inadequately non-Asian minorities are doing. The document points out that the NAEP results display the same patterns as SAT scores, which correlate well with grades and class rank.

The task force describes the problem of underachievement as emerging "very early" and minces no words about the fact that black and Hispanic kids "at virtually all socioeconomic levels do not perform nearly as well on standardized tests as their White and Asian counterparts." In fact, the racial gap in academic achievement is widest among middle-class students from educated families. The scores of black and white youngsters whose parents lack even a high school degree are more alike.

Proponents of preferential admissions often argue that underachieving black and Hispanic students will catch up in college. But the College Board report admits that the best predictor of academic performance is prior academic performance. Do well in high school, and success in college follows—although black students do worse than their SATs suggest they should. The report refers to the "cultural attributes of home, community, and school," and talks at length about the attitudes toward school and hard work that Asian parents transmit to their children.

There is obviously much overlap between the Jencks and Phillips volume and the College Board report. Both are moving beyond racial preferences as a panacea. In fact, the task force refers to "affirmative development"—a term that implies the need for multifaceted and sustained action to address a problem. No quick fixes, which depend on fudging inconvenient facts. The College Board hasn't given up on race-based programs; it explicitly embraces them. But implicit in the report is an acknowledgment that in many public institutions of higher education, preferences may not survive; and that, in any case, after 30 years of using preferences, black students are appallingly behind whites and Asians in basic, absolutely essential academic skills.

The College Board is no profile in political courage; it would not have issued this report had it not felt safe in doing so. This report— together with the Bush speech, Jencks and Phillips, and other recent writings and statements—signals a change in the framework of the race debate, at least when it comes to education, the nation's most important race-related issue. Tom Daschle can call the GOP "anti-minority"; Democrats can play the race card from now until November 2000 and beyond; but they cannot stop the old rhetorical order from continuing to unravel.

Change the discourse, and the old policies themselves are placed in jeopardy. The whole structure of going-nowhere race-conscious policies—whose proponents have been satisfied with good intentions but few results—may be crumbling. If so, we are seeing the first steps towards honestly and seriously addressing the undeniable problem of ongoing racial inequality. Better late than never.

· ·

Loco, Completamente Loco

The Many Failures of "Bilingual Education"

Glenn Garvin

This selection first appeared in *Reason* Magazine's January 1998 edition. Glenn Garvin is a contributor editor for *Reason* Magazine and author of the *Reason* articles "No Fruits, No Shirts, No Service" (April 1995) and "Bringing the Border War Home" (October 1995), which were finalists for the National Magazine Award.

Rosa Torres had been dreading this call. Her daughter Angelica's first-grade teacher wanted to come over and talk. The teacher didn't say what she wanted to discuss, but Rosa knew. There had been a program on television, and the unfamiliar English words had rung in her head like a fire alarm: learning disorder. Surely that was what little Angelica had.

Every afternoon when she came home from school, Rosa asked the same question: What did you do in school today? And every day Angelica gave the same answer: Nothing. She seemed bored, listless, maybe even—though Rosa didn't see how it was possible for a six-year-old—depressed.

Rosa wondered how a child developed a learning disorder. Certainly there had been no sign of it a couple of years before, when Angelica started preschool at the YMCA. Rosa had been so worried, sending her little girl off without a word of English to spend a day among the American children. But everything had worked out just fine. Angelica rolled through there like a snowball, picking up more and more English every day. Soon she spoke it much better than Rosa, and after a while she spoke it much better than Spanish.

Of course, that wasn't surprising. After all, Angelica was an American, born just a few miles down the freeway from their home in Redwood City, a scruffy working-class town 30 miles south of San Francisco. It was her parents Rosa and Carlos who were the immigrants. They left Cuzco, the ancient Inca city in central Peru, with plans to study in America, learn English, get college degrees, live the good life.

Like most immigrants, they found out it wouldn't be all so easy as that—American landlords and shopkeepers wanted to be paid in cash, not dreams. Classes gave way to jobs, the kind you get when you can't speak English. Carlos was baking pizzas for a little more than minimum wage, Rosa babysitting for a little less. She spent her days with the children massaging the little bit of English she'd picked up in a couple of community college classes; the three- and four-year-olds were patient professors, never complaining about her fractured sentences, content to point at the big white thing in the kitchen and repeat the word refrigerator a hundred times if that was what it took for Rosa to get it. For adult company, she watched television while they napped, puzzling over Oprah's vocabulary as much as her ethos, smiling in secret delight whenever she got one of Regis and Kathie Lee's jokes.

The life, if not exactly the one she'd dreamed, wasn't a bad one. No one was sick, no one went to bed hungry. There was a roof over their heads. Little by little, they were adjusting to America. But now there was this trouble with Angelica. Apprehensively, Rosa waited, tried to steel herself to hearing the words *learning disorder* not from a disembodied voice on TV but from the teacher's lips; not affixed to some unfortunate, not-quite-real children from another part of the planet, but to her own daughter, right here, right now.

The teacher turned out to be a Japanese lady (well, American, really; Rosa had to keep reminding herself how it worked here) with a manner that was at once kindly and intense. "I think you need to go talk to the principal at the school about Angelica," she said after they settled in. "What about her?" Rosa said, stomach churning, knowing the answer, dreading it.

"I think you need to get her into an English-speaking classroom," the teacher replied. "She understands English perfectly. And she doesn't like taking lessons in Spanish. I think it's really holding her back. It's damaging her."

"What do you mean, Spanish?" Rosa asked, silently cursing Oprah and Kathie Lee, who had obviously failed her, because this teacher wasn't making any sense.

"Spanish, that's what we're teaching her in," the teacher said. "Didn't anyone tell you? She's in a bilingual education program. Just go tell the principal she speaks English, and you want her out." When the teacher left, Rosa still found it hard to believe the whole conversation hadn't been some horrendous translation glitch. The teacher had explained that Angelica, because she was Hispanic, had been swept into a class full of immigrant children from Mexico and El Salvador who spoke little or no English. OK, Rosa could understand how that might have happened. But why were the children being taught Spanish instead of English? How were they ever going to learn English if the school didn't teach it to them?

Nonetheless, a conversation with Angelica confirmed it. All day long, her teacher spoke Spanish. The books were in Spanish. Even the posters on the classroom wall were in Spanish.

Only for a few minutes in the afternoon did the language switch to English. "And then we just learn some baby words like *bread* or *paper*," Angelica complained. Summoning the most malevolent curse in her six-year-old vocabulary, she cried: "*It's dumb!*" Finally Rosa understood her daughter's moody shuffling of the past few months.

The solution, unfortunately, was not as simple as the teacher promised. When Rosa went in to see the school administrators a few days later, her request to transfer Angelica into an English-speaking class met with withering disapproval. "That's not in your daughter's best interests," one of the school officials said. They flashed incomprehensible charts around, used a lot of language Rosa didn't understand, but the message came through loud and clear: *We know better, we're the teachers.*

Rosa was doubtful. The idea that kids would learn English by being taught in Spanish all day seemed, well, kind of nuts—especially for Angelica, whose best language was English. But . . . but . . . who was she to question them? An immigrant babysitter lady who spent her days in pathetic conversations with four-year-olds about who was smarter, Big Bird or the Cookie Monster? When Rosa left the office, her daughter was still enrolled in the Spanish class.

Each morning for the next two years, she watched Angelica mope off to a school that bored her nearly to tears. Each afternoon, when she checked the girl's homework, it was in Spanish. Rosa began to wonder why the program was called "bilingual." The principal had promised Rosa that the amount of English in the lessons would increase, but there was no sign of that happening.

And it never did. It wasn't until the family moved 20 miles south to Cupertino, a Silicon Valley suburb on the edge of San Jose, that Angelica got any English education. Then she had to have a lot of it. "Your daughter isn't reading anywhere near a third-grade level," the teacher told Rosa. "And she's behind in math and science, too." But Cupertino (fortunately, as far as Rosa was concerned) had no bilingual program. So Angelica stayed in the class, though all year she had to take special after-school English lessons with newly arrived Chinese immigrant children.

This is what bilingual education did for my daughter, Rosa thought bitterly. It stole two years out of her life.

It was a hard fight, but Angelica won them back. Nobody in the house likes to recall that ugly year she spent in the third grade, but when it was over, she had caught up to the other kids. And as the years passed, her mother and father started catching up, too, to those immigrant dreams that, for a time, had faded into the distance. They became U.S. citizens. Carlos went to school, got a job as a graphic designer. Rosa stopped babysitting and started cleaning houses, which paid better. Her English blossomed. She began taking accounting courses at a community college. Two more babies arrived: Nathan and Joshua.

Nathan entered school without incident. But in 1996, when Joshua was ready for the first grade, school administrators called Rosa. They were starting this new bilingual program, and . . .

As they talked, Rosa flashed back to that conversation nine years before, when a shy, frightened babysitter with a Peruvian passport let a bunch of school administrators overrule her common sense. She recalled the price her daughter paid. And she said: "No way."

Rosa Torres isn't alone. Bilingual education was born 30 years ago from a good-hearted but vague impulse by Congress to help Spanish speakers learn English. Instead, it has become a multi-billion-dollar hog trough that feeds arrogant education bureaucrats and militant Hispanic separatists. And now poor immigrant parents increasingly see it as the wall around a linguistic ghetto from which their children must escape if they want to be anything more than maids or dishwashers. Like Rosa Torres, they are starting to say "no way":

- At 9th Street Elementary School in Los Angeles, located on the edge of the city's garment district, parents held about 90 children out of class for two weeks to force the school to start teaching English. "The only time they spoke English at the school was during lunch and recess," said Luisa Hernandez, a sweatshop worker from Mexico whose nine-year-old daughter Yanira attends the school. "I want my daughter to learn English. All the exams for things like lawyers and doctors are in English. Without English, she would have to take a job like mine."

- One hundred fifty Hispanic families in Brooklyn's Bushwick neighborhood sued the state of New York to force the release of their children from a bilingual program. Ada Jimenez, one of the plaintiffs, said her grandson spoke only English when he entered the Bushwick school system. "We were told that because my grandson has a Spanish last name, he should remain in bilingual classes," she said. Result: He flunked kindergarten. "He is now in seventh grade and cannot read in either English or Spanish," Jimenez said in an affidavit for the lawsuit.

Denver is considering a change that would limit students to three years in its bilingual program instead of the six that many of them have been staying. Leading the charge is school board member Rita Montero, who originally championed bilingual education—until her own son was enrolled. "The kids were doing work way below the regular grade level," she said. "I was furious." She yanked him from the program and enrolled him in another school across town: "I had to think, what is more important to me? To keep my child in a program where perhaps he'll learn some Spanish and that'll make me happy? Or do I want my child to be able to come out of public education with the ability to compete for scholarships, to be able to go to the college of his choice?"

An October 1997 poll by the *Los Angeles Times* showed that California voters favored a proposed ballot measure to limit bilingual education by an astonishing 4–1 margin. The support was greatest among Hispanics: 84 percent. "Wake up call for *los Maestros* . . . If you are into Bilingual Ed. your days are numbered," the bilingual paper San Diego *La Prensa* warned teachers. "We, *los Chicanos*, are responsible for putting you in . . . and you betrayed us. Bilingual Ed. has been turned into a full employment program for your own agenda that has nothing to do with our kids . . . that's why 84% of *la gente en* Los Angeles voted against you . . . YOU BLEW THE PROGRAM."

In Los Lunas, New Mexico, high school students walked out to protest the lack of English tutoring. In Dearborn, Michigan, the school board junked a proposal for $5 million in federal money to begin a bilingual program after parents complained. In Princeton, New Jersey, immigrant parents raised so much hell about rules that made it difficult to get their children out of bilingual programs that the state legislature stepped in to change them.

Though usually poorly organized and often relatively powerless—they often aren't U.S. citizens and sometimes aren't even legal residents—the parents are starting to make themselves heard. Michigan has adopted reforms in its bilingual programs. Bethlehem, Pennsylvania, did away with its bilingual program altogether. So did Orange County and three smaller school districts in California. In November, when Orange County voters were asked what they thought of the change, a crushing 86 percent approved.

An even bigger blow may be on the way in California, where voters in 1998 will consider a ballot initiative making bilingual education optional. Under the "English for the Children" initiative, non–English-speaking children would normally be placed in a short-term "structured immersion" program; parents could, however, apply for a waiver to have their children instead placed or kept in a bilingual or English-only program. If it wins the sweeping victory that current polls predict, the proposition is bound to turn bilingual education into a hot-button issue around the rest of the country—just as previous California ballot initiatives on property taxes and affirmative action have started dominoes tumbling. At press time, it was unknown whether the initiative would be on the ballot in June or November.

The proposition is the brainchild of Silicon Valley millionaire Ron Unz, who got the idea from reading newspaper stories about the boycott of 9th Street Elementary in Los Angeles. Unz had long been skeptical about bilingual education, but it was only after speaking with some of the 9th Street Elementary parents that he realized how deep the discontent ran in California's Hispanic community.

"Immigrant parents always understood how damaging this was to their children," he says, "but it was hard for them to make their voices heard." Unz, a one-time Republican gubernatorial candidate, had the political and financial clout to turn up the volume. And as a longtime supporter of immigration—he was one of a tiny handful of Republican politicians to publicly oppose California's anti-immigrant Proposition 187 three years ago—he was immune to the inevitable charges of racism from bilingual advocates. Assembling a campaign around a nucleus of anti-bilingual Hispanic teachers (including Jaime Escalante, the math teacher whose success in East Los Angeles inspired the film *Stand and Deliver*), Unz has turned bilingual education into California's top political issue.

But the bilingual forces won't yield without a fight, certainly not to mere parents. When those buttinsky parents in Princeton were demanding the right to put their kids in English-speaking classrooms, Joseph Ramos, the co-chairman of the New Jersey Bilingual Council, advised the school board to tell them to mind their own business. "Why would we require parents unfamiliar with our educational system to make such monumental decisions," he asked, "when we as bilingual educators . . . are trained to make those decisions?" *We know better, we're the teachers.*

Some years ago, a newspaper sent me to interview S.I. Hayakawa, by then a retired senator from California. Hayakawa was legendarily combative: Asked once during a campaign stop what he thought about a local referendum on legalizing greyhound tracks, he snapped: "I'm running for the U.S. Senate. I don't give a good goddamn about dog racing." When I spoke with him, he had recently lashed out at bilingual education. It seemed paradoxical, to say the very least: Hayakawa was a native of Canada whose parents were born in Japan; he grew up speaking Japanese. He had authored a widely used book on linguistics. "Senator," I began the interview, "why are you against people learning to speak two languages?" He looked at me as though I were daft. "Who said anything about that?" he demanded. "Only an idiot would be against speaking two languages. I'm against *bilingual education.*"

That's still the biggest misconception among people who've never had a personal brush with bilingual education. It is *not* a program where two sets of children learn one another's language at the same time. That's called dual, or two-way, immersion. Only a few well-heeled school districts can afford to offer it, always as an elective, and the only complaint about it is that there usually aren't enough slots to go around. Another thing bilingual education is not is a program conducted mostly in English, where the teacher occasionally translates a particularly difficult concept, or offers extra language help to children with limited English skills. Known variously as English as a Second Language, sheltered English, or structured English *immersion*, these are all wrinkles in a technique that educators call immersion, because the students are expected to wade into English quickly.

As Hayakawa explained to me that day, when educators use the term *bilingual education*, it's shorthand for "transitional bilingual education," which is the other major technique for teaching languages. TBE, as it is often called, was originally structured around the idea that students would take the main curriculum in their native language while they learned English, so that they wouldn't fall behind in other subjects. But over the past two decades or so, most school districts have reshaped their TBE programs to reflect the ideas of the so-called "facilitation" theorists of language education. The facilitation theorists believe that children cannot effectively learn a second language until they are fully literate in the first one, a process that can take four to seven years. (A new study from TBE advocates at the University of California at Riverside ups the ante to 10 years.)

During that time, a TBE student is supposed to be taught almost entirely in his native language, by a teacher fluent in that language, using books and films and tapes in that language. Gradually increasing bits of English are worked into the mix. At some point—bingo!—the child hits his "threshold" in the first language. Now he's ready to suck up English like a human vacuum cleaner.

The idea that a kid will learn English by being taught in Spanish does not usually strike people outside the education field as very plausible—"*loco, completamente loco*" was the reaction of Luisa Hernandez when the principal at 9th Street Elementary in Los Angeles explained it to her—but the theory is so inculcated in many teachers that they rarely question it. When they do, it can be a shattering experience. Rosalie Pedalino Porter, director of the Research in English Acquisition and Development Institute, taught Spanish bilingual classes in kindergarten and elementary school for five years in Springfield, Massachusetts. As a six-year-old kid right off the boat from Sicily, Porter had done just fine without TBE, but education school had filled her with missionary zeal for the theory. She vividly remembers the day that she began to wonder if the bilingual god had failed.

It was a lesson in colors. "*Juan, que color es este?*" Porter asked one little boy, waving a box in her hand.

"Green," he replied.

"*Verde,*" she corrected with the Spanish word.

"Green," Juan repeated.

"*Verde,*" Porter corrected him again.

"Green," Juan answered again.

What in the hell am I doing? Porter wondered to herself. *Why am I telling him not to speak English?* Pretty soon, once her classroom door was closed, Porter was giving lessons in English. "I wasn't the only one, either," she says.

It seems certain that, on the day in 1967 that he introduced the first piece of bilingual-education legislation, Ralph Yarborough had no idea his handiwork would one day lead to the concept of English teacher as guerrilla warrior. Yarborough was a liberal senator from Texas who was disturbed about the high dropout rate among Mexican Americans and Puerto Ricans, which by some accounts ran as high as 40 percent. Yarborough asked for a paltry $7.5 million to set up some programs "not to stamp out the mother tongue and not to try to make their mother tongue the dominant language, but just to try to make those children fully literate in English."

In those twilight days of the Great Society, the Bilingual Education Amendment passed easily, triggering no alarms. Yarborough always said he didn't know and didn't much care what method was used to teach the kids. The concept of TBE didn't exist, and it would be another decade before facilitation theory came slithering out of the primordial linguistic ooze.

Yet, in retrospect, the warning signs were there. Hispanic activists flocked to testify for the bill, and very few of them said anything about learning English. Instead, they argued that the high dropout rate was due to the fact that Hispanic kids had low self-esteem because they weren't being taught in their native language ("or their parents' native language," as NYU historian Diane Ravitch acidly noted later).

And one witness, after suggesting that children might get some of their lessons in Spanish, admitted: "The Spanish-speaking parent is going to be opposed to this in many cases. Just last night at a little barbecue, we were talking about this bill . . . and one fellow said, 'Well, my wife doesn't want any of this for her children.' I should explain that this was a group of—all of us were Spanish-speaking, and we were speaking Spanish at the time. . . . These people were afraid of the bill or what it might do because they felt it would slow their children down in learning English. I want to say to them that there is nothing to fear."

But there was. Militant Chicano activists immediately began demanding that the money from Yarborough's bill bankroll Spanish-language instruction. Within three years, what was then the U.S. Department of Health, Education, and Welfare was issuing guidelines making bilingual programs compulsory for school districts. In 1974, the Supreme Court ruled in *Lau v. Nichols* that non–English-speaking children (in this case, a Chinese student in San Francisco) had the right to special language programs. The next year HEW said that meant bilingual programs, period—and not just for kids who couldn't speak English. Now bilingual education was expanded to include any child from a home where English wasn't the primary language. Even a kid who spoke like an Oxford don was headed for bilingual classes if his parents preferred Spanish or Chinese. By 1980, HEW had bludgeoned 500 school districts nationwide into creating bilingual programs, with more on the way.

All this had happened without a scrap of evidence that bilingual education worked at all, much less that it was the best way to teach language. Then, in the late 1970s, facilitation theory was born. Its foundation was a 1976 study of two groups of children who migrated from Finland to Sweden, one before entering the third grade, one after. The study found that the children who emigrated after the third grade—whose Finnish language skills would presumably be more developed—performed better in Swedish than the children who came earlier.

But there are two major problems with the study. One is that its statistics have come under ferocious attack from other researchers. The second is that the study neglected to mention that Swedish is the second official language of Finland and is taught in Finnish schools beginning in the third grade. So the older students had already been studying their "new" language when they arrived in Sweden, in some cases for several years.

"I visited Finland a few years ago and talked to linguists there, and nobody could believe we take that study seriously in the United States," says Rosalie Pedalino Porter. "They thought it was comical—the study has been discredited there for years."

No matter. Here, it gave rise to facilitation theory, which in turn gave a patina of intellectual respectability not only to bilingual education but to gringo bashing. The writings of Canadian linguist Jim Cummins, one of the big academic guns of facilitation theory, are studded with denunciations of "coercive relations of power" created by a "curriculum that reflects only the experience and values of white middle-class English-speaking students." If you doubt him, you surely are among the ranks of the "intellectual xenophobes" or "cultural hegemonists."

What Cummins and other TBE advocates don't like to admit is that they turn a blind eye to a multitude of acts of intellectual xenophobia and cultural hegemony *every day* in schools with bilingual curriculums. Here's one of the dirty little secrets of TBE: It's just for Spanish speakers. "When you talk about bilingual education, people will get absolutely hysterical over how kids will be cognitively deprived if they're not taught in their native tongue," says Christine Rossell, a political science professor at Boston University who has observed hundreds of classrooms in her research on bilingual education. "And yet, thousands and thousands of children are not taught in their native tongue every day, and no one cares. Polish kids don't get taught in their native tongue. Vietnamese kids don't get taught in their native tongue. Russian kids don't, and Greek kids don't. Even though all these principles of bilingual education are supposedly universal, bilingual education is basically just Spanish, and no one seems to notice. I figure it's some kind of mass delusion. That's the only way you can explain it."

There are some true TBE classes in other languages. More often, though, a class labeled TBE in anything but Spanish will include at most a token nod to the native language. Doug Lasken, who teaches at Ramona Elementary School in Los Angeles, for a time presided over what was supposedly a TBE class for second- and third-grade Armenian-speaking children. "I certainly don't speak a word of Armenian, and never told anyone I did," Lasken remembers. "It was mysterious. I wondered what I was doing there sometimes. But it was a fun class, with great kids, and we spoke English. They had learned it all by themselves, without any special help at all." About the only hint of TBE in the classroom was some battered turn-of-the-century Armenian textbooks that were rarely opened.

One reason other languages have been discreetly pitched overboard is that any attempt to supply TBE for everyone who theoretically needs it would bankrupt the country before lunch. Schools in the state of New York include kids who speak 121 different languages. In the city of Seattle, 76. In Alexandria Avenue Elementary School in Los Angeles, 19—including Tagalog, Lao, Twi, Urdu, Punjabi, Hindi, Bengali, and Sinhalese. For each of these languages, a full curriculum would have to be planned, textbooks would have to be purchased, and certified teachers would have to be hired. It is a prospect that daunts even the most madcap tax-and-spend liberal.

But even if we invaded Saudi Arabia and seized all its oil to fund full-service TBE, we couldn't provide it. The teachers simply don't exist. When California's Little Hoover Commission, Sacramento's version of the General Accounting Office, investigated bilingual education in 1993, it discovered a statewide shortage of 20,000 teachers. Even among Spanish-speaking teachers, in by far the most plentiful supply, there was a 60 percent shortfall. When it came to Romanian, Farsi, Pashto, and Lahu, forget it. Of course, if anyone had applied for all those empty jobs, there was no way for California to evaluate their competence; the state had teacher certification tests for only nine of the dozens of languages spoken by its schoolchildren.

Some languages simply can't be taught at all in TBE, because they have no written forms. (Remember, the whole point is that students must not merely *speak* their native language but *read and write* it well before they move on to English.) That has not stopped the educrats from trying. In Massachusetts, school officials actually created an alphabet so that Kriolu—an obscure spoken-only dialect of Portuguese used in parts of the Cape Verde Islands—could be written for the first time. Textbooks and a curriculum followed, and now Massachusetts boasts the only schools in the entire world where classes are taught in Kriolu. (The unenlightened schools of the Cape Verde Islands continue to teach in Portuguese.) Massachusetts even sends home report cards and school bulletins in Kriolu. The parents have no idea whatsoever what this stuff says—none of them can read Kriolu—but their opinion hardly matters, does it? *We know better, we're the teachers.*

It is tempting to label the Kriolu classrooms as the all-time most harebrained product of bilingual education, but in considering TBE, caution is always advised; this is a field lush with opportunities for stupidity. A better choice may be experiments during the 1970s in New York City and Laredo, Texas, where teachers were trained to speak "Spanglish" ("Hey, Maria, *vamanos por el cine* Orpheum, they're having a festival *de peliculas de directores de Cuba* tonight"), supposedly the native language of local schoolchildren. Furious Puerto Rican parents snuffed the idea before it got anywhere in New York, but the Laredo program is still cited in bilingual literature as "the concurrent approach."

Here's another crazy aunt locked away in the bilingual attic: TBE administrators ruthlessly and routinely shanghai English-speaking kids into the program. What happened to Rosa Torres's daughter Angelica is by no means uncommon, and it is far from the most extreme example. Nor is it something that only happens to the children of easy-to-bully new immigrants.

Exhibit A: Seven-year-old Tony, a third-generation American who speaks English like a kid who grew up in Ames, Iowa, or Manhattan, Kansas. Favorite TV show: *Sesame Street.* A member of the Children's Book of the Month Club. And here's the acid test: A recent visitor to Tony's home heard him playing by himself in his bedroom, barking English commands to his GI Joes. In other words, there's no earthly reason for Tony to be in a TBE class.

But Tony doesn't live in Iowa or Kansas. And to the officials in his school district in the Southern California city of Hawthorne, there was only one relevant factor: his last name, Velasquez. When he started first grade in 1995, they put him in TBE. The school did notify his mother Ericka, who offered no objection. She heard the word *bilingual* and figured it meant he was in a class where he would study both Spanish and English. Ericka and her husband speak both languages and wanted to make sure Tony did, too. But after a few weeks, she began to have doubts.

"All his spelling words, every day, were in Spanish," Ericka recalls. "I began to wonder, is this really bilingual? Or is it just Spanish?" Finally she paid a visit to the school, where she discovered Tony's class spent just a few minutes a day on English. "I want him out of here," she told the teacher. Nonetheless, it took an entire year of skirmishing before he moved to an English classroom. "I was so mad," Ericka says, brow knitting as she thinks about it. "All that time wasted! He was so confused—why was he in Spanish classes when he knew English? He wants to be in English like the other kids. . . . Now, for the first time, he likes doing his schoolwork."

What still makes her sad is remembering the immigrant children from El Salvador and Nicaragua who stayed behind when Tony left his TBE classroom. "These kids come from other countries, and I don't know how they're going to learn English if they keep feeding them the language of their native countries," Ericka says. "But they're stuck there. I'm an American, I know the ropes, and it still took me a year to get Tony out. Those kids' parents will never be able to do it."

The idea that those children must be taught in Spanish is ludicrous to Ericka. The daughter of a Nicaraguan immigrant, as a child she never heard English in her own home and spoke none at all when she started school. Yet she speaks it perfectly now, in the stop-and-go cadences (though not the loopy vocabulary) of the Valley Girls who shared her all-English classroom. "If children can't learn English without a special program," she wonders, "how do you explain me?"

School systems shunt kids into TBE all the time strictly on the basis of a Hispanic name. When Linda Chavez was director of the U.S. Commission on Civil Rights, she was amazed to discover that the Washington, D.C., schools had placed her son Pablo in a TBE class—despite the fact that he didn't speak a word of Spanish.

But even school systems that pretend to use more sophisticated techniques for evaluating students often misroute English speakers into foreign-tongue classrooms. Typically, the district conducts a "home language survey" of new students to determine which ones come from a non–English-speaking background, then uses a standardized achievement test to zero in on kids who will be placed in TBE.

Home language surveys, however, are hopelessly broad. They typically ask if *anyone* in the home speaks another language, a fatal flaw when dealing with immigrant households that often include three generations with widely varying language patterns. If Grandma was already 60 when she came to the United States from Saigon or Havana and never learned to speak English, little Tuyen or Rodrigo has to take the test, regardless of the fact that he speaks *nothing* but English.

Nor will the tests necessarily save them. Most school districts will designate any child who scores below a certain percentile—generally somewhere between the 30th and 40th—as "limited-English proficient" and whisk them off to TBE classes. The godawful fallacies in such an approach are obvious to anyone without an advanced degree in education:

- The achievement test shows only the student's attainment in English, not in the other language. So a kid who scores 29 goes into TBE even if he doesn't speak a word of Spanish.

- The achievement test does nothing to identify the *reason* for the low score. A child who scores 25 may indeed need help with his English; or he may just need remedial education, period. There's no way to tell from the test score itself.

- Last and certainly not least, 40 percent of the children taking an achievement test will *always*, by definition, score in the lowest 40th percentile. And it doesn't necessarily say anything about whether they know enough English to understand history or math lessons.

"These tests are designed to break the students who take them into 100 categories and rank them," says Boston University's Rossell, who has written extensively on the testing issue. "They don't include anything at all about basic English communication skills, because they're designed for English-speaking students who for the most part have those skills." As critical as she is of the achievement tests, which are given to older children, Rossell actually shudders when she talks about the oral tests given to incoming kindergarten and first-grade students.

"I have a professor friend whose kid was given an English oral proficiency test because he had a Hispanic name," she said. "The kid tested as limited-English proficient even though he didn't know any language besides English. But he's kind of an odd kid, just wouldn't answer some of the questions, and acted bored. That's not exactly uncommon with five-year-olds. They may not feel confident enough to answer questions asked by a stranger, or they may just not feel like talking at all at that moment."

The failures of standardized tests are much more than theoretical. When the U.S. Department of Education investigated federally funded bilingual programs in Texas in 1982, it found 90 percent of the students designated limited-English proficient actually spoke better English than Spanish. A 1980 study of several California school districts showed only about half the Hispanic limited-English proficient students spoke better Spanish than English; 40 percent spoke no Spanish at all.

Attempts to develop language aptitude tests that would do a better job of identifying TBE candidates haven't met with much success. As an experiment, one such test was given to Chicago students who spoke English only and were above-average readers. Almost half of them wound up classified as non- or limited-English-speaking. A later experiment with English-only Cherokee Indian students had nearly identical results.

The victims of testing malpractice, by the way, are almost always kids from poor families. "There's a ton of research showing that students from economically disadvantaged households score lower than the rest of the population on standardized tests," says Rossell. Yet the church and civil rights groups who would undoubtedly be in a blood frenzy if these tests were being used against poor kids for virtually any other purpose are curiously quiet about TBE.

On the other hand, maybe it's not curious at all. For they didn't say anything, either, when the *San Francisco Examiner* discovered that more than 750 black students had been arbitrarily dumped into the city's Spanish or Chinese classrooms to fulfill school district integration policies. (The *Examiner* also found 325 children who used something besides English at home were put in Spanish or Chinese TBE classes on the grounds that they needed bilingual education, even if it was in a language they didn't speak.) One elementary school principal candidly admitted that he knew he was supposed to ask parents before transferring students into TBE, but never did. "If I went and asked everybody," he explained, "I'd get too many no's." *We know better, we're the teachers.*

The *Examiner* story ran in 1991, but the practice continues. "I meet with black parents all the time whose kids have gotten trapped in this thing," says attorney Cynthia McClain-Hill, who has squared off with the Los Angeles schools several times. "I can tell you this is a smoldering volcano in the African-American community."

Some of TBE's shortcomings might be argued away, or at least choked down, if bilingual education actually worked. But it doesn't. "When this all started out, we didn't know anything, so we adopted bilingual education on a leap of faith," says Rosalie Pedalino Porter of the Research in English Acquisition and Development Institute. "Thirty years later, we know better. The effects have been almost uniformly negative."

Sifting through social science research is always tricky for a layman; there are so many studies, their methodologies obscured in thick layers of jargon, their outcomes in impenetrable mathematics. Fortunately, when it comes to bilingual education, someone has done the academic grunt work for us. Christine Rossell and her research partner Keith Baker, who directed several studies of bilingual education for the U.S. Department of Education, sifted through scientific evaluations of 300 bilingual programs. Their first conclusion: Most of the research was just plain rotten. "It's as bad as the dueling psychologists you see in criminal courtrooms," Rossell says. Of the 300 evaluations, Rossell and Baker found only 72 that were methodologically sound.

Then they compiled a scorecard based on the results. The outcome was devastating for TBE. In head-to-head comparisons with the various versions of immersion teaching on reading, grammar, and math, TBE lost every time. That is, there were always more studies showing immersion therapy produced superior results. Often, lots more. For instance, 83 percent of the studies comparing TBE to "structured immersion" teaching (essentially, using simple English) showed kids learned to read better in the structured immersion classes; not a single one showed TBE to be superior.

Perhaps the single most calamitous statistic was in the comparison between TBE and *doing nothing at all*. An amazing 64 percent of the studies found kids learned grammar better in sink-or-swim classes without any special features whatsoever than they did in TBE. Many critics have seized on another way of evaluating TBE's results: the length of time it takes students to "graduate" into mainstream classes. Many school districts don't even compile those statistics—do they fear the results, or do they just not care? and which is worse?—but where they're available, the numbers are sad.

A 1994 study in New York City showed only about half the children who enter TBE in kindergarten have been mainstreamed within three years. For kids who enter in the second grade, the number drops to 22 percent. And in the sixth grade, just 7 percent. By contrast, 80 percent of students who enter immersion programs in kindergarten, 68 percent of those who enter in the second grade, and 33 percent of those who enter in the sixth grade are mainstreamed within three years.

A 1985 report on TBE in Boston showed more than half the TBE students in high school or middle school had been in the program six years or more. Across the country in Seattle, a 1993 study showed the annual exit rate from TBE was 10.6 percent. In California, it's less than 6 percent. These rates are low even according to TBE theory, which says kids should be ready for English classes in four to seven years. Not everyone agrees that exit rates are terribly significant. "Transition out of TBE is a function of local politics and test scores on very unreliable tests, not whether or not you know English," says Rossell. "The reality is that teachers inside the program are cheating, teaching English even though they're not supposed to. So the good news is that bilingual education is not as harmful as people think."

Try arguing that point to Alice Callaghan, who runs the Las Familias del Pueblo family center in the Los Angeles garment district, and she has an easy comeback. It's a paper written by one of the little boys who comes to her center each day after school, a veteran of six years of TBE: *"I my parens per mi in dis shool en I so I feol essayrin too old in the shool my border o reri can grier das mony putni gire and I sisairin aliro sceer."*

"The school district says this boy is doing very well and he's nearly ready to leave bilingual classes," says Callaghan, shaking her head. "As far as I'm concerned, that says it all."

It was at Callaghan's center that the boycott of 9th Street Elementary was conceived. For an entire year, the immigrant parents of the kids in her after-school program had been trying to meet with administrators at the school to ask for more English in the curriculum. No thanks, said the school officials. *We know better, we're the teachers.*

The parents gathered at the center to try to figure out their next step and asked Callaghan for some suggestions. Well, she said, we could write letters to state officials. We could pass around a petition. We could boycott, pull the kids out of class until the school officials do what we're asking. We could—"Boycott! Boycott!" shouted one of the mothers, jumping out of her chair. "Let's do the boycott!"

"It was instantaneous," recalls Callaghan. "Everybody agreed. I was shocked, frankly. A lot of these people don't have legal papers. For them to do this, to call public attention to themselves, it shows you the frustration they were feeling. And they were right. Without the boycott, I think we might as well have gone outside and talked to the tires on our cars. That's how much progress we were making."

School administrators reacted to the boycott like plantation overseers to a slave revolt, calling police out to try to break up the parents' picket line, then phoning them at the garment factories where they work to warn them that keeping their children out of school was illegal.

In the end, though, the bright light of publicity generated by the boycott caused the school officials to scuttle for the corners. They capitulated, though later some would hint darkly that the parents had somehow been duped and manipulated by Callaghan. It is a charge that puzzles the parents. "It was our idea, we were the ones who wanted to do it," says Juana Losara, a Mexican seamstress whose three children attend the school. "I knew my children needed help. I would hear somebody speaking English on the street or on TV, and I would say to the kids, 'What's he saying?' And they would all answer, 'I don't know.' They were born here, but they don't speak any English."

When Losara found out her children were spending less than an hour a day on English, she went to the school. "All the other American children are speaking English at this age," she told an official. "Why aren't mine?" The answer—be patient—was not good enough. "If they don't learn English at this age, at 9 or 10, they aren't going to speak it when they grow up," she said.

Losara knows how hard it is to learn English later: After 15 years in this country, she barely speaks a word. She knows the cost, too: "If I could get English, maybe I could get a job I like better. But the first question is always, 'Do you speak English?'" So, like her husband, she stays at the big sewing machines in the garment factories, toiling away for minimum wage.

Going back to Mexico, though, never crosses her mind. "I want to stay here," she says quietly. "I want my children to be something. My husband and I are nothing. But we're struggling so they can be something."

Perhaps the most telling argument of all against bilingual education is the high school dropout rate among Hispanic students: 30 percent, more than double that for blacks or whites. Those who have difficulty with English are far more likely to drop out. The message has gotten through to Hispanic parents. The *Los Angeles Times* poll showing their support for the anti-bilingual ballot proposition in California was hardly the first to reflect their skepticism about TBE. A 1996 survey of

Hispanic parents in Houston, San Antonio, Miami, New York, and Los Angeles showed that they regard teaching English as the single most important thing that schools do. Second: math, history, and other academic subjects. Spanish finished a distant third.

But Hispanic politicians and activists, wildly out of touch with their own communities, continue to wave the bloody bilingual flag. Characteristic is their reaction to the California proposition. Although the proposition would establish "sheltered English" or "structured immersion" as the educational norm in California, it would by no means make TBE illegal or force schools to do away with it. Any parents who want to place their children in TBE could do so by asking for a waiver.

You'd never know that, though, from the way opponents talk. "If we lose bilingual education in California today, we could easily lose it everywhere tomorrow," warns Antonia Hernandez, president of the Mexican-American Legal Defense Fund. Chimes in Rep. Xavier Becerra (D-Calif.), chairman of the Congressional Hispanic Caucus: "Hopefully, our community will see this as another case of immigrant bashing and react."

Even more hysterical has been the reaction of academicians. James Lyons, executive director of the National Association of Bilingual Education, recently predicted that without TBE, children would no longer be able to speak with their grandparents. "That isn't what we want in America," he implored.

Rosalie Pedrino Porter believes TBE's champions will conduct a scorched-earth campaign in its defense, no matter what polls show about what parents really want. "It's now wrapped up in politics— ethnic politics, victimhood, which of course gives you preferential status through affirmative action," she says. "It's wrapped up in money and power and control. Now we have a huge bureaucracy of administrators, bilingual psychologists, textbook publishers producing books in Spanish. Whether anybody wants to admit it or not, there's a huge investment in keeping this going. The fact is you can't make changes in this program very easily."

The financial incentives to keep TBE on life support are considerable. Because the money is scattered across thousands of budgets at the state, local, and federal level, and often not plainly labeled, it's difficult to come up with a reliable estimate of TBE's costs, but they probably approach $2 billion. In California, bilingual certification can mean up to $5,000 extra a year for a teacher.

Even more important, though, may be the groupthink that afflicts TBE's chattering-class supporters. The integrationist impulse of the 1960s is dead. Liberal chic in the 1990s is segregation, dressed up as identity-group politics. It's embarrassing enough that immigrants believe in an American dream that liberals long ago declared mythical and absurd. But that they want to drag their children into it, too!

"A lot of my friends were just scandalized when I started saying I supported the anti-bilingual initiative," says Alice Callaghan. Callaghan, who describes herself as "a Teddy Kennedy liberal," had impeccably politically correct credentials until she got involved in the 9th Street Elementary boycott: An Episcopal priest who's spent 16 years working with sweatshop workers and their kids, she's the veteran of many a civil rights sit-in—even has an arrest record. But the price of supporting English education for the children at her center has been far higher than any she ever had to pay for opposing U.S. military adventures or its support for South Africa. Just for starters, the University of Southern California—a stronghold of TBE theory—has just canceled a $238,000 grant to her center.

And her movement friends who still speak to her do so in tones of pity. "It must be tough being out there all alone," one said recently. "It's not so lonely," Callaghan replied. "There may not be any liberals out here with me, but there are plenty of the people that liberals say they want to help."

Still, there may be hope. People *do* change. Fernando Vega did. Vega, in a very real sense, is responsible for everything that happened to Rosa Torres, the Peruvian immigrant whose daughter got snarled up in Redwood City's TBE program. Fernando, you see, was the guy who got the Redwood City schools started down the bilingual path nearly three decades ago.

Not that he meant Rosa any harm. In fact, his story is, in many ways, similar to hers. Fernando is an American—born in Houston, he grew up right on the border in Brownsville, Texas—but his parents were Mexican immigrants. They spoke only Spanish, but Fernando's dad was a demon about learning English. Sometimes he would make the boy come out with him and lug backbreaking loads of shingles under that scorching Brownsville sun. "It's hot, no?" his father would ask after they'd been at it for a while. "Yes, Papa," Fernando would gasp. "Remember it, then," his father commanded. "And stay in school."

Fernando did, until World War II broke out. Then he enlisted in the Army Air Corps and learned to fix planes. After the war he got a job with

Pan Am. He was such a good mechanic that after a while, the airline asked him to train others. So in 1958 he left Brownsville for San Francisco. With his wife and six children, Fernando settled in Redwood City.

It was a small town in those days, without many Hispanics. But Fernando never had any trouble until his eldest son Oscar was ready for high school. Together the two of them sat down and planned the courses Oscar would need to go to college. Algebra, civics, biology. But when Oscar came home from his first day of school, he had a new schedule: general math, ceramics, and woodworking.

"This is not what I want for my son," Fernando told the guidance counselor. "You never consulted me about these changes."

"The courses you wanted for him are reserved for kids who are going to college," the counselor explained. "And, let's be realistic, Oscar isn't going to college. But if he comes to these classes every day and behaves himself, he'll get a diploma."

"This school doesn't belong to you!" Fernando growled. "I pay taxes for this place!" He stomped out. After some angry talk at a school board meeting, he got Oscar back into the college prep classes. But every time one of his children started high school, Fernando had to go through the whole damned thing again. After a while, other Hispanic parents were calling, asking for his help with their kids. He got to be so good at it that he was elected to his own seat on the school board.

It was around 1970, when Fernando was visiting one of the schools, that a teacher approached him. "Mr. Vega, you know we're starting to get a lot of immigrants from Mexico here," she said. "And some of the children don't speak a word of English. I've got three in my class right now and I don't know what to do with them. Is there any money we could use to hire some teachers' aides who speak Spanish? Just to get them started."

Fernando called the superintendent, who remembered getting a notice that there was some federal money available for a new program called bilingual education, taught partly in Spanish, partly in English. Fernando, bemused, gave it some thought. Back in Brownsville, he'd learned English sink-or-swim in the first grade, and things had worked pretty well—not just for Fernando, but for a lot of Mexican kids who were allowed to attend school on the American side of the border. One of them even became the valedictorian of his high school class.

On the other hand, you had to be open to new ways of doing things. When Fernando started out in the Army Air Corps, everybody carried a slide rule to calculate things like fuel consumption. But these days, all the pilots and flight engineers carried little electronic calculators. That was progress. This bilingual education, it was progress too. "Let's get some of that money," he told the superintendent.

Fernando couldn't believe how quickly things moved after that. They hired teachers, not aides, with the federal money—and because bilingual teachers were hard to come by, they accepted some who Fernando privately didn't think were very good. But there wasn't much he could do about it. They needed more bilingual teachers every year, because the program was getting huge—new waves of immigrants were pouring in, but none of the kids seemed to be moving over into English classes. It was all a little disquieting, but before it reached the point of alarm, Fernando left the school board. His kids had all graduated, and it was time to do something new. He won a seat on the city council, then became an official in the state Democratic Party, finally a national organizer. The problems of Redwood City's schools were a distant memory.

Until the day in 1988 that Oscar stopped by the house. Fernando's eldest son now had a little boy of his own, Jason, who just two weeks ago had started the first grade. Funny thing, though—his class was taught in Spanish, a language the child didn't know. When Oscar went over to the school to ask that Jason be moved into an English classroom, the principal said there weren't any.

"Besides, he needs to learn Spanish," the principal added. "It's a shame he doesn't know his native language."

"English is his native language," Oscar retorted. "He's an American. He's never even been to Mexico." The principal just shrugged.

"What am I going to do, Dad?" Oscar asked after he'd told the story. "They won't listen to me at all."

Fernando didn't answer for a minute. He was still marveling at the insane mutation of a small act of kindness to some immigrant kids two decades earlier. He had gotten involved with the schools in the first place because they were trying to segregate his children under the guise of academic tracking. Now they were trying to do it again, to his grandchildren, under the guise of language instruction.

Finally he spoke. "I guess you're going to have to do what I did, when they wouldn't listen to me about your classes," he counseled Oscar. "You're going to have to run for the school board."

Oscar did. He won—it turned out that a lot of Redwood City parents had been hoping someone would voice their discontent about TBE—and though it took some time, he helped rein in the program's worst excesses.

Now, at 73, Fernando is mostly retired from politics. But last fall, when he heard about the California ballot proposition that would cut back TBE, he stopped by one of the campaign offices to find out what it was all about. Impressed at the explanation, he took home some signs bearing the proposition's slogan, "English for the Children," in both English and Spanish. He stuck them in his front lawn.

That evening, the doorbell rang. "Excuse me, mister," a woman—a Salvadoran, by the sound of her Spanish—asked when Fernando answered. "I saw your sign. Do you teach English here? My children need to learn it."

"I'm sorry, the sign is about something else," Fernando replied. "But why do you need an English teacher? Don't your children go to school?"

"Of course they do," the woman replied sadly. "But at the school, they only teach Spanish."

· ·

Defining Disability Down
Why Johnny Can't Read, Write, or Sit Still

Ruth Shalit

This selection first appeared in *The New Republic* on 25 August 1997. Ruth Shalit is a frequent contributor to *The New Republic* and other national publications.

In July of 1995, Jon Westling, the provost of Boston University, traveled to Australia to attend the Winter Conversazione on Culture and Society, a highbrow tete-a-tete for globetrotting pundits and savants. Westling, a protege of former B.U. President John Silber, is an avowed conservative; and the subtitle of his speech, "The Culture Wars Go to School," seemed to portend the usual helping of red meat for the faithful. But instead of decrying deconstruction, or puncturing the pretensions of tenured radicals, Westling took aim at an unexpected target—the learning-disabled. He told the story of a shy yet assertive undergrad, "Somnolent Samantha," who had approached him one day after class and presented him with a letter from the Office of Disability Services. The letter explained that Samantha had a learning disability "in the area of auditory processing" and would require certain "accommodations," including time-and-a-half on quizzes, double time on the midterm, examinations administered in a room separate from all other students, copies of Westling's lecture notes, and a reserved seat at the front of the class. Samantha also notified Westling that she might doze off in class, and that he should fill her in on any material she missed while snoozing.

The somnolent undergrad, Westling contended, was not alone. A new, learning-disabled generation was coming of age in America, a generation "trained to the trellis of dependency on their special status and the accommodations that are made to it." Citing a Department of Education estimate that up to 20 percent of Americans may be learning-disabled, Westling mused on the evolutionary ramifications of such a diagnosis. "There may be as many as 50 million Americans," he observed. "What happened? Did America suffer some silent genetic catastrophe?"

Westling's speech, it turns out, was a prelude to action. Shortly after returning from Melbourne, the aggrieved provost took a cleaver to B.U.'s bloated Office of Learning Disabilities Support Services, a half-million dollar fiefdom whose policies had, in the words of *The New York Times*, earned B.U. a "national reputation" as a haven of support for the learning-impaired. He stepped up standards for documentation, and he issued a blanket prohibition on waivers of the school's math and foreign language requirements, contending that there was no medical proof that students with learning disabilities are unable to learn these subjects. Henceforth, he declared, all requests for learning-disabled accommodations would be routed through his office. Westling then made a final announcement. In 1996, he said, he would become president of the university.

The learning-disability establishment was dumbfounded. "Here was someone coming in with no knowledge, taking the national model and destroying it," says Anne Schneider, the Park Avenue fund-raising doyenne who spearheaded the creation of B.U.'s program a decade ago, after her learning-disabled daughter Andrea nearly washed out of the university—due, Schneider says, to a lack of services. Schneider, whose personal fund-raising efforts have kept the office flush with cash, sees Westling's assault on her brainchild as analogous to "taking a seeing-eye dog away from a blind person." Janet Cahaley, mother of learning-disabled sophomore Michael, agrees: "These kids are the most vulnerable people on campus. Before, they were treated with humanity and decency and kindness. Now, they're hopeless and helpless."

Well, maybe not so helpless. Westling's putsch brought howls from disabled-rights advocates and from the media, which pounced upon the revelation that Somnolent Samantha was a fictitious composite—a "rhetorical trope," as Westling somewhat sheepishly admitted. And on July 15, 1996, ten students filed a lawsuit against Westling, claiming his unkind words and arduous new requirements amounted to illegal discrimination under the 1990 Americans with Disabilities Act. In their complaint, the students alleged that Westling's new standard for documentation—requiring applicants to submit an evaluation that is less than three years old and prepared by a physician or licensed psychologist—amounted to an "unduly burdensome prerequisite" that would screen out learning-disabled students from receiving their legally mandated accommodations. Also unlawful, the students contended, was Westling's prohibition on waivers of academic requirements. Finally, in their most enterprising claim, the students accused Westling of creating a "hostile learning environment" for the disabled, inflicting needless "emotional distress" and crushing their hopes of collective advancement. A ruling by Judge Patti B. Saris of Boston Federal District Court is expected by the end of August.

Recent rulings by other judges suggest that the learning-disabled students may well prevail in court. But even then the questions begged by Somnolent Samantha will remain. Westling and B.U.'s new guard insist that they have no animus against those with "genuine" learning impairments; they simply want to weed out the impostors. Yet, in holding up a trendy diagnosis to the bright light of public scrutiny, B.U. officials have raised issues that go to the core of a debate that has grown as civil rights law has expanded to cover not merely the halt, the lame, and the blind, but the dysfunctional, the debilitated, and the drowsy.

Should "learning-disabled" even be a protected category under federal law? What, exactly, is a learning disability? Are the B.U. plaintiffs at the vanguard of a new generation of civil rights warriors, as their supporters contend? Or is their lawsuit the reductio ad absurdum of identity politics and tort madness—Harrison Bergeron meets Perry Mason in The Case of the Litigious Lollygaggers?

The recent announcement by the Equal Employment Opportunity Commission that the Americans with Disabilities Act covers not only physically but mentally handicapped individuals has occasioned a flurry of hand-wringing editorials. Worried employers have painted a scary scenario of a law that will coddle murderous lunatics, endanger the welfare of unsuspecting customers, and transform America's factories and foundries into dystopias of dementia. In some ways, however, it is the entrenchment of learning disability—a comparatively undersung, and seemingly more benign, "hidden impairment"—that poses the more subversive challenge to basic notions of fair play, professionalism, and equal protection under the law.

No one would deny that an individual who is unfortunate enough to be afflicted with one of the classically defined mental disorders—schizophrenia, paranoia, manic depression, and so on—suffers from a clearly defined and clearly recognizable infirmity, one that is likely to impair significantly her educational achievements and career prospects. (Whether employers should be legally compelled to overlook these mental disabilities is another matter.) The diagnosis of a learning disability, in contrast, is a far more subjective matter. For many of the more recently discovered learning maladies—math disability, foreign-language disability, "dysrationalia"—there are no standard tests. To be sure, real and debilitating learning disabilities do exist. But there are no good scientific grounds to believe that some of the more exotic diagnoses have any basis in reality. Yet, thanks to the interlocking protections of three powerful federal disability laws, refusal to accommodate even the most dubious claims of learning impairment is now treated by the courts and by the federal government as the persecution of a protected minority class.

Modern disability law was inspired by the most humane of motives, to protect the disabled from prejudices that deprived them of equal opportunities in the workplace and in the classroom. From the outset, however, this grand aspiration was framed in the fuzziest of terms. The statutory framework for modern disability law was established in the Rehabilitation Act of 1973, which mandated assistance measures for the disabled in federal facilities. Here is how Section 504 of the act defined a learning disability: "a disorder in one or more of the basic psychological processes involved in understanding or in using language, spoken or written . . . [which] may manifest itself in imperfect ability to listen, think, speak, read, write, spell or do mathematical calculations." This remarkably broad definition is echoed in all subsequent disability laws, notably the 1975 Individuals with Disabilities Education Act, which mandated an array of services for disabled public school students, and the 1990 Americans with Disabilities Act, which extended the protections of the Rehabilitation Act into the private sector. All three laws are equally vague in their description of how people with disabilities must be treated. As the ADA puts it, in the case of any individual possessing a "disability" that results in "substantial impairment" of a "major life activity," schools and employers cannot "discriminate" and must provide "reasonable accommodation." The meaning of these legal appelations, as interpreted by the courts and the regulatory agencies, would turn out to be remarkably expansive.

There were some limits written into the disability laws. For instance, only "otherwise qualified" individuals are entitled to protection; accommodations are only mandated if they do not result in "undue hardship." But recently a number of rulings by federal courts and government enforcement agencies have revealed how flimsy these limits are.

Although compliance with federal disability law is not supposed to come at the expense of education or job performance standards, the Department of Education's Office of Civil Rights has delivered stinging rebukes to schools that refuse to exempt learning-disabled students from academic requirements. Last May, a student afflicted with dyscalculia— math disability—filed a complaint with the San Francisco Office for Civil Rights after her college declined to waive the math course required of all business majors in paralegal studies. Despite the college's earnest attempts to accommodate her impairment—the student would receive extensive tutoring and extra time on tests—OCR issued a finding of discrimination anyway, writing on May 30 that "[a]bsolute rules against any particular form of academic adjustment or accommodation are disfavored by the law." When the school asked if they could require learning-disabled students to at least try to pass a required course, OCR said no way, arguing that "it is discriminatory to require the student to consume his or her time and jeopardize his or her grade point average taking a particular mathematics course when the person qualified to administer and/or interpret the psychometric data has determined that the student, due to his or her disability, is highly unlikely to pass the course with any of the accommodations the institution can identify and/or deliver." OCR added that this rule should apply even to borderline dyscalculics, that "substantial group of students for whom interpretation of psychometric measures provide no clear prediction of success in a particular mathematics course."

This is the new frontier, the learning disability as an opportunistic tautology. The fact that one displays a marked lack of aptitude for a particular intellectual discipline or profession establishes one's legal right to ensure at least a degree of success in that discipline or profession. That is not a fanciful conceit, but an adjudicated reality. Several judges have recently ventured the enterprising claim that any person who is not performing up to his or her abilities in a chosen endeavor suffers from a learning disability within the meaning of the ADA.

Consider the lawsuit filed in 1993 by an aspiring attorney named Marilyn J. Bartlett. Bartlett graduated in 1991 from Vermont Law School, where she received generous accommodations of her reading disability and disability in "phonological processing." Nonetheless, Bartlett did not do well, graduating with a GPA of 2.32 and a class standing of 143 out of 153 students. She then went to work as a professor of education at Dowling College, where, according to court documents, she "receives accommodations at work for her reading problems in the form of a full-time work-study student who assists her in reading and writing tasks."

When it came time to take the bar exam, Bartlett petitioned the New York Board of Law Examiners for special arrangements. She wanted unlimited time for the test, access to food and drink, a private room, and the use of an amanuensis to record her answers. Acting on the advice of its own expert, who reported that Bartlett's test data did not support a diagnosis of a reading disorder, the board refused Bartlett's demands. Three times, Bartlett attempted the exam without accommodation. After her third failure, she sued the board.

On July 3, 1997, Judge Sonia Sotomayor ruled in Bartlett's favor. Ordering the board to provide the accommodations Bartlett had requested, she also awarded Bartlett $12,500 in compensatory damages. Judge Sotomayor did not challenge the board's contention that Bartlett was neither impaired nor disabled, at least not in the traditional sense. In an enterprising new twist, however, she declared that Bartlett's skills ought not to be compared to those of an "average person in the general population" but, rather, to an "average person with comparable training, skills and abilities"—i.e., to her fellow cohort of aspiring lawyers. An "essential question" in the case, said the judge, was whether the plaintiff would "have a substantial impairment in performing [the] job" of a practicing lawyer. The answer to this question was "yes," the judge found. And this answer—the fact that Bartlett would have a very hard time meeting the job requirements of a practicing lawyer—was, in the judge's opinion, precisely the reason why Bartlett had a protected right to become a practicing lawyer. Thus, Judge Sotomayor ruled that Bartlett's "inability to be accommodated on the bar exam—and her accompanying impediment to becoming bar-admitted—exclude her from a 'class of jobs' under the ADA," and could not be permitted.

To drive home her point, Judge Sotomayor triumphantly cited Bartlett's performance during a courtroom demonstration of her reading skills. "Plaintiff read haltingly and laboriously, whispering and sounding out some words more than once under her breath before she spoke them aloud," the judge recalled. "She made one word identification error, reading the word 'indicted' as 'indicated.'"

It could, of course, be argued that the ability to read is an essential function of lawyering; that any law school graduate who cannot distinguish "indicated" from "indicted," who cannot perform cognitive tasks under time constraints, is incapable of performing the functions of a practicing lawyer and therefore, perhaps, should not be a practicing lawyer. But one would be arguing those things in the teeth of the law. Thanks to the Americans with Disabilities Act, the Individuals with Disabilities Education Act and Section 504 of the Rehabilitation Act of 1973, Bartlett and her fellows among the learning-disabled are now eligible for a lifelong buffet of perks, special breaks, and procedural protections, a web of entitlement that extends from cradle to grave.

Jon Westling is a crusty chain smoker with owlish glasses and a stuffy, orotund manner, an easy figure to mock. But, as it turns out, his portrait of Somnolent Samantha was hardly a wild flight of fancy. Before beginning his formal audit of LDSS's practices, Westling asked its director, Loring Brinckerhoff, whether the office had ever turned down a single request for special dispensation on the grounds that the student hadn't presented enough evidence. When Brinckerhoff answered no, Westling asked to see folders and accommodation letters for the twenty-eight students who had most recently requested and received adjustments to their academic program. Of these twenty-eight, Westling pronounced no fewer than twenty-seven to be insufficiently documented. And, indeed, copies of the students' files, exhumed during the discovery phase of the lawsuit and now available as courthouse exhibits, seem to provide some support for this harsh assessment.

For starters, some of the diagnosticians themselves appeared somewhat impaired. One evaluator wrote that "taking notes and underlying [sic] while reading" would help a student "maintain her attention." Another student, a female, was erroneously referred to as "Joe" by the evaluator who pronounced her to be learning-disabled. Even more troubling, though, was LDSS's seemingly reflexive acquiescence to students' wish lists. Michael Cahaley, one of the plaintiffs in the lawsuit, was, according to Westling's affidavit, described by his doctor as having "minimal" deficits: "this very intelligent youngster should do well in high school and college."

Nonetheless, Cahaley had requested—and was granted—double time on all of his examinations. In another case, the clinical psychologist who examined a student reported that his "skill deficits" were "not severe enough to be a learning disability"; but a learning specialist misread the report and recommended accommodation anyway, on the grounds that "the student was evaluated and found to have a learning disability."

Sometimes the evaluator's recommendations seemed just bizarre. In one case, a student's psychologist opined that a student who "appears to have subtle verbal processing difficulties" should not be "asked to recall very specific data or information." As Westling dryly observed in his affidavit, requests for "very specific data or information" constituted "an essential element of every course and academic program offered by Boston University."

At the trial, the student plaintiffs came off as something other than inspiring champions for disabled rights. Elizabeth Guckenberger, a third-year law student who was diagnosed as having "a visual and oral processing disability" while a freshman at Carleton College, admitted she had received every accommodation she had ever requested under the Westling regime, including extra time on exams, a reduced course load, and priority registration in the law school section of her choice. Benjamin Freedman, a senior with dysgraphia ("really, really bad handwriting," he says), also got everything he wanted, including double time on exams, the option to be tested orally, and the services of a professional note-taker.

Plaintiff Jordan Nodelman, who claimed he suffered from attention deficit disorder (ADD), also had received every accommodation he ever requested, including the right to take all tests in a distraction-free environment with extra time. At trial, he admitted that his attention deficit waxed and waned. When "something's very important to me," he explained at trial, he "forc[ed] [him]self to concentrate." Nodelman had a 3.6 GPA, had made the Dean's List, and had taken his tests untimed in every class except Zen Guitar.

Perhaps the least compelling plaintiff was sophomore Scott Greeley, who testified that he suffers from an "audio-visual learning processing deficit." At B.U., Greeley had been provided with a note-taker, time-and-a-half on tests, and an open-ended right to have any test question "clarified" by the instructor. But the perks didn't help much—as Greeley explained at trial, after the accommodations were provided his GPA improved to a less-than-stellar 1.9. Over the course of the trial, B.U. attorneys established that this shoddy showing was perhaps not wholly attributable to societal persecution of the disabled. Queried about his spotty attendance record in a science course for which he received a "D" grade, Greeley explained that "part of my disability is that I need a structured schedule." "Would you say you missed over half the classes?" persisted the judge. "Probably around that, yes," replied the undergrad.

It would be comforting to think that B.U.'s "disabled" plaintiffs represent an exception to the norm, but this does not seem to be the case. Over the years, proposed reforms to disability law have been effectively vanquished by televised testimony from sobbing children in wheelchairs. Increasingly, however, individuals with grave physical handicaps comprise only a small portion of the people who claim special privilege under the federal disability laws. As Manhattan Institute fellow Walter Olson points out in *The Excuse Factory*, complaints by the traditionally disabled—the deaf, blind and paraplegic—have accounted for only a tiny share of ADA lawsuits. According to 1996 EEOC figures, only 8 percent of employment complaints have come from wheelchair users and a mere 6 percent from the deaf or blind, bringing the total for these traditional disabilities to a skimpy 14 percent.

The diagnosis of learning disability, by contrast, is experiencing something of a boom. In the space of only a few years, the number of children diagnosed with attention deficit disorder, reading disability, and math disability, has swollen by hundreds of thousands. Of the 5.3 million handicapped children currently on Individual Education Programs (specially tailored, often costly regimens of technology, therapy, and one-on-one tutoring that public schools are mandated to provide to every child with a disability), the U.S. Department of Education estimates that just over half (51 percent) are learning-disabled. According to the authors of the book *Promoting Postsecondary Education for Students with Learning Disabilities*, up to 300,000 students currently enrolled in college have proclaimed that they are learning-disabled and need special accommodations.

The National Collegiate Athletic Association, meanwhile, is under intense legal pressure from the Justice Department to relax the initial eligibility standards that require student athletes to get a cumulative score of 700 on their SATs and to maintain at least a 2.0 grade point average in core courses. These standards are meant to offer a slight safeguard against the tendency of universities to enroll and graduate young men and women whose ability to pass a ball exceeds their ability to pass their courses. Not so fast, said Justice Department lawyer Christopher J. Kuczynski. In a March 1996 letter to the NCAA, Kuczynski warned that the association's academic standards may "have the affect [sic] of excluding students with disabilities from participation in college athletics." NCAA spokesman Kevin Lennon says the association is in the process of revising its policy "to accommodate students with learning disabilities."

The most common estimate cited by advocacy groups and frequently repeated in government documents is that between 15 and 20 percent of the general population have learning disabilities. Any hypochondriac can test himself: In a recent booklet, the American Council on Education supplies a checklist of symptoms for adults who suspect they may be learning-disabled. Some of us will be disturbed to recognize in the checklist possible symptoms of our own: According to the council, telltale signs of adult learning-disablement include "a short attention span," impulsivity, "difficulty telling or understanding jokes," "difficulty following a schedule, being on time, or meeting deadlines," and "trouble reading maps."

As the ranks of the learning-disabled swell, so too do the number of boutique diagnoses. Trouble with numbers could signal dyscalculia, a crippling ailment that prevents one from learning math. Lousy grammar may stem from the aforementioned dysgraphia, a disorder of written expression. Dozing in class is evidence of latent ADD, perhaps even ADHD (attention deficit/hyperactivity disorder). Many tykes also exhibit the telltale symptoms of ODD—oppositional defiant disorder. According to the American Psychiatric Association, the defining feature of ODD is "a recurrent pattern of negativistic, defiant, disobedient, and hostile behavior . . . characterized by the frequent occurrence of at least four of the following behaviors: losing temper, arguing with adults, actively defying or refusing to comply with the requests or rules of adults, deliberately doing things that will annoy other people, blaming others for his or her own mistakes or misbehavior." Rates of up to 16 percent have been reported.

A tongue-tied toddler could have dysphasia, otherwise known as a "difficulty using spoken language to communicate." Boorish behavior may be a sign of dyssemia, defined as a "difficulty with signals [and] social cues." (According to the Interagency Commission on Learning Disabilities, social skills are a domain in which a learning disability can occur.) An even more sinister malady is dysrationalia, defined in an October 1993 issue of *The Journal of Learning Disabilities* as "a level of rationality, as demonstrated in thinking and behavior, that is significantly below the level of the individual's intellectual capacity." A checklist of childhood precursors include "premature closure, belief perseverance . . . resistance to new ideas, dogmatism about beliefs, and lack of reflectiveness."

These neo-disabilities are likely to strike the nonspecialist as an exercise in pathologizing childhood behavior, and the nonspecialist would be on to something. Increasingly, scholars and clinicians in the field of learning disability are speaking out against the dangers of promiscuous diagnosis of disablement. "In the space of twenty years, American psychiatry has gone from blaming Johnny's mother to blaming Johnny's brain," says Dr. Lawrence Diller, an assistant clinical professor of behavioral pediatrics at the University of California at San Francisco. The problem, says Dr. Diller, is that in a variant of the Lake Woebegone effect, "Bs and Cs have become unacceptable to the middle classes. Average is a pejorative." And yet, as he points out, "someone has got to be average."

Some scholars have even begun to question the notion that there is such a thing as a learning disability. In a recently published book, Off Track, one of its authors, Robert Sternberg, a Yale professor of psychology and education, presents a powerful case for why the concept of learning disability ought to be abandoned. Drawing on the latest research into the physiology of the human brain, Sternberg argues that there is no evidence to support the view that children who are labeled as learning-disabled have an immutable neurological disability in learning. From a medical standpoint, he writes, there is no scientific proof that children labeled as learning-disabled actually have a discernible biological ailment "in terms of the underlying cognitive abilities related to reading." Says Sternberg: "I'm not denying that there are dramatic disparities in the speed with which people learn. . . . But, most of the time, what you're talking about here is a garden-variety poor reader. You're talking about someone who happens to be not very good in math."

To be sure, there is no question that children who are intellectually normal, and sometimes even unusually bright, can have genuine, serious difficulties in learning how to read or to do math; and that educators should do everything in their power to put these students back on track developmentally. But as their clinics swarm with hordes of pushy parents and catatonic collegians, all hankering for a diagnosis of intractable infirmity, a growing number of diagnosticians are crying foul. "The way the diagnoses [of attention deficit disorder and learning disabilities] are being used right now, a backlash against the conditions is inevitable," says Diller. "We've created a paradox where the more problems you have, the better off you may be. That's a prescription for societal gridlock."

It's no puzzle, of course, why the learning-disability movement insists that learning disability is an immutable, brain-based disorder—a malady that is "fundamentally neurological in origin," according to the National Center for Learning Disabilities. For it is this understanding of learning disability that justifies its inclusion as a protected category under the ADA. If learning disability is an innate neurological defect that "artificially" lowers test performance, then it follows that learning-disabled individuals should be able to take tests under special conditions that will neutralize the effects of this handicap. In *Help Yourself: Advice for College-Bound Students with Learning Disabilities*, author Erica-lee Lewis stresses that asking for an untimed administration of your SATs "does NOT give you an unfair advantage; it just reduces the unfair disadvantage by providing you with equal access and opportunity. You deserve that and the law protects you against anything short of that fairness!"

There's just one tiny problem: The two major studies on the subject say that precisely the opposite is true. As Dr. Warren W. Willingham, a psychometrician with the Educational Testing Service, points out in his widely respected textbook *Testing Handicapped Students*, institutions have long relied on standardized tests because such tests, for all their faults, tend to be highly reliable in their estimation of how well a particular applicant will actually perform in college or on the job. The case of learning-disabled students, in contrast, "presents a very different picture," writes Willingham. When students diagnosed with learning disabilities were allowed to take the SAT on an untimed or extended-time basis, the "college grades of learning-disabled students were substantially overpredicted," suggesting that "providing longer amounts of time may raise scores beyond the level appropriate to compensate for the disability." The other study—by Marjorie Ragosta, one of ETS's own researchers—confirms Willingham's pessimistic diagnosis.

Both researchers raise a troubling question: whether, as Willingham puts it, "the nonstandard version of the SAT is seriously biased in favor of [learning-disabled] students." The concern is not just theoretical. There is reason to suspect that fast-track students, and their parents, have figured out that a little learning disability can be an advantageous thing—can make the difference, in a hypercompetitive setting, between getting into (and getting successfully out of) the right school. The privilege of taking the SAT on an untimed basis raises students' scores by an average of 100 points, according to the College Board. In the last couple of years, testing agencies have been bombarded with requests from students who proclaim that they are learning-disabled and will therefore need additional time. According to Kevin Gonzales, a spokesman for the Educational Testing Service, 18,000 learning-disabled examinees received "special administration" for the SAT in 1991–92. By 1996–97, that number had more than doubled, to 40,000. Requests for accommodation on Advanced Placement exams, meanwhile, have quadrupled—in 1996, 2,244 learning-disabled eggheads took their A.P. tests untimed. To reap the benefits of this particularly useful perk, ETS requires only a letter of verification from a school special education director or a state-licensed psychologist or psychiatrist.

Certification and licensure exams—long, carefully standardized examinations that function as gatekeepers into the professions—are also under assault. In 1995, the National Board of Medical Examiners administered over 450 untimed Medical College Admissions Tests—a fivefold increase from 1990. Lawyers, too, are requesting special dispensation. This year, in New York alone, more than 400 aspiring attorneys have asked to take the bar exam untimed. "The requests have increased tremendously," says Nancy Carpenter, who heads up the New York Board of Legal Examiners. "ADD is becoming much more common. We have a lot of dysgraphia. Some dyscalculia . . . . Most applicants just say, 'unspecified learning disability.' They are all over the lot."

ETS officials do not like to talk about the Willingham and Ragosta studies. Indeed, far from planning to toughen up its accommodations policy, the agency seems poised to eliminate its only check on spurious claims—the marking, or "flagging," of a score to indicate that an applicant took the test under nonstandard conditions. For years, the learning disability industry has railed against the asterisk, arguing that it violates a student's right to keep his or her disability a secret. Now ETS seems prepared to agree. "We are taking a good, hard look at the whole issue of flagging," says ETS's newly appointed director of disability services, Loring Brinckerhoff. "I'm not prepared to say it's going to go away overnight. . . . My gut feeling is that it may well be a Section 504 violation." Yes, that's the same Loring Brinckerhoff who recently re-signed under pressure by Jon Westling from his B.U. sinecure. "Isn't it ironic," muses Brinckerhoff. "I'm told by Boston University that I'm unqualified to do my job. Yet here I am—at the biggest testing agency in the world—determining accommodations for hundreds of thousands of people with disabilities."

Of course, a legally recognized disability means more than just extra time on tests—or even extra privileges in the classroom. Under the Individuals with Disabilities Education Act, a diagnosis of L.D. also qualifies a child for an Individual Education Program—a handcrafted educational program, replete with techno-goodies and other kinds of specialized attention. The law, which states that "all children with dis-abilities" ought to have available to them "a free and appropriate public education," encourages parents to be bound not by what the school dis-trict can offer, but by what they think their child needs. It specifies that, in the event that the parents don't care for their child's IEP, the local school district must convene a "an impartial due process hearing"—a trial-like proceeding in which both parties have the right to be repre-sented by a lawyer, the right to subpoena, confront, and cross-examine witnesses, and the right to present evidence. If a school district loses the due process hearing, it must pay the parents' attorneys' fees. The result, says Raymond Bryant, director of special education for Maryland's Montgomery County public schools, has left school districts vulnerable to parental tactics bordering on extortion. "It used to be that kids didn't try hard enough, or didn't work hard enough," says Bryant. "Now, it's ADD or L.D. . . . They want their child to read half the material. They want him to do half the homework. They don't want him to take the same tests. But guess what? They want him to get the same grades!"

In prosperous, sun-dappled school districts around the country, ex-otic new learning disabilities are popping up, each requiring its own costly cure. In Orange County, where "executive function disorder" (difficulty initiating, organizing, and planning behavior) reigns, parents have begun demanding that schools foot the bill for horseback riding lessons. "This is now supposed to be the way to help kids with EFD," says Peter Hartman, superintendent of the Saddleback Unified School District. "There's some stable in the area that they all go to." In Holliston, Massachusetts, parents of children with attention deficit/hyperactivity disorder hanker for a trendy new treatment called "educational kinesthesiology," a sort of kiddie Pilates for angst-ridden tots. "Unfortunately, the treatment can only be done by a, quote, licensed educational kinesthesiologist," sighs Margaret Reed, special-ed administrator for Holliston Public Schools. "And it seems there's only one in the district. And she charges $50 an hour."

Sometimes, it seems, the problem is less inattentive children than overattentive parents, many of whom are unwilling to believe their progeny is less than perfect. Consider the case of Michael F., whose plight was thrashed out at length at a 1996 hearing after his parents expressed discontent with his Individual Education Program. Michael, then a ninth grader, was thriving at his high school—earning "A's" in honors courses and demonstrating "overall cognitive functioning in the very superior range (99th percentile)." He had also written a book, played in the school band and, according to the hearing officer, "successfully completed bar mitzvah training."

At the hearing, it emerged that Michael did all of this while fighting off the ravages of "attention deficit disorder, language-based specific learning disabilities, neuro-motor dysfunction, and tactile sensitivity." These numerous handicaps had made Michael eligible for a generous dose of special-education services. Under the terms specified in his IEP, Michael received three and three-eighths hours a week of special tutoring; extra time on homework assignments and tests: "allowance of standing up, stretching and/or walking around in class"; "permission to chew gum or hard candy to help him concentrate and focus"; "seat assignments in close proximity to the teacher"; and "access to a tape recorder, transcripts of lectures, outlines and notes and/or a laptop computer if needed." Now Mr. and Mrs. F. wanted even more. Michael's low grade on his Honors Geometry midterm, they argued at the hearing, revealed evidence of a new, previously unsuspected disability "with the concepts of quadratic equations and the Pythagorean theorem." They blamed the school for numerous "procedural violation[s]," including "failure to pursue a math reevaluation of Michael" after he received a 65 on his midterm. Now, they said, their son would experience "substantial regression" over the summer, unless his high school saw fit to furnish him with "extended summer programming in the form of math tutoring."

This, the hearing officer would not do. True, she wrote, Michael's poor showing on his geometry midterm might well be "related to his learning disability and/or ADD." On the other hand, she boldly ventured, it could also be that "math remains a subject where Michael will not receive As in an Honors track."

Ensconced in his pleasantly stuffy office, an Anglophile's fantasy of elephant ear plants and bas-relief cornucopias in carved wood, Jon Westling awaits the decision of Judge Patti B. Saris. He is resigned to the knowledge that, whatever is decided, the learning-disabled activists and their supporters will regard him as a villain. "This is a cause where the support and commitment verges almost on fanaticism," he says, puffing on one Marlboro Light, then another. "And whenever you have less than ideal science coupled with something close to fanaticism, you can move beyond appropriate use into areas of abuse."

The students say that, whatever the outcome, the litigation has salved their faltering self-esteem. Ben Freedman, a twenty-one-year-old senior who has maintained a 3.6 GPA despite a reading and writing disability and dysgraphia, likens his crusade to the civil rights movement of the 1960s. "I don't want to compare myself to Dr. King, but there are great similarities," he says.

Anne Schneider, too, says she's achieved closure on the whole re-grettable incident. To the true believers, it seems, there's an explanation for everything; and it's usually the same explanation. "I've been think-ing about Jon Westling," she tells me one evening. "For all his bragging about his Rhodes scholarship, he didn't do the final paper. He's not a finisher." Schneider lets out a reflective sigh. "To tell the truth," she says, "I've always thought: learning disability."

. . . .

Why Ritalin Rules

Mary Eberstadt

This selection first appeared in the April/May 1999 issue of *Policy Review*. Mary Eberstadt is consulting editor to *Policy Review*.

There are stories that are mere signs of the *Times*, and then there are stories so emblematic of a particular time and place that they demand to be designated cultural landmarks. Such a story was the *New York Times*'s front-page report on January 18 appearing under the tame, even soporific headline, "For School Nurses, More Than Tending the Sick."

"Ritalin, Ritalin, seizure drugs, Ritalin," in the words of its sing-song opening. "So goes the rhythm of noontime" for a typical school nurse in East Boston "as she trots her tray of brown plastic vials and paper water cups from class to class, dispensing pills into outstretched young palms." For this nurse, as for her counterparts in middle- and upper-middle-class schools across the country, the day's routine is now driven by what the *Times* dubs "a ticklish question," to wit: "With the number of children across the country taking Ritalin estimated at well over three million, more than double the 1990 figure, who should be giving out the pills?"

"With nurses often serving more than one school at a time," the story goes on to explain, "the whole middle of the day can be taken up in a school-to-school scurry to dole out drugs." Massachusetts, for its part, has taken to having the nurse deputize "anyone from a principal to a secretary" to share the burden. In Florida, where the ratio of school nurses to students is particularly low, "many schools have clerical workers hand out the pills." So many pills, and so few professionals to go around. What else are the authorities to do?

Behold the uniquely American psychotropic universe, pediatrics zone—a place where "psychiatric medications in general have become more common in schools" and where, in particular, "Ritalin dominates." There are by now millions of stories in orbit here, and the particular one chosen by the *Times*—of how the drug has induced a professional labor shortage—is no doubt an estimable entry. But for the reader struck by some of the facts the *Times* mentions only in passing—for example, that Ritalin use more than doubled in the first half of the decade alone, that production has increased 700 percent since 1990, or that the number of schoolchildren taking the drug may now, by some estimates, be approaching the 4 million mark—mere anecdote will only explain so much.

Fortunately, at least for the curious reader, there is a great deal of other material now on offer, for the explosion in Ritalin consumption has been very nearly matched by a publishing boom dedicated to that same phenomenon. Its harbingers include, for example, Barbara Ingersoll's now-classic 1988 *Your Hyperactive Child*, among the first works to popularize a drug regimen for what we now call attention deficit disorder (ADD, called ADHD when it includes hyperactivity). Five years later, with ADD diagnoses and Ritalin prescriptions already rising steeply in the better-off neighborhoods and schools, Peter D. Kramer helped fuel the boom with his best-selling *Listening to Prozac*—a book that put the phrase "cosmetic pharmacology" into the vernacular and thereby inadvertently broke new conceptual ground for the advocates of Ritalin. In 1994, most important, psychiatrists Edward M. Hallowell and John J. Ratey published their own best-selling *Driven to Distraction: Recognizing and Coping with Attention Deficit Disorder from Childhood to Adulthood*, a book that was perhaps the single most powerful force in the subsequent proliferation of ADD diagnoses; as its opening sentence accurately prophesied, "Once you catch on to what this syndrome is all about, you'll see it everywhere."

Not everyone received these soundings from the psychotropic beyond with the same enthusiasm. One noteworthy dissent came in 1995 with Thomas Armstrong's *The Myth of the ADD Child*, which attacked both the scientific claims made on behalf of ADD and what Armstrong decried as the "pathologizing" of normal children. Dissent also took the form of wary public pronouncements by the National Education Association (NEA), one of several groups to harbor the fear that ADD would be used to stigmatize minority children. Meanwhile, scare stories on the abuse and side effects of Ritalin popped out here and there in the mass media, and a national controversy was born. From the middle to the late 1990s, other interested parties from all over—the Drug Enforcement Administration (DEA), the Food and Drug Administration (FDA), the medical journals, the National Institutes of Health (NIH), and especially the extremely active advocacy group CHADD (Children and Adults with Attention Deficit Disorder)—further stoked the debate through countless reports, conferences, pamphlets, and exchanges on the Internet.

To this outpouring of information and opinion two new books, both on the critical side of the ledger, have just been added: Richard DeGrandpre's iconoclastic *Ritalin Nation: Rapid-Fire Culture and the Transformation of Human Consciousness* (Simon & Schuster, 1999), and physician Lawrence H. Diller's superbly analytical *Running on Ritalin: A Physician Reflects on Children, Society and Performance in a Pill* (Bantam Books, 1998). Their appearance marks an unusually opportune moment in which to sift through some ten years' worth of information on Ritalin and ADD and to ask what, if anything, we have learned from the national experiment that has made both terms into household words.

Let's put the question bluntly: How has it come to pass that in *fin-de-siècle* America, where every child from preschool onward can recite the "anti-drug" catechism by heart, millions of middle- and upper-middle-class children are being legally drugged with a substance so similar to cocaine that, as one journalist accurately summarized the science, "it takes a chemist to tell the difference"?

What Is Methylphenidate?

The first thing that has made the Ritalin explosion possible is that methylphenidate, to use the generic term, is perhaps the most widely misunderstood drug in America today. Despite the fact that it is, as Lawrence Diller observes in *Running on Ritalin*, "the most intensively studied drug in pediatrics," most laymen remain under a misimpression both about the nature of the drug itself and about its pharmacological effects on children.

What most people believe about this drug is the same erroneous characterization that appeared elsewhere in the *Times* piece quoted earlier—that it is "a mild stimulant of the central nervous system that, for reasons not fully understood, often helps children who are chronically distractible, impulsive and hyperactive settle down and concentrate." The word "stimulant" here is at least medically accurate. "Mild," a more ambiguous judgment, depends partly on the dosage, and partly on whether the reader can imagine describing as "mild" any dosage of the drugs to which methylphenidate is closely related. These include dextroamphetamine (street name: "dexies"), methamphetamine (street name: "crystal meth"), and, of course, cocaine. But the chief substance of the *Times*'s formulation here—that the reasons why Ritalin does what it does to children remain a medical mystery—is, as informed writers from all over the debate have long acknowledged, an enduring public myth.

"Methylphenidate," in the words of a 1995 DEA background paper on the drug, "is a central nervous system (CNS) stimulant and shares many of the pharmacological effects of amphetamine, methamphetamine, and cocaine." Further, it "produces behavioral, psychological, subjective, and reinforcing effects similar to those of *d*-amphetamine including increases in rating of euphoria, drug liking and activity, and decreases in sedation." To put the point conversely, as Richard DeGrandpre does in *Ritalin Nation* by quoting a 1995 report in the Archives of General Psychiatry, "Cocaine, which is one of the most reinforcing and addicting of the abused drugs, has pharmacological actions that are very similar to those of methylphenidate, which is now the most commonly prescribed psychotropic medicine for children in the U.S."

Such pharmacological similarities have been explored over the years in numerous studies. DeGrandpre reports that "lab animals given the choice to self-administer comparative doses of cocaine and Ritalin do not favor one over another" and that "a similar study showed monkeys would work in the same fashion for Ritalin as they would for cocaine." The DEA reports another finding—that methylphenidate is actually "chosen *over* cocaine in preference studies" of non-human primates (emphasis added). In *Driven to Distraction*, pro-Ritalin psychiatrists Hallowell and Ratey underline the interchangeable nature of methylphenidate and cocaine when they observe that "people with ADD feel focused when they take cocaine, *just as they do when they take Ritalin* [emphasis added]." Moreover, methylphenidate (like other stimulants) appears to increase tolerance for related drugs. Recent evidence indicates, for example, that when people accustomed to prescribed Ritalin turn to cocaine, they seek higher doses of it than do others. To summarize, again from the DEA report, "it is clear that methylphenidate substitutes for cocaine and *d*-amphetamine in a number of behavioral paradigms."

All of which is to say that Ritalin "works" on children in the same way that related stimulants work on adults—sharpening the short-term attention span when the drug kicks in and producing equally predictable valleys ("coming down," in the old street parlance; "rebounding," in Ritalinese) when the effect wears off. Just as predictably, children are subject to the same adverse effects as adults imbibing such drugs, with the two most common—appetite suppression and insomnia—being of particular concern. That is why, for example, handbooks on

ADD will counsel parents to see their doctor if they feel their child is losing too much weight, and why some children who take methylphenidate are also prescribed sedatives to help them sleep. It is also why one of the more Orwellian phrases in the psychotropic universe, "drug holidays"—meaning scheduled times, typically on weekends or school vacations, when the dosage of methylphenidate is lowered or the drug temporarily withdrawn in order to keep its adverse effects in check—is now so common in the literature that it no longer even appears in quotations.

Just as, contrary to folklore, the adult and child physiologies respond in the same way to such drugs, so too do the physiologies of *all* people, regardless of whether they are diagnosed with ADD or hyperactivity. As Diller puts it, in a point echoed by many other sources, methylphenidate "potentially improves the performance of anyone–child or not, ADD-diagnosed or not." Writing in the *Public Interest* last year, psychologist Ken Livingston provided a similar summary of the research, citing "studies conducted during the mid seventies to early eighties by Judith Rapaport of the National Institute of Mental Health" which "clearly showed that stimulant drugs improve the performance of most people, regardless of whether they have a diagnosis of ADHD, on tasks requiring good attention." ("Indeed," he comments further in an obvious comparison, "this probably explains the high levels of 'self-medicating' around the world" in the form of "stimulants like caffeine and nicotine.")

A third myth about methylphenidate is that it, alone among drugs of its kind, is immune to being abused. To the contrary: Abuse statistics have flourished alongside the boom in Ritalin prescription-writing. Though it is quite true that elementary schoolchildren are unlikely to ingest extra doses of the drug, which is presumably kept away from little hands, a very different pattern has emerged among teenagers and adults who have the manual dexterity to open prescription bottles and the wherewithal to chop up and snort their contents (a method that puts the drug into the bloodstream far faster than oral ingestion). For this group, statistics on the proliferating abuse of methylphenidate in schoolyards and on the street are dramatic.

According to the DEA, for example, as early as 1994 Ritalin was the fastest-growing amphetamine being used "non-medically" by high school seniors in Texas. In 1991, reports DeGrandpre in *Ritalin Nation*, "children between the ages of 10 and 14 years old were involved in only about 25 emergency room visits connected with Ritalin abuse. In 1995, just four years later, that number had climbed to more than 400 visits, which for this group was about the same number of visits as for cocaine." Not surprisingly, given these and other measures of methylphenidate's recreational appeal, criminal entrepreneurs have responded with interest to the drug's increased circulation. From 1990 to 1995, the DEA reports, there were about 2,000 thefts of methylphenidate, most of them night break-ins at pharmacies—meaning that the drug "ranks in the top 10 most frequently reported pharmaceutical drugs diverted from licensed handlers."

Because so many teenagers and college students have access to it, methylphenidate is particularly likely to be abused on school grounds. "The prescription drug Ritalin," reported *Newsweek* in 1995, "is now a popular high on campus—with some serious side effects." DeGrandpre notes that at his own college in Vermont, Ritalin was cited as the third-favorite drug to snort in a campus survey. He also runs, without comment, scores of individual abuse stories from newspapers across the country over several pages of his book. In *Running on Ritalin*, Diller cites several undercover narcotics agents who confirm that "Ritalin is cheaper and easier to purchase at playgrounds than on the street." He further reports one particularly hazardous fact about Ritalin abuse, namely that teenagers, especially, do not consider the drug to be anywhere near as dangerous as heroin or cocaine. To the contrary: "they think that since their younger brother takes it under a doctor's prescription, it must be safe."

In short, methylphenidate looks like an amphetamine, acts like an amphetamine, and is abused like an amphetamine. Perhaps not surprisingly, those who value its medicinal effects tend to explain the drug differently. To some, Ritalin is to children what Prozac and other psychotropic "mood brightening" drugs are to adults—a short-term fix for enhancing personality and performance. But the analogy is misleading. Prozac and its sisters are not stimulants with stimulant side effects; there is, ipso facto, no black market for drugs like these. Even more peculiar is the analogy favored by the advocates in CHADD: that "Just as a pair of glasses help the nearsighted person focus," as Hallowell and Ratey explain, "so can medication help the person with ADD see the world more clearly." But there is no black market for eyeglasses, either—nor loss of appetite, insomnia, "dysphoria" (an unexplained feeling of sadness that sometimes accompanies pediatric Ritalin-taking), nor even the faintest risk of toxic psychosis, to cite one of Ritalin's rare but dramatically chilling possible effects.

What is methylphenidate "really" like? Thomas Armstrong, writing in *The Myth of the ADD Child* four years ago, probably summarized the drug's appeal best. "Many middle- and upper-middle- class parents," he observed then, "see Ritalin and related drugs almost as 'cognitive steroids' that can be used to help their kids focus on their schoolwork better than the next kid." Put this way, the attraction to Ritalin makes considerable sense. In some ways, one can argue, that after-lunch hit of low-dose methylphenidate is much like the big cup from Starbucks that millions of adults swig to get them through the day—but only in some ways. There is no dramatic upswing in hospital emergency room visits and pharmacy break-ins due to caffeine abuse; the brain being jolted awake in one case is that of an adult, and in the other that of a developing child; and, of course, the substance doing the jolting on all those children is not legally available and ubiquitous caffeine, but a substance that the DEA insists on calling a Schedule II drug, meaning that it is subject to the same controls, and for the same reasons of abuse potential, as related stimulants and other powerful drugs like morphine.

What Is CHADD?

This mention of Schedule II drugs brings us to a second reason for the Ritalin explosion in this decade. That is the extraordinary political and medical clout of CHADD, by far the largest of the ADD support groups and a lobbying organization of demonstrated prowess. Founded in 1987, CHADD had, according to Diller, grown by 1993 to include 35,000 families and 600 chapters nationally. Its professional advisory board, he notes, "includes most of the most prominent academicians in the ADD world, a veritable who's who in research."

Like most support groups in self-help America, CHADD functions partly as clearing-house and information center for its burgeoning membership—organizing speaking events, issuing a monthly newsletter (*CHADDerbox*), putting out a glossy magazine (named, naturally enough, *Attention!*), and operating an exceedingly active website stocked with on-line fact sheets and items for sale. Particular scrutiny is given to every legal and political development offering new benefits for those diagnosed with ADD. On these and other fronts of interest, CHADD leads the ADD world. "No matter how many sources of information are out there," as a slogan on its website promises, "CHADD is the one you can trust."

One of CHADD's particular strengths is that it is exquisitely media-sensitive, and has a track record of delivering speedy responses to any reports on Ritalin or ADD that the group deems inaccurate. Diller quotes as representative one fund-raising letter from 1997, where the organization listed its chief goals and objectives as "conduct[ing] a proactive media campaign" and "challeng[ing] negative, inaccurate reports that demean or undermine people with ADD." Citing "savage attacks" in the *Wall Street Journal* and *Forbes*, the letter also went on to exhort readers into "fighting these battles of misinformation, innuendo, ignorance and outright hostility toward CHADD and adults who have a neurobiological disorder." The circle-the-wagons rhetoric here appears to be typical of the group, as is the zeal.

Certainly it was with missionary fervor that CHADD, in 1995, mounted an extraordinary campaign to make Ritalin easier to obtain. Methylphenidate, as mentioned, is a Schedule II drug. That means, among other things, that the DEA must approve an annual production quota for the substance—a fact that irritates those who rely on it, since it raises the specter, if only in theory, of a Ritalin "shortage." It also means that some states require that prescriptions for Ritalin be written in triplicate for the purpose of monitoring its use, and that refills cannot simply be called into the pharmacy as they can for Schedule III drugs (for example, low-dosage opiates like Tylenol with codeine, and various compounds used to treat migraine). Doctors, particularly those who prescribe Ritalin in quantity, are inconvenienced by this requirement. So too are many parents, who dislike having to stop by the doctor's office every time the Ritalin runs out. Moreover, many parents and doctors alike object to methylphenidate's Schedule II classification in principle, on the grounds that it makes children feel stigmatized; the authors of *Driven to Distraction*, for example, claim that one of the most common problems in treating ADD is that "some pharmacists, in their attempt to comply with federal regulations, make consumers [of Ritalin] feel as though they are obtaining illicit drugs."

For all of these reasons, CHADD petitioned the DEA to reclassify Ritalin as a Schedule III drug. This petition was co-signed by the American Academy of Neurology, and it was also supported by other distinguished medical bodies, including the American Academy of Pediatrics, the American Psychological Association, and the American Academy of Child and Adolescent Psychiatry. Diller's account of this episode in *Running on Ritalin* is particularly credible, for he is a doctor who has himself written many prescriptions for Ritalin in cases where he has judged it to be indicated. Nevertheless, he found himself dissenting strongly from the effort to decontrol it—an effort that, as he writes, was "unprecedented in the history of Schedule II substances" and "could have had a profound impact on the availability of the drug."

What happened next, while CHADD awaited the DEA's verdict, was in Diller's words "a bombshell." For before the DEA had officially responded, a television documentary revealed that Ciba-Geigy (now called Novartis), the pharmaceuticals giant that manufactures Ritalin, had contributed nearly $900,000 to CHADD over five years, and that CHADD had failed to disclose the contributions to all but a few selected members.

The response from the DEA, which appeared in the background report cited earlier, was harsh and uncompromising. Backed by scores of footnotes and well over 100 sources in the medical literature, this report amounted to a public excoriation of CHADD's efforts and a meticulous description, alarming for those who have read it, of the realities of Ritalin use and abuse. "Most of the ADHD literature prepared for public consumption and available to parents," the DEA charged, "does not address the abuse liability or actual abuse of methylphenidate. Instead, methylphenidate is routinely portrayed as a benign, mild stimulant that is not associated with abuse or serious effects. In reality, however, there is an abundance of scientific literature which indicates that methylphenidate shares the same abuse potential as other Schedule II stimulants."

The DEA went on to note its "concerns" over "the depth of the financial relationship between CHADD and Ciba-Geigy." Ciba-Geigy, the DEA observed, "stands to benefit from a change in scheduling of methylphenidate." It further observed that the United Nations International Narcotics Control Board (INCB) had "expressed concern about non-governmental organizations and parental associations in the United States that are actively lobbying for the medical use of methylphenidate for children with ADD." (The rest of the world, it should be noted, has yet to acquire the American taste for Ritalin. Sweden, for example, had methylphenidate withdrawn from the market in 1968 following a spate of abuse cases. Today, 90 percent of Ritalin production is consumed in the United States.) The report concluded with the documented observations that "abuse data indicate a growing problem among school-age children," that "ADHD adults have a high incidence of substance disorders," and that "with three to five percent of today's youth being administered methylphenidate on a chronic basis, these issues are of great concern."

Yet whatever public embarrassment CHADD and its supporters may have suffered on account of this setback turned out to be short-lived. Though it failed in the attempt to decontrol Ritalin (in the end, the group withdrew its petition), on other legislative fronts CHADD was garnering one victory after another. By the end of the 1990s, thanks largely to CHADD and its allies, an ADD diagnosis could lead to an impressive array of educational, financial, and social service benefits.

In elementary and high school classrooms, a turning point came in 1991 with a letter from the U.S. Department of Education to state school superintendents outlining "three ways in which children labeled ADD could qualify for special education services in public school under existing laws," as Diller puts it. This directive was based on the landmark 1990 Individuals with Disabilities Education Act (IDEA), which "mandates that eligible children receive access to special education and/or related services, and that this education be designed to meet each child's unique educational needs" through an individualized program. As a result, ADD-diagnosed children are now entitled by law to a long list of services, including separate special-education classrooms, learning specialists, special equipment, tailored homework assignments, and more. The IDEA also means that public school districts unable to accommodate such children may be forced to pick up the tab for private education.

In the field of higher education, where the first wave of Ritalin-taking students has recently landed, an ADD diagnosis can be parlayed into other sorts of special treatment. Diller reports that ADD-based requests for extra time on SATs, LSATs, and MCATs have risen sharply in the course of the 1990s. Yet the example of such high-profile tests is only one particularly measurable way of assessing ADD's impact on education; in many classrooms, including college classrooms, similar "accommodations" are made informally at a student's demand. A professor in the Ivy League tells me that students with an ADD diagnosis now come to him "waving doctor's letters and pills" and requesting extra time for routine assignments. To refuse "accommodation" is to risk a hornet's nest of liabilities, as a growing caseload shows. A 1996 article in *Forbes* cites the example of Whittier Law School, which was sued by an ADD-diagnosed student for giving only 20 extra minutes per hour-long exam instead of a full hour. The school, fearing an expensive legal battle, settled the suit. It further undertook a preventive measure: banning pop quizzes "because ADD students need separate rooms and extra time."

Concessions have also been won by advocates in the area of college athletics. The National College Athletic Association (NCAA) once prohibited Ritalin usage (as do the U.S. and International Olympic Committees today) because of what Diller calls its "possible acute performance-enhancing benefits." In 1993, citing legal jeopardy as a reason for changing course, the NCAA capitulated. Today a letter from the team physician will suffice to allow an athlete to ingest Ritalin, even though that same athlete would be disqualified from participating in the Olympics if he were to test positive for stimulants.

Nor are children and college students the only ones to claim benefits in the name of ADD. With adults now accounting for the fastest-growing subset of ADD diagnoses, services and accommodations are also proliferating in the workplace. The enabling regulations here are 1997 guidelines from the Equal Employment Opportunity Commission (EEOC) which linked traits like chronic lateness, poor judgment, and hostility to coworkers—in other words, the sorts of traits people get fired for—to "psychiatric impairments," meaning traits that are protected under the law. As one management analyst for the *Wall Street Journal* recently observed (and as CHADD regularly reminds its readers), these EEOC guidelines have already generated a list of accommodations for ADD-diagnosed employees, including special office furniture, special equipment such as tape recorders and laptops, and byzantine organizational schemes (color coding, buddy systems, alarm clocks, and other "reminders") designed to keep such employees on track. "Employers," this writer warned, "could find themselves facing civil suits and forced to restore the discharged people to their old positions, or even give them promotions as well as back pay or reasonable accommodation."

An ADD diagnosis can also be helpful in acquiring Supplemental Security Income (SSI) benefits. SSI takes income into account in providing benefits to the ADD-diagnosed; in that, it is an exception to the trend. Most of the benefits now available, as even this brief review indicates, have come to be provided in principle, on account of the diagnosis per se. Seen this way, and taking the class composition of the ADD-diagnosed into account, it is no wonder that more and more people, as Diller and many other doctors report, are now marching into medical offices demanding a letter, a diagnosis, and a prescription. The pharmacological charms of Ritalin quite apart, ADD can operate, in effect, as affirmative action for affluent white people.

What Is Attention Deficit Disorder?

Another factor that has put Ritalin into millions of medicine cabinets has to do with the protean nature of the disorder for which it is prescribed— a disorder that was officially so designated by the American Psychiatric Association in 1980, and one that, to cite Thomas Armstrong, "has gone through at least 25 different name changes in the past century."

Despite the successful efforts to have ADD construed as a disability like blindness, the question of what ADD is remains passionately disputed. To CHADD, of course, it is a "neurobiological disorder," and not only to CHADD; "the belief that ADD is a neurological disease," as Diller writes, also "prevails today among medical researchers and university teaching faculty" and "is reflected in the leading journals of psychiatry." What the critics observe is something else—that "despite highly successful efforts to define ADD as a well-established disorder of the brain," as DeGrandpre puts it in a formulation echoed by many, "three decades of medical science have yet to produce any substantive evidence to support such a claim."

Nonetheless, the effort to produce such evidence has been prodigious. Research on the neurological side of ADD has come to resemble a Holy Grail-like quest for something, anything, that can be said to set the ADD brain apart—genes, imbalances of brain chemicals like dopamine and serotonin, neurological damage, lead poisoning, thyroid problems, and more. The most famous of these studies, and the chief grounds on which ADD has come to be categorized as a neurobiological disability, was reported in *The New England Journal of Medicine* in 1990 by Alan Zametkin and colleagues at the National Institute of Mental Health (NIMH). These researchers used then-new positron emission tomography (PET) scanning to measure differences in glucose metabolizing between hyperactive adults and a control group. According to the study's results, what emerged was a statistically significant difference in the rates of glucose metabolism—a difference hailed by many observers as the first medical "proof" of a biological basis for ADD.

Diller and DeGrandpre are only the latest to argue, at length, that the Zametkin study established no such thing. For starters—and from the scientific point of view, most important—a series of follow-up studies, as

Diller documents, "failed to confirm" the original result. DeGrandpre, for his part, details the methodological problems with the study itself—that the participants were adults rather than children, meaning that the implications for the majority of the Ritalin-taking population were unclear at best; that there was "no evidence" that the reported difference in metabolism bore any relationship to behavioral activity; that the study was further plagued by "a confounding variable that had nothing to do with ADD," namely that the control group included far fewer male subjects than the ADD group; and that, even if there had been a valid difference in metabolism between the two groups, "this study tells us nothing about the cause of these differences."

Numerous other attempts to locate the missing link between ADD and brain activity are likewise dissected by Diller and DeGrandpre in their books. So too is the causal fallacy prevalent in ADD literature—that if a child responds positively to Ritalin, that response "proves" that he has an underlying biological disorder. This piece of illogic is easily dismissed. As these and other authors emphasize, drugs like Ritalin have the same effect on just about everybody. Give it to almost any child, and the child will become more focused and less aggressive—one might say, easier to manage—whether or not there were "symptoms" of ADD in the first place.

In sum, and as Thomas Armstrong noted four years ago in *The Myth of the ADD Child*, ADD remains an elusive disorder that "cannot be authoritatively identified in the same way as polio, heart disease, or other legitimate illnesses." Instead, doctors depend on a series of tests designed to measure the panoply of ADD symptoms. To cite Armstrong again: "there is no prime mover in this chain of tests; no First Test for ADD that has been declared self-referential and infallible." Some researchers, for example, use "continuous performance tasks" (CPTS) that require the person being tested to pay attention throughout a series of repetitive actions. A popular CPT is the Gordon Diagnostic System, a box that flashes numbers, whose lever is supposed to be pressed every time a particular combination appears. Yet as numerous critics have suggested, although the score that results is supposed to tell us about a given child's ability to attend, its actual significance is rather ambiguous; perhaps, as Armstrong analyzes, "it only tells how a child will perform when attending to a repetitive series of meaningless numbers on a soulless task."

In the absence of any positive medical or scientific test, the diagnosis of ADD in both children and adults depends, today as a decade ago, almost exclusively on behavioral criteria. The diagnostic criteria for children, according to the latest Diagnostic and Statistics Manual (DSM-IV), include six or more months' worth of some 14 activities such as fidgeting, squirming, distraction by extraneous stimuli, difficulty waiting turns, blurting out answers, losing things, interrupting, ignoring adults, and so on. (To read the list is to understand why boys are diagnosed with ADD three to five times as often as girls.) The diagnostic latitude offered by this list is obvious; as Diller understates the point, "what often strikes those encountering DSM criteria for the first time is how common these symptoms are among children" generally.

The DSM criteria for adults are if anything even more expansive, and include such ambiguous phenomena as a sense of underachievement, difficulty getting organized, chronic procrastination, a search for high stimulation, impatience, impulsivity, and mood swings. Hallowell and Ratey's 100-question test for ADD in *Driven to Distraction*, an elaborately extrapolated version of the DSM checklist, illustrates this profound elasticity. Their questions range from the straightforward ("Are you impulsive?" "Are you easily distracted?" "Do you fidget a lot?") to more elusive ways of eliciting the disorder ("Do you change the radio station in your car frequently?" "Are you always on the go, even when you don't really want to be?" "Do you have a hard time reading a book all the way through?"). Throughout, the distinction between what is pathological and what is not remains unclear—because, in the authors' words, "There is no clear line of demarcation between ADD and normal behavior."

Thus the business of diagnosing ADD remains, as Diller puts it, "very much in the eye of the beholder." In 1998, partly for that reason, the National Institutes of Health convened a conference on ADD with hundreds of participants and a panel of 13 doctors and educators. This conference, as newspapers reported at the time, broke no new ground, and indeed could not reach agreement on several important points—for instance, how long children should take drugs for ADD, or whether and when drug treatment might become risky. Even more interesting, conference members could not agree on what is arguably the rather fundamental question of how to diagnose the disorder in the first place. As one panelist, a pediatrician, put it succinctly, "The diagnosis is a mess."

Who Has ADD?

To test this hypothesis, I gave copies of Hallowell and Ratey's questionnaire to 20 people (let's call them subjects) and asked them to complete it and total up the number of times they checked "yes." "These questions," as Hallowell and Ratey note, "reflect those an experienced diagnostician would ask." Although, as they observe, "this quiz cannot confirm the diagnosis" (as we have seen already, nothing can), it does "offer a rough assessment as to whether professional help should be sought." In short, "the more questions that are answered 'yes,' the more likely it is that ADD may be present."

In a stab at methodological soundness, I had equal numbers of males and females take the test. All would be dubbed middle or upper middle class, all but one are or have been professionals of one sort or another, all are white, and the group was politically diverse—which is to say, the sample accurately reflects the socioeconomic pool from which most of the current Ritalin-taking population is drawn. As to the matter of observer interference, although some subjects may have guessed what the questionnaire was looking for, all of them (myself excepted, of course) took the test "blind," that is, without any accompanying material to prejudice their responses.

We begin with results at the lower end of the scale. Of the 18 subjects who completed the test, two delivered "yes" scores of 8 and 10 (a professor of English and his wife, an at-home mother active in philanthropy). These "yes" results, as it turned out, were at least threefold lower than anyone else's. In "real" social science, according to some expert sources, we would simply call these low scores "outliers" and throw them out for the same reason. We, however, shall include them, if only on the amateur grounds of scrupulousness.

The next lowest "yes" tallies—29 in each case—were achieved by an editorial assistant and a school nurse. That is to say, even these "low scorers" managed to answer yes *almost a third of the time* (remember, "the more questions that are answered 'yes,' the more likely it is that ADD may be present"). After them, we find a single "yes" score of 33 (an assistant editor). Following that, fully six subjects, or a third of the test-finishers, produced scores in the 40s. These include this magazine's editor, two at-home mothers (one a graphic designer, the other a poet), a writer for *Time* and other distinguished publications, *Policy Review's* business manager, and—scoring an estimable 49—the headmaster of a private school in Washington.

Proceeding into the upper echelons, a novelist who is also an at-home mother reported her score as 55, and a renowned demographic expert with ties to Harvard and Washington think tanks scored a 57. A male British journalist and at-home father achieved a 60, and a female American journalist and at-home mother (me) got a 62. Still another at-home mother, this one with a former career in public relations, garnered a 65.

In the lead, at least of the test-finishers, was a best-selling satirist whom we shall call, for purposes of anonymity, Patrick O'Rourke; he produced an estimable score of 75. "Mr. O'Rourke" further advanced the cause of science by answering the questions on behalf of his 16-month-old daughter; according to his proud report, 65 was the result. Then there were the two subjects who, for whatever reason, were unable to complete the test in the first place. One of these subjects called to say that he'd failed to finish the test because he'd "gotten bored checking off so many yes answers." When I pressed him for some, any, final tally for me to include, he got irritated and refused, saying he was "too lazy" to count them up. Finally he said "50 would be about right," take it or leave it. He is a Wall Street investment banker specializing in the creation of derivative securities. Our last subject, perhaps the most pathological of all, failed to deliver any score despite repeated reminding phone calls from the research team. He is the professor mentioned earlier, the one who reported that ADD is now being used as a blanket for procrastination and shirking on campus.

Now on to interpreting the results. Apart from the exceedingly anomalous two scores of ten and under, all the rest of the subjects reported answering "yes" to at least a quarter of the questions—surely enough to trigger the possibility of an ADD diagnosis, at least in those medical offices Diller dubs "Ritalin mills." (As for the one subject who reported no result whatsoever, he is obviously entitled to untold ADD bonus points for that reason alone.) Fully 15 of the finishers, or 80-plus percent, answered yes to one-third of the questions or more. Eight of the finishers, or 40-plus percent of the sample, answered yes more than half of the time, with a number of scores in the high 40s right behind them. In other words, *roughly half of the sample answered yes roughly half of the time.*

My favorite comment on the exercise came from the school nurse (who scored, one recalls, a *relatively* low 29). She has a background in psychiatry, and therefore realized what kind of diagnosis the questionnaire was designed to elicit. When she called to report her result, she said that taking the test had made her think hard about the whole ADD issue. "My goodness," she concluded, "it looks like the kind of thing almost anybody could have." This brings us to the fourth reason for the explosion of ADD and its prescribed corollary, Ritalin: The nurse is right.

What Is Childhood?

The fourth and most obvious reason millions of Americans, most of them children, are now taking Ritalin can be summarized in a single word that crops up everywhere in the dry-bones literature on ADD and its drug of choice: *compliance*. One day at a time, the drug continues to make children do what their parents and teachers either will not or cannot get them to do without it: Sit down, shut up, keep still, pay attention. That some children are born with or develop behavioral problems so severe that drugs like Ritalin are a godsend is true and sad. It is also irrelevant to the explosion in psychostimulant prescriptions. For most, the drug is serving a more nuanced purpose—that of "help[ing] your child to be more agreeable and less argumentative," as Barbara Ingersoll put it over a decade ago in *Your Hyperactive Child.*

There are, as was mentioned, millions of stories in the Ritalin universe, and the literature of advocates and critics alike all illustrates this point. There is no denying that millions of people benefit from having children take Ritalin—the many, many parents who will attest that the drug has improved their child's school performance, their home lives, often even their own marriages; the teachers who have been relieved by its effects in their classrooms, and have gone on to proselytize other parents of other unruly children (frequently, it is teachers who first suggest that a child be checked for the disorder); and the doctors who, when faced with all these grateful parents and teachers, find, as Diller finds, that "at times the pressure for me to medicate a child is intense."

Some other stories seep through the literature too, but only if one goes looking for them. These are the stories standing behind the clinical accounts of teenagers who lie and say they've taken the day's dose when they haven't, or of the children who cry in doctor's offices and "cheek" the pill (hide it rather than swallow, another linguistic innovation of Ritalinese) at home. These are the stories standing behind such statements as the following, culled from case studies throughout the literature: "It takes over of me [sic]; it takes control." "It numbed me." "Taking it meant I was dumb." "I feel rotten about taking pills; why me?" "It makes me feel like a baby." And, perhaps most evocative of all, "I don't know how to explain. I just don't want to take it any more."

But these quotes, as any reader will recognize, appeal only to sentiment; science, for its part, has long since declared its loyalties. In the end, what has made the Ritalin outbreak not only possible but inevitable is the ongoing blessing of the American medical establishment–and not only that establishment. In a particularly enthusiastic account of the drug in a recent issue of *The New Yorker*, writer Malcolm Gladwell exults in the idea that "we are now extending to the young cognitive aids of a kind that used to be reserved exclusively for the old." He further suggests that, given expert estimates of the prevalence of ADD (up to 10 percent of the population, depending on the expert), if anything "too few" children are taking the drug. Surely all these experts have a point. Surely this country can do more, much more, to reduce fidgeting, squirming, talking excessively, interrupting, losing things, ignoring adults, and all those other pathologies of what used to be called childhood.

. . . .

The Scandal of Special Ed

Robert Worth

This selection first appeared in *The Washington Monthly*'s June 1999 issue. Robert Worth is a contributing editor to *The Washington Monthly*.

If you've ever wondered what the words "special education" mean, consider Saundra Lemons. A tall, gangly 19-year-old senior in a Washington, D.C., public high school, she is quiet and attentive. Like the vast majority of children in special ed, she's not blind or deaf or confined to a wheelchair; instead she has had trouble learning to read. If dollars were education, Saundra would be in fine shape. D.C. pours almost a third of its total education budget into the 10 percent of its students who are special ed. In theory—or rather, in wealthy school districts—this money buys kids like Saundra all kinds of assistance: special tutoring sessions, a modified curriculum, specially trained therapists and consultants, even untimed tests.

But Saundra wasn't born in a wealthy suburb. So when she started having trouble in first grade, she was placed—like many kids in D.C.— into a dead-end classroom where she learned nothing. In her case, it was a class for the mentally retarded. It took six years for a teacher to notice that Saundra wasn't retarded at all. Now she's catching up, but probably not fast enough to attend college next year. "You can never make up for that lost time," says one social worker who has helped Saundra.

Twenty-five years after the passage of the nation's special ed law, the Individuals with Disabilities Education Act (IDEA), the real scandal is not simply that we spend too much to educate handicapped kids. It's the inequity in the way the law is applied. At an estimated $35 billion a year, special education is like a huge regressive tax—helpful to those wealthy enough to take advantage of it, and often harmful to those who are not.

Furthermore, poor children like Saundra who get shunted into dead-end classrooms aren't the only victims. In order to pay for special ed's enormous, ineffectual bureaucracy and skyrocketing enrollments, school districts are being forced to cheat their conventional students. Unlike general education, special ed is a federal mandate: School districts can be sued (and routinely are) for not providing every service parents think is appropriate for their disabled kids. It's also massively underfunded. When IDEA was passed in 1975, the feds offered to pay up to 40 percent of the costs. They've averaged less than 10 percent ever since, and states don't make up the difference. This is not the kind of program you can fund with bake sales. One southern California district has seen its special ed layouts grow from $3 million to almost $11 million in just the past three years. School districts face a painful choice: Raise local property taxes or cut back on students. "We are cannibalizing our regular education budget," says Joe Quick, an administrator in the Wisconsin public school system. "For the first time since 1975, teachers are saying 'why are those kids here?' . . . it's really starting to drive a wedge between regular ed and special ed."

Republicans in Congress have pounced on this issue, declaring Clinton a hypocrite for announcing new school initiatives without promising to increase special education funding first. "What President Clinton isn't saying about this new budget is how he has decided to . . trim special education funding," declared Rep. Bill Goodling (R-Pa.), a former teacher and superintendent and chair of the House Education and the Workforce Committee, in March. "The president decided not to provide funding for our most vulnerable children," added Senate Majority Leader Trent Lott. The irony here is delicious: The party that tried to abolish the Department of Education and slash the federal role in education has now become a cheerleader for the most regulated and costly federal program under the sun.

Democrats counter that their plan to hire 100,000 new teachers will reduce the need for referrals to special ed in the first place. But neither party has even tried to reform special ed's mountainous bureaucracy and skewed incentives. It's not hard to see why. "If you criticize [IDEA] you will be publicly vilified as anti-handicap," says James Fleming, superintendent of the Capistrano Unified school district, near Los Angeles. "But what is happening now will absolutely destroy public education before the next decade is out."

The Road to Hell

There's no question that the special ed law served a crying need. Before Congress passed it in 1975, an estimated one million handicapped kids were not getting any education at all, and vastly disproportionate numbers of black children were being warehoused under the rubric "educably mentally retarded." The new law's intention was to remedy these conditions by mandating "specially designed instruction" for each child and "related services to meet his unique needs," including transportation, physical therapy, speech therapy, psychological counseling, occupational therapy, social work and services, and virtually anything else a child might conceivably need. To ensure that no one was left out, Congress mandated that each handicapped child receive an Individualized Education Plan from a multidisciplinary team, which would specify long- and short-term goals, and describe required services and special equipment. Furthermore, handicapped children had to be taught in the "least restrictive environment."

IDEA has achieved some of its main goals. Far fewer handicapped children sit at home staring at the walls, and the number attending college has more than tripled since 1978. According to the Department of Education, 62 percent of people with disabilities age 16 to 24 were employed in 1994, compared with 31 percent in the 16 to 64 age range—which suggests that far more are entering the workplace than ever before.

At first, accommodating the handicapped didn't seem like such a big job; total costs were about $1 billion in 1977. Yet little by little, Congress has added new categories to the original list of 13 disabling conditions. Children age three to five are now included, as are those with autism and traumatic brain injuries—both categories that require intensive supervision and therapy. In March, the Supreme Court ruled that an Iowa school district must pay for full-time nursing care for a high school sophomore named Garret Frey who is paralyzed from the neck down. Meanwhile the most porous special ed category, "learning disabilities," exploded as parents realized it could be made to include virtually any child who isn't living up to his potential. "It's just like a nightmare," says April Port, special ed director for Marin County, Calif. "They keep opening the barn door wider and wider, and the burden is always on the school." Currently, special ed costs the nation about $25 billion, with some estimates running closer to $60 billion.

In almost any individual case, it's hard not to sympathize with the family. Garret Frey is a likeable, smart kid, who has no trouble keeping up with his peers academically. For all we know, he could become a great scientist like the wheelchair-bound Stephen Hawking, the theorist of space-time. But he won't be able to do so unless someone pays for his medical supervision. Handicapped kids often struggle heroically to get by in school, and it's no wonder their parents feel entitled to extra help. One father told me in a voice choking with rage about how he had gone to school to confront a teacher who had taunted and bullied his boy, who has severe learning disabilities. "You hear about some parents demanding horseback riding lessons for their autistic kids, and it sounds ludicrous," another parent told me. "But when you see what they're going through, believe me, you want to do anything you can if there's any chance it would help."

The trouble is that the law pits the single interest of every disabled child against the broader interest of the school and arms his parents with a legal right to a "free and appropriate public education" in the "least restrictive environment." Needless to say, the vagueness of these words is a recipe for litigation. A whole cottage industry of lawyers and advocates has grown up to help parents get what they want out of the school system. Furthermore, school districts must pay parents' court fees if they lose. Overburdened, underfunded, and without the expert legal advice parents can draw on, schools tend to give in rather than face a case that could bankrupt them. "Districts will provide services they don't think are appropriate because they can't afford to go to court," says April Port. One southern California school district pays for a severely brain-damaged boy to attend a specialized school in Massachusetts, and to fly his parents and sister out for regular visits, at an annual cost of roughly $254,000. The superintendent only balked when the family demanded extra visits for the boy's sister.

Parents of severely disabled kids also regularly try to shoehorn them into mainstream classes, even when it would do little good for the child and plenty of harm to the rest of the class. It's true that for years schools were too quick to put seriously handicapped kids into classes of their own, where they often learned little and got no experience interacting with ordinary people. But special ed teachers tend to agree that the pendulum has now swung too far in the other direction. "It's hard for parents to give up the dream that their kid is normal," says April Port. The 1997 amendments to the IDEA strengthen the parents' hands: Teachers must prove that a child would be better off in separate classes before they move them, and that can be very hard to do. "Often you'll have a kid with a 40 or 50 IQ, at a pre-kindergarten level, with very little language," says one California elementary teacher. "The kid is all over the place, and the teacher has no idea what to do." In response, many districts are paying for aides—babysitters really—to sit with the student all day long. "Mainstreaming is creating a huge financial burden," says Port.

Defining Disability Down

Still, if special ed were merely a matter of accommodating physically disabled kids like Garret Frey, it would be a relatively straightforward affair. Unfortunately, the special ed law has inflated the meaning of "disability," encouraging wealthier families to capitalize on their weaknesses at the expense of their peers. "We are talking about kids who get tired," says Superintendent James Fleming of Capistrano Unified. "We are talking about people thinking any problem their kid has is a handicap." At worst, the handicap designation—designed to protect kids from discrimination—can become a protection against any sort of discipline. "We found one kid with enough pot on him to be selling," says Fleming. "We suspended him. Then the parents were contacted by an advocate who said, 'all you have to say is that you're handicapped.' Sure enough, the kid was back in school the next day. The kids he sold to were expelled." The 1997 amendments to IDEA gave schools a little more latitude in disciplining violent special ed kids, but the problem remains.

Meanwhile, the largest area of disability inflation, known as "specific learning disabilities," remains unaddressed. Learning disabilities, or LDs, account for over 51 percent of all children in special ed, and the numbers are growing at astounding speed. Technically, the 1975 law defines LD as "a disorder in one or more of the basic psychological processes involved in understanding or in using language, spoken or written, which disorder may manifest itself in imperfect ability to listen, think, speak, read, write, spell, or do mathematical calculations." Lest this be an open invitation to anyone who has trouble with their homework, the regulations stipulate that a diagnostic team shall identify as LD those students who show a "severe discrepancy" between their achievement in one or more subject areas and their intelligence, usually as measured by an IQ test.

Yet even with this diagnostic testing, LD is a notoriously plastic category. There are 50 state definitions in addition to the federal one, and the methods used to determine intelligence vary wildly. More than 80 percent of all school children in the United States could qualify as learning-disabled under one definition or another, according to University of Minnesota researcher James Ysseldyke. Even if LDs do exist as a legitimate category, it is not a foregone conclusion that learning-disabled children should receive more help than garden-variety poor readers. Why should a kid with a genius IQ but only above-average reading skills get extra help, while his average-scoring peers get none—no matter what obstacles they've overcome? It seems especially unfair that the rules should specifically exclude kids whose learning problems derive from "environmental, cultural, or economic disadvantage."

LD advocates respond by citing voluminous studies purporting to demonstrate that LDs are real, and that they respond to treatment. But the scientific status of LDs is still cloudy at best, and it's not clear that LD students respond any better than their undiagnosed peers. Indeed, "[T]here is considerable evidence that non-LD pupils would benefit from higher levels of educational inputs, and even stronger evidence that as a group, if not in each individual case, those diagnosed with LDs have been remarkably unresponsive to the costly special education that has been provided to them," write Mark Kelman and Gillian Lester in their 1998 book, *Jumping the Queue: An Inquiry into the Legal Treatment of Students with Learning Disabilities.* "There is very scant evidence that dyslexics, for instance, benefit more from the interventions of reading specialists than do garden-variety poor readers."

Furthermore, the LD diagnosis is often little more than an expression of class bias. As Kelman and Lester write, "a student is viewed as LD when the observer finds it *surprising* that he or she is performing poorly." These expectations, of course, are likely to be informed by the parents' social status. Learning disabilities grew out of a grassroots movement by middle-class parents in the 1950s and '60s who wanted a label—and extra help—for what they saw as their "under-achieving" children. That's not to say that some bright kids don't suffer from dyslexia and other serious reading problems. But there's little doubt that the meaning of the LD diagnosis depends, in large measure, on who your parents are.

Consider Michael, a slender, sandy-haired fourth grader in a public school in Marin, one of California's wealthiest counties. Michael's teacher says he has an IQ in the high 120s, but he's about two years behind his classmates in reading. His parents are both wealthy professionals who don't have much time to spend with him—which may account for his reading problems. But his teachers didn't want lawsuits, so they wrote an education plan that includes a modified curriculum with separate tests, special reading sessions in a "resource" room, a buddy to read with, and books on tape to keep him on track. If his problems persist, his parents will see to it that he gets any other accommodations the school can offer, including untimed tests, and eventually, an untimed SAT, to increase his chances of going to Stanford as Mom and Dad did. "We get a lot of referrals junior year," says another teacher in Michael's school. "Parents want to cut their kid a break. And it's starting a lot earlier." The words LD, she adds, no longer have any tainting stigma. Yale psychologist Robert J. Sternberg, who has spent years preparing a book on LDs, agrees. "That's the funny thing—before, no one would want that label. Now it's almost a cachet."

Despite the fact that LD isn't meant to apply to kids whose problems derive from poverty, teachers in poorer schools routinely bend the rules in order to get more attention for kids who are failing. Crowded and decaying inner-city classrooms are a handicap in their own right, and poverty itself can cut deeply into a child's learning. According to the Children's Defense Fund, middle-class children starting first grade have been exposed to 1,000 to 1,700 hours of one-on-one reading, while their low-income counterparts have been exposed to only *25 hours*. It's little wonder that so many of these kids get referred to special ed.

But these efforts often backfire when the students end up in dead-end classrooms where they'll be even less likely to learn. "You need to look at who gets the benefits of being diagnosed LD and who gets the bad side," says Mark Kelman. Tony, an African-American boy from northeast Washington, D.C., is fairly typical. He was diagnosed with learning disabilities a few years ago at roughly the same age as Michael. Like many kids in large urban school systems, he didn't get any help at all, and began falling further behind. Unhappy with his failures, he began "acting out" in class, whereupon he was reassessed and classified "emotionally disturbed" and put into separate classes. There he was taught nothing and his behavior got worse, because many of his genuinely disturbed classmates picked fights with him. By the sixth grade he barely knew the alphabet. Yet Tony is neither stupid nor disturbed. A public interest lawyer managed to work a minor miracle, getting him assessed and transferred to a private school, where he has thrived. "If he'd had the appropriate intervention in third or fourth grade," says the lawyer, "who knows where he'd be now."

According to researchers who have studied trends in the treatment of LD across the country, these patterns apply nationwide. Kelman and Lester argue that the current system "continues to permit relatively privileged white pupils to capture high-cost or non-stigmatic in-class resources that others with similar educational deficits cannot obtain while, at the same time, allowing disproportionate numbers of African-American and poor pupils to be shunted into self-contained classes."

Bureaucrazy

Why does special ed serve the poor so badly? Part of the answer has to do with its massive, ineffectual, and self-perpetuating bureaucracy. Beneath the federal Office of Special Education Programs, which does research and audits states and school districts, there is a state office, and a localized Special Education Local Plan Area office, and a school district office. This is all on top of whatever counselors, psychologists, therapists, and "educational evaluators" a given school may have working for it. And in some individual states and cities, the situation is even worse. New York City, for instance, has its own separate bureaucracy, jokingly called the "Board of Special Ed," thanks to a consent decree that grew out of a lawsuit by advocates for special ed students in 1979.

Given this focus on legal liability and procedure, it's little wonder that teaching takes a back seat to paper-pushing. "[Special ed teachers] complain they're spending 50 to 60 percent of their time filling out forms," says Kim Reid, a professor at Columbia Teachers College. This constant bureaucratic drain makes it that much harder to recruit talented young people. It's bad enough dealing with disabled or disturbed children and their grieving, angry parents all day. The job is so stressful that the average shelf life of special ed teachers is three years, says Reid. The Department of Education website, which proudly displays the voluminous 1997 amendments to the IDEA, notes tersely a 'chronic' shortage of special education teachers who are fully certified in their positions."

The burden of this teacher crisis, and the top-heavy bureaucracy that fuels it, falls disproportionately on the poor. Wealthier parents, after all, can use the law to force schools to accommodate them or place their child in a private school. In Washington, D.C., such private placements account for over a third of the District's entire $167 million special ed budget, even though less than one-sixth of the District's special ed students attend private school. (The special ed budget itself comprises almost a third of the *entire* school budget, even though only one-tenth of the District's students are in special ed.)

What is left over for the students whose parents lack the money or know-how to work the system to their advantage? Precious little. Despite all those bureaucrats hired to evaluate and place students, more than 250 students in D.C. haven't received an initial evaluation, and almost 2,200 are overdue for their second evaluation. Many of these kids are like Saundra Lemons, languishing in inappropriate classes until an "evaluator" notices them. Often it's far too late by that time, since the crucial learning years are the earliest, and catching up is far more difficult when children are older. And being evaluated doesn't always help. "Often the kid ends up in a class with 20 kids, all with different disabilities, and a teacher who's trained in one of those," says Nancy Opalack, a D.C. social worker. "No one learns anything." Teachers in the District estimate that half the kids in special ed drop out by 10th grade.

Gross Inequalities

Yet anyone who's spent time in an inner-city classroom can tell you that the challenges the average poor kid faces are often hard to distinguish from those you'll find in special ed. This may be the greatest absurdity of the special ed law: It fails to acknowledge "environmental, cultural, or economic disadvantage" as disabling conditions. Why should a child with a broken back be guaranteed round-the-clock, state-of-the-art medical care, no matter what the cost, while the millions of kids whose difficulties stem from poverty and neglect are left to hope that their teachers will break the rules so they can get some extra help? Should we really be spending $10 billion (at least) a year on "learning disabilities" when we still don't adequately fund Head Start and Title I, the federal programs that were designed to help poor children catch up with their wealthier peers?

If the goal of public education is to give everyone a roughly equal start by the time they reach adulthood, it simply doesn't make sense to privilege obstacles that can be given a medical diagnosis over those that derive from poverty—which may be the greatest handicapping condition of all. The fact that the special ed bureaucracy often *prevents* poor kids from getting the help they need, by making them wait until they've been properly evaluated, only adds insult to injury.

Reforming IDEA is no easy task. Any politician who touches it runs the risk of being branded a cold-hearted enemy of kids in wheelchairs. But before we start pouring billions more into the program, Congress should ask whether it's really serving the goal of equal opportunity for all. And if special ed has become a kind of band-aid for schools that lack money to teach their kids adequately, or for kids whose parents never prepared them in the first place, then perhaps it's time to address those problems head-on. Kids like Garret Frey deserve a shot at success—but not at the expense of kids like Saundra Lemons.

STANDARDS AND ACCOUNTABILITY

·····································

Developing and Implementing Academic Standards

A Template for Legislative Reform

Lance T. Izumi

The following is a "Fact Sheet" summary of *Developing and Implementing Academic Standards*, the second in the three-part policy series *Templates for Legislative and Policy Reform*. The other two templates address the issues of school choice and charter schools. The series recommends best practices and legislative language, and highlights problem areas that arise when policy deviates from those best practices. Lance Izumi is the director of the Pacific Research Institute's Center for School Reform.

Developing and Implementing Academic Standards is a groundbreaking document focusing on five important standards-related issues. First, it defines and outlines the critical components of a successful academic standards system using examples of good and bad standards to illustrate key points. In addition, it offers analyses, discussion, and recommendations in four other crucial areas: tests aligned to the standards; categorization of student achievement through performance standards; implementation and accountability systems to guarantee that the standards become a reality in the classroom; and communications strategies to disseminate information about the standards to parents, teachers, and local school officials. Unless each of these components is both present and of high quality, a system of education standards will most likely fail to improve achievement.

Academic content standards set out the essential subject knowledge and skills students must master at defined intervals in their school careers. During the 1990s, a consensus has developed on the qualities that should be embodied in any good set of standards. According to a wide range of experts, a good set of academic content standards, in whatever subject, should be

1. Rigorous;
2. Intelligible;
3. Measurable;

4. Specific;

5. Comprehensive;

6. Academic;

7. Balanced;

8. Manageable; and

9. Cumulative.

Examples of academic content standards meeting these requirements include California's math and reading standards and Japan's math standards.

Crafting the content standards is just one part of a comprehensive system. Without an assessment device, there can be no way of knowing if the content standards are being met in the classroom. Further, if the assessment device does not accurately measure the knowledge content, then it will be impossible to determine if the standards are being met. An assessment device tests students' subject knowledge and skills and the results are reported to officials and the public. In deciding upon the type of assessment device to use, policymakers should bear in mind issues such as

1. Depth vs. breadth;

2. Time and cost of scoring;

3. Ability to generalize;

4. Factual knowledge vs. higher order thinking skills;

5. Memorability;

6. Equivalency; and

7. Validity.

Performance standards designate the achievement levels on the state test (e.g., "advanced," "proficient," "basic," and "below basic") and what the cut-off scores for the achievement levels will be on the test. It is important that the cut-off scores not be pegged artificially low so that, for example, more students score at the "advanced" level than is warranted by the students' actual knowledge. In crafting performance standards, the following steps should be observed:

1. Set the number of performance standards.

2. Name the performance levels.

3. Provide content and quality of performance at each level.

4. Develop and administer test items.

5. Decide cut scores.

6. Provide student work samples.

A high-stakes implementation and accountability system must be put in place so that local school districts have an incentive to make sure the standards actually make it into the classroom. Such a system cannot consist of more money thrown at districts which underperform. Rather, schools and districts where students fail to meet the standards should be targeted for reforms guaranteed to shake the status quo. Policymakers should therefore consider these implementation and accountability strategies:

1. Performance contracting with outside firms to provide educational services;

2. Merit pay for teachers linked to student achievement on standards-aligned tests;

3. Teacher selection and renewal based on performance;

4. Targeted school-choice demonstration programs in districts where students fail to meet the standards;

5. Improving teacher training programs by increasing content-area requirements; and,

6. Improving professional development for existing teachers by emphasizing standards-aligned content-area knowledge.

Finally, a communications plan must be formulated that informs parents, teachers, local school officials, the media, and the general public about details of the standards, assessments, performance standards, and accountability mechanisms.

. . . .

The War Against Testing

David W. Murray

This selection first appeared in *Commentary*'s September 1998 edition. David W. Murray is director of the Statistical Assessment Service in Washington, D.C.

It is safe to say that Thomas Jefferson never took a standardized test, and would probably consider them hopelessly inadequate as measures of what an educated person should know. Yet Jefferson, in his way, was the inspiration behind our present vast apparatus for assessing academic aptitude and achievement. Looking toward America's future, he imagined an educational system that would seek young people from "every condition of life," students of "virtue and talents" who would someday form a "natural aristocracy" to replace the old-fashioned kind based on wealth and family background.

The U.S. of course has never fully achieved this ideal. But particularly in the period after World War II, as ever larger numbers of Americans entered colleges and universities, Jefferson's educational vision did begin to appear closer than ever to being realized. To an extent unimaginable a few generations earlier, access to American universities, and especially the elite ones, became based on considerations of merit. The chief instrument of this transformation was the standardized test—mass-administered, machine-scored, and utterly indifferent to every characteristic of a student save his ability to get the answers right.

And yet, for all its obvious benefits in helping to identify Jefferson's "natural aristocracy," and for all its widespread acceptance—this year, the Educational Testing Service (ETS), the organization that does the bulk of such evaluation, will administer its tests to some nine million students—the enterprise of testing has never been free from criticism. Today, in fact, its critics are more numerous and more vociferous than ever.

Indignant over the recent drop in minority enrollment at some state universities as a result of bans on affirmative action, the foes of standardized assessment argue with bitterness that America's vaunted meritocracy has never served all its citizens equally well. As they see it, moreover, the real issue is not the abilities of the test-takers, minority or otherwise. Rather, it is the tests themselves, and the unreasonable emphasis placed on them by the gatekeepers of American higher education.

The oldest and most familiar accusation against standardized tests is that they are discriminatory. As the advocacy group FairTest puts it, a seemingly objective act, namely, "filling in little bubbles" with a No. 2 pencil, conceals a process that is "racially, culturally, and sexually biased."

The prime evidence for this charge is the test results themselves. For many years now, the median score for blacks on the Scholastic Assessment Test (SAT) has fallen 200 points short of that for whites (on a scale of 400 to 1600, divided equally between math and verbal skills). Less dramatic, but no less upsetting to groups like the Center for Women's Policy Studies, has been the persistent 35-point gender gap in scores on the math section of the SAT.

The SAT produces such disparate results, say critics, because its very substance favors certain kinds of students over others. Thus, fully comprehending a reading selection might depend on background knowledge naturally available to an upper-middle-class white student (by virtue, say, of foreign travel or exposure to the performing arts) but just as naturally unavailable to a lower-class black student from the ghetto. The education writer Peter Sacks calls this the "Volvo effect," and has offered for proof an ETS study according to which, within certain income brackets, the difference between the test scores of white and black students disappears.

At the same time, women are said to be put at a disadvantage by the multiple-choice format itself. Singled out for blame are math questions that emphasize abstract reasoning and verbal exercises based on selecting antonyms, both of which supposedly favor masculine modes of thought. "[F]emales process and express knowledge differently, and more subtly," explains FairTest's Robert Schaeffer. "They look for nuances, shades of gray, different angles."

In fact, so biased are the tests, according to their opponents, that they fail to perform even the limited function claimed for them: forecasting future grades. The SAT, says Peter Sacks, consistently "underpredicts" the college marks of both women and minorities, which hardly inspires confidence in its ability to measure the skills it purports to identify. As for the Graduate Record Exam (GRE), required by most academic graduate programs, a recent study of 5,000 students found that their scores told us almost nothing, beyond what we might already know from their grades, about how they would perform in graduate school.

Another line of attack against the tests grants their accuracy in measuring certain academic skills but challenges the notion that these are the skills most worth having. High test scores, opponents insist, reveal little more than a talent for—taking tests. According to a 1994 study by the National Association of School Psychologists, students who do well on the SAT tend to think by "rote" and to favor a "surface approach" to schoolwork. Low scorers, by contrast, are more likely to delve into material, valuing "learning for its own sake."

It is likewise contended that no mere standardized test can capture the qualities that translate into real-world achievement. Thus, when it emerged last year that American children ranked dead last among the major industrial nations in the Third International Mathematics and Science Study, the Harvard education expert Howard Gardner declared himself unconcerned. The tests, after all, "don't measure whether students can think," just their exposure to "the lowest common denominator of facts and skills." Besides, Gardner observed, at a time when America enjoys unrivaled prosperity, what could be more obvious than that "high scores on these tests . . . aren't crucial to our economic success"?

In a similar vein, the social commentator Nicholas Lemann has called for a reassessment of what we mean by meritocracy. Our current view of it, he argued recently in the New York Times, is "badly warped." If universities are to regain the "moral and public dimensions" that once connected them to the wider society, instead of being mere instruments for "distributing money and prestige," they should begin to select not those students who excel on standardized tests but those with the skills necessary to lead "a good, decent life."

This varied chorus of critics has already won some significant concessions from the current testing regime. For one thing, ETS, faced with both adverse publicity and threats of legal action by activists and the U.S. Department of Education, has tried to remedy differences in group performance. On the Preliminary Scholastic Assessment Test (PSAT), which is used for choosing National Merit Scholars, a new method of scoring was recently introduced in the hope that more women might garner the prestigious award. The old formula, which assigned equal weight to the math and verbal sections of the test, was replaced by an index in which the verbal score, usually the higher one for female test-takers, was doubled. The point, as a prominent testing official put it, was "to help girls catch up."

More widely publicized was the massive "recentering" of SAT scores that went into effect with the 1996 results. Though the declared aim of ETS was a technical one—to create a better distribution of scores clustered around the test's numerical midpoint—the practical effect was a windfall for students in almost every range. A test-taker who previously would have received an excellent score of 730 out of 800 on the verbal section, for example, is now granted a "perfect" 800, while the average scores for groups like blacks and Hispanics have received a considerable boost.

But since neither "recentering" nor any other such device has succeeded in eliminating disparities in scores, opponents of tests have had to look elsewhere. At universities themselves, affirmative action has long been the tool of choice for remedying the alleged biases of tests. With racial preferences now under siege, economic disadvantage is being talked about as a new compensating factor that may help shore up the numbers of minority students. The law school at the University of California at Berkeley, for instance, has introduced a selection system that will consider a "coefficient of social disadvantage" in ranking applicants.

Some schools go farther, hoping simply to do away with standardized tests altogether. There are, they insist, other, less problematic indicators of student merit. High school grades are a starting point, but no less important are essays, interviews, and work portfolios that offer a window into personal traits no standardized test can reveal.

Bates College in Maine, like several other small liberal arts schools, has already stopped requiring applicants to take the SAT. According to the college's vice president, William Hiss, standardized scores are far less meaningful than "evidence of real intelligence, real drive, real creative abilities, real cultural sensitivities." These qualities, moreover, are said to be especially prominent in the applications of minority students, whose numbers at the school have indeed shot upward since the change in policy.

Taken as a whole, the campaign currently being mounted against standardized testing constitutes a formidable challenge to what was once seen as the fairest means of identifying and ranking scholastic merit. Since that campaign shows every sign of intensifying in the years ahead, it may be relevant to point out that every major premise on which it rests is false.

In the first place, the SAT and GRE are hardly the meaningless academic snapshots described by their critics. Results from these tests have been shown to correspond with those on a whole range of other measures and outcomes, including IQ tests, the National Assessment of Educational Progress, and the National Educational Longitudinal Study. Though each of these uses a different format and has a somewhat different aim, a high degree of correlation obtains among all of them.

This holds true for racial and ethnic groups as well. Far from being idiosyncratic, the scoring patterns of whites, blacks, Hispanics, and Asians on the SAT and GRE are replicated on other tests as well. It was in light of just such facts that the National Academy of Science concluded in the 1980's that the most commonly used standardized tests display no evidence whatsoever of cultural bias.

Nor do the tests fail to predict how minority students will ultimately perform in the classroom. If, indeed, the purported bias in the tests were real, such students would earn better grades in college than what is suggested by their SAT scores; but that is not the case. As Keith Widaman, a psychologist at the University of California, showed in a recent study, the SAT actually *over*estimates the first-year grades of blacks and Hispanics in the UC system.

Foes of testing are a bit closer to the mark when they claim that women end up doing better in college than their scores would indicate. But the "underprediction" is very slight—a tenth of a grade point on the four-point scale—and only applies to less demanding schools. For more selective institutions, the SAT predicts the grades of both sexes quite accurately.

As for the claim that test scores depend heavily on income, the facts again tell us otherwise. Though one can always point to exceptions, students who are not of the same race but whose families earn alike tend, on average, to perform very differently. A California study found, for example, that even among families with annual incomes over $70,000, blacks still fell short in median SAT scores, trailing Hispanics by 79 points, whites by 148 points, and Asians by 193 points.

This suggests that universities turning to economic disadvantage as a surrogate for racial preferences will be disappointed with the results. And this has already proved to be the case. When the University of Texas medical school mounted such an effort, it found that most of its minority applicants did not qualify for admission, coming as they did from fairly comfortable circumstances but still failing to match the academic credentials of less-well-off whites and others. In fact, as a University of California task force concluded last year, so-called economic affirmative action, by opening the door to poor but relatively high-scoring whites and Asians, might actually *hurt* the prospects of middle-class blacks and Hispanics.

What about relying less on tests and more on other measuring rods like high school grades? Unfortunately, as everyone knows, high schools across the country vary considerably, not only in their resources but in the demands they make of students. An A– from suburban Virginia's elite Thomas Jefferson High School of Science and Technology cannot be ranked with an A– from a school in rural Idaho or inner-city Newark, especially at a time of rampant grade inflation aimed at bolstering "self-esteem." It was precisely to address this problem that a single nationwide test was introduced in the first place.

Nor is it even clear that relying more exclusively on grades would bump up the enrollment numbers of blacks and Hispanics, as many seem to think. While it is true that more minority students would thereby become eligible for admission, so would other students whose gradepoint averages (GPAs) outstripped their test scores. A state commission in California, considering the adoption of such a scheme, discovered that in order to pick students from this larger pool for the limited number of places in the state university system, the schools would have to raise their GPA cut-off point. As a result, the percentage of eligible Hispanics would have remained the same, and black eligibility actually would have dropped.

In Texas, vast disparities in preparation have already damped enthusiasm for a much-publicized "top-10-percent" plan under which the highest-ranking tenth of graduates from any Texas high school win automatic admission to the state campus of their choice, regardless of their test scores. Passed in the wake of the 1996 *Hopwood* case (1996), which scuttled the state university's affirmative-action program, the plan has forced many high schools to discourage their students from getting in over their heads when choosing a college. As one guidance counselor quoted in the *Chronicle of Higher Education* warned her top seniors, "You may be sitting in a classroom where the majority of students have demonstrated . . . higher-order thinking skills that are beyond what you have. You'll have to struggle."

Grades aside, what of the various less measurable signs of student potential? Should not a sterling character or artistic sensitivity count for something? What of special obstacles overcome?

Certainly, such things should count, and always have counted—more so today than ever, to judge by the sorts of questions most schools currently ask of applicants. But gaining a fuller picture of a particular student's promise is a difficult business, especially in an admissions process that very often involves sorting through thousands of individuals. Moreover, it can only go so far before it ceases to have anything to do with education. What a student is like outside the classroom is surely significant, but until we are prepared to say outright that the heart of the matter is something other than fitness for academic work, a crucial gauge of whether a student is going to be able to pass a biology final or write a political science research paper will remain that old, much-maligned SAT score.

There are, to be fair, social commentators who acknowledge this ineluctable fact, and who therefore urge us to direct all our remedial efforts toward improving the test scores of American blacks.* But for the true opponents of testing, such efforts—the work of generations—are clearly beside the point. Basically, what these critics are hoping to do is to achieve the ends of affirmative action by other, more politic means.

Hence the search for supposedly more "nuanced" measures of scholastic merit like "creativity" and "leadership," tacitly understood as stand-ins for skin color. But there is no reason to think that minority students possess these qualities in greater abundance than do their peers. The attempt to substitute them for test scores will thus only perpetuate the corrupt logic of affirmative action by piling deception upon deception.

Whatever the euphemism used to describe it, only counting by race and gender can produce the result that will satisfy the most determined critics of standardized testing. If they have their way, and such testing wholly or partly disappears, we will have forfeited our best and most objective means of knowing how our schools are doing, as well as any clear set of standards by which students themselves can judge their own educational meritocracy will have come to an end. How this will benefit the poor and disadvantaged among us, or help them get ahead, is anybody's guess.

---

* See "America's Next Achievement Test" by Christopher Jencks and Meredith Phillips in the September-October 1998 *American Prospect.*

STRUCTURING EDUCATION

SPENDING

Making America's Schools Work

Eric A. Hanushek

This selection first appeared in the Fall 1994 issue of *The Brookings Review*. Eric Hanushek is the Paul and Jean Hanna Senior Fellow on Education Policy at the Hoover Institution and a member of Hoover's Koret Task Force on K–12 Education.

No one is happy with America's schools. Students, parents, politicians all call for schools to do a better job. The news media regularly report the failures of U.S. education, whether in the poor showing of American students in international test score competition or in the deficiencies of graduates entering the workplace.

Often the blame is placed on tightfisted government officials and taxpayers. Teachers' salaries, it is said, are too low. Class sizes are too big. The school year is too short. Educational reformers emphasize the need for renewed commitment to schooling—a commitment that is often translated into an appeal for expanded resources for schools.

But in fact, the nation has been spending more and more to achieve results that are no better and perhaps worse. Between 1960 and 1990, while student performance on such tests as the SAT and the National Assessment of Educational Progress faltered, real (inflation-adjusted) public spending on elementary and secondary education in the United States rose from just over $50 billion to almost $190 billion. Real per-student spending more than tripled—from $1,454 in 1960 to $4,622 in 1990.

Surprisingly, the increased costs, combined with public dissatisfaction with school performance, have aroused few protests or demands to stop the growth in spending. One explanation for the public's silence may be that the dramatic 1970–90 drop in the school-age population masked overall spending increases by offsetting much of the rise in per-pupil instructional costs. But if that is the case, trouble lurks on the horizon. For the population of school-age children is on the rise again, and with it, fiscal pressures.

America's lunar-landing approach to school reform—devote sufficient energy and resources to the problem and the nation will crack it—is not sustainable. Education faces stiff competition for society's limited resources. The nation will not, indeed cannot, continue to spend more and more on education to achieve flat or falling performance.

More Money, Better Schools?

Nor is there any *reason* to continue to pour ever more money into the schools, given their current organization. Over the past quarter century, researchers have made the surprising discovery that there is little systematic relationship between school resources and student performance. For every study that finds that increases in basic school resources promote higher achievement, another study shows just the opposite.

Take class size, for example. The intuitively appealing idea that smaller classes will improve student learning is a perennial cornerstone of educational reform. As a result, the pupil-teacher ratio in American schools is always on the decline. The ratio, which stood at 35–1 in 1890, fell to 28–1 in 1940, 20–1 in 1970, and less than 16–1 in 1990.

But econometric experimental evidence shows vividly that across-the-board reductions in class size are unlikely to yield discernible gains in overall student achievement. That is not to say that small classes are never useful. Some situations may lend themselves to smaller classes, while others can accommodate larger classes. For example, individual tutorial programs can substantially improve the achievement of poorly performing primary school students, while other students in various situations can be placed in larger classes without jeopardizing their achievement—so holding overall cost constant. Indeed, in Japan teachers and administrators expressly trade large class size for more time for teacher preparation. But so far, U.S. schools have made little effort to learn which uses of resources, for smaller classes or other purposes, best promote student achievement.

As the public school system is now organized, some schools appear to use money and resources effectively, but others do not. In fact, resources are spent ineffectively so often that there is simply no reason to expect overall improvement from increased resources. School administrators today are not monitoring the performance of their programs or the effectiveness of resource use. Schools have no way to know what does and does not work. What's more, few incentives push toward improved schooling and higher student performance.

Put the Money Where It Works

The highest priority for America's schools today is to use existing resources more efficiently. When economists try to interject the economic principle of efficiency into the education debate, however, they often meet with stout resistance—largely because of misunderstandings. Efficiency does not mean that educators should measure both the costs and benefits of various approaches to education—and choose the approach that maximizes the excess of benefits over costs. In simplest terms, funds devoted to schools should be put to their best possible use. If two programs are competing for limited funds, put the money into the one that achieves the best results. If a program does not improve student performance, do not fund it.

These notions are so commonsensical that resistance to them would seem out of the question. But as America's schools are now run, virtually no one in them has a serious interest in improving performance or conserving resources. And all are reluctant to face the uncertainty that change would entail.

The best way to improve performance is to establish mechanisms that directly reward improvement. In general, school systems can be run in two ways: through regulation and through performance incentives. Regulation is a centralized command and control system. Central management creates a system of rules. Results can be satisfactory if the rules are appropriate and useful, if the schools can be adequately monitored, and if punishments for violating rules are sufficient to ensure that rules are obeyed. Performance incentives, on the other hand, rely more on rewards within a centralized system of decisionmaking. Central management specifies its goals and rewards those who achieve them. Typically, incentive systems specify what is to be achieved and leave it up to the agent to decide how, while regulatory regimes attempt to specify both what and how.

Today's schools rely far more heavily on regulation than on incentives, even though education is inherently a highly decentralized activity. Almost all productive work is done in classrooms. It is next to impossible to create a single set of regulations capable of identifying, hiring, and mobilizing America's almost 3 million teachers. Still, despite the evident difficulty of applying strong regulatory regimes to education, schools today make little use of performance incentives—with results that are all too evident.

People respond to incentives, be they financial, emotional, or some other form. When rewarded for an action, people do it. Students, teachers, and other school personnel are no different. Moreover, every organization, either implicitly or explicitly, sets up incentives for action. Unfortunately, few incentives within today's schools relate to student performance. If school reform is to work, that must change.

Learning about Incentives

It is not enough simply to exhort schools to "use performance incentives." Performance incentives come in many forms, and incentives that work in one school system may not work in another. If there is a single, glaring lesson to be learned from past attempts at school reform, it is that no single overarching reform can solve the problems of every school. Policymakers must decentralize school systems to allow local decisionmakers to devise programs appropriate for their situations. They must also help provide the discipline to ensure that those programs are effective.

The school reform landscape is dotted with proposals for new programs of educational incentives. The ideas behind them are conceptually appealing, but so far we have little experience with the programs in practice. Somewhat hesitantly, schools have begun to experiment with a variety of new programs that differ both in how they define "good" performance and how they reward it. For example, charter schools enable teachers to set up new schools to try out new educational ideas in exchange for performance commitments. School choice and educational vouchers give students and their parents an important voice in determining whether schools are good by allowing them to decide which to attend. Merit pay for teachers and principals, together with attempts to contract educational services to private firms, provide still other performance definitions and incentives.

Applications of these new programs have, nonetheless, been very limited. All will need to be tested far more widely, and much greater effort will have to go into evaluating their performance and disseminating information about their results. The field of medicine has made great strides by wide and systematic experiments to test the efficacy of new treatments and publicize their success or failure. Schools should do likewise.

In some ways the discussion about performance incentives has become confused with notions of decentralized decisionmaking. Considerable legislation and local change has been devoted to promoting decentralized decisions through such means as site-based management or semi-autonomous subdistricts. But decentralization alone is not enough—for it has been tried widely and has frequently failed to lead to general improvement. Decentralization must be combined with well-crafted performance initiatives based on clear definitions of good performance. These definitions, in turn, require agreement on the goals and objectives of the schools.

Measurement and Evaluation

An essential ingredient of reform will therefore be clear measurement of student performance—a subject that is itself controversial. Naturally, people differ on what they think schools should accomplish, on how those things are best evaluated, and, ultimately, on what part of student performance should be attributed to schools.

The starting point must be a plain delineation of goals and objectives. While defining a good education is politically difficult, performance in core academic areas should be paramount. If schools fail to prepare students properly with basic literacy, numeracy, and analytical skills, they will never be judged successful.

One aspect of performance measurement that is being hotly debated is the appropriateness of currently available standardized tests. Many participants in that debate, however, can agree on three points. First, good measures of student performance are essential to educational improvement. Second, while the appropriate testing instrument depends considerably on the purpose of measurement, existing tests, though far from perfect, do provide useful information in assessing schools' performance. Third, although test measurements can and should be improved, evaluation of schools should not await development of the perfect instrument.

One confusion about performance measurement involves judging the contribution of schools. When student test scores are made public, many people immediately judge the performance of schools solely on the basis of these scores, implicitly ignoring the fact that student performance is the result of much more than just the schools. Inevitably it involves a mixture of schooling, education in the home, innate abilities, and the like. Thus for example, a teacher or school that must deal with students unprepared for their current grade level should not be penalized for poor student preparation. Instead, attention should be focused on what the teacher or school contributes—on their "value added" to learning. This focus is particularly appropriate when student performance is incorporated in incentive systems. Concentrating on value-added is also essential to program evaluations that attempt to uncover effective approaches to schooling. Indeed, when value-added is appropriately measured, we may well find that some schools with high average scores are really contributing little to students' performance and vice versa.

Altered Roles

Moving toward a school system that uses resources effectively, emphasizes incentives, and recognizes the importance of evaluation will require all participants to take on new roles and responsibilities, which will, of course, vary across states and districts.

Teachers, perhaps the most important element of our schooling system, must take an active part in improving schools. Yet teaching under a new system based on performance incentives and decentralized decision-making promises different challenges—and requires new experience, training, and expectations—than teaching today. One way to introduce changes into teaching without completely alienating current teachers is two-tier employment contracts. New teachers' contracts would offer fewer tenure guarantees, more risks, and greater flexibility and rewards. Existing teachers could either continue under existing employment rules for tenure, pay, and work conditions or opt for the new-style contract. The expectations that today's teachers had when they entered the profession cannot be arbitrarily revoked if we expect schools to improve.

State governments should put aside many of their old tasks—laying down school curricula and procedures—and instead promote local experimentation with new incentive systems and then help produce and disseminate evaluation results. States should define performance standards and explicit student goals. Finally, states share with the federal government a role in ensuring equality of opportunity. Disadvantaged students may well require additional resources, even when all schools are using resources effectively. Moreover, states must monitor the performance of local districts. When performance is unacceptably low, states must intervene through school choice programs or voucher systems that will enable students in poorly performing districts to move to better schools elsewhere.

The federal government should join states in setting goals and standards, developing performance information, supporting evaluation, and disseminating results. It should also take the lead in supporting supplemental programs for disadvantaged and minority students. (Programs for the disadvantaged should themselves follow the same guidelines as all other programs but may also involve expansions of earlier childhood education, integrated health and nutrition programs, and other supplemental interventions.)

Local school districts' responsibilities—making curricular choices and managing teacher and administrative personnel—would remain nominally the same but would actually change significantly if states removed many of their restrictions on instruction and organization. Moreover, if major decisions devolved to local schools, new emphasis would be placed on management and leadership.

Businesses too could take on a new role. While businesses frequently lament the quality of workers being turned out by the schools, they have never worked closely with schools in defining the skills and abilities they want. Closer consultation with schools, perhaps coupled with long-term hiring relationships, could aid both schools and businesses. Moreover, businesses could give students valuable incentives to perform well in school by making it clear that hiring decisions are based on school transcripts. And experienced business managers might have much to teach schools about how to manage performance incentives.

Finally, parents, who often have few opportunities to play an active part in schools today, would have a crucial role in many incentive-based systems of school management. Systems of choice require parents to decide which school offers the best opportunities for their children.

Systems of decentralized management give parents a chance to become more actively involved in running schools, and indeed may require it.

An Overriding Perspective

Reforming America's schools does not require more money. On the contrary, the cause of reform will best be advanced by holding overall real spending constant. Schools must acquire the discipline imposed by economic efficiency. They must learn to consider tradeoffs among programs and operations. They must learn to evaluate performance and eliminate programs that are not working. They must learn to seek out and expand on productive incentive structures and organizational approaches. In short, they must make better use of existing resources.

Inefficiencies in the current structure of schools are widespread, but there is little interest or pressure to eliminate them. Where such interest exists, it is often thwarted by regulations or contract restrictions that do not permit reasonable adjustments in personnel, classroom organization, the use of new technologies or other approaches that might improve performance for existing spending. If America's schools are to improve, they must embrace the basic principles of economics, with its attention to effectiveness of expenditures and to establishing appropriate incentives.

In the long run, the nation may find it inappropriate to increase school spending. It is simply hard to tell at this point. But it is clear that expanding resources first and looking for reform second is likely to lead only to a more expensive system, not a better one.

. . . .

Half of Choice Schools Spend Less than State Allots

Joe Williams

This selection first appeared in the *Milwaukee Journal Sentinel* on 22 May 2000. Joe Williams is a staff writer for the *Milwaukee Journal Sentinel*.

Nearly half of the schools participating in Milwaukee's private school choice program had to return money to the state last year—in two cases, more than $100,000 each—because, hard as they tried, they couldn't spend the $4,894 they were given to educate each of their choice students, records show.

As Milwaukee Public Schools officials prepare to approve a budget for 2000–2001 that comes to about $9,500 per student, audits of schools in the choice program show they are struggling to spend just half of what is spent by their public counterparts.

"We don't have to pay for a huge administration and a lot of red tape," said Lois Maczuzak, an administrator at St. John Kanty School, 2840 S. 10th St., which spent $3,096 to educate each student, making it the lowest-cost school in the choice program.

Under the program, which lets low-income students attend private and religious schools at taxpayer expense, students in 1998–99 received vouchers worth either $4,894 or the choice school's cost to educate each pupil, whichever was less. This year, the vouchers are worth slightly more than $5,000.

MPS' per-pupil costs tend to be higher than those of most private schools due to the expense of services to special-needs students, transportation (including busing for some private-school students), and costly benefits packages for MPS employees.

According to audits filed with the state Department of Public Instruction, 39 of 82 schools that had choice students last school year spent less than $4,894, resulting in return payments of nearly $1.2 million to the state.

In St. John Kanty's case, the school paid $93,047 back to the state because of its low cost.

Many private schools in the city for years have survived by keeping costs as low as possible, in turn keeping tuition affordable for students' families.

"Our teachers sacrifice a whole lot in terms of their salaries," Maczuzak said. "I can't compete with MPS in payroll. Our teachers bring in a lot of materials on their own, and that helps to keep costs down as well."

At St. John Kanty, parents volunteer to supervise recess, lunch hour, and field trips, eliminating the need for paid employees to do such non-teaching work. While the Archdiocese of Milwaukee provides some help in administering programs, the school is largely left to its own devices, Maczuzak said.

"At the Catholic schools, the buck stops here," Maczuzak said. "We don't have the costs that come with a lot of red tape, but we also are the ones who are responsible for what happens in our schools."

Much of the difference between the city's public and private schools comes down to salaries and benefits. A recent University of Wisconsin–Milwaukee study showed that salaries in the city's private schools tend to be about half those paid to local public-school teachers.

Richard Gottschalk, administrator at Oklahoma Avenue Lutheran School, 5335 W. Oklahoma Ave., has been a private-school educator for 33 years—including 21 years as an administrator—and still hasn't hit the $40,000-per-year salary mark. The average salary for an MPS teacher is more than $42,000.

"Our starting salaries are $18,000," Gottschalk said.

Oklahoma Avenue spent $3,725 per pupil, but only 25% of the school's students come through the choice program.

The problem for schools such as Oklahoma Avenue is that if they raise costs to the amount covered by the vouchers, they end up having to raise tuition for non-choice students.

"We are committed to the mission of the school and to keeping the tuition affordable," Gottschalk said. "If we raised the pupil costs so that our salaries were in line with the public school, 75% of the students would have to pay higher tuition."

Gottschalk said per-pupil costs for this year will be even less than $3,725 because the 1998–99 cost included one-time infrastructure expenses.

The local group Partners Advancing Values in Education has begun working with private schools to find ways to increase teacher salaries using money from the choice program. But the fewer students a school has in the choice program, the harder it is to spend more money without raising tuition.

"I was just talking with a group of Catholic-school principals, and they are all wondering how they can increase teacher salaries without raising tuition for the non-choice students," said Dan McKinley, PAVE's executive director. "It's an interesting situation."

While public schools in Wisconsin have their budgets capped by state-imposed revenue limits, private schools' spending tends to be capped by market forces. If tuition becomes too high, private schools hurt their own ability to compete for student customers.

Thirteen schools in the choice program didn't break the $4,000 mark per student. Two schools had to pay back more than $100,000 because their expenses were so low: Catholic East Elementary ($107,852) and St. Anthony's School ($123,807).

DPI officials said all of the money has been paid back. Under the program, choice schools get payments during the school year equal to the $4,894 maximum value of each voucher, then reconcile the accounts in the summer, after financial reports and audits are completed. It is impossible to determine a school's annual cost per student until the school year is over.

Some private schools spent considerably more per student than the maximum value of the vouchers, but no additional tuition can be charged to choice students. Milwaukee Montessori School spent $10,933 per student, the most in the program.

About 8,000 students are participating this year in Milwaukee's choice program.

. . . .

Money and School Performance

Lessons from the Kansas City Desegregation Experiment

Paul Ciotti

This selection first appeared as Cato Institute *Policy Analysis* No. 298 on 16 March 1998. Paul Ciotti lives in Los Angeles and writes about education.

Executive Summary

For decades critics of the public schools have been saying, "You can't solve educational problems by throwing money at them." The education establishment and its supporters have replied, "No one's ever tried." In Kansas City they did try. To improve the education of black students and encourage desegregation, a federal judge invited the Kansas City, Missouri, School District to come up with a cost-is-no-object educational plan and ordered local and state taxpayers to find the money to pay for it.

Kansas City spent as much as $11,700 per pupil—more money per pupil, on a cost of living adjusted basis, than any other of the 280 largest districts in the country. The money bought higher teachers' salaries, 15 new schools, and such amenities as an Olympic-sized swimming pool with an underwater viewing room, television and animation studios, a robotics lab, a 25-acre wildlife sanctuary, a zoo, a model United Nations with simultaneous translation capability, and field trips to Mexico and Senegal. The student-teacher ratio was 12 or 13 to 1, the lowest of any major school district in the country.

The results were dismal. Test scores did not rise; the black-white gap did not diminish; and there was less, not greater, integration. The Kansas City experiment suggests that, indeed, educational problems can't be solved by throwing money at them, that the structural problems of our current educational system are far more important than a lack of material resources, and that the focus on desegregation diverted attention from the real problem, low achievement.

The Kansas City Story

In 1985 a federal district judge took partial control over the troubled Kansas City, Missouri, School District (KCMSD) on the grounds that it was an unconstitutionally segregated district with dilapidated facilities and students who performed poorly. In an effort to bring the district into compliance with his liberal interpretation of federal law, the judge ordered the state and district to spend nearly $2 billion over the next 12 years to build new schools, integrate classrooms, and bring student test scores up to national norms.

It didn't work. When the judge, in March 1997, finally agreed to let the state stop making desegregation payments to the district after 1999, there was little to show for all the money spent. Although the students enjoyed perhaps the best school facilities in the country, the percentage of black students in the largely black district had continued to increase, black students' achievement hadn't improved at all, and the black-white achievement gap was unchanged.[1]

The situation in Kansas City was both a major embarrassment and an ideological setback for supporters of increased funding for public schools. From the beginning, the designers of the district's desegregation and education plan openly touted it as a controlled experiment that, once and for all, would test two radically different philosophies of education. For decades critics of public schools had been saying, "You can't solve educational problems by throwing money at them." Educators and advocates of public schools, on the other hand, had always responded by saying, "No one's ever tried."

In Kansas City they did try. A sympathetic federal judge invited district educators literally to "dream"—forget about cost, let their imaginations soar, put together a list of everything they might possibly need to increase the achievement of inner-city blacks—and he, using the extraordinarily broad powers granted judges in school desegregation cases, would find a way to pay for it.

By the time the judge took himself off the case in the spring of 1997, it was clear to nearly everyone, including the judge, that the experiment hadn't worked. Even so, some advocates of increased spending on public schools were still arguing that Kansas City's only problem was that it never got enough money or had enough time. But money was never the issue in Kansas City. The KCMSD got more money per pupil than any of 280 other major school districts in the country, and it got it for more than a decade. The real issues went way beyond mere funding. Unfortunately, given the current structure of public education in America, they were a lot more intractable, too.

An Average American City

Unlike New York or Los Angeles, Kansas City has a low-key, sleepy feel to it. There's no sense of pounding humanity on the downtown streets or even much in the way of traffic congestion. The poorer residential areas have a strangely depopulated feel to them. Some old tree-lined streets have three or four fading frame houses in a row followed by a series of concrete steps leading to grassy vacant lots where houses once stood. In downtown Kansas City there are skyscrapers and even a new convention center (it looks like a cross between a Mississippi River steamboat and the Brooklyn Bridge), but overall, expectations are modest and so are ambitions. It is not surprising that Kansas City, which sits in the middle of the country, has an average amount of culture, an average amount of poverty, and an average amount of crime. What it didn't have by the late 1970s was an average number of good schools. In the three decades following the Supreme Court's 1954 decision in *Brown v. Board of Education*, which banned separate-but-equal schools, white flight totally reversed the demographics of the KCMSD—enrollment slowly declined from 70,000 to 36,000 students, and racial composition went from three-fourths white to three-fourths nonwhite (mostly blacks, with small percentages of Hispanics and Asians).[2]

As whites abandoned the schools, the school district's ability to raise taxes disappeared. The last year that the voters approved a tax increase for the schools was 1969, the same year that blacks first became a majority. Over the next two decades, the voters of the district declined to approve a tax increase for the school district 19 times in a row.[3] After middle-class whites pulled their children out of the school district, leadership declined. It was hard to find people to run for the school board. Those who did run tended not to be particularly sophisticated, usually earned less than $30,000 a year, and had difficulty dealing with complex financial issues.[4] With neither adequate leadership from the school board nor sufficient funding from taxpayers, the school system basically collapsed—test scores plummeted, assaults rose, the good teachers either burned out or accepted better offers elsewhere. By the time the plaintiffs (originally, schoolchildren and the school district itself) filed suit against the state of Missouri in 1977, wooden windows in the school buildings had rotted to the point where panes were literally falling out, ceiling tiles were coming down, and the halls reeked of urine. There were exposed electrical boxes, broken lights, crumbling asbestos falling from overhead pipes, nonworking drinking fountains, and rainwater running down the stairwells. Textbooks were decades out of date, with pages missing and the covers torn off. Emergency doors were chained shut. Boilers were so erratic that in some classrooms students wore coats and gloves all winter while in other classrooms in the same school it was so hot that the windows had to be kept open in the coldest weather.[5] When plaintiffs' attorney Arthur Benson took mature men, presidents of corporations, into those schools in the 1980s, they came out with tears in their eyes. Years later Judge Clark, an unpretentious man who wore cowboy boots on the bench, would remark that in all his years as a judge he had never seen a prison in as bad shape as the Kansas City schools.[6]

Winning Big in Federal Court

In the mid-1970s, in response to what appeared to be the imminent financial and educational bankruptcy of the school system, a group of mothers and educational activists took over the KCMSD school board. Then in 1977, with the schools in collapse and the voters unwilling to approve levy increases or school bond measures, members of the school board, the school district and two (later increased to ten) plaintiff schoolchildren brought suit against the state of Missouri and assorted federal agencies, alleging that the state, the surrounding school districts, and various federal agencies had caused racial segregation within the district.[7] Federal Judge Russell Clark, who had just been appointed to the federal bench by President Jimmy Carter, got the case shortly thereafter. The following year he dropped the federal agencies from the case and realigned the school district, making it a defendant rather than a plaintiff[8] (in practice, however, the district and the plaintiffs always had a "friendly adversary" relationship).[9]

In April 1984, after five months of trial, Clark rendered his first major decision, releasing the suburban districts from the case.[10] Three years later he found that the district and the state were "jointly and severally liable" for the segregated conditions in the Kansas City schools, a decision that meant that if Clark ordered the district to spend money to improve the schools and the district didn't have it, the state had to make up the difference.[11]

Originally, the plaintiffs' goal had been to get the judge to consolidate Kansas City's dozen small suburban districts with the KCMSD to create one big district that would then be subdivided into three or four smaller districts, each with a mandatory busing plan for integrating the schools. But when Judge Clark dismissed the suburban districts from the case, the plaintiffs were forced into a radical shift in strategy.[12]

Because the KCMSD was already 73 percent nonwhite, the only way to really integrate it was to bring in white children from the suburbs. Although critics had told Benson that such a plan wouldn't work—whites simply wouldn't go to majority black schools—Benson was operating on a Field of Dreams theory—"If you build it, they will come." As he saw it, parents didn't care about race. They didn't care how long the bus ride was. They didn't care what kind of neighborhood the school was in. What they wanted was a good, safe school that would provide their children with a good education. Benson considered it his job, therefore, to build a school system that would give students a better education than they could get anywhere else in the area. Then, as suburban middle-class whites flooded into the district, they would integrate the schools, and their middle-class aspirations would change the school culture from one of failure to one of success, whereupon blacks' achievement would rise to match that of whites.[13]

Because the judge had no expertise in devising a plan that would both desegregate the district and provide a quality education for the students, he asked the state and the plaintiffs each to come up with a remedy and he would chose between the two.

The state took the aggressive but (as events would later show) not entirely irrational position that most of what was wrong with the KCMSD had more to do with crime, poverty, and dysfunctional families than it did with the failure of the state to meet its constitutional obligations. Under the circumstances, the state argued, all that was legally required was a little reroofing, patching, painting, and carpet repair coupled with curriculum reform and emphasis on better teaching.

The plaintiffs, on the other hand, encouraged by what they saw as the increasing sympathy of the judge for their position, decided to "go for the moon"—to ask for far more than they thought they could ever get.

The choice for Clark was a stark one—he could go with the state's plan, which in the words of Harvard researcher Alison Morante was "laughably insufficient," or he could go with the plaintiffs' plan, which was basically a wish list of everything they had ever wanted. Given the choice between doing hardly anything and giving the plaintiffs the moon, Clark decided to go for the moon.[14]

Once Clark decided for the plaintiffs, he didn't ask them to do things on the cheap. When it came time to fill in the plan's specifics, he invited them to "dream"[15]—to use their imaginations, push the envelope, try anything that would both achieve integration and raise student scores. The idea was that Kansas City would be a demonstration project in which the best and most modern educational thinking would for once be combined with the judicial will and the financial resources to do the job right. No longer would children go to schools with broken toilets, leaky roofs, tattered books, and inadequate curricula. The schools would use the most modern teaching techniques; have the best facilities and the most motivated teachers; and, on top of everything else, be thoroughly integrated, too. Kansas City would show what could be done if a school district had both the money and the will. It would be a model for educational reformers throughout the nation.

When estimates of the cost of the initial version of the plan came back, the lawyers and education activists who had designed the plan were shocked at their own audacity.[16] The $250 million cost was a staggering amount in a district whose normal budget was $125 million a year. But that was only the start. By the time he recused himself from the case in March 1997, Clark had approved dozens of increases, bringing the total cost of the plan to over $2 billion—$1.5 billion from the state and $600 million from the school district (largely from increased property taxes).

With that money, the district built 15 new schools and renovated 54 others. Included were nearly five dozen magnet schools, which concentrated on such things as computer science, foreign languages, environmental science, and classical Greek athletics. Those schools featured such amenities as an Olympic-sized swimming pool with an underwater viewing room; a robotics lab; professional quality recording, television, and animation studios; theaters; a planetarium; an arboretum, a zoo, and a 25-acre wildlife sanctuary; a two-floor library, art gallery, and film studio; a mock court with a judge's chamber and jury deliberation room; and a model United Nations with simultaneous translation capability.

To entice white students to come to Kansas City, the district had set aside $900,000 for advertising, including TV ads, brochures, and videocassettes. If a suburban student needed a ride, Kansas City had a special

$6.4 million transportation budget for busing. If the student didn't live on a bus route, the district would send a taxi. Once the students got to Kansas City, they could take courses in garment design, ceramics, and Suzuki violin. The computer magnet at Central High had 900 interconnected computers, one for every student in the school. In the performing arts school, students studied ballet, drama, and theater production. They absorbed their physics from Russian-born teachers, and elementary grade students learned French from native speakers recruited from Quebec, Belgium, and Cameroon.[17]

For students in the classical Greek athletic program, there were weight rooms, racquetball courts, and a six-lane indoor running track better than those found in many colleges. The high school fencing team, coached by the former Soviet Olympic fencing coach, took field trips to Senegal and Mexico.[18]

The ratio of students to instructional staff was 12 or 13 to 1, the lowest of any major school district in the country.[19] There was $25,000 worth of beads, blocks, cubes, weights, balls, flags, and other manipulatives in every Montessori-style elementary school classroom.

Younger children took midday naps listening to everything from chamber music to "Songs of the Humpback Whale." For working parents the district provided all-day kindergarten for youngsters and before- and after-school programs for older students.

A District Overwhelmed

For the KCMSD such a sudden change in fortune was overwhelming. Within a few years, a small neglected inner-city school district that never paid its bills on time, had horrible credit, couldn't balance its books at the end of the year, and suffered from a grossly bloated bureaucracy had as much as an extra $300 million a year coming in over the transom.[20]

It was more than the district could handle. District expenditures took quantum leaps from $125 million in fiscal year 1985 to $233 million in FY88 to $432 million in FY92.[21] There were too much largesse, too many resources, and too little security. A woman in the Finance Department went to jail for writing checks to her own account. Hundreds of thousands of dollars worth of equipment and supplies were lost to "rampant theft" every year.[22] "It was like taking a Third World country, a totally deprived community, and giving them unlimited wealth," said one local activist. "And that's how they acted—like kids in a candy store. They misused it, mismanaged it, and misappropriated it. They were just not prepared for what Judge Clark thrust upon them."[23]

Perhaps the worst problem for what one school board president called the district's "modestly qualified" administrators was the sheer volume of paperwork.[24] When the judge started building schools and inviting school principals to order whatever they wanted, purchase orders flooded into the central administrative office at the rate of 12,000 a month. Clerks were overwhelmed, devastated, and too ashamed to admit they couldn't handle the crush. The system just collapsed.[25]

There was such a rush to build or remodel so many schools in so short a time that contractors were starting work before educators had fully decided exactly what they wanted to build. Equipment arrived before the schools were ready to receive it. Everything moved so fast that, as one former board member would later recall, "it was like building a train while it was rolling down the tracks."[26]

To outsiders, it appeared that the KCMSD had gone on a spending binge. At $400 million, Kansas City's school budget was two to three times the size of those of similar districts elsewhere in the country. The Springfield, Missouri, school district, for instance, had 25,000 students, making it two-thirds as big as the KCMSD. Yet Springfield's budget ($101 million) was only one-quarter to one-third the size of Kansas City's ($432 million at its peak).[27]

Everything cost more in Kansas City.[28] Whereas nearby districts were routinely building 500-student elementary schools for around $3 million, in Kansas City comparably sized schools cost $5 million to $6 million. Whereas the nearby Blue Valley district built a 1,600-student high school at a cost of $20.5 million, including furniture and equipment, in Kansas City the 1,200-student Central High cost $33 million (it came with a field house larger than those of many colleges, ubiquitous computers, and an Olympic-sized swimming pool).[29]

Warehouses filled up with equipment that schools had ordered but later decided they didn't want. One school ordered light fixtures that cost $700 apiece. Principals of some schools ordered replacements for desks and light fixtures that were in perfectly good condition. (The workmen who were installing the new desks and fixtures took the discards to their home districts and installed them in their own schools.) The district spent $40,000 for a display case for a high school that had no trophies. It bought 286- and 386-model computers and then left them sitting on the shelves so long they became obsolete without ever having been in a classroom. At one point, complained state attorney general Jay Nixon, the district couldn't account for some 23,000 items, including TV sets, CD players, bookcases, office furniture, and (temporarily) a baby grand piano.[30]

The Desegregation Monitoring Committee, which Clark had appointed to oversee the district under his direction, was irate at the district's nonchalance toward money. "The attitude has been prevalent throughout the . . . program that money is no object and the court will provide all that is necessary and no one will take any punitive action," complained the committee's 1992 report.[31]

With some 600 employees for a district of 36,000 students, the KCMSD had a central administration that was three to five times larger than the administrations of other comparably sized public school districts. It was also 150 times larger than the administration of the city's Catholic school system, in which four people—one superintendent, two assistant superintendents, and a part-time marketing manager—ran a school district of 14,000 students.[32] The KCMSD was so top-heavy that a 1991 audit discovered that 54 percent of the district's budget never made it to the classroom; rather, it was used for food service, transportation, and, most of all, central administration.[33]

At one point, complained Nixon, 44 percent of the entire state budget for elementary and secondary education was going to just the 9 percent of the state's students who lived in Kansas City and St. Louis.[34] Missouri was spending more on desegregation than it was spending on prisons, courts, the highway patrol, and the state fire marshal combined.[35]

To parents in the state's 529 other school districts, it seemed extraordinarily unfair that Kansas City was awash in money while their districts had to cope two years in a row with funding declines that forced them to hold bake sales and car washes to finance programs, sell hot dogs and sodas to buy school athletic uniforms, and clip soup coupons to buy computers.

To replace the money that the state sent to St. Louis and Kansas City, other districts in the state had to cancel field trips and extracurricular activities, defer maintenance, fire teachers, and freeze salaries.[36] The decline in state revenue cost the Springfield school district $4 million—4 percent of its entire budget. As there was no slack in the budget, Springfield had to fire 19 employees; defer grouting the mortar on 100-year-old brick buildings; cancel public speaking classes; dispense with water safety courses; and beg for money to send students to the Civil War battlefield at Wilson's Creek, an annual trip that had been made for decades.[37] In the meantime, the KCMSD was spending $50,000 a month to bring students to school in taxis, sending its fencing team to Senegal, and dispatching the district superintendent on a goodwill mission to Moscow.[38]

In some parts of the country, such excesses wouldn't have caused much of an outcry. "But these were Midwesterners and it was too much for their sensibilities," one Kansas City legislator noted. "If [Judge Clark] had gone slowly, built a few schools, renovated a few others, they wouldn't have minded so much. But there was this huge excess. And it was too much."[39]

From time to time, Clark did try to rein in the district. Once when the district tried to appoint someone with no magnet experience to be the principal of a magnet school, the judge forced the district to rescind the appointment. Another time he fined the school district when it failed for two years in a row to order books for the start of school. "The school district is like a small child," he once commented. "They'll push their parents as far as they can push them."[40]

Still, because Clark lived and worked in Springfield, 175 miles south of Kansas City, there was only so much he could do in person. Even more important, early on he made a conscious decision not to try to micromanage the school district. Clark felt that Arthur Garrity, the Boston federal judge who had earlier tried to implement his own remedy in that city's troubled schools, had failed dismally. Clark didn't want to make the same mistake.[41]

The Poster Boy of the Imperial Judiciary

Because the state was paying 75 percent of the desegregation costs, Clark wanted to equalize the burden by having the school district increase property taxes. But local voters, the majority of whom were older and white, repeatedly refused, whereupon Clark, taking matters into his own hands, ordered that property taxes in the district be doubled (from $2.05 to $4 for each $100 of assessed value). Later, to help pay for what would eventually become a 40 percent raise for teachers, he ordered a further increase—to $4.96.[42] He also ordered a 1.5 percent surcharge on income earned by people who worked in Kansas City but lived elsewhere.

It was one thing to take control of a local school district. It was another thing entirely for a judge to take the view that citizens weren't taxing themselves enough. In the ensuing outcry, editorial writers and news commentators denounced Clark as "King George" and "the poster boy of the imperial judiciary."[43] "Politicians do polls and get their negatives rated," Benson later commented. "He is the most un-popular man in Jackson County and he doesn't even live here."[44] He began to get death threats, enough hostile letters to fill two big file drawers, and so many phone calls from outraged citizens that he quit answering the phone.[45]

For politicians who needed something or someone to run against, Judge Clark was a godsend. Not only did state and federal representa-tives run against him, but so did council members in other cities. "The animosity was mind-boggling," said former school board president Sue Fulson. For three years running, whenever citizens tried to lobby the legislature, they got back a form letter lamenting that, much as their representative would like to help, the matter was out of his hands—"All the money is going to Kansas City. Write Judge Clark."[46]

Clark was unswayed. "I had to balance two constitutional issues," he later said. "One was no taxation without representation and the other was the kids' right to an equal opportunity. I decided it in favor of the school children."[47]

A group of local taxpayers and property owners, represented by the Landmark Legal Foundation, appealed the order. Eventually, the issue got to the U.S. Supreme Court, which, by a five-to-four vote, decided in April 1990 that (1) Judge Clark did not have the right to raise taxes by himself but that (2) he could order the district to raise taxes to satisfy its debt obligations.[48] Justice Byron White justified the tax increase with the argument that "a local government with taxing authority may be ordered to levy taxes in excess of the limit set by state statute where there is reason based in the Constitution for not observing the statutory limitation."[49] In dissent, Chief Justice William Rehnquist and Justices Anthony Kennedy, Sandra Day O'Connor, and Antonin Scalia com-plained of the majority's "casual embrace of taxation imposed by the unelected, life-tenured federal judiciary."[50]

In the meantime, the Eighth Circuit Court of Appeals rescinded Clark's 1.5 percent income surcharge (which had brought in $32 million the first year, double what had been expected) on the grounds that it was an entirely new tax requiring the creation of a new tax collection bu-reaucracy and thus unconstitutionally interfered with the right of local jurisdictions to manage their own affairs.[51]

Although the tax issue upset voters all over the state, what especially irked Kansas City parents was the district's inept running of its magnet school busing plan. To achieve the best possible racial balance within the Kansas City schools (as well as to transport those white suburban students who wanted to attend district schools), the desegregation plan called for a massive criss-crossing, door-to-door busing system. Once the magnet plan started, the district suddenly went from having 100 bus routes to having 850. At a given bus stop, it was not uncommon to find 10 kids going to 10 different schools.[52]

The opening of school each year was a media circus—and every year the buses were late. The Kansas City Star once ran a picture of two little girls sitting on a street corner hours after their buses were supposed to have come. On another occasion, a little girl who fell asleep on the bus ended up with frostbite when she found herself locked in the bus all night. Eventually, the district brought in a professional transportation manager who finally was able to make the buses run on time, but by then parents hated the magnet busing plan[53] and Kansas City had earned a reputation as a district that couldn't do anything right.

The atmosphere at school board meetings didn't help. There were so much paranoia and shouting and so many accusations that board president Sue Fulson had to walk on eggs.[54] If she didn't call on some board members, they would claim that they had been slighted. White liberals who came on the board thinking of themselves as "good guys" found their commitment to blacks constantly in question. Some members of the black community thought that the white board members told the black board members how to vote. Black board members regularly asked white colleagues, "What are you getting out of this?"[55]

The school board tried to do something about the antagonism, at one point calling in an attorney to hold up a little flag of truce when things got too far out of hand and, on another occasion, holding a weekend retreat in the country, but nothing helped—the races didn't trust each other.[56]

Teacher Competence versus the Community's Need for Jobs

The school board's obsession with racial politics greatly complicated its efforts to hire a superintendent who was qualified to handle a $300 million to $400 million budget and yet willing to work with the school board. "Race is the first and foremost consideration in almost anything to do with the district," said former school board president Sue Fulson.

"Once you decide which way you are going on [race] then you make the decision on the merits of whatever is left. And it has been that way for years."[57]

Kansas City never did solve that problem. Candidates with national reputations voluntarily took themselves out of consideration for the Kansas City superintendent's position once they actually met the school board.[58] Furthermore, once a superintendent was hired, the antagonism only got worse. The board rode one superintendent so relentlessly that he developed suicidal tendencies, took multiple out-of-state trips, and faked a back injury (for which he was subsequently fired) to avoid going back to work.[59] When Judge Clark recused himself from the case, he noted in his final state-of-the-district order that the KCMSD had had 10 superintendents in the last nine years, most of them bought out or fired (at one point the district had five superintendents on the payroll simultaneously). With such turnover, he complained, it was hard to hold anyone accountable.[60]

The turnover problem also left the district with neither the ability nor the political will to do anything about improving the quality of teachers and principals. Promotions to principal were based less on merit than on race. "We so desperately need good principals and we just continue to support hacks," Benson complained.[61]

Before the desegregation plan, the KCMSD could always argue that for more than 30 years it had not had the money to offer high enough salaries to attract a first-class teaching staff. But even after the desegregation money started rolling in, the district still didn't do anything to upgrade instructional personnel. It was less traumatic to concentrate on what Benson called the "easy expensive" things (new buildings, new equipment, busing plans) than to tackle the "difficult inexpensive" things that really make a difference in children's lives—appointing qualified principals, supervising instructional practices, developing a curriculum, providing incentives, hiring good teachers, and firing bad ones.[62]

The result, education activist and gadfly Clinton Adams maintained, was that 50 percent or more of the teachers in the district were "not focused, rather vacuous, totally devoid of intellectual capacity, ill suited for the mission at hand."[63] Benson, more tactful, argued that only 20 percent of the teachers were "totally incompetent" and that another 20 percent could be brought up to speed with retraining.[64]

The biggest problem faced by KCMSD superintendents was that they didn't have a free hand when it came to personnel decisions. In Kansas

City the two largest employers of middle-class blacks were the post office and the school district. Just the rumor of a dismissal sent tremors through the entire black community—there was no other place to go; the community needed the jobs. At the same time, school district employees were the mainstay of the black churches. (Kansas City mayor Emanuel Cleaver, a Methodist minister, had 200 teachers in his parish.)[65] The black preachers closely monitored the district's hiring and promotion practices, with the result that the district essentially couldn't fire anyone.[66]

Since it could do nothing about inadequate teachers, the district sidestepped the matter by simply raising everyone's (including cafeteria workers' and janitors') salary 40 percent.[67] But that didn't so much attract better teachers as convince poor teachers to stick with the district as long as they could because they were getting salaries they couldn't get anywhere else.[68]

The Kansas City Plan Goes Awry

When Clark first authorized the desegregation plan, he made what he now regards as a serious error—he ordered enough schools built to accommodate the 5,000 to 10,000 suburban students he believed would flock to Kansas City to enroll in the new magnet schools.[69]

But despite a $900,000 television advertising budget and a $6.4 million special budget for door-to-door transportation of suburban students, the district did not attract the 5,000 to 10,000 white suburban students the designers of the desegregation plan had envisioned. The largest number it ever enrolled was 1,500, and most white students returned to their old suburban schools or to local private schools after one year, which forced the district to recruit a whole new cohort of white students every fall.[70] Even that modest number drastically declined after the Supreme Court's 1995 ruling that the judge had no authority to spend taxpayer dollars to transport suburban students into the district. By the 1996–97 school year, only 387 suburban students were still attending school in the KCMSD.[71] Given that the district's annual desegregation budget was approximately $200 million, the cost of attracting those suburban students was half a million dollars per year per child.

Some people in the black community regarded the white reluctance to attend school in the KCMSD as further proof of white racism— "You can't just build a $6 million school facility, call it a magnet, offer some romantic courses and think all the white students are going to come," said Kansas City mayor Emanuel Cleaver.[72] But to others the problem wasn't so much racism as hard-nosed parental realism. What suburban white parents really wanted were schools that would enable their children to compete effectively and successfully in the market-place. The real reason whites wouldn't send their children to school in Kansas City was quite simple—the KCMSD couldn't offer white students as good an education as they were already getting in their neighborhood suburban schools.[73]

The desegregation plan called for the district to close old schools as new ones were built, but because of objections from the community, which suspected the district of trying to close schools in black neighborhoods, the district found it difficult to raze even the oldest and most dilapidated buildings.[74] As a result of that (and the never-realized tide of suburban enrollees), the district ended up with seats for a maximum of 54,000 students even though actual enrollment never exceeded 37,000.[75] Not only were the high schools of Kansas City "rattlingly empty," they were financial white elephants.[76] "It's my fault we built a school system the tax base can't support," Clark concluded.[77] Finally, in the summer of 1997, with state desegregation funding rapidly ending, the school board voted to do what it could never find the political will to do before—close two high schools and a middle school.[78]

Results of the Kansas City Experiment

By the time Judge Clark took himself off the case in March 1997, he was a deeply frustrated man. For more than 20 years he had devoted 20 percent of his time as a judge to the Kansas City case.[79] And despite all the effort he had made to order the plan, fund the plan, and keep the plan on track—often in the face of intense opposition from the very people he was trying to help—the plan wasn't working. The number of white suburban students attracted to the district by all the new magnet schools was less than 10 percent of the number that Clark had expected.[80] Year after year the test scores would come out, the achievement levels would be no higher than before, and the black-white gap (one-half a standard deviation on a standard bell curve) would be no smaller.[81]

Although the initial gap was small, by the 12th grade, blacks' scores on standardized tests were about three years behind those of whites (10.1 vs. 13.1).[82] At Central High School, which tended to attract suburban white computer hackers, white males were five years ahead of black males on standardized tests.[83] "While there is some good teaching and learning going on in KCMSD schools," Clark concluded in his March 1997 final order, "there is a great deal of poor teaching and little learning in many schools."[84]

Despite intense and unrelenting effort, the district also found it impossible to eliminate almost-all-black schools. The reason wasn't racism, either—the district had a black school superintendent, a majority black school board, and a black school board president. In 1996 nonwhite enrollment exceeded 90 percent at 4 high schools, 2 middle schools, and 10 elementary schools.[85] Clark could have ordered intradistrict transfers to distribute whites equally, but he feared that the white parents would do what other whites had done in the past—enroll their children in private schools or pull up stakes and leave the district or even the state. The border between Kansas City, Missouri, and Johnson County, Kansas, runs right down the middle of the metropolitan area. For people wanting to escape the reach of the court by leaving Missouri entirely, doing so was in some cases as simple as moving across the street.[86]

Although the district had once hoped to have enough white suburban students to bring down the black/white ratio to 60 percent black, 40 percent white, the percentage of nonwhites (blacks, Hispanics, and Asians) increased every year, going from 73 percent at the start of the desegregation plan to 80 percent in the spring of 1997.[87]

In his final order, Judge Clark blamed the failure on the district: "Because of the KCMSD's troubled past, the district has lost the confidence of many of its staff, students, parents, and the community at large—already low achievement scores have fallen in the last year or two and the debacles of the School Board have provided near constant fodder for the news media."[88]

The average black student's reading skills increased by only 1.1 grade equivalents in four years of high school.[89] At Central High, complained Clark, black males were actually scoring no higher on standardized tests when they graduated as seniors than they had when they enrolled as freshmen four years before.[90] Most annoying to the judge, the district seemingly had no idea what it really spent on various budget line items. Instead of adhering to a budget, Clark wrote, the district simply "threw" some money into a given account, and the departments could overspend or underspend as they saw fit. Despite repeated requests from the court, the district couldn't put together a security plan, a staff development program, or a core curriculum—something it had needed since the desegregation plan had gone into effect 12 years earlier.[91]

Clark had reason to be annoyed. Back in 1985 his chief educational adviser had sat on the witness stand in his court and had confidently assured him that, if he funded the proposed plan, student achievement on standardized tests would climb above state averages in less than five years.[92] But then Kansas City got all the money any school district could ever want, and essentially nothing changed.

"I don't know who sold the judge that bill of goods [that students would meet state norms in five years]," Annette Morgan, a Kansas City Democrat and chairwoman of the Missouri House Education Committee, said in 1995. "I always thought that was ludicrous. If they had done that they would have achieved the attention of everyone else because that has not been done any place I know of."[93]

No one was more disappointed than former school board president Sue Fulson. "I truly believed," she told the Harvard Project on School Desegregation in 1992, "if we gave teachers and administrators everything they said they needed that they would truly make a huge difference. I knew it would take time, but I did believe by five years into this program we would see not just results, but dramatic results, educationally. And [the fact we didn't] is my bitterest disappointment."[94]

Judge Clark was so disappointed that at one point he suggested that he would keep control of the district until test scores reached national norms. That left Missouri in a bit of a bind. For one thing, no big city school district had ever met national norms (they had their own standard—big city norms), and, as Justice Scalia pointed out in exasperation when the case finally got to the Supreme Court, by definition, "half the country is below national norms!"[95] The other problem was one of incentives. As long as Clark kept control, the state was obligated to send the district upwards of $100 million a year with no say in how the money was spent. Furthermore, given the extensive facilities and new programs the district had created, it was money the district couldn't do without. If the district did unexpectedly and unaccountably happen to raise test scores to national norms, the money would cease, and the district would go bankrupt.

The Kansas City plan did have some successes. The district had perhaps the best facilities in the country. The equipment was state of the art. One former student won a Rhodes scholarship. Some of the students got an opportunity to visit other parts of this country or Europe. David Armor, an educational consultant and sociologist who testified in

Clark's court on educational achievement in January 1997, found that the desegregation plan did integrate the system "as far as was possible," given the conditions that existed in Kansas City. "But educationally," he noted, "it hasn't changed any of the measurable outcomes."[96] Scores on standardized tests didn't go up at all. And the average three-grade-level black-white achievement gap was as big as it always had been.

In perhaps the biggest surprise, Armor's studies found that black elementary students who go to magnet schools (which have the highest percentages of whites) score no better on standardized tests than do blacks who go to all-black nonmagnet schools.[97] In short, Armor found that, contrary to the notion on which the whole desegregation plan was founded—that going to school with middle-class whites would increase blacks' achievement—the Kansas City experiment showed that "integration has no effect."[98]

How the Desegregation Plan Hurt Kansas City

The most pressing problem with the Kansas City schools, which were mostly black to begin with, was not that they weren't integrated but that the schools were falling down and the students weren't learning. However, the lawsuit filed by the plaintiffs' attorney didn't concentrate on learning—it focused on segregation. One reason was that Benson initially assumed that segregation was the cause of poor achievement among blacks and once you cured that, bringing up test scores would be a trivial matter.[99]

There was also the practical question of finding a way to pay for the buildings, equipment, programs, amenities, transportation, and salary hikes. As one high school guidance counselor observed, "It's not unconstitutional to give the students a lousy education; it's only unconstitutional to give them a segregated one."[100] If the goal is to get a federal court to pour a billion dollars into a district, Landmark Legal Foundation's then-president Jerald Hill noted in 1995, "you have to come up with a constitutional violation."[101]

In Kansas City, segregation had become the constitutional tail that wagged the educational dog. Back before it became clear that there was no way the district could ever meet the prescribed desegregation ratio of 60 percent black to 40 percent white, Judge Clark's Desegregation Monitoring Committee was forever badgering the district: "Show us your progress. What are we getting for our money? How much integration have you got? How many white kids from the suburbs? What are your [black/white] ratios? What is the disparity index?"[102]

By worrying so much about integration in a district that was already three-quarters nonwhite, the judge and the plaintiffs ended up ignoring a whole list of far more likely reasons for students' lack of achievement. Because of steadfast union opposition, the district rejected merit pay for teachers.[103] It promoted principals on the basis of their race instead of their merit (which it had no systematic way to assess in any event). Because it failed to develop a core curriculum, many teachers simply geared their teaching to the Iowa Test of Basic Skills, a standardized multiple choice exam—a short-run strategy that hurt students long term.[104] For fear such a plan would reduce enrollment and jobs (and possibly show up the school district), the district rejected an initiative by 50 private schools to take 4,000 Kansas City students and educate them in return for vouchers for one-third to one-half of what the district was currently spending.[105] The KCMSD also rejected an offer by the Missouri Department of Education to run a demonstration school in the district because the state insisted on the right to pick its own teachers.[106]

An overzealous commitment to their desegregation plan sometimes led proponents of the plan to take positions seemingly at odds with their ultimate goal of helping inner-city blacks. At one point the Landmark Legal Foundation had to go to court to stop the district from enforcing a quota that allowed desks to sit empty in new magnet schools (waiting for whites who never came) while some overcrowded all-black schools had to house their students in trailers.[107] If a white suburban student wanted to go to a magnet school, admission was automatic because that brought the district closer to the 60/40 black/white ratio ordered by the judge. If a black student wanted to go to the same school, however, that student often ended up on a waiting list. As a result, some black parents registered their children as white in order to get them into certain schools.[108]

Finally, the district had discovered that it was easier to meet the court's 60/40 integration ratio by letting black students drop out than by convincing white students to move in. As a result, nothing was done in the early days of the desegregation plan about the district's appalling high school dropout rate, which averaged about 56 percent in the early 1990s (when desegregation pressures were most intense) and went as high as 71 percent at some schools (for black males it was higher still).[109]

Although the plan was ostensibly designed to benefit black inner-city students, in practice it required spending hundreds of millions of dollars on fancy facilities to attract white suburban students—who didn't need help—while neglecting the needs of inner-city blacks for health care, counseling, and basic instruction in reading, writing, and arithmetic.[110] That seeming perversion of logic left some black parents confused and angry and less than eager to give their full support to a desegregation plan that pulled their children out of neighborhood schools for the questionable benefits of riding across town to go to school with whites whose parents, in some cases, had left the Kansas City schools to avoid blacks in the first place.[111]

The fact that the desegregation plan called upon the district to abandon neighborhood schools in favor of a massive magnet busing plan also weighed heavily on Judge Clark. In successful school districts, neighborhood schools are the hub of much community social activity. When students are bused clear across the district to a faraway magnet school, the fabric of the community is torn apart. Such considerations notwithstanding, Clark still came down on the side of busing for desegregation. "There were two objects to the Kansas City plan," he later said. "One was integration and the other was a quality education, and you can't necessarily have both."[112]

Finally, in June 1995, with $1.6 billion in desegregation funding down the drain and no end in sight, the U.S. Supreme Court made its third ruling in the case, telling Clark to quit trying to solve social problems beyond his purview; forget about what Chief Justice Rehnquist called "desegregative attractiveness" (building a school system so fancy it will attract students from other districts); quit holding the state hostage until test scores reach national norms; focus his energy on overcoming the vestiges of any remaining discrimination; and, as soon as possible, return control to local authorities.[113]

Although irked by what he regarded as the Court's faulty understanding of the issues,[114] Judge Clark bowed to the inevitable and two years later in March 1997 began the process of dismantling the desegregation plan by approving an agreement between the state of Missouri and the school district that would end the state's annual $110 million desegregation payment to the KCMSD after 1999.[115]

Clark's final order left many people wondering how the KCMSD would manage to survive without state desegregation funding. Not only would the district lose approximately $110 million a year from the state, it also stood to lose an additional $75 million provided by Clark's $4.96 property tax levy. Eventually the court would have to relinquish control of the district to local authorities (called "restoring unitary status"). Once it did that, legal authority for the district's court-ordered property tax increase would expire, allowing the rates to drop back down to the state-ordered minimum of $2.75 per $100 of assessed value. That $75 million drop, on top of the already negotiated $110 million a year drop in state funding, would leave the district—assuming it got no additional help—with a budget of about $140 million.

Although there are many similarly sized school districts around the country that are surviving quite well on budgets that size, such as Montgomery County, Alabama, and Richmond County (Augusta), Georgia, the KCMSD would probably need a minimum of $240 million a year to survive.[116] It had too many built-in expenses. The magnet school busing plan alone cost $30 million a year. The district had too many schools that were only half full. Many schools had extensive landscaping and athletic facilities, as well as expensive high-tech heating and air conditioning systems.[117] Just the cost of heating the much-ballyhooed 650,000-gallon Olympic-sized swimming pool at Central High ran to several hundred thousand dollars a year.

For his part, Judge Clark was miffed at what seemed to him to be some kind of informal collusion between the state and the district to convince him to withhold unitary status (and thus keep his property tax levies from expiring). "It is not the duty of this court to ensure funding for the KCMSD," he pointed out in his final order. If the district needed more money after the court orders expired, it ought to submit a property tax increase to the voters, or the state legislature ought to put together some kind of long-term financial aid package.

Even so, in his final order of March 1997, Judge Clark expressed deep concern over what would happen to the KCMSD when a subsequent court finally did return control of the district to local authorities. Given its past performance, he wrote, the district would probably cut school services rather than reduce its "lavish" administration. To prevent that, he urged whatever judge took his place on the case to consider appointing a special master to run the district until such time as it proved itself capable of handling its own affairs. "The KCMSD must come to grips with fiscal reality," he wrote. "It cannot continue to spend money on either excess or incompetent personnel."[118]

What Went Wrong

At one time the Kansas City experiment was going to be a progressive light unto the educational nation. Instead, it became the most expensive desegregation plan in the nation and, in terms of achievement-bang-for-the-educational-buck, the biggest failure, too. Kansas City did all the things that educators had always said needed to be done to increase student achievement—it reduced class size, decreased teacher workload, increased teacher pay, and dramatically expanded spending per pupil—but none of it worked.

Although official class size in the KCMSD ranged from 22 per room in kindergarten to 25 in high school, so many students cut classes that the effective class size was often closer to 15.[119] If such small class sizes were helping achievement, it didn't show up on exams. Neither did attempts to reduce the teacher workload. At Central High, complained Clark, teachers taught only three classes per day, but student scores on standardized tests were lower at Central than they were at schools where teachers taught six daily classes.[120]

Although Kansas City did increase teacher pay a total of 40 percent to an average of about $37,000 (maximum was $49,008 per year for Ph.D.s with 20 years experience), test scores for the district were consistently below state and national averages.[121] Parochial school teachers, in contrast, earned an average of $24,423, but their students' test scores were consistently above state and national averages.[122]

In fact, the supposedly straightforward correspondence between student achievement and money spent, which educators had been insisting on for decades, didn't seem to exist in the KCMSD. At the peak of spending in 1991–92, Kansas City was shelling out over $11,700 per student per year.[123] For the 1996–97 school year, the district's cost per student was $9,407, an amount larger, on a cost-of-living-adjusted basis, than any of the country's 280 largest school districts spent.[124] Missouri's average cost per pupil, in contrast, was about $5,132 (excluding transportation and construction), and the per pupil cost in the Kansas City parochial system was a mere $2,884.[125]

The lack of correspondence between achievement and money was hardly unique to Kansas City. Eric Hanushek, a University of Rochester economist who testified as a witness regarding the relationship between funding and achievement before Judge Clark in January 1997, looked at 400 separate studies of the effects of resources on student achievement.

What he found was that a few studies showed that increased spending helped achievement; a few studies showed that increased spending hurt achievement; but most showed that funding increases had no effect one way or the other.[126]

Between 1965 and 1990, said Hanushek, real spending in this country per student in grades K–12 more than doubled (from $2,402 to $5,582 in 1992 dollars), but student achievement either didn't change or actually fell. And that was true, Hanushek found, in spite of the fact that during the same period class size dropped from 24.1 students per teacher to 17.3, the number of teachers with master's degrees doubled, and so did the average teacher's number of years of experience.[127]

As Hanushek saw it, the real problem in American public education wasn't so much financial as structural. There were no incentives in the current system to improve student performance—nothing rested on whether students achieved or not. The KCMSD should have been looking at incentives to increase academic productivity, such as merit pay, charter school vouchers, rewards for successful teachers, and penalties for unsuccessful ones. But the KCMSD, along with virtually the entire educational establishment, was institutionally biased against the notion of competition. As a result, state and federal governments had "spent tens of billions of dollars on school reforms over the last 15 years with nothing to show for it."[128] That didn't mean that money couldn't ever be important, Hanushek said, only that "in the current structure it doesn't help."[129]

Conclusion

All the money spent in Kansas City brought about neither integration nor higher levels of achievement. The lessons of the Kansas City experiment should stand as a warning to those who would use massive funding and gold-plated buildings to encourage integration and improve education:

- The political realities of inner-city Kansas City made it impossible to fire incompetent teachers and principals and hire good ones.

- Because the community regarded the school system as much as an employment opportunity as an educational institution, less than half the education budget ever made it to the classroom.

- School superintendents found it hard to function because every decision was second-guessed by the court-appointed monitoring committee; the attorney for the plaintiffs; and the state of Missouri, which was paying most of the bills.

- Because the designers of the Kansas City plan assumed that inner-city blacks couldn't learn unless they sat in classrooms with middle-class whites, the district wasted exorbitant amounts of time and money on expensive facilities and elaborate programs intended to attract suburban whites instead of focusing its attention on the needs of inner-city blacks.

- By turning virtually every school in the district into a magnet school, the Kansas City plan destroyed schools as essential parts of neighborhoods, fractured neighborhoods' sense of community, and alienated parents.

- The mechanism used to fund improvements to the school system (a federal desegregation lawsuit) deflected attention from the real problem—the need to raise black achievement.

- The ideological biases of local educators and politicians, and the federal court, made them reject solutions that might have worked, such as merit pay, charter schools, or offers by private schools to educate students in return for vouchers.

- Because the district had no way to evaluate the performance of teachers and administrators, promotions couldn't be based on merit.

- The desegregation plan created inverse achievement incentives—the district got hundreds of millions of extra dollars in court-ordered funding each year but only if student test scores failed to meet national norms.

Postscript: Confirmation from Sausalito

People who believe there's a strong connection between money spent on education and student achievement have a hard time explaining what's going on in the tiny 284-student Sausalito, California, Elementary School District. The district spends more than $12,300 per student each year—nearly three times the state average.[130] Students go to school in freshly painted buildings, with manicured lawns and new playground equipment. Class size is a mere 16 students per room, half that of many larger districts. The district has special instructors for art, drama, science, and computers. Yet, when it comes to student achievement, none of that seems to matter. Test scores are the lowest in Marin County; a third of the students are in special education classes; classrooms are "chaotic"; teachers are "frustrated, distressed and exhausted" and afraid to "turn their backs" on their classes.[131]

How could that happen in Sausalito, a wealthy liberal community of some 7,200 artists, writers, and professionals just across the bay from San Francisco at the northern end of the Golden Gate Bridge? "Why," asked one *Los Angeles Times* reporter, "aren't children performing better in a district that wants for nothing money can buy?"[132]

One reason, certainly, is parental influence, or lack thereof. Sausalito shares its school district with an unincorporated area called Marin City, a federal housing project built to house the families of workers who flocked to area shipyards to build oil tankers during World War II. The contrast between Marin City and Sausalito couldn't be more striking. Sausalito, which is 94 percent white, has an average family income of $107,500, an unemployment rate of 3.8 percent, and hillside homes that overlook San Francisco Bay. Marin City, in contrast, suffers from a 38 percent unemployment rate; two-thirds of its 2,000 residents live in public housing best known for fostering dependence on welfare, crime, alcoholism, and drug abuse.[133]

Even so, the situation of the schools was stable until 1990, when the Department of Defense closed three nearby bases. When the military left, a lot of social stability went with it and the schools quickly began to deteriorate. Concerned white parents began to transfer their children from the local public schools to private schools. By 1997 only 13 of the estimated 200 elementary-school-age children in Sausalito were going to school in their own school district.[134] Eighty percent of the district's students were black, and most came from Marin City.

Their chaotic home life came with them to the classroom. Students were "disruptive, ill-trained, ill-prepared, often without the most basic academic and social skills."[135] During the 1996–97 school year, teachers and principals called the police on 50 different occasions. According to a Marin County civil grand jury report, the district lacked strong leadership, the teachers were demoralized, and the students were so violent that the teachers feared "turning their backs" on them.[136]

When parents complained, some board school members blamed low test scores on poverty, unemployment, and drugs. But a group of concerned parents pointed out that there were schools in San Francisco and nearby San Rafael where students had just as many disadvantages and those students were doing fine.

Many people have suggested ideas for improving the schools: replacing the school board; hiring a dean and a full-time counselor for troubled children; coming up with a new curriculum; encouraging parental involvement, now close to nonexistent; and improving communication.[137] So far, however, no one has suggested solutions that might actually work. One reason is that school officials are so wedded to the notion that money is the solution to low achievement that, when they have money and it doesn't help, they don't know what to do.

In the meantime, they ignore ideas that might work. They might fire poor teachers and reward good ones with merit pay, give parents vouchers so they could send their children to private schools, or stop trying to solve the problem of dysfunctional families after the fact and look upstream for a solution—the elimination of welfare to end the resulting social chaos.

Notes

1. Jenkins v. Missouri, 959 F. Supp. 1151 (W.D. Mo., 1997), order of Judge Russell Clark. [Hereinafter Clark, order.]

2. Arthur Benson, *School Segregation and Desegregation in Kansas City*, www.bensonlaw.com/deseg/deseg_history.htm, work in progress, Spring 1995 with 1996 epilogue.

3. Interview with attorney Arthur Benson (Aug. 24, 1995).

4. Interview with Sue Fulson, former Kansas City school board president (September 13, 1995).

5. Benson, *supra* note 3.

6. Interview by Alison Morantz, Harvard graduate student, with Judge Russell Clark for the Harvard Project on School Desegregation (September 2, 1992). The project published *Money, Choice and Equity in Kansas City* in April 1994. Morantz provided the author transcripts of the interviews she conducted.

7. School District of Kansas City, Missouri v. Missouri, 438 F. Supp. 830 (W.D. Mo., 1977).

8. School District of Kansas City, Missouri v. Missouri, 460 F. Supp. 421 (W.D. Mo., 1978).

9. Jenkins v. Missouri, 593 F. Supp. 1487 (W.D. Mo., 1984).

10. Id.

11. Jenkins v. Missouri, 672 F. Supp. 400 (W.D. Mo., 1987).

12. Benson, *supra* note 3.

13. Id.

14. Interview with Alison Morantz (September 8, 1995).

15. Stephen Chapman, *An Educational Experiment Yields Some Astonishing Sobering Lessons*, CHICAGO TRIBUNE, June 22, 1995.

16. Interview by Alison Morantz with Sue Fulson for the Harvard Project on School Desegregation (August 26, 1992).

17. Benson, *supra* note 3.

18. Interview with Jay Nixon, Missouri attorney general (September 13, 1995).

19. Interview with David Armor, George Mason University sociologist (July 24, 1997).

20. Fulson, *supra* note 4.

21. Desegregation Division, Missouri Department of Elementary and Secondary Education.

22. Lynn Horsley, *Audit Suggests Possible Savings*, KANSAS CITY STAR, August 8, 1997.

23. Interview with Clinton Adams, Kansas City attorney (September 8, 1995).

24. Fulson, *supra* note 4.

25. Benson, *supra* note 3.

26. Interview with Paul Ballard, former school board member (September 19, 1995).

27. Interview with Ed Payton, Springfield attorney (September 15, 1995).

28. Interview with John Munich, Missouri state attorney (September 14, 1995).

29. Lynn Horsley, *Costs of KC's Improvements*, KANSAS CITY STAR, November 18, 1991.

30. Nixon, *supra* note 18.

31. Quoted in Jim Mosely, *Kansas City's Plush Schools Lure Students*, ST. LOUIS POST DISPATCH, FEBRUARY 9, 1992.

32. Interview with Sister Anne Shepard, Kansas City Catholic Diocese School Superintendent (August 20, 1997).

33. Lynn Horsley & Tim O'Connor, *KC School District Lacks Leadership and Vision*, KANSAS CITY STAR, January 24, 1991.

34. Nixon, *supra* note 18.

35. Charles Crumpley & Lynn Horsley, *Who Pays the Price?*, KANSAS CITY STAR, May 10, 1994.

36. Payton, *supra* note 27.

37. Id.

38. Interview with Richard Miller, Kansas City attorney (September 13, 1995). Miller filed a petition with the court on behalf of black parents asking Clark to approve a voucher plan to allow black children to attend desegregated private schools. The matter was dropped after Miller's "angel" ran out of money.

39. Interview with Annette Morgan, state legislator (September 14, 1995).

40. Morantz, *supra* note 6.

41. Id.

42. Interview with Mark Bredemeir, Landmark Legal Foundation attorney (August 8, 1995).

43. Blake Hurst, *Runaway Judge*, AMERICAN ENTERPRISE, May–June 1995, 53–56.

44. Benson, *supra* note 3.

45. Interview with Judge Russell Clark (September 15, 1996).

46. Fulson, *supra* note 4.

47. Clark, *supra* note 45.

48. Missouri v. Jenkins, 110 S. Ct. 1651 (1990).

49. Id. at 1666.

50. Id. at 1667.

51. Jenkins v. Missouri, 855 F.2d 1295 (8th Cir., 1988).

52. Ballard, *supra* note 26.

53. Fulson, *supra* note 4.

54. Id.

55. Ballard, *supra* note 26.

56. Id.

57. Fulson, *supra* note 4.

58. Benson, *supra* note 3.

59. Ballard, *supra* note 26.

60. Clark, order at 1174.

61. Benson, *supra* note 3.

62. Id.

63. Adams, *supra* note 23.

64. Benson, *supra* note 3.

65. Interview by Alison Morantz with Emanuel Cleaver, Kansas City mayor, for the Harvard Project on School Desegregation (August 3, 1992).

66. Benson, *supra* note 3.

67. Id.

68. Adams, *supra* note 23.

69. Twenty-five percent of the KCMSD's 37,000 students were white. Thus, to meet the court-mandated ratio of 40 percent white to 60 percent black, the district needed to attract 10,000 additional white students.

70. Interview with Gene Eubanks, professor of education at the University of Missouri, Kansas City (September 12, 1995)

71. Desegregation Division, Missouri Department of Elementary and Secondary Education.

72. Morantz, *supra* note 65.

73. Adams, *supra* note 23.

74. Benson, *supra* note 3.

75. Munich, *supra* note 28.

76. Benson, *supra* note 3.

77. Clark, *supra* note 45.

78. Phillip O'Connor & Lynn Horsley, *Three Schools Slated to Close*, KANSAS CITY STAR, August 2, 1997.

79. Clark, *supra* note 45.

80. Desegregation Division, Missouri Department of Elementary and Secondary Education.

81. Clark, order at 1160.

82. Id.

83. Interview with Edward Newsome, school board president (September 12, 1995).

84. Clark, order at 1173.

85. Id. at 1165.

86. Fulson, *supra* note 4.

87. Clark, order at 1165.

88. Id. at 1178.

89. Id. at 1158.

90. Id.

91. Id. at 1173, 1174.

92. Chapman, *supra* note 15.

93. Morgan, *supra* note 39.

94. Morantz, *supra* note 16

95. Jenkins v. Missouri, 115 S. Ct. 2038 (1995).

96. Armor, *supra* note 19.

97. Id.

98. Id.

99. Benson, *supra* note 3.

100. Interview with Dorothy Phillips, school counselor (September 12, 1995).

101. Interview with Jerald Hill, president of Landmark Legal Foundation (October 4, 1995).

102. Benson, *supra* note 3.

103. Id.

104. Id.

105. Interview with John Coons, law professor at the University of California, Berkeley, School of Law (September 7, 1995).

106. Morgan, *supra* note 39.

107. Hill, *supra* note 101.

108. Id.

109. Id.

110. Newsome, *supra* note 83.

111. Hill, *supra* note 101.

112. Clark, *supra* note 45.

113. Missouri v. Jenkins, 115 S. Ct. 2054, 2054, 2055.

114. Clark, *supra* note 45.

115. Clark, order at 1152.

116. Benson, *supra* note 3.

117. Lynn Horsley, *Fine Schools Will Need Years of Expensive Care*, KANSAS CITY STAR, November 18, 1991.

118. Clark, order at 1177.

119. Armor, *supra* note 19.

120. Clark, order at 1177.

121. Salary data from KCMSD Research Office.

122. Shepard, *supra* note 32.

123. Desegregation Division, Missouri Department of Elementary and Secondary Education.

124. Clark, order at 1170.

125. Average cost is from the Desegregation Division, Missouri Department of Elementary and Secondary Education. The Kansas City parochial figure is from Shepard.

126. Interview with Eric Hanushek (July 7, 1997).

127. Eric Hanushek, *Remedial Math*, NEW DEMOCRAT, December 1995, 25–27.

128. Id.

129. Hanushek, *supra* note 126.

130. Peter Fimrite, *Sausalito Schools Get Low Grades*, SAN FRANCISCO CHRONICLE, August 22, 1997.

131. Id.

132. Maria L. LaGanga, *Audit Sees 'Chaos' in Sausalito Schools*, LOS ANGELES TIMES, September 26, 1997.

133. Maria L. LaGanga, *Sausalito Schools: Money Isn't Enough*, LOS ANGELES TIMES, May 16, 1997.

134. Id.

135. Fimrite, *supra* note 130.

136. Id.

137. LaGanga, *supra* note 132.

VOUCHERS

Public Schools: Make Them Private

This article first appeared in the *Washington Post* on 19 February 1995. Milton Friedman is a senior research fellow at the Hoover Institution; he won the Nobel Prize for Economic Sciences in 1976.

Our elementary and secondary educational system needs to be radically reconstructed. That need arises in the first instance from the defects of our current system. But it has been greatly reinforced by some of the consequences of the technological and political revolutions of the past few decades. Those revolutions promise a major increase in world output, but they also threaten advanced countries with serious social conflict arising from a widening gap between the incomes of the highly skilled (cognitive elite) and the unskilled.

A radical reconstruction of the educational system has the potential of staving off social conflict while at the same time strengthening the growth in living standards made possible by the new technology and the increasingly global market. In my view, such a radical reconstruction can be achieved only by privatizing a major segment of the educational system—i.e., by enabling a private, for-profit industry to develop that will provide a wide variety of learning opportunities and offer effective competition to public schools. Such a reconstruction cannot come about overnight. It inevitably must be gradual. The most feasible way to bring about a gradual yet substantial transfer from government to private enterprise is to enact in each state a voucher system that enables parents to choose freely the schools their children attend. I first proposed such a voucher system 40 years ago.

Many attempts have been made in the years since to adopt educational vouchers. With minor exceptions, no one has succeeded in getting a voucher system adopted, thanks primarily to the political power of the school establishment, more recently reinforced by the National Education Association and the American Federation of Teachers, together the strongest political lobbying body in the United States.

(1) The Deterioration of Schooling

The quality of schooling is far worse today than it was in 1955. There is no respect in which inhabitants of a low-income neighborhood are so disadvantaged as in the kind of schooling they can get for their children. The reason is partly the deterioration of our central cities, partly the increased centralization of public schools—as evidenced by the decline in the number of school districts from 55,000 in 1955 to 15,000 in 1992. Along with centralization has come—as both cause and effect—the growing strength of teachers' unions. Whatever the reason, the fact of deterioration of elementary and secondary schools is not disputable.

The system over time has become more defective as it has become more centralized. Power has moved from the local community to the school district to the state, and to the federal government. About 90 percent of our kids now go to so-called public schools, which are really not public at all but simply private fiefs primarily of the administrators and the union officials. We all know the dismal results: some relatively good government schools in high-income suburbs and communities; very poor government schools in our inner cities with high dropout rates, increasing violence, lower performance, and demoralized students and teachers.

These changes in our educational system have clearly strengthened the need for basic reform. But they have also strengthened the obstacles to the kind of sweeping reform that could be produced by an effective voucher system. The teachers' unions are bitterly opposed to any reform that lessens their own power, and they have acquired enormous political and financial strength that they are prepared to devote to defeating any attempt to adopt a voucher system. The latest example is the defeat of Proposition 174 in California in 1993.

(2) The New Industrial Revolution

A radical reconstruction of our educational system has been made more urgent by the twin revolutions that have occurred within the past few decades: a technological revolution—the development, in particular, of more effective and efficient methods of communication, transportation, and transmission of data; and a political revolution that has widened the influence of the technological revolution.

The fall of the Berlin Wall was the most dramatic event of the political revolution. But it was not necessarily the most important event. For example, communism is not dead in China and has not collapsed. And yet beginning in 1976, Premier Deng initiated a revolution within China that led to its being opened up to the rest of the world. Similarly, a political revolution took place in Latin America that, over the course of the past several decades, has led to a major increase in the fraction of people there who live in countries that can properly be described as democracies rather than military dictatorships and that are striving to enter open world markets. The technological revolution has made it possible for a company located anywhere in the world to use resources located anywhere in the world, to produce a product anywhere in the world, to be sold anywhere in the world. It's impossible to say, "this is an American car" or "this is a Japanese car," and the same goes for many other products.

The possibility for labor and capital anywhere to cooperate with labor and capital anywhere else had dramatic effects even before the political revolution took over. It meant that there was a large supply of relatively low-wage labor to cooperate with capital from the advanced countries, capital in the form of physical capital, but perhaps even more important, capital in the form of human capital—of skills, of knowledge, of techniques, of training.

Before the political revolution came along, this international linkage of labor, capital, and know-how had already led to a rapid expansion in world trade, to the growth of multinational companies, and to a hitherto unimaginable degree of prosperity in such formerly underdeveloped countries in East Asia as the "Four Tigers." Chile was the first to benefit from these developments in Latin America, but its example soon spread to Mexico, Argentina, and other countries in the region. In Asia, the latest to embark on a program of market reform is India. The political revolution greatly reinforced the technological revolution in two different ways. First, it added greatly to the pool of low-wage, yet not necessarily unskilled labor that could be tapped for cooperation with labor and capital from the advanced countries. The fall of the Iron Curtain added perhaps a half-billion people and China close to a billion, freed at least partly to engage in capitalist acts with people elsewhere.

Second, the political revolution discredited the idea of central planning. It led everywhere to greater confidence in market mechanisms as opposed to central control by government. And that in turn fostered international trade and international cooperation.

These two revolutions offer the opportunity for a major industrial revolution comparable to that which occurred 200 years ago—also spread by technological developments and freedom to trade. In those 200 years, world output grew more than in the preceding 2000. That record could be exceeded in the next two centuries if the peoples of the world take full advantage of their new opportunities.

(3) Wage Differentials

The twin revolutions have produced higher wages and incomes for almost all classes in the underdeveloped countries. The effect has been somewhat different in the advanced countries. The greatly increased ratio of low-cost labor to capital has raised the wages of highly skilled labor and the return on physical capital but has put downward pressure on the wages of low-skilled labor. The result has been a sharp widening in the differential between the wages of highly skilled and low-skilled labor in the United States and other advanced countries.

If the widening of the wage differential is allowed to proceed unchecked, it threatens to create within our own country a social problem of major proportions. We shall not be willing to see a group of our population move into Third World conditions at the same time that another group of our population becomes increasingly well off. Such stratification is a recipe for social disaster. The pressure to avoid it by protectionist and other similar measures will be irresistible.

(4) Education

So far, our educational system has been adding to the tendency to stratification. Yet it is the only major force in sight capable of offsetting that tendency. Innate intelligence undoubtedly plays a major role in determining the opportunities open to individuals.

Yet it is by no means the only human quality that is important, as numerous examples demonstrate. Unfortunately, our current educational system does little to enable either low-IQ or high-IQ individuals to make the most of other qualities. Yet that is the way to offset the tendencies to stratification. A greatly improved educational system can do more than anything else to limit the harm to our social stability from a permanent and large underclass.

There is enormous room for improvement in our educational system. Hardly any activity in the United States is technically more backward. We essentially teach children in the same way that we did 200 years ago: one teacher in front of a bunch of kids in a closed room. The availability of computers has changed the situation, but not fundamentally. Computers are being added to public schools, but they are typically not being used in an imaginative and innovative way.

I believe that the only way to make a major improvement in our educational system is through privatization to the point at which a substantial fraction of all educational services are rendered to individuals by private enterprises. Nothing else will destroy or even greatly weaken the power of the current educational establishment—a necessary precondition for radical improvement in our educational system. And nothing else will provide the public schools with the competition that will force them to improve in order to hold their clientele. No one can predict in advance the direction that a truly free-market educational system would take. We know from the experience of every other industry how imaginative competitive free enterprise can be, what new products and services can be introduced, how driven it is to satisfy the customers—that is what we need in education. We know how the telephone industry has been revolutionized by opening it to competition; how fax has begun to undermine the postal monopoly in first-class mail; how UPS, Federal Express, and many other private enterprises have transformed package and message delivery; and, on the strictly private level, how competition from Japan has transformed the domestic automobile industry.

The private schools that 10 percent of children now attend consist of a few elite schools serving at high cost a tiny fraction of the population, and many mostly parochial nonprofit schools able to compete with government schools by charging low fees made possible by the dedicated services of many of the teachers and subsidies from the sponsoring institutions. These private schools do provide a superior education for a small fraction of the children, but they are not in a position to make innovative changes. For that, we need a much larger and more vigorous private enterprise system. The problem is how to get from here to there. Vouchers are not an end in themselves; they are a means to make a transition from a government to a market system. The deterioration of our school system and the stratification arising out of the new industrial revolution have made privatization of education far more urgent and important than it was 40 years ago.

Vouchers can promote rapid privatization only if they create a large demand for private schools to constitute a real incentive for entrepreneurs to enter the industry. That requires first that the voucher be universal, available to all who are now entitled to send their children to government schools, and second that the voucher, though less than the government now spends per pupil on education, be large enough to cover the costs of a private profit-making school offering a high-quality education. If that is achieved there will in addition be a substantial number of families that will be willing and able to supplement the voucher in order to get an even higher quality of education. As in all cases, the innovations in the "luxury" product will soon spread to the basic product.

For this image to be realized, it is essential that no conditions be attached to the acceptance of vouchers that interfere with the freedom of private enterprisers to experiment, to explore, and to innovate. If this image is realized, everybody, except a small group of vested interests, will win: parents, students, dedicated teachers, taxpayers—for whom the cost of the educational system will decline—and especially the residents of central cities, who will have a real alternative to the wretched schools so many of their children are now forced to attend.

The business community has a major interest in expanding the pool of well-schooled potential employees and in maintaining a free society with open trade and expanding markets around the world. Both objectives would be promoted by the right kind of voucher system.

Finally, as in every other area in which there has been extensive privatization, the privatization of schooling would produce a new, highly active, and profitable private industry that would provide a real opportunity for many talented people who are currently deterred from entering the teaching profession by the dreadful state of so many of our schools.

This is not a federal issue. Schooling is and should remain primarily a local responsibility. Support for free choice of schools has been growing rapidly and cannot be held back indefinitely by the vested interests of the unions and educational bureaucracy. I sense that we are on the verge of a breakthrough in one state or another, which will then sweep like a wildfire through the rest of the country as it demonstrates its effectiveness.

To get a majority of the public to support a general and substantial voucher, we must structure the proposal so that (1) it is simple and straightforward so as to be comprehensible to the voter, and (2) it guarantees that the proposal will not add to the tax burden in any way but will rather reduce net government spending on education. A group of us in California has produced a tentative proposition that meets these conditions. The prospects for getting sufficient backing to have a real chance of passing such a proposition in 1996 are bright.

· ·

School Choice: Beyond the Numbers

Joseph P. Viteritti

This selection first appeared in *Education Week* on 23 February 2000. Joseph Viteritti is a research professor of public administration in the Wagner School of Public Service at New York University in New York City, where he is the director of the Program on Education and Civil Society. He is the author of *Choosing Equality: School Choice, the Constitution, and Civil Society* (Brookings Institution Press, 1999).

There are two distinct approaches to school choice. A market model, taken from economics, is based on the empirical proposition that introducing competition to education will improve the performance of school systems and their students. An equity model, derived from a concept of justice, is based on the normative proposition that all parents deserve an equal opportunity to select the schools their children attend. The two approaches are inextricably related, but often confused and misapplied in debates about the desirability of school choice. The validity of an empirical model is tested by the assembly of measurable data that reasonable people can agree are relevant. Normative models are assessed according to deep-seated values that parties to a discussion claim to share.

Behind the choice debate that has occupied policymakers so intensely for the past 10 years is the fantastic notion that some day a group of dispassionate experts will objectively reach a judgment to determine whether or how it is safe to translate the explosive idea into policy without incurring unwitting harm. Of all the issues up for discussion among educational researchers, none is so packed with emotion. Many of the underlying premises to the debate are plainly irrational. Choice opponents defend the status quo by arguing that if we provided parents with the means to remove their children from traditional public schools, an overwhelming number would. Education is the only profession where the providers' lack of confidence in their own product is used as a rationale for rejecting an alternative.

Market purists, skeptical about the capability of the public sector to accomplish anything worthwhile, expect government officials to enact a revolutionary choice policy that is not only efficient but also just. Presently, there is little evidence that the market alone is capable of serving the needs of disadvantaged communities, whether the commodity in question is housing or groceries, recreation or health care. Equally absurd, however, is the assertion that we should not try choice until it can be proven to work, since it is impossible to demonstrate the viability of any idea that has not been given a chance.

Most people trace the market model to the writing of economist Milton Friedman, dating back to 1955. Troubled by the monopolistic nature of education in America, the Nobel laureate advocated a system of vouchers that parents could use at any school, public or private. His expectation was that competition would force low-performing schools to close, and provide the rest with an incentive to improve. Convinced that private schools would outperform public schools, he envisioned a system of education that was publicly financed and privately run, with a minimal governmental role in either operating or regulating institutions. Since the market had not yet been tested in education, Mr. Friedman's model was purely theoretical; because the operation of the market had been uneven in other sectors, his message rang hollow to most who heard it. And if the culture of the public education profession was inhospitable to the concept of competition, it was downright hostile to the prospect of privatization.

The choice question was brought into the mainstream of policy circles in 1990, with the publication of John E. Chubb and Terry M. Moe's *Politics, Markets, and America's Schools*. As the issue moved to center stage through the next decade, both the dialogue and the characters began to change, so that the script originally written by Milton Friedman was barely recognizable. Charter schools, which by the first of this year were instituted in 36 states and the District of Columbia, provided public school advocates with a way to enjoy the benefits of choice and experiment with competition without crossing over into the voucher camp. Voucher programs became a reality for 8,000 low-income students in Milwaukee and 4,000 in Cleveland, while Florida began to launch a statewide program for children who attend chronically failing public schools.

Unlike the universal voucher plan put forward by Milton Friedman, the current voucher programs are targeted at disadvantaged and underserved populations. They are advanced in the name of equity as well as efficiency. Like the many charter proposals that were enacted in state legislative bodies once resistant to change, these voucher plans were put forward by unusual political coalitions that included free-market champions, concerned business leaders, and representatives of minority communities who were fed up with the quality of local public schools, demonstrating that the constituency for choice had expanded beyond the Republican right. Polls today indicate that the most consistent and vocal supporters of school choice are black and Hispanic parents.

The case for choice is no longer built on abstract economic models; and advocates are unwilling to wait for expert evidence decreeing that it is all right to advance the cause. The demand erupts from an on-the-ground understanding by parents that there is no future for children consigned to failing schools, parents who reject the unjust arrangement that limits choice to families that have the economic means to either acquire a private school education or live in communities where public schools provide a decent education. Economically disadvantaged people, who historically have not been well served by either public education or the market, are not likely to be taken in by romanticized notions of one or the other. But they understand that both public schools and the market respond to clients who have the power to grant or withhold revenues needed for institutional survival. It is not the market that makes choice work for the poor, so much as giving poor people the resources to prod the market. When choice is properly designed, it is a form of redistributive public policy: providing public resources for disadvantaged people to purchase private (or public) goods (or services) in accord with a larger public interest.

There is no reasonable response to the demand that all parents, regardless of economic status, should be allowed to select the schools their children attend—other than to argue that if poor people were granted choice, they would fail to exercise it in the best interests of their own children. It is an untenable position on many counts. History shows that those who have made such crucial decisions for poor children in the past usually have not done so to the children's benefit; if a disproportionate number of poor children attend failing schools, it is not because their parents want them there. Anyone who has a child knows that there isn't any person or institution that is more inclined to act in the best interest of the child than that child's own parents. This natural sentiment is not compromised by economics, but the ability to act on it is.

In addition to the charter and voucher programs already mentioned, philanthropists have inaugurated privately supported, voucher-style scholarship programs that reach more than 100,000 students across the nation. This wide range of experience has been informative. The record shows that there is a strong demand for choice among poor and minority parents. This is demonstrated by the long waiting lists of applicants that accompany all choice programs—charters, vouchers, and private scholarships alike. Last year, when the Children's Scholarship Fund announced a lottery for 40,000 partial-tuition scholarships, the foundation received 1.25 million applications from low-income parents. These parents were willing to forgo a free public education and absorb the balance of tuition payments for the opportunity to exercise choice.

When parents who have exercised choice are asked to identify the characteristics that attracted them to their children's new schools, their responses usually focus on several factors: high academic standards, a safe, nurturing environment, opportunities for meaningful parental involvement, and, for those in parochial schools, the religious values within the curriculum.

After their children attend such schools, they register higher levels of satisfaction on these same factors in comparison to their previous public schools. Contrary to what some would believe, poor parents are capable of making intelligent decisions in selecting schools for their children.

The most controversial empirical debate that rages around choice programs concerns student performance. If students who have opted into charter schools and voucher programs are not exhibiting higher levels of academic achievement, then, even conceding the best intentions among choice advocates and parents, what's the point? At this juncture, there is no definitive evidence with regard to charter schools, although a major federal study is under way. Early studies of privately financed voucher programs in New York, San Antonio, Milwaukee, and Indianapolis are encouraging, but skeptics question their methodological rigor. The same can be said for the public voucher programs in Milwaukee and Cleveland, although the quality of the later evaluations is generally better.

Scholars have been fighting over whether private and parochial schools outperform public schools since the late James S. Coleman posed the question in 1983. I happen to agree with him that parochial schools do a better job mediating the effects of poverty among inner-city minority children. I find the recent spate of comparative studies on graduation rates in urban schools especially persuasive. But not everyone would agree. Nor will they ever, at least not in the educational lifetimes of those children whose parents are waiting for some authoritative body to declare that they should have the opportunity to exercise choice that most middle-class families take for granted.

In the end, choice constitutes good public policy because it is fair, not because its effects are measurable by academicians who would not dream of sharing the decision about where to send their own children to school.

For those empiricists who need reassurance, I would suggest for the sake of argument that we call it a draw. Let us assume that there is an equal proportion of high-quality schools in the public and private sectors. Acknowledging the overall shortage of good schools in poor urban communities, let us assume that the parent in search of an educational opportunity has the same probability of finding a desirable placement in both. Certainly there is no evidence to contradict that assumption; even skeptical scholars could accept such a randomized assertion. A well-crafted voucher program targeted for poor and underserved communities would simply expand the number of decent options for a population that wants and needs more options; and it would empower parents whose opportunity to act in the best interest of their own children has been impeded by financial hardship.

A final consideration brings us back to where we began: Would the competition engendered by choice provide an incentive for low-performing schools to improve? Unfortunately, that question cannot be fully addressed with the current assortment of charter and voucher programs because most have been designed to limit real competition. As a result of the legislative horse-trading imposed by choice opponents, most charter school laws set strict limits on the number of schools allowed, and on average, these new schools receive about 80 cents for every dollar allocated to regular public schools. The same is true for voucher programs. When the Milwaukee program began, a cap was set so that only 1 percent of the school population was allowed to participate. It is now at 15 percent. About 4,000 children participate in the Cleveland program, but the waiting list of applicants exceeds 17,000.

It seems that children who participate in choice programs are forced to incur certain "opportunity costs" in terms of educational expenditures. The further one moves from the traditional public school run by a local district, the higher the cost. For example, in Cleveland, per-capita public spending for children who attend regular public schools is $7,746; for charter school students, it is $4,518; and for students who use vouchers, it is $2,250. This is an unfair competitive arrangement. It is also inequitable. Considering that many of the children who participate in choice programs come from disadvantaged backgrounds, the practice turns the idea of compensatory education on its head.

Yes, theoretically the effect of market competition is measurable empirically, but no, we can not fully assess it under the existing plans. Of course, there are some skeptics who will continue to deny that competition, even unencumbered, with all the artificial constraints removed, will work to improve public education. I don't share their cynicism. Even if they are wrong, but especially if they are right, the most compelling argument for choice remains a plea for fairness. We don't need numbers to prove that.

. . . .

Fighting for School Choice: It's a Civil Right

Alveda C. King

This selection first appeared in *The Wall Street Journal* on 11 September 1997. Alveda C. King is chairman of the Atlanta-based King for America and a senior fellow with the Alexis de Tocqueville Institution.

Thirty years ago, my uncle Martin Luther King Jr. talked about America's "promissory note" to deliver to all its people the unalienable rights to life, liberty, and the pursuit of happiness. He dreamed of an

America where all children, regardless of their color or religion or other circumstance, would enjoy the full exercise of those rights.

For our children, a decent education is an integral part of life, liberty, and the pursuit of happiness. For parents faced with school violence, pervasive drug use, and sexual license, a choice among different types of education is no less important. This may not make a decent education an "entitlement," but it certainly gives rise to parents' desire to direct a process so vital to their children's future.

Is it moral to tax families, compel their children's attendance at schools, and then give them no choice between teaching methods, religious or secular education, and other matters? Is it consistent to proclaim, meanwhile, that America is a nation that prides itself on competition, consumer choice, freedom of religion, and parental responsibility?

I can't presume to know exactly what my uncle would say about the current debate over school vouchers and choice. But I know what principles he taught, and I know that he not only preached but also practiced them. Martin Luther King Jr. and his siblings were products of public and private education. In turn, they educated their children in both public and private schools—and impressed upon my generation the importance of faith and family in effective schooling.

In this spirit, House Majority Leader Dick Armey (R., Texas), Sen. Joe Lieberman (D., Conn.), Rep. Floyd Flake (D., N.Y.), and several other congressmen have proposed the District of Columbia Student Opportunity Scholarship Act. The measure, which the Senate will likely vote on next week as part of an appropriations bill, is designed to rescue Washington's public schools by using public and private compensation and incentives.

Under the act, 2,000 low-income students in Washington would receive tuition scholarships of up to $3,200 per year, which would enable them to attend the public or private school of their choice. The act would also provide 2,000 public school students with vouchers for extra tutoring assistance, worth up to $500 a year.

In the name of civil rights, some oppose such relief for religious parents who want their children to attend a religious school. In the name of helping poor and minority children, opponents of "opportunity scholarships" want to continue business as usual in the Washington schools—which today remain closed, bankrupt, and not even up to fire code.

The District of Columbia public school system allocates $10,180 per student, the highest in the nation, according to the U.S. Department of

Education. Yet according to the Annie Casey Foundation, 80% of fourth-graders in the Washington public schools score below their grade on basic math skills. The National Assessment of Educational Progress reports that 72% of Washington's fourth-graders test below "basic proficiency."

In response to this appalling failure, Washington's families are choosing alternatives to the deteriorating school system—19.7% send their children to private schools, significantly higher than the national average of 13.1%. Washington public school teachers send their own children to nongovernment schools at a rate of 28.2%, more than double the national average of 12.1%. More than one-third of all Washington teachers, both public and private, send their children to nongovernment schools; the national average is 17.1%. And here's a statistic for the so-called civil-rights leaders: African-Americans comprise two-thirds of Washington's population, yet 61% of the city's families that send their children to private schools are white, and only 12% of the families that do so are black.

These statistics show that a "choice" has already been made. Washington's families and teachers favor a right to choose the paths of education for their families. Of course, there are also those who choose to remain in the public school system. The issue is not what families choose, but rather, that they be allowed and empowered to do so.

Herein lies the challenge. What happens to families who cannot afford to choose a private school over a public school? In part, this is a question of a parent's civil right to determine what is best for a child who cannot make that mature, responsible decision for himself.

U.S. citizenship guarantees all parents an education for their children. This is a true civil right. Yet some children receive a better education than others due to their parents' abilities to pay for benefits that are often missing in public schools. This inequity is a violation of the civil rights of the parents and children who are so afflicted by lack of income and by the mismanagement endemic to so many of the country's public school systems.

The District of Columbia Student Opportunity Scholarship Act is designed specifically to alleviate this inequality—to restore parents' and children's civil rights. This is not an attempt to destroy public schools. Indeed, all Americans should want the public schools to be the very best that they can be. But we must make it possible for all people to choose the best educational settings for their children, no matter what their circumstances.

. . . .

Whittling Away the Public School Monopoly

Thomas Toch

This selection first appeared in *The Wall Street Journal* on 15 November 1999. Thomas Toch is a guest scholar at the Brookings Institution.

Edison Schools Inc., a company that has run public schools for profit since 1995, became a $760 million business last Thursday when its stock began trading on the Nasdaq exchange. Its initial public offering marks the return of company founder and chief executive Christopher Whittle, the flamboyant former owner of *Esquire* magazine and Channel One, whose high-profile publishing and marketing company, Whittle Communications, crashed and burned in the mid-1990s.

More importantly, Edison's successful IPO reflects the momentum behind a market-based movement that is changing the very nature of public education. With 79 schools and 38,000 students, Edison is merely the largest of many new providers of public education that are now vying with traditional public schools for students. Churches, YMCAs, universities, at least two dozen for-profit companies, and many other types of organizations are operating publicly funded charter schools and, in Edison's case, traditional public schools under contract to local school boards.

The company knew from the outset that it would have to attract students away from conventional public schools. So it created a school design with attractive features such as home computers linked to school-based networks, and it lengthened both the school day and the school year so as to give students the equivalent of four extra years of instruction.

The company delivers its upscale school design not to rich suburban kids but primarily to disadvantaged urban students—kids conventional public schools haven't educated very well. Nearly half of Edison's students are black, and 60% are from impoverished families. The average Edison student comes to the company's school scoring at the 30th percentile on standardized tests. Symbolizing Edison's devotion to the poor, Mr. Whittle is planning to move its headquarters from midtown Manhattan to Harlem.

Edison has proved that the market forces are just as likely to spur innovation in public education as in other sectors. With its survival as a business tied directly to its performance in the classroom, Edison has come up with several ingenious solutions to pedagogical problems.

When the company opened its first middle schools three years ago, it found that its reading curriculum was far too advanced for its many students who could barely read. So the company hired the creators of Wilson Reading, a highly regarded adult literacy program, to adapt the program for preteens. As a way of shrinking staff expenses and enabling outstanding teachers to reach more students, Edison this summer entered a partnership with APEX, a company launched by Microsoft co-founder Paul Allen, to make Advanced Placement courses available to Edison high schools via the Internet.

Edison tracks student achievement and school performance to a degree unprecedented in public education. Every student's progress in basic subjects is measured monthly, and the results are delivered to the company's headquarters. Edison surveys parent, teacher, and student satisfaction in every school annually. Edison principals are awarded performance-based bonuses of up to about 20% of their salaries. And the company swiftly fires principals and teachers who don't perform.

Have such steps produced better-educated students? In a handful of scientific studies comparing Edison students' classroom performance over several years against that of students with similar backgrounds, Edison students have registered greater gains. And on the 300 or so state and national tests students have taken in different Edison schools, their passing rates have risen or their scores have ratcheted up faster than expected about 75% of the time. Student attendance is generally high in Edison's schools, and dropout rates are low.

Critics argue that for-profit companies aren't necessary to introduce such reforms and that the money Edison makes in profit should be returned to students. But it's clear that outside catalysts are necessary to bring about real change. In Toledo, Ohio, facing the prospect of Edison opening a local charter school, the local teachers' union joined forces with the school system to reconstitute a traditional public school to look a lot like an Edison school. They lengthened the school day and school year and brought in the same highly regarded reading curriculum that Edison uses. They abandoned seniority-based hiring in order to ensure that they got the best possible teachers.

Edison hasn't been successful everywhere. Several of its schools have foundered, and last spring it temporarily suspended two struggling high schools. Some Edison schools have inadequately served special-education students. Many of Edison's teachers have failed to use its expensive technology effectively in their classrooms. And most of the new Edison schools that opened this year lacked books and supplies (some even lacked desks) because of purchasing blunders. In response, the company sacked its entire purchasing staff.

Nor has Edison yet turned a profit; it lost $27.6 million last year. Losses have led to cost-cutting moves. The company has trimmed back expensive features of its school design—cutting the length of its typical school year from 210 days to 200 (the public school average is 180) and beginning its home-computer program in third grade rather than in kindergarten. And Edison cannot profitably operate schools in much of the South, the Rocky Mountain states, and California because of low state education spending. As a result the company has turned to philanthropy; it opened eight schools in California with the help of millions of dollars donated by Don and Doris Fisher, founders of the Gap.

Edison's model is not excessively expensive. The company received an average of $5,555 a student last year, less than the $6,392 that the average public school spent per pupil. The company is counting on such things as cheaper computers and economies of scale to put the company into the black. If the company grew to about 700 schools, it would have the revenues of a Fortune 500 company.

Whatever Edison's flaws, the mostly disadvantaged kids on Edison's campuses are by and large in more attractive, safer schools with higher standards, more resources, and a greater sense of purpose than the traditional public schools most would otherwise attend. And that's not because Edison employs a bunch of educational magicians. It's because the company has to compete for every student it enrolls.

. . . .

A Private Solution

*Increasingly, School Districts Are Turning to Private
Companies to Serve At-Risk Kids*

Lawrence Hardy

This selection first appeared in *The American School Board Journal*'s April 1999 issue.
Lawrence Hardy is an associate editor of *The American School Board Journal*.

"It's boring," says 16-year-old Amonte Porter. And maybe that's OK.
Relaxing around a table with his four classmates, Amonte laments the
lack of sports at his school and the kind of excitement only a big high
school can bring.

The sprawling Fairfax County Public Schools in northern Virginia
has plenty of big high schools, including six with more than 2,000 students. And then there is Richard Milburn High School, this tiny school
in a frame house on the rougher edge of town.

Amonte has been expelled from regular school. So have his classmates. But they still dream about the future.

Amonte wants to be a musician. Or maybe a teacher. Or maybe a
counselor, to help kids like himself. He smiles, looks at the ceiling. He
really doesn't know.

At regular school, Kim Ryals, 16, was tempted by her friends to skip.

"Here," she says, pulling back her long blond hair, "there's no reason to."

History and English teacher A.T. Johnson is a big, soft-spoken man
who can calm you with his gaze. A retired Air Force master sergeant, he
has just finished the afternoon class, a special segment on heroes that
coincides with Black History Month.

"These kids are no different than anyone else," Johnson says. "It just
takes a little extra effort and a lot of patience."

Privately Run

But Richard Milburn High School is different, and not just because of
its size. It is a private school operating within the nation's 11th largest
school system.

Fairfax sends up to 100 students a year to two Richard Milburn campuses. Mainly serving students who have been expelled, Richard Milburn is what Fairfax County administrator Douglas Holmes calls "a program of last resort" for students who otherwise would be on the street. It is a privately run school among the vast array of district-run alternative programs.

Why turn to a private company? Robert H. Crosby, president of the Woodbridge, Va., business, explains: "We'll take your most difficult kids. We'll keep them in school—85 percent of our kids stay in school or graduate—and we'll do it for approximately the same per-pupil costs as the school district's cost."

Or perhaps for considerably less. Fairfax spends more than $7,000 per student throughout the district, but only about $3,500 for the typical student at Richard Milburn. This represents the cost of six courses—and few of the amenities of a regular high school. Parents are responsible for transportation. Lunch is not provided.

In addition to offering lower costs, privately run schools can tailor their programs to the specific populations they serve, making them better equipped to help these students, industry leaders say.

"Would it ever be the priority of a public school or system" to teach at-risk kids? Timothy P. Cole, president of Youth Services International, Inc., which operates schools for adjudicated youth and hopes to get into the at-risk market, raises that question, then answers it himself: "If it was, would we be having this problem now?"

But some educators are wary. "Contracting out" might be a legitimate option for transportation and food services, they say, but the practice raises practical and philosophical problems when applied to instruction.

Some school board members and administrators are concerned about the loss of day-to-day control. Some fear private companies will be overly concerned with the bottom line. Others say that turning over some educational services to a profit-making enterprise could create a separate group of second-class students.

"I'm a heavy-duty skeptic on contracting out delivery of educational services," says John S. Davis, a member of the Tacoma Park School Board, in Tacoma Park, Wash.

Davis says school boards should not leap to the often-popular notions that government is, by nature, wasteful, and that the profit motive is the most powerful incentive for achieving excellence. He points to

Washington state's efforts to raise student achievement and increase the accountability of schools and districts.

"Those conditions are as big an incentive to local schools as profits are to a company," Davis says.

Contracting Out

The practice isn't new. Contracting out various educational services to public agencies—and, at times, private companies—has long been an option for districts that have small numbers of students with special needs. For example, a child with a relatively rare condition such as autism might be better served by an agency specially suited to handle that disability.

But increasingly, districts are looking to private companies to serve a broader population of students deemed "at risk," says John M. McLaughlin, president of the Education Industry Group, a trade organization in Sioux Falls, S.D. "At risk" is a designation that can mean anything from students who have been expelled or suspended to those with a variety of academic problems. And with the sheer numbers of students expected to rise through at least 2006, the number of children needing alternative schools will grow as well.

"I have a feeling that school boards over the next 5 to 20 years are going to be looking more at outsourcing instructional services," McLaughlin says.

According to Private Options for Public Schools, a 1995 report from the National School Boards Association (NSBA), districts have been far more likely to contract out for management services than for instruction. Among instructional programs cited in the NSBA report, special education led the way with 14 percent of districts opting for privatization. Eight percent used private technology programs, and 7 percent contracted for at-risk programs.

Urban districts were more likely to privatize instructional programs, the report said. Fourteen percent of urban districts had privatized at-risk programs, compared with 6 percent of suburban districts and 5 percent of rural districts.

Among the larger companies serving at-risk students are Richard Milburn High School; Ombudsman Educational Services of Libertyville, Ill.; Kids 1 of East Brunswick, N.J.; and Options for Youth in La Crescenta, Calif.

The benefits of contracting out aren't only economic, McLaughlin says. It has been estimated that 95 percent of management time is spent on 5 percent of the students, he says, adding: "When solutions are found for these students, then the energy, the resources of the school can be turned in another direction."

That is what is happening in the Houston Independent School District, where a private company, Community Education Partners, is charged with educating certain students who have been expelled or are in danger of expulsion. According to the district's contract, CEP is required to raise the math and reading achievement of each student attending for 180 days to a level specified by the state's alternative education standards, says Susan Sclafani, the district's chief of staff for educational services. If CEP cannot meet this goal, it must provide its services free of charge until the student attains it. Students attending between 90 and 180 days must advance at least one grade level in reading and math, Sclafani says.

The program's cost, at $8,500 per student, is higher than the district's average per-student cost of $5,400 but less than the $10,000 average per-pupil cost at the now-defunct alternative schools that used to educate these students.

The company pays its teachers less than the district does but pays teacher aides more than the district, says Gayle Fallon, president of the Houston Federation of Teachers. And the staff has been unionized, she says: "We organized everything that moved that was not administration."

Fallon's response to the program might seem unusual for a union leader.

"It's one of the most impressive educational programs I've ever looked at," she says. ". . . They're dealing with children who we're about to expel but who have not yet been picked up by the police."

Filling a Niche

Richard Milburn High School was founded in 1975 in Quantico, Va., to teach basic skills and GED, or high school equivalency, instruction to soldiers in the U.S. Marine Corps. Now operating in eight states, the company offers nontraditional secondary education programs for students in more than 40 districts. The school's two Fairfax locations offer three-hour sessions in mornings and afternoons.

The Fairfax students who attend Richard Milburn represent a fraction of the 2,000 district high school students attending alternative programs, says Holmes, hearing officer for the district's Hearing and Legal Office. He says Richard Milburn is more isolated than other programs, and less comprehensive. For example, unlike Fairfax's small alternative high schools, Richard Milburn doesn't offer laboratory sciences or elective courses.

But the school fills an important niche for students who have been expelled because of disciplinary problems.

"It keeps kids in school who otherwise would probably face the street," Holmes says.

Ombudsman Educational Services, another large company in the field, operates alternative programs in 10 states. The programs serve 2,500 students in about 200 school districts.

"I think probably the bottom line is economics," says Ombudsman President James P. Boyle. "If school districts are doing it themselves, they're probably spending two or three times as much."

"Usually," he adds, "they're trying to create something from nothing. They reinvent the wheel."

Boyle says Ombudsman can cut costs by offering three sessions a day, with students attending three hours a day. Instructional programs are individualized and, unlike the instruction at Richard Milburn, are heavily computer-based.

"The model is essentially the same in all areas," Boyle says. "We teach our teachers like McDonald's teaches people to fry hamburgers."

Like Richard Milburn's Crosby, Boyle says 85 percent of his company's students are successful, meaning they either graduate or return to their regular schools.

Founded in 1991, Youth Services International, Inc., concentrates mainly on adjudicated youth. The company, which recently merged with Correctional Services Corporation, operates 28 residential programs in 12 states and 9 after-care programs in 7 states. However, President Cole says YSI hopes to contract with school districts to serve at-risk students.

It's a niche market that he says is growing.

"It requires a special program and a special mentality to work with these kids," Cole says. "A lot of teachers don't want to function in the combat zone."

And public school systems, he adds, "don't want to deal with them. They either expel them or push them through."

In a 1995 guidebook published by NSBA—Guidelines for Contracting with Private Providers for Educational Services—McLaughlin says that privatization expands the number of options available to districts. But they need to answer a variety of questions before taking that route.

Are their needs being met under the present arrangement? If not, why not? And do state laws give boards the power to enter into private contracts for educational services?

"It doesn't work the same way in any of the 50 states," McLaughlin says.

If a district is seriously considering contracting, it should initiate a Request for Proposals as part of an open and competitive bidding process, McLaughlin says. The contract's length should be addressed, as well as the scope of the proposed services and a well-specified description of the quality expected.

Ivan Hernandez, who directs alternative education programs at the Lincoln County School District in Newport, Ore., says his district will be reviewing its contract with a regional consortium that educates students who have been expelled or are on the verge of expulsion. He is concerned about student absenteeism—50 percent of the students are gone 25 percent of the time, he says—and wonders if the contract should contain more performance criteria.

One benefit of the arrangement is that the district pays part of the teachers' salaries. "That link is critical, I think, for the future success of the program," Hernandez says.

But whether or not districts use their own teachers, they still have to answer for the quality of the education provided. And regardless of whether they decide to keep instructional services "in-house" or turn some over to private businesses, they remain ultimately responsible.

"They do not lose—and they cannot by law lose—that right and responsibility," McLaughlin says. "That responsibility still rests with the school district."

. . . .

Class Acts

How Charter Schools Are Revamping Public Education in Arizona—and Beyond

James K. Glassman

This selection first appeared in *Reason* Magazine's April 1998 edition. James Glassman is a resident fellow at the American Enterprise Institute, host of the website TechCentralStation.com, and co-author of *Dow 36,000* (Times Books, 1999).

Three years ago, Arizona passed a law that allows almost any reasonably serious person to start a school and receive a little more than $4,000 in state funds for every student enrolled. Such "charter schools," as they're called, are public schools that operate with more autonomy than conventional ones—a vague definition, perhaps, but the best one available. Twenty-nine states and the District of Columbia have laws permitting them. In the short time they've been around in Arizona, charters have attracted more than 25,000 students, or roughly 3 percent of the state's public school population, and the number is still rising by 10,000 annually. Arizona, with one-fiftieth of the nation's population, has about one-third of its 780 charter schools. Arizona has twice as many charters as California, which has eight times as many children under age 18.

Over the past year, I've visited Arizona three times to see how well its charter schools are working. I especially wanted to find out whether charters were providing competition to traditional public schools and whether, in response, those public schools were trying to improve. I am not an expert on education—far from it—but I write about business and economics, and I've long suspected that one reason public schools fail is that, as government-protected near-monopolies, they lack the feedback mechanisms built into market systems. As a result, they can't get the sort of information that would help them do a better job. Ultimately, they're operated more for the benefit of administrators and teachers than for parents and students—for producers rather than consumers. When charter schools started pulling some of those consumers away from traditional public schools, my hypothesis went, the latter would have no choice but to get better in order to lure the kids back.

Although it's early in the process and the evidence is not yet conclusive, that's precisely what I found when I traveled to the Grand Canyon State. What's more, if a major goal of educational reform is to open the public school system to the salutary effects of competition, charters have more immediate political appeal than vouchers (which would allow families to use state money to send their kids to private schools) and are probably just as effective.

One dramatic illustration of how charters have forced traditional schools to respond was the full-page advertisement—yes, an advertisement—that the Mesa Unified School District ran in local newspapers last summer. The headline blared: "There's no better place to learn than in the 68 Mesa public schools! . . . Don't miss out!" Mesa, a fast-growing, prosperous city of 350,000 east of Phoenix, is a hotbed of charter schools, with 23 of them currently operating in the area. (The 68 schools to which the ad refers are traditional public schools—although technically all 91 schools are public.)

"We're not afraid of a little competition," says Judi Willis, a school district spokesperson. In fact, Mesa has no choice but to make its conventional public schools better. It's already losing about $10 million a year in funds that are going to charters. From 1996 to 1997, the total public school enrollment in Mesa rose by 1,870, with conventional schools losing 69 students and charters gaining close to 2,000. In fact, Mesa's charter schools have even been hiring school bus drivers away from traditional public schools, offering them 10 percent more pay plus a bonus.

In the Roosevelt Elementary School District in Phoenix, one of the poorest neighborhoods in the state, another superintendent, John Baracy, is feeling the heat as well. In his office at an administrative headquarters that is itself as big as a typical school, Baracy tells me that 300 students have left so far for charters—a drain of more than $1 million, or 2 percent to 3 percent, from his budget. He calls these departures "a wake-up call" and says he was moved to phone "our customers that left us" to find out why. "The main theme that's coming across is that we have not been sensitive to the needs of the parents," he explains.

The departure of students is the sort of unambiguous market signal that was heavily muffled before charters came on the educational scene. Baracy won't be specific about how he'll respond to student needs, but he's gotten the message. "It's an incentive for schools to reflect on themselves and reassess where they're at," he says, adding, "I'm a supporter of charter schools. If parents feel the opportunity is better with them, then they should have that option."

The precise effects of competition on educational quality are difficult to measure, but in a study released last year, Harvard economist Caroline Hoxby found that when families are given a "large increase" in the number of schools to which they can send their children conveniently—defined roughly as a jump from two schools to ten—interesting things happen. First, per-pupil spending drops by about $400, or 7 percent. Second, increased competition improves measures of student performance—including test results, the probability of finishing high school, and future income—by about 5 percent. "The striking thing is the opposite directions of the spending and achievement results," says Hoxby. "This has powerful implications for productivity." None of this should be surprising: Lower costs and higher quality are the results that competition produces in the private sector. Why should public education be very different?

The first of the country's charter schools opened its doors in St. Paul, Minnesota, in 1992. Some 290 new charter schools were launched last fall alone, but the average state has only about two dozen, and in most cases established interests, led by the teachers' unions, have placed restrictions on the freedom of educators to run the schools the way they want. These rules often go beyond the onerous; some even prescribe exact qualifications for teachers and micromanage how instruction is given.

In Arkansas, for example, the union "essentially wrote the charter law," says Joe Nathan, director of the Center for Social Change at the University of Minnesota. "And the Arkansas law is a joke." A joke, that is, on students and parents: Students can't move to a charter school; they have to be matriculating at a conventional one that converts. Also, all teachers have to participate in the statewide collective bargaining agreement. As a result, Arkansas has zero charter schools.

Arizona is at the other end of the spectrum. Students have to meet detailed statewide academic standards in math, language, science, arts, foreign language, and health. And schools have to be run on a sound financial basis and be audited annually. But as far as oversight goes, that's about it. Schools use their own forms of teaching, ranging from back-to-basics curricula to the Montessori method. They can concentrate on the arts or agriculture, on science or school-to-work programs. They have to be nonsectarian and can't display religious objects, but one school, Gan Yeladeem in Scottsdale, teaches Hebrew as a second language (though only about one-third of its 96 students are Jewish), and several Mormon schools have converted to charters (though no Catholic schools have done so). Arizona charters don't have to give preference to "at-risk" students (though there are special charter schools for the hearing-impaired and for pregnant teens and mothers), and they don't have to strive for racial balance. They do, however, have to admit all comers (the arts schools can't even hold auditions) and, if too many students want to enroll, admit them at random.

The key to Arizona's success is that charters for new schools can be bestowed not just by local school boards—which aren't eager to engender competition—but by a state board for charter schools or by the state board of education, headed by Lisa Graham Keegan, the elected superintendent of public instruction. By contrast, in most states, only local school boards—or county boards, on appeal—can charter a school.

The city of Mesa illustrates the importance of a multi-sited charter certification process: None of its 23 charter schools was approved by its local board (given entrenched interests, that's hardly surprising). Two, in fact, were chartered by boards from other parts of the state. One of the neat wrinkles in the law is that any board can charter schools anywhere in Arizona and receive a licensing commission in the process. Because of this open-door policy, four for-profit national chains have secured charters in Arizona: The Tesseract Group (formerly Education Alternatives Inc.), based in Minneapolis; Sabis Educational Systems Inc., of Eden Prairie, Minnesota; Leona Academies of East Lansing, Michigan; and Advantage Schools Inc., of Boston. Chris Whittle's Edison Project, which operates public schools enrolling 13,000 student in eight states (some in charters, others through management contracts with conventional public school boards), is another likely entrant in Arizona.

Superintendent Keegan, who is rumored to have aspirations for higher office, was the driving force behind the charter law as a state legislator. It passed almost by a fluke. Originally, Keegan and her colleagues tried to pass a voucher law that would have given parents money they could have used to enroll their kids in private schools. When it became clear that the unions stood in the way, she switched to charters, which the opposition assumed—mistakenly, it turns out—would be less threatening to the public school monopoly.

Indeed, one thing I learned in Arizona is that, from an educational standpoint, charters make the question of whether the alternatives to conventional public schools are public or private less pressing. In terms of creating better schools, the key is that parents have wide choices and that the schools are as close to independent as possible. When I asked Susan Heller, principal of Gan Yeladeem, if parents were happy with her school, which she founded in 1996 and which already has a waiting list, she said simply, "Well, if they aren't happy, they have the choice to leave, and nearly every child has stayed." So far, Arizona's minimal academic requirements haven't played mischief with the charters' diverse personalities and approaches to learning.

The financial oversight has been pretty hands-off, too. In fact, only two schools—less than 1 percent of the total—have lost their charters because they failed to meet the state's fiscal standards. In one case, there was out-and-out fraud; in the other, the state didn't trust the school's enrollment numbers. Those failures actually point out a major strength of the charter system. As Keegan wrote in January in a letter to the editor in *The New York Times*: "Our public system has at times been rife with mismanagement, yet before the advent of charter schools Arizona had never been able to take such strong actions on behalf of students. Closing a failing school is not a travesty, it is progress." Like any other business, a school should fail if it messes up financially or if it can't deliver what its customers want. When you have trial and error, you have error—and it has to be punished. Bad schools should go bankrupt. The idea, after all, is to create a resilient system, not a fault-free one.

The only deficiency of Arizona's law—and it's a big one—is that the state stipend is not supplemented to account for buildings and other capital costs. Arizona charters receive the same amount, per student, as conventional public schools do for operations. But the charters, unlike regular public schools, have to use some of that money to pay rent on their buildings.

"At $4,200 [a student], your margins are so thin that if you hiccup, you're going to lose money," explains John Golle, chairman of The

Tesseract Group. When it opens its charters over the next few years, Tesseract will be Arizona's largest charter school operator, with 16 sites and a total of 6,650 students in grades K–12 (it already runs a private school in Scottsdale, with annual tuition averaging about $6,700). This is the same company that, before changing its name from Education Alternatives Inc. last December, ran schools under management contracts with boards in Baltimore and Hartford. Those deals came apart at the seams, in large part because of opposition from the unions.

In Arizona, Tesseract's challenge is more economic than political, though hardly less daunting: How do you stay in business given the state's relatively stingy stipend? Golle's idea is to run his charters like a movie house, profiting from the popcorn, not the film. In this case, the popcorn includes preschools that feed into the charter, post-secondary classes for adults, summer programs, and special classes in computer skills.

If Superintendent Keegan gets her way, though, charter school operators will see their margins fatten up a bit. She is now pushing for an extra $640 per student as a capital stipend. The ultimate goal, she told me, is to "strap dollars on the back of students." That's a concept that could, of course, lead to a voucher-style system, where the money accompanies students to private schools (which enroll about one in eight kids nationwide). Whether that ultimately happens, the odds look fairly good that Keegan will succeed in getting a capital stipend for charters. If and when she does, says Jaime Molera, the 29-year-old top assistant on education to Gov. Jane Dee Hull, "Charter schools could grow exponentially."

John Graham, a Phoenix real estate developer, concurs. He says that firms like Tesseract and Edison have asked him to build schools in his suburban subdivisions and lease them back to the charter operators for free, or at a token rental, to encourage families to buy houses there. It's a nice deal for the educational firms, he says, but one that doesn't do much for the builder. "As a businessman, it doesn't make sense," says Graham. But, he points out, if a developer could pull in $600 per student, or $180,000 in annual rent from an enrollment of 300, it does.

I visited with Graham (who is, incidentally, Keegan's ex-husband; Phoenix is that sort of small town) last November. A little later that same day, I toured a school in a central-city neighborhood that is worlds apart from Graham's commodious developments. The school has 359 elementary students, nearly all of them Hispanic, and is located in a former shopping center. It's run by Advantage, a typical start-up company with enthusiastic founders, high expectations, and little else.

Currently, Advantage has only one other charter school, in Rocky Mount, North Carolina, and another set to go in New Jersey this fall. Advantage has received a total of $5 million in venture-capital funding from Bessemer Venture Partners and Fidelity Capital, a division of Fidelity Investments, the huge mutual fund house.

Critics accuse charters of "skimming" the best students from public systems, which is often a coded way of claiming they have predominantly wealthy, white students. But the Advantage school's large minority student body is actually pretty typical for charters. A study released last May by the U.S. Department of Education found that 48 percent of charter school students are minorities, compared with 34 percent for all public schools nationwide. In Arizona, the study found that 45 percent of charter students come from families with incomes low enough to qualify for the free or reduced-price lunch program, compared with 40 percent for all public schools in the state. Nationally, 13 percent of charter school students are in special education programs, vs. 10 percent at regular public schools.

Far from skimming the best students, then, charter schools often wind up with those who are having problems. The reasons for this are not hard to fathom. As researchers Chester Finn, Gregg Vanourek, Bruno Manno, and Louann Bierlein suggest in their extensive 1997 study of charter schools for the free-market–oriented Hudson Institute, the most comprehensive review yet of the existing charter school literature: "Well-to-do parents of successful youngsters are not likely to enroll their progeny in new, unproven schools that have not yet established firm reputations. . . . The families streaming into charter schools are plenty needy, and many of their children have been poorly served elsewhere."

That's certainly the case at Advantage, where 90 percent of the children are on free or reduced lunch (the generally used poverty standard for schools). While most of the parents are Hispanic, the teaching language is English. Both the school day and the school year are longer than in normal Phoenix public schools. But that doesn't seem to bother the kids. The principal, Pepe Quintero, a 27-year veteran of teaching, is a bundle of energy, and the students, all in neat uniforms, are almost frighteningly attentive to teachers using a highly scripted curriculum called Direct Instruction that stresses reading skills.

Each classroom has rules posted on the wall: "Be responsible. Be kind. Tell the truth. Persevere." Encouragement is everywhere. In a fifth-grade room, a sign says, "We are the world's best class." And there's a remarkable amount of respect shown to the kids by the teachers and administrators. For example, when Quintero brings me into a classroom, he says to the second-graders, "Excuse me, ladies and gentlemen, for interrupting."

Anyone who has visited an inner-city public school would find the sense of order at Advantage astonishing. But not surprising: The parents of these kids want discipline and structure in their children's schools; that's one of the main draws of Advantage. Clearly, the power of self-selection is intense and effective. It helps everything run more smoothly.

"Everybody is here by choice, not by assignment," says Stephen Wilson, the president of Advantage and formerly director of strategic planning for the commonwealth of Massachusetts. And he's referring not just to the students and their parents but to the teachers and the principal as well.

Wilson's partner is Theodor Rebarber, who was an aide to former Minnesota Rep. Steve Gunderson and who authored a 1997 Reason Public Policy Institute study on charters. Like any other businessmen, they're out to make a profit by giving customers what they want. But staying in the black is no easy task given Arizona's level of per-student funding. "Phoenix, for us, is a great business challenge," says Wilson. "If we can make it here, we can make it anywhere." Next on his list are Washington, D.C.; Worcester, Massachusetts; Kalamazoo, Michigan; and Chicago. If Advantage goes public, Wilson says, teachers will get stock options.

To my admittedly untutored eye, the Advantage school appears to be an enormous educational success. But it just opened its doors in September, so no student test results are available yet. Similarly, there are not yet any substantive data from other Arizona charter schools.

The Hudson Institute study, however, suggests cautious optimism regarding charter schools, noting that the "early signs are promising. . . . [A]t six of eight Massachusetts charter schools where students have been tested, academic gains were greater than is typically found in regular public schools. (The other two cases were inconclusive.) In Lawrence, second-, third-, and fourth-grade students at Community Day Charter School advanced an average of 1.5 years in eight months. In Springfield, where Sabis (a for-profit firm) took over the town's worst elementary school, students in grades second through seven gained 1.5 years in seven months."

Reports of similar gains are trickling in from other parts of the country. The Fenton Avenue Charter School in Los Angeles, with an enrollment that is nearly all poor, boosted test scores more than 20 percent in two years. The Academy of Charter Schools in Colorado reports that students have advanced an average of 13 percentile points in "basic battery" categories for the past two school years.

As important, parents are convinced that charter schools are working for their kids. As part of their study, the Hudson Institute group surveyed the parents of 2,978 students at 30 charter schools in nine states. They found that of parents who said that their children's performance was "below average" at their previous school, 32 percent responded that performance at the charter was now "excellent" or "above average." Fifty-five percent said it was "average." Only 13 percent of the kids remain below average in the view of their parents. Not quite Lake Wobegon (where all the children are famously above average), but it's very impressive when 87 percent of parents see a significant improvement.

But to return to the question that prompted my travels: Are conventional public schools reacting to charter competition in a positive way? Yes. In Arizona's Queen Creek school district, the local elementary school changed its curriculum to a back-to-basics approach in direct response to the opening of a charter school in the district. Flagstaff last year opened a "school within a school" for 100 students, who can focus on either arts or on math and science. As *Investor's Business Daily* reported, Flagstaff schools spokesman Gary Leatherman minced no words as to why, saying simply, "We did that to stem the flow of students."

The same *IBD* story notes that after Lansing, Michigan, lost 900 students (about 5 percent of its base, at a cost of more than $5 million) to charters last year, the public school district "announced tough new goals— like higher test scores and reduced dropout rates—with specific targets in place for the next five years." While the announcement of a five-year plan sounds like the typical reaction of a large bureaucracy, in this case it's clear that Lansing's public school administrators are getting the right message.

The massive Hudson Institute report, surveying charter schools around the country, helps flesh out how competition with charters will enrich conventional public education. While Finn and his colleagues stress that at this point they "only have clues" and that they're "not quite certain what a 'critical mass' of charter schools will be," the signs of charters' positive effects on traditional public schools are not hard to find. They write, "We've . . . been to places where the appearance of a charter school (or two or three) in the community leads to beneficial effects from competition, heightened entrepreneurship on the part of the 'regular' schools, a scramble to find efficiencies, even 'copycat' schools that borrow a popular curriculum, disciplinary strategy, or special service from the charter school."

For example, the researchers found that one charter school in Massachusetts offered full-day kindergarten, prompting the local public school to offer the same. In Detroit, where charter schools just began operating this year, the superintendent of public schools has said, "We're finding the charter idea is helping encourage other schools in our district to examine what they are doing. I don't agree with those who are defensive. We are proud of many things about the Detroit schools. But we can, and must, do better. Charter schools are helping us move in the right direction."

Traditional public schools in San Carlos, California, have been using the charter school there as a research and development laboratory, to see what works. According to the Hudson Institute study, it has "instituted the use of personalized learning plans, thematic instructional units, multi-age classrooms, and technology-based instruction. Other schools in the district are now adopting these approaches."

This evidence, I'll admit, is anecdotal—and sparse—but all signs suggest that charter schools are having an important dual effect: Not only do charters provide their own students with a quality education, they are having a significant impact on non-charter public schools, too. The dynamics unleashed by charter competition may not be the perfect solution to bad schools, but it's hard to see what's better—or more immediately available.

Much of the success of charters depends on the excitement, energy, and drive they generate in all involved. That was evident at the very first charter I visited, the Arizona School for the Arts, in downtown Phoenix. The director, Mark Francis, has for 15 years had a vision of the school he wanted to start—"a school where the arts go hand-in-hand with personal and intellectual development." Says Francis, a Ph.D. in musical arts, "We're a college prep school that allows students to work with performing artists." Education experts will tell you that a school that has such a clear-cut idea guiding it is more likely to succeed than one with the vague mission of simply "teaching" students. When parents, students, teachers, and administrators all know where they are headed, it becomes much easier to arrive at a particular educational destination.

Like most charter entrepreneurs, Francis got the school off the ground himself—recruiting a board, hiring teachers, finding a building (in a church) and, in his special case, making arrangements with a ballet company, a theater company, and the local symphony to give his students instruction. He found the head of the school's academic program, Diane Jarrell (who has a Ph.D. in education) by putting a "little bitty ad in the newspaper. I had something in there that said that certification is not necessary, excellence is."

In its second year, the school has 275 students in grades 6 through 12—and a waiting list for the middle grades. The state provides an average of $4,500 per student (annual stipends vary by grade), for a total of about $1.2 million. Francis would like more money, but so far he's in the black. Teachers are paid $24,500 to start, with more experienced ones earning $32,000—similar to traditional public school pay in Phoenix. "We prefer to get younger teachers," Francis says, "and bring them up our own way."

Students don't receive grades, but they're subjected to tough oral exams three times a year, and teachers send home a one-page assessment. It's a system that seems to please everyone. And the kids are smart and alert. I visited a social studies class that discussed the economics of art: how, for instance, painters make a living. Some of the students had parents who were artists who also gave lessons or held down other part-time jobs, and they talked about their own experiences. The discussion turned to artists in Renaissance Italy, and the teacher, frankly and accurately, pointed out how the rise of a rich merchant class helped the arts flourish.

Interestingly, Francis says that running a charter has moved him closer to the libertarian camp. "I just want people to have more choices," he says. "And this is a liberal Democrat talking." I ask him what he thought of federal grants to state education agencies for charter schools, which President Clinton is pushing. Not much, he replies: "It costs more to hire someone to do the paperwork." And he fears the strings that are always attached to Washington's money.

Francis reminds me of the owner of any start-up business (I used to be one myself). The school is the fruit of his own imagination, and he's desperate to make it succeed. It's precisely this spirit that's missing from public schools, where bloated power structures make it difficult for students, parents, teachers, and administrators to have much of a personal stake or to believe their involvement can really make a difference. Educators like Francis lead by example—and the schools they're creating in Arizona and elsewhere are likely to lead by example, too—even helping kids sitting in conventional public school classrooms.

Such a powerful ripple effect is one reason why Jaime Molera, the assistant to Arizona Governor Hull, likes to quote his boss as saying that her goal is for all of Arizona's schools to be charter schools—that is, schools of such spectacular variety and independence that parents choose them for their kids.

. . . .

Healthy Competition

David Osborne

This selection first appeared in *The New Republic Online* on 16 September 1999. David Osborne is a managing partner of Public Strategies Group, a consulting firm, and co-author of *The Reinventor's Fieldbook: Tools for Transforming Your Government* (Jossey-Bass, 2000).

A decade ago, a group of parents in Forest Lake, Minnesota, decided they wanted to create a Montessori elementary school. They had kids in a Montessori preschool, and some had older children in the local public school. The parents were afraid the love of learning they saw emerging in their preschoolers, who were encouraged to follow their interests and initiate their own projects, would be squelched in the public school. They looked into starting a private school but quickly realized they couldn't afford the tuition. So they approached their school district and proposed a public Montessori school. And they got nowhere.

"Every meeting resulted in, 'No, we can't do this,'" said Mark Gilchrist, a public school teacher in another district. "And the reasons weren't that it was an educationally poor concept. In fact, every school administrator and teacher we talked to agreed that this was very sound educationally. But it was, 'We don't know how we would arrange the busing,' or 'We don't have magnet schools, we have neighborhood schools,' or 'How would we train teachers?' It was, 'Yes, this is a good program, but we can't do it, we can't do it, we can't do it.'"

Then, in 1991, the Minnesota legislature passed the nation's first charter school law, which allowed parents and others to create new public schools that would be free from most district regulations, contingent upon local school board approval. The parents passed the hat, hired a consultant to help them draft a charter school proposal, and made their case to the school board.

These were voters, so the board members didn't want to say no. But the board members also knew that, if they authorized the school, several hundred thousand dollars would be deducted from their district budget each year to fund the charter school. "You could see them adding and subtracting the amounts of money that each child represented," said Jane Norbin, one of the parents.

Finally, one board member asked, "Why don't we find a way to do this in the public school?" The board directed the administration to work with the parents, and, when they met, it was as if night had become day, according to Norbin. "One at a time, all the barriers that just weeks before were there, we started finding ways around. It was just amazing how those could be taken down when you wanted to take them down." The result was not a charter school but a better public school—a small Montessori-school-within-a-school that provided exactly what the parents had wanted all along.

This fall, eight years after the initial charter school law was passed, some 350,000 students will enroll in 1,684 charter schools in 32 states and the District of Columbia. Since the first charter school opened in 1992, the debate over whether to expand the number of charter schools has focused almost exclusively on the performance of individual schools. But those who invented charter schools were not just out to create a few thousand good schools. Rather, they wanted to improve all 88,000 public schools in the country by creating enough competition for money and students to force school districts to innovate. They wanted to create a public school system in which the Forest Lake story was repeated—in different permutations—thousands of times each year.

The most important question policymakers should ask about charter schools is whether they are achieving this goal. Until recently, the evidence was anecdotal. But, over the past year, several empirical studies have demonstrated that, indeed, competition works just as the reformers predicted. Unfortunately, it only happens when state charter laws unleash true competition for funds and students—and that still occurs all too infrequently.

Charter schools can be created by parents, teachers, nonprofits, or, occasionally, for-profit companies. They typically have three- to five-year charters—that is, performance contracts—with the government organizations that authorize them: local school boards, city councils, county boards, state boards of education, or, in some states, even colleges and universities. They are schools of choice, and their public funding normally comes with the students who choose them, from the district the students leave. To succeed, they must attract—and keep—enough students to finance their operations.

Although Albert Shanker, the legendary former American Federation of Teachers president, played a pivotal role in putting charter schools on the political agenda, most teachers' unions and administrators' associations still resist them. In state after state, these organizations have fought to kill or weaken charter school bills. The big issue is competition: They don't want to see public school districts laying off teachers and administrators because they have lost funding to charter schools. Unions also fear losing bargaining rights and teacher tenure in charter schools. For the adults in the system, competition can be painful—no matter how much it helps the children.

Sometimes opponents talk openly about this issue, accusing charter school proponents of trying to "destroy" the public schools. Since charter schools are public schools—forbidden by law from charging tuition, using selective admissions, teaching religion, or discriminating by race, religion, or gender—this argument is specious on its face. So, more often, the unions and their allies accuse charter schools of being elitist or of "skimming"—luring the best students out of inner-city schools. Occasionally, they allege that charters are outright scams perpetrated by con artists who seek to profit at the expense of children. Perhaps the most-often-heard argument, however, is that we should go slowly until we know whether charter schools really work. Unions have used this argument repeatedly to win and protect statewide caps on the number of charter schools, as well as provisions that charters must be approved by local school boards—the same local monopoly that charter schools are designed to break.

There is ample evidence to prove that no "skimming" effect exists in charter schools. Indeed, their percentages of minority students are equal to or higher than those of other public schools in their states. As for the argument that some charters are outright scams, the few bad apples have been quickly closed down by their chartering authorities—something that rarely happens to failing public schools. And the numbers are hardly cause for concern: The Center for Education Reform reports that charter-granting authorities had closed only 28 schools—2.3 percent of the total—by last January.

And how about the "go slowly" argument—do we know whether existing charter schools are working? Unfortunately, it's hard to prove anything related to performance, because little meaningful data exists. In the few areas where test scores are available to allow a comparison among charter schools and their surrounding districts, the data usually measures absolute test scores, not student gains from one year to the next. Hence, it doesn't tell us whether charter schools are creating more educational gains or whether they started with students who were already ahead.

One thing is certain, though: Charter schools are passing the market test. Their number continues to expand rapidly, and 70 percent of them have waiting lists, according to the most recent annual report published by the U.S. Department of Education. In a nationwide survey, 65 percent of parents rated their children's charter schools better than their former public schools; fewer than 6 percent rated them worse.

But what about the competitive effect? Have charter schools really jolted education bureaucracies into greater innovation? The first nationwide empirical study of this question was published last year by an independent research unit of the University of California at Berkeley called Policy Analysis for California Education. Doctoral candidate Eric Rofes, now an assistant professor of education at Humboldt State University, interviewed 227 administrators, principals, teachers, and charter school founders in 25 school districts. He included eight states and the District of Columbia, all of which had at least two years of experience with charter schools.

Rofes found that, when charter schools took enough students and dollars away from school districts, the districts usually made significant changes. Overall, six districts "had responded energetically to the advent of charters and significantly altered their educational programs," opening new schools organized around themes or methodologies, adding courses at existing schools, and creating their own charter schools. In Bartow County, Georgia, the district had turned eight of its ten elementary schools into charter schools. Colorado's Adams County School District Twelve had "chartered numerous schools," "responded to parent requests for more 'back-to-basics' programs, and created stronger thematic programs in its traditional schools."

Another six districts exhibited what Rofes called a "moderate" response. But even these had made significant changes: Boston had responded by creating nine charterlike "pilot schools," each with a particular focus such as health sciences or dropout prevention; Mesa, Arizona, had launched all-day kindergarten and new "back-to-basics" schools; and Grand Rapids, Michigan, had opened a new school focused on environmental education and had plans for additional thematic schools. "Charter laws throughout the nation have spurred a revival of the alternative educational programs popular in the 1960s and '70s," Rofes added, "and expanded open-classroom, Montessori, Waldorf-type programs, and developmental-focused pedagogies within public schooling."

Competition has a very clear psychological effect, an administrator in Grand Rapids told Rofes. "It's a morale issue in terms of the staff. At first, they have some initial fear: Is the government out to destroy public schools? Then there's an urgency, people recognizing we're in a competitive market. When you visit a staff room in a building located near a charter school, you sense an immediate change in psychology: now we're in competition with the charter. We have to market our schools."

Indeed, the day after a charter school was awarded in one Massachusetts town, the superintendent walked into an administrators' meeting, tossed a copy of David Halberstam's book *The Reckoning* on the table, and asked, "Who do you want to be—Honda or General Motors?" As the superintendent told Rofes, "Our middle school, which is the school at which the charter school is aimed, was by any rational standard the least successful school in the district. Its test scores were mediocre. . . . It had a faculty that was defensive and complacent."

"The charter school was a wake-up call, like it or not," the superintendent continued. "The fact is that the parents of more than a hundred kids said, 'We want our kids out. . . .' Charter schools served notice to everybody that complacency wasn't an option."

Rofes is not the only one who has uncovered evidence of charter schools' success. Separate studies on Arizona, Michigan, Massachusetts, and Los Angeles came to similar conclusions. The study in Arizona, undertaken by researchers at James Madison University, found that the mere possibility of competition from charters was enough to prompt "low-cost" reforms such as teacher training, while actual competition stimulated "high-cost" reforms such as all-day kindergarten programs and significant changes in curriculum. The Michigan study, by researchers at Western Michigan University, found that charter schools were stimulating districts to create all-day kindergarten programs, before- and after-school programs, and more foreign-language programs, while encouraging more parental involvement and more attention to performance on standardized tests.

The lone discordant note has come from a study done by a research team at the University of California at Los Angeles, focusing on ten school districts in California. That study found little or no perception of pressure "to change the way they do business." But, with the exception of one very large urban district with 15 charter schools, the other nine had a total of just 24 charter schools among them. Five of the districts were large urban districts where charters had not drained enough resources to pose a real threat to the system, according to lead investigator Amy Stuart Wells. In the five rural and suburban districts, Wells reports, administrators had used the law to begin creating their own charter schools. Hence, they had seized on the charter law as a way to innovate before any outside pressure emerged.

It doesn't always take competition to spark innovation. But, particularly in the larger districts, bureaucracy stifles all but the most capable and persistent reformers. Those who run the monopoly—in this case, the school board, the superintendent, the central administration, and the principals—usually want to do what's best for the children. The problem is that innovation requires taking risks. Ted Kolderie, a pioneer of the charter school movement, explains the dynamic well: "As they consider proposals for change, the superintendent, board, principal, union, and teachers weigh the potential benefits to the kids against the risk of creating 'internal stress.' They want to help the kids. But upsetting people might create controversy. It might produce a grievance. It might lose an election. It might cause a strike. It might damage a career." Robert Wright, a teacher in San Jose, California, who once founded a public-school-within-a-school, calls it "the rule of the ringing telephone." Change brings complaints, and when the phone rings often enough—no matter how trivial the complaints are nor whom they are from—the typical administrator clamps down.

Competition forces administrators to take the initiative. If they don't shake things up, their districts and schools will shrink. They will have to lay teachers off. Angry voters may overthrow school boards, angry boards may fire superintendents, and angry superintendents may even fire principals. Consider what has happened in Massachusetts, where David J. Armor and Brett M. Peiser studied the impact of interdistrict choice for the Pioneer Institute. They conducted detailed surveys and interviews in nine of the ten school districts that had seen the most students leave for other districts. Those that lost the most students (5 to 6 percent) and felt the most financial pain made the most changes to increase their competitiveness; those that felt the least financial pain did nothing. In general, it took a loss of 2 to 3 percent of the students to wake a district up and stimulate significant innovation.

Charter schools add power to public school choice by creating both new choices and excess capacity in the system. "The important part of school choice is that we have lots of different choices," explained former Minnesota State Representative Becky Kelso, another sponsor of the original charter school law. "If your only choice is another public school right next door that's just like the public school you're in, that's not much of a gift. I think charter schools are a part of that choice system that means there will be new and unique choices, and that's a very critical ingredient."

In many school systems, there are so few empty seats that, while parents theoretically have choices, most of the schools they would choose don't have room for new students. In a closed market such as this, schools face very little real competition for their dollars. But if new schools are springing up all the time, creating excess capacity in the system, the competition increases dramatically. As new schools emerge, other schools shrink, losing money. When they lose enough to feel the pain, they begin making changes to win back their customers.

So why aren't there more charter schools already? At the national level, the idea has support from presidential front-runners Al Gore and George W. Bush. Yet many state legislatures continue to stall. While there are 37 charter school laws on the books, fewer than a dozen of those laws create significant competition. As Bryan Hassel, author of *The Charter School Challenge*, explained in a recent Progressive Policy Institute brief: "Fifteen of the first 35 charter laws allow local school boards to veto applications. Fifteen make charter schools part of their local school districts, denying them legal independence. Only 17 of the laws permit full per-pupil operating funding to follow the child from a district to a charter school; fewer than five allow capital funding to follow the child. And many laws restrict the number of charter schools that can open, the types of people and organizations that can propose charter schools, or both."

Consider California, which jumped on the charter school bandwagon back in 1992 and is considered to have a fairly aggressive program. Those who want to start a charter school still have to ask the local school board for approval. If their request is denied, they can appeal to the county board of supervisors. But elected officials on school boards are often quite influential with their elected colleagues on county boards, so winning such an appeal can be hard. When Wright considered starting a charter school, he knew he couldn't get his school board to vote for it, so he talked with the president of the county board, a charter school supporter. But the board president couldn't get the votes either. So Wright created a school-within-a-school instead, which the district bureaucracy quickly neutered. California law was amended last year, and prospective charter operators can now appeal to the state Board of Education. But no one knows yet how well that will work; the board has rejected the only appeal so far. San Jose, a city of 900,000 in the heart of the hyperinnovative Silicon Valley, still awaits its first charter school.

Charter schools can create sufficient competition to force existing districts to reform, but only if the conditions are right: if there are enough charter schools, if diverse groups can create them, if they can get charters from somebody other than the local monopoly, if they take significant money away from the monopoly, and if they are free to operate independently from any district bureaucracy. In the states where all or most of these conditions exist—such as Arizona, Michigan, Massachusetts, Minnesota, North Carolina, and Texas—the competition strategy is working. Why shouldn't more states allow their own citizens the same opportunities?

. . . .

The Elixir of Class Size

Chester E. Finn, Jr.
Michael J. Petrilli

This selection first appeared in the *Weekly Standard* on 9 March 1998; copyright News America Incorporated. Chester E. Finn, Jr. is the John M. Olin Fellow at the Hudson Institute and president of the Thomas B. Fordham Foundation. Michael J. Petrilli is a researcher at the Hudson Institute and is certified in Michigan to teach social studies.

The president has proposed to shrink class sizes in the early grades by hiring 100,000 more teachers at federal expense. This is quintessential Clintonism—a warm Labrador puppy of a policy notion, petted by teachers and parents alike, but destined to bite when it grows up.

There is precious little evidence that smaller classes help students— achievement may even go down if the new teachers are mediocre—but don't try telling this to voters. Smaller classes are a pollster's delight. The idea is so popular that many states and communities have jumped the gun. Indiana shrank its primary classes more than a decade ago. California's Pete Wilson was hailed when he said the state's surplus should be used for this purpose. Class-size reduction was part of the successful campaign platform of Virginia's new Republican governor, Jim Gilmore, who has promised 4,000 new teachers in the state over the course of his four-year term. Similar proposals await legislative action in Alabama, Delaware, New York, and many other jurisdictions.

Why this lemming-like rush off the class-size cliff? "Teachers are thrilled, parents are thrilled," explained a California elementary school principal in response to the president's plan. Parents simply take for granted that smaller classes mean better education. Teachers cheer because their jobs get easier with fewer students per classroom. Unions get more members. Administrators get more staff. And most local school boards welcome any move by Uncle Sam to pay teacher salaries.

Congress will therefore likely end up saying yes. But it shouldn't. The administration's plan—and others like it—is bad for at least five reasons.

First, the conventional wisdom that students do better in smaller classes is flat wrong. After surveying all the relevant research, economist Eric Hanushek of the University of Rochester concludes that "there is little systematic gain from general reduction in class size." Besides, classes have been shrinking for decades—today's national average of 22 kids per classroom is down from 30-plus in the 1950s—with no commensurate gains in learning, although the cost has been immense. (No "reform" is more expensive than smaller classes.) The Asian lands that trounce us on international assessments have vastly larger classes, often 40 or 50 youngsters per teacher. Yes, there are one or two studies indicating that fewer *kindergarten* children in a classroom is linked with modest test-score gains. But put it this way: If smaller classes were a drug, the FDA would not let it onto the market. Additional experiments might be warranted, but no scientist would say that its efficacy has been proven.

There's a simple reason why small classes rarely learn more than big ones: Their teachers don't do anything differently. The same lessons, textbooks, and instructional methods are typically employed with 18 or 20 children as with 25 or 30. It's just that the teacher has fewer papers to grade and fewer parents to confer with. Getting any real achievement bounce from class shrinking hinges on teachers who know their stuff and use proven methods of instruction. Of course, knowledgeable and highly effective teachers would also fare well with classes of 30 or 35. Jaime Escalante, renowned as the "best teacher in America," packs his classroom every year with 30-plus "disadvantaged" teenagers and consistently produces scholars who pass the tough Advanced Placement calculus exam. But such teaching is not the norm in U.S. schools, and adding teachers to the rolls won't cause it to be. (Indeed, a federal program hell-bent on raising achievement would probably do better by firing rather than hiring 100,000 teachers. Students would be in larger classes but with better teachers, who could be paid more with the salary moneys freed up by the layoffs.)

Second, those 12 billion new dollars (over seven years) would likely do more good if spent in other—politically riskier—ways. $1.7 billion a year would, for example, furnish $4,000 scholarships to 425,000 low-income children to escape from grim urban schools into private or charter (or suburban public) schools. That's equivalent to liberating every boy and girl in Washington, Baltimore, and Philadelphia from the educational carnage that now surrounds them. Alternatively, such sums would pay for *all* current U.S. teachers to take more university courses. The leading problem in many classrooms, after all, isn't the pupil body count. It's teachers who never mastered the content. The Education Department reports that 36 percent of public-school teachers of academic subjects neither majored nor minored in their main teaching field. To get them up to speed, the amount Clinton proposes to spend on class-size reduction would yield a $4,500 tuition grant for every one of the nation's 2.7 million teachers.

Which brings us to the third flaw in his scheme. It's embedded in a larger "teacher improvement" package that has little to do with the quality of the current teaching force, will strengthen the ed-school and certification monopolies for future teachers, and will weaken halting state efforts to develop sound alternatives. The White House will, for example, require communities that want to participate in the class-reduction scheme to ensure that every person hired is (or soon will be) "fully certified."

At first glance, "certified teachers" looks like another warm puppy of a policy. Who could want anything else? Yet in practically every state, the only way to get certified today is to take lots of "methods" courses in colleges of education rather than immersing oneself in the subject to be taught. It's certification that blocks millions of able adults from teaching in public schools. (Charter and private schools are often free from these rules—and plenty of well-educated people queue up at their doors for every teaching job.) It's certification that keeps low-quality education schools in business.

Fourth, bringing 100,000 teachers onto direct federal support will create another permanent program, a virtual entitlement sure to grow over time. What happens in Year Eight, after Clinton's $12 billion is spent? Easy. The program will be extended. Indeed, if 18 children per class is good, the next politician will claim that 16 must be better. If Uncle Sam is going to provide the country with smaller classes through third grade, why not through fourth, then fifth? The Clinton version is just a preview of coming attractions.

Finally, across-the-board class reductions can leave needy kids worse off. Take California, for example. When Pete Wilson shrank primary classes throughout the state, veteran teachers left inner-city schools in droves, lured by the higher pay and cushier working conditions of suburban systems that suddenly had openings.

President Clinton is not the only politician now eyeing this path to voters' hearts. Congressmen and senators on both sides of the aisle are hastening to craft their own measures. They like teachers—and puppies—too. Most pending proposals (like the White House "teacher improvement" package) lift their ideas from the National Commission on Teaching and America's Future, a private group funded by the Rockefeller and Carnegie foundations and chaired by longtime North Carolina governor Jim Hunt. Its members include the heads of both national teachers' unions and a blue-ribbon list of ed-school professors, deans, and presidents. This crew contends that the central weakness in U.S. teacher training is that candidates don't spend enough time in "professional development programs," that states lack "professional standards" boards, that certification requirements need to be strengthened, and that all teacher training programs should jump through the same "accreditation" hoops.

The commission's recommendations boil down to teachers' spending more time in ever-more-uniform education schools and barring the classroom door to everyone else. It's no surprise that the administration has bought this line. But why Congress?

If there's money burning to be spent, Congress should give it to states to underwrite novel approaches to the training, pay, and licensing of teachers. Cajole the states to break the ed-school hammerlock, loosen the certification stranglehold, and blaze alternative paths into teaching so that well-educated liberal arts graduates and experienced professionals can enter the classroom from many directions. States could also demand that every teacher—veteran and novice alike—master the subjects they are expected to teach—and hold them accountable for pupil achievement by scrapping tenure and substituting multi-year contracts that reward results and penalize failure.

Such suggestions lack the instant appeal of Clinton's new pooch. Unlike class-size reduction, which has no known enemies, serious attention to quality means attacking the school establishment's strongest redoubts: the unions, teacher colleges, state regulatory apparatuses, and interlocking special-interest groups. It's much easier just to call for more adult bodies in the classroom (and confine all "quality control" provisions to newcomers.) Schools won't improve. Kids won't learn more.

But the politicians will score points with the public—and with the unions. We understand why Bill Clinton needs such points nowadays. But his proposal is really a dog of an idea. Congress should shop at a different pet store.

. . . .

Where Everybody Knows Your Name

William R. Capps and Mary Ellen Maxwell

This selection first appeared in *The American School Board Journal*'s September 1999 issue. William R. Capps is an education professor at Troy State University in Dothan, Alabama. Mary Ellen Maxwell, a school board member in Moyock, North Carolina, is immediate past president of the National School Boards Association.

For months, the nation has attempted with little success to decipher the cultural forces that led to the tragic high school shooting in Littleton, Colo. The political, media, and psychological pundits notwithstanding, about the only self-evident truth that can be gleaned from our soul-searching is that we have elevated finger-pointing to a fine and expedient art.

There is one convincing body of research, however, that invites the attention of school board members and administrators as they ponder how best to respond to the repercussions of Littleton. That research addresses the issue of school size.

The American character has been shaped in many ways by the concept of bigness—the bigger, the better. We glorify wide-open spaces, the Big Sky, the Big Gulp, and the Super-Sized. We are fascinated with the big and powerful. But sadly, we have lost our attachment to the beauty of smallness—a loss that has had a profound effect on our nation's schools.

The move toward ever-larger schools has been going on through most of the 20th century. This trend was validated in the late 1950s when Harvard University President James B. Conant and other nationally recognized education leaders began to advocate the creation of consolidated, comprehensive high schools. The best feature of such schools, they believed, was that they could offer students a wider variety of academic and vocational courses. Underlying this rationale were the principles of efficiency and economy of scale espoused by business and industry.

In retrospect, there is a troubling irony: Conant believed an enrollment of just 400 students was sufficient for the delivery of a comprehensive high school curriculum. He did not foresee that his advocacy of the comprehensive high school would be used to justify creating enormous schools. Today, 25 percent of U.S. secondary schools enroll more than 1,000 students. Columbine High School, the site of the Littleton massacre, has nearly 2,000 students. The largest high school in the country—John F. Kennedy High School in the Bronx—has 5,300.

The Merits of Smallness

The trend toward bigness and consolidation continues unabated. It is driven by political, economic, social, and demographic considerations, rather than by the extensive research indicating that school size has a demonstrable effect on how well we educate students. School officials who are contemplating consolidation, new school construction, or the prevention of school violence would do well to consider what this research says about the merits of small schools.

Kathleen Cotton, a research specialist at the Northwest Regional Educational Laboratory in Portland, Ore., conducted an exhaustive review of the available data on school size and concluded that "research has repeatedly found small schools to be superior to large schools on most measures and equal to them on the rest." (Cotton's 1996 report, *School Size, School Climate, and Student Performance*, can be found online at http://www.nwrel.org/scpd/sirs/10/c020.html.) For example, the teachers in small schools know the students well, so they are more likely to notice if a child is having academic or emotional problems. In addition, small schools, on average, have fewer discipline problems, better student attendance rates, and fewer dropouts than large schools. (These attributes should be especially appealing to school officials in states that have instituted accountability standards that measure school success on the basis of these criteria.)

Cotton notes that these findings are consistent across all grade levels (K–12), regardless of the students' abilities and the type of community—rural, suburban, or urban.

Deciding what constitutes a "small" school is still a matter of discussion, however. Although there is no official definition, many researchers say that the appropriate size for an elementary school is from 300 to 400 students and that the enrollment of a secondary school should not exceed 800. In our experience, we have found these are good parameters.

School size is also a factor in adolescent alienation, which has been the subject of much of the public dialogue on school violence. The research shows that students who attend small schools have a greater sense of belonging than those who attend large schools. In fact, minimizing the alienation that commonly afflicts adolescents appears to be one of the most redeeming qualities of small schools. Large and impersonal high schools can obviously cloak the more severe manifestations of student alienation to a much greater degree than small schools.

In a May 2, 1999, opinion piece for the *Washington Post*, Lakis Polycarpou, a 1990 graduate of Columbine High School, eloquently portrayed the realities of suburban alienation—the increasing mobility of American culture, the "absolute interchangeability of place," and the difficulty of feeling part of a community. "We never knew our neighbors except in passing," he wrote; "we certainly never had a social connection to them."

Small schools can overcome these realities because they are more likely to foster a greater sense of community among students. The evidence shows that students in smaller schools are more likely to bond with their teachers and peers, and that they more readily identify with their schools. Parent involvement is also higher in small schools.

All these factors work together to help make small schools places that have positive and unique cultures. In their 1999 book *Shaping School Culture: The Heart of Leadership*, Terrence Deal, a professor of education at Vanderbilt University, and Kent Peterson, an education professor at the University of Wisconsin, define school culture as "deep patterns of values, beliefs and traditions which have been formed over the course of time." Recognition of the cultural framework within a school gives students a "system of meaning," they write. Small schools are more apt to have strong cultures, with the result that students see teachers enjoying their jobs, teacher absenteeism is rarely a problem, and students are more motivated to learn.

Academics, Activities, and Discipline

Despite such findings, the prevailing wisdom in some education circles holds that students attending small schools are academically penalized when it comes to achievement comparisons with their peers in large schools. Cotton's review of the research shows that this is not the case: The academic achievement of students attending small schools is comparable to or better than that of students in large schools. These findings are not limited to standardized test data, Cotton says; they also apply to "school grades, test scores, honor roll membership, subject area achievement, and assessment of higher-order thinking skills." And, what is especially gratifying, these results hold true for minority students and students from poor families.

In addition, Cotton reports, students enrolled in small schools have higher levels of participation in extracurricular activities, and they are active in a greater number of these activities than are their peers in large schools. Again, this participation was found among all students regardless of race, ethnicity, or family income.

School size, not surprisingly, also has a definite effect on social interaction. Media reports from Columbine indicate there was tension between student athletes, the "Trenchcoat Mafia," and perhaps other student cliques. Cliques are a part of the social scene in any high school, of course, but the animosity they create is much greater in large schools, where many students do not know each other personally. In fact, the research documents the polarization of student groups in large schools. Small schools, in contrast, are less likely to experience the same sense of fragmentation and peer alienation.

It makes sense, then, that small schools experience fewer discipline problems than large schools. Put simply, antisocial behavior is less prevalent at small schools because there is a greater sense of knowing who's who and what they're up to. The interpersonal relationships found among students, teachers, and other staff members in small schools are stronger than those found in larger schools. Beyond that, there is a more caring atmosphere and a familiarity among students and teachers that fosters a desire to do the right thing—something not found in the anonymity of most large, comprehensive high schools.

Advocates of consolidation argue that large schools are cheaper to operate than small schools. The research Cotton reviewed, however, does not substantiate this claim. It appears that cost-efficiency is more a function of school management than school size. "Researchers have found that the relationship between size and cost varies depending on individual school circumstances," Cotton writes. "Many small schools are operated very economically, while many large ones have exorbitant per-pupil costs."

Certain costs, in fact, tend to be higher in bigger schools, especially those that have been consolidated. For example, the number of administrators tends to grow as schools are consolidated and enrollments increase. In addition, the costs associated with student transportation are higher due to the increased number of miles buses must travel daily. And administrators in consolidated schools often find it necessary to increase teacher-student ratios to save money.

Some researchers argue that the human costs of consolidation should also be factored into the equation. It is not uncommon, for instance, for students in geographically large districts to spend one to two hours every morning and afternoon on a bus, increasing the likelihood of safety and discipline problems on the bus.

Clearly, the move toward larger schools during the last century has exacted many intangible, social, and educational costs. We need to reclaim the small school's sense of community, caring, and meaning. Our children need to know school as a place where they feel a personal connection, a place where someone knows their dreams and fears, a place where they are safe—and, we would hope, a place where everybody knows their names.

FEDERAL AID TO EDUCATION AND THE POOR

Title I's $118 Billion Fails to Close Gap

Program Has Been Unable to Lift Academic Level of Poor Students, Research Shows

Ralph Frammolino

This selection first appeared in the *Los Angeles Times* on 17 January 1999. Ralph Frammolino is a staff writer for the *Los Angeles Times*.

The federal government's largest education grant program, despite spending $118 billion over the last three decades, has been unable to meet its goal of narrowing the achievement gap between rich and poor students, interviews and documents show.

Title I, which started with idealistic fervor in the 1960s' War on Poverty, provides $7.4 billion each year to help one of every five pupils in the nation's public schools.

Recent evaluations by the U.S. Department of Education found that the extra computers, tutoring, and more than 132,000 classroom positions paid for by the massive investment have been "insufficient to close the gap" in reading and math performance between poor students and their more affluent peers.

The program has been "a failure up to now," said Maris A. Vinovskis, a University of Michigan education expert who has reviewed independent studies assessing the effectiveness of Title I. "The real losers in this are not just the taxpayers [but] the kids. . . . We haven't been able to deliver."

One reason, experts agree, is that Title I funds are spread too thin among the nation's poor students to do much good. And, of the billions of dollars allocated each year, most are spent on tutoring and other remedial efforts that have produced marginal improvement in test scores.

Much of the blame for the program's shortcomings has been directed at the more than 50,000 school aides and teacher assistants hired with Title I funds. A nationwide movement to replace these "paraprofessionals" with certified teachers has sparked controversy and led to considerable anxiety.

Under increasing pressure to show results, the program now finds itself on a collision course with its past—and the aides are caught in the middle, experts say.

"It's a classic situation where yesterday's reform becomes today's obstacle," said Jerome T. Murphy, dean of Harvard University's Graduate School of Education, who helped write Title I legislation 34 years ago.

Title I, which comes before Congress for reauthorization this year, was created to tackle perhaps the most daunting task in all of education: to help students overcome the inherent barriers that poverty poses to academic achievement.

While no one expects the federal government to eliminate such a formidable deficit, supporters contend that Title I has become a victim of unrealistic expectations. They credit the program with focusing attention on the needs of low-income students, but they also argue that Title I is no match for the challenges presented by poverty and problems such as racial tensions, language barriers, crime, violence, and drug use.

Title I "can change some services, but it cannot change the lives of hundreds of thousands of kids," said Jack Jennings, director of the Center on Education Policy in Washington and a former general counsel of the House Labor and Education Committee.

A special evaluation report last fall by the Department of Education found that the gap between 9-year-olds attending "high-poverty" and "low-poverty" schools either stayed the same or increased from the mid-1980s to the mid-1990s. This gap left poor students nearly four grade levels behind affluent pupils in reading and two levels behind in math.

In addition, a separate study commissioned specifically to assess Title I concluded in 1997 that the massive spending has had little effect on the achievement gap.

The 1997 Education Department report found that Title I failed to make a significant dent in the achievement gap from 1991 to 1994 in part because it tolerates low academic standards for poor and minority students.

Many Title I programs "reinforced low expectations for student achievement," the report says. "Students in high-poverty schools were exposed to a 'watered down' and non-challenging curriculum when compared to other students."

Squandering of Funds on Clerks, Aides Cited

Also part of the problem, according to high-ranking education officials and other experts, is that schools squander Title I funds on clerical workers and classroom aides who lack the expertise to teach poor students the kind of high-level skills needed to compete with their more affluent peers.

Reformers have seized on these findings and urged the removal of classroom aides to pay for retraining teachers or to hire new ones. The push even comes from the top of the Clinton administration's Education Department.

"It's pretty significant that half of the instructional staff under Title I were paraprofessionals," said Val Plisko, who supervises independent evaluations for the Education Department's Planning and Evaluation Service. "For children who are most at risk, you want the best-educated, the most knowledgeable, the most effective teachers."

Mary Jean LeTendre, a top federal education official who oversees Title I and other programs for disadvantaged students, said that in some cases employment of Title I aides has amounted to "a jobs program for members of the community." She added, "I am one who believes that this program needs to be focused on the needs of the kids."

LeTendre vowed in a recent interview to "work with every ounce of my energy" to shift Title I spending from aides to more qualified teachers. She added that federal officials are considering whether to eventually limit or prohibit the use of Title I funds to hire teacher aides.

Unfavorable Ratios of Aides to Teachers

In California, the latest available figures indicate that the ratio of aides to teachers paid for by Title I funds is 4 to 1. At Los Angeles Unified, the nation's second-largest school district, the ratio is about 7 to 1. And most of the instructors on the district's Title I payroll rarely teach; instead they serve as program coordinators at their individual schools, officials said.

The winds of change already are being felt at LAUSD, where all but 2 of 30 schools facing a takeover by the superintendent's office for dismal student performance are considered Title I schools. In all, 465 of 641 LAUSD schools have student populations that are predominantly poor.

Supt. Ruben Zacarias recently ordered the spending of $10 million in Title I funds for extra tutoring at the district's lowest-performing schools. In an interview, Zacarias added that he may dip further into those federal funds to pay for other student intervention programs as well as teacher training—moves that he said might spell "crunch time" for teacher aides. "If the priorities mean that we're going to have to reduce our . . . aides, then we're going to have to bite that bullet," he said.

At Pacoima Elementary, one of the 30 schools on Zacarias' list for academic probation, Principal Lawrence D. Gonzales is already tasting the gunpowder.

In a bid to kick-start student scores languishing in the bottom 25% of the LAUSD, Gonzales is investing $100,000 of the school's $800,000 Title I allotment into an intensive reading program for each of Pacoima's 70 classrooms. Some of the money comes from reductions in Title I classroom aides through attrition, said Gonzales.

"We have to put up or shut up," he said.

But the retrenchment has been slow and difficult. Not only are LAUSD aides unionized, they are among the most visible and popular features of a Title I program that has become deeply embedded in some neighborhoods as a source of steady employment that increased the presence of adults in schools.

The Title I aides, who work for significantly lower wages than teachers, are widely used in classrooms to work one-on-one or with small groups of students to reinforce lessons. They also serve nonnative students.

Mary Castro has been on the Title I payroll as an aide for 22 years, the last 11 at James A. Garfield High School in East Los Angeles. The soft-spoken great-grandmother works seven hours a day shelving books, shushing students in the library, and preparing due-date notices.

Castro is one of 6,540 part-time paraprofessionals whose employment consumes nearly 40% of LAUSD's Title I budget this year. By comparison, 21% of the district's Title I funds are spent on instructors and teacher training. The remaining expenditures include instructional materials and support staff, such as school psychologists.

As part of its $1.1 million annual allotment in Title I funds, Garfield employs 22 aides—all but five work in classrooms, budget figures show.

Since her job isn't directly related to classroom instruction, Castro may be a prime candidate for dismissal. At 62, Castro is not volunteering to quit her $10.84-an-hour position.

"It's not easy to say I'd get another job, because I'm old," she said.

Nor is anyone likely to force her out at Garfield, which is facing administrative takeover due to dismal academic performance. Alex Fuentes, Garfield's Title I coordinator, said that downsizing would put him in a bind, even in cases of non-classroom aides like Castro.

"She's providing services—maybe not the services she did when she was young, but I'm not getting any complaints," said Fuentes. "What do you say to someone like that? 'Oh, Mary, it's time for you to go out to pasture'?"

Question at Heart of Rehabilitation Effort

Indeed, that question—with all its personal and policy implications—is at the heart of the latest push to rehabilitate Title I.

Considered the keystone of the War on Poverty, Title I was fashioned during the country's civil rights struggle by President Lyndon B. Johnson, who muscled it through Congress in a breathtaking 89 days as part of a sweeping school aid bill.

"I will never do anything in my entire life, now or in the future, that excites me more or benefits the nation I serve more," said Johnson, a former teacher, after he signed Title I into law in 1965 in front of a one-room schoolhouse in Texas.

The program was predicated on an academic truism: Family income is closely linked to educational success.

Johnson hoped to make up for the disadvantages of poverty by providing a jolt of federal dollars earmarked for extra tutoring and other add-on programs targeted at low-income students.

In a symbolic gesture, Johnson set the initial Title I appropriation at $1 billion. The program has since grown to seven times that size.

Title I currently pays an average of $685 per poor child as defined by the U.S. Census, but its spending formula has been so politicized that the actual amounts vary widely among states.

California, home of the largest concentration of impoverished students, receives only $573 per pupil—an amount that is less than the funding provided to 49 other states and territories.

The money flows from Washington to 46,000—or nearly half—of the nation's schools. It is intended for students who are considered educationally "at risk." In California, such students are identified as children from welfare families or children who qualify for free or reduced-price lunches.

The ultimate decision on how to spend the money, however, remains with each school. Across the country, school administrators have invested Title I dollars in "pull-out" programs, in which low-income students are taken out of their regular classes for 30-minute tutoring sessions each day that incorporate new materials and computers.

And they've hired more than 50,000 school and classroom aides. Typically, the aides were parents or activists from surrounding neighborhoods. They monitored lunchrooms, ran off dittos on the mimeograph, put up bulletin boards.

Teacher aides have had the biggest effect in the classroom, working individually with poor students to reinforce lessons. This is particularly true in elementary schools, where the aides have become fixtures.

As a condition of employment, more than 5,000 classroom "teaching aides" in Los Angeles are required to enroll in college courses or degree programs to become certified educators, said Margaret A. Jones, LAUSD director of specially funded programs.

"I've seen some teaching assistants who are better than some of the teachers we have," Jones said, scoffing at the movement by critics to replace aides.

An additional 1,500 resource aides are not required to enroll in college courses, but some are still used in classrooms and contend they do a good job.

Sharon Watanabe has outlasted three principals and all but a few teachers as a $12.26-an-hour Title I aide for the last 19 years at Hoover Street Elementary School, near downtown Los Angeles.

"I think I make a big difference in the classroom with the children because I've seen it," said Watanabe, who works three hours each morning. "In the beginning of the year, some [students] wouldn't speak in English. Now they come up to me and make a conversation with me."

Few have challenged such claims, especially during the 1970s and early 1980s, when test scores among minority students—who receive the bulk of Title I services—began catching up, narrowing the achievement gap by about a third. But in the mid-1980s, scores for minority students stalled and the gap widened. Critics, particularly political conservatives, have heaped blame on Title I ever since.

"It's a waste," Chester E. Finn, Jr., former assistant secretary of Education under President Reagan, said in a recent interview. "It's accomplishing nothing other than the expenditure of money."

Finn noted that the program remains popular in Washington because Title I funds go to most congressional districts. "The fiercest fights in Congress are not over whether it accomplishes anything but over the distribution formula for the money."

Complaints by Black Parents Are Described

Even longtime advocates such as Phyllis McClure, a former NAACP Legal Defense and Education Fund monitor who kept a watchful eye on Title I compliance, now raise questions about the efficacy of the program. McClure recalled hearing complaints from black parents that the program was relegating their children to a second-class education.

"When black parents were taking their kids out of Title I because . . . they weren't getting the regular math, they were getting something low-level . . . I changed my mind," said McClure, who six years ago led a federal task force to assess Title I. "This program isn't working as it was intended to work."

In 1993, the Education Department released preliminary results of an ongoing, comprehensive study that measured Title I's effect on 40,000 students and the achievement gap. The study found that Title I assistance "did not compensate for the initial deficiencies of the disadvantaged students." It also pointed out that the lowest-achieving poor students often received instruction from Title I aides.

Some Title I advocates complain that aides are scapegoats for a program that, at last count, contributed only 2 cents of every local, state, and federal dollar spent on public education. Title I accounts for 42% of every federal dollar spent on education from kindergarten through high school.

Congress made sweeping changes in its 1994 reauthorization of Title I, requiring that students in the program be held to the same academic standards as other children. It also required for the first time that aides have at least a high school diploma.

LeTendre, the department's director of Title I, said she was "incensed" that Congress set such a minimal requirement for aides who often help instruct students. She said surveys show that only 13% of the Title I aides hold college degrees.

And while she applauded efforts that encouraged Title I aides to get their teaching degrees, she said it was an "absolute must" that more certified instructors be hired with program money.

A new comprehensive assessment of these reforms will not be finished until the spring; early indications are that the number of aides nationwide is declining.

But the cutbacks have not come easily.

After much coaxing and coalition-building, school officials in Pueblo, Colo., laid off 62 aides this summer, said Paul Ruiz, partner of the Education Trust, a Washington nonprofit group that helped broker the change. Most of those receiving pink slips were Latino "moms and dads, some of whom worked as teacher aides for 10, 15 years," he said.

The money saved from the dismissal of school aides will be redirected into professional training for teachers, Ruiz said.

Education Trust abandoned a similar effort in Hartford, Conn., Ruiz said, where local officials could not muster the "political will."

··

Special Ed

Factory-Like Schooling May Soon Be a Thing of the Past

Britton Manasco

This selection first appeared in *Reason* magazine's July 1996 edition. Britton Manasco is founder and executive director of the high-tech consulting firm Quantum Era Enterprises. He also is editor and publisher of *Knowledge, Inc.*, an executive newsletter exploring business opportunities in the emerging knowledge economy.

> *School days, I believe, are the unhappiest in the whole span of human existence. They are full of dull, unintelligible tasks, new and unpleasant ordinances, brutal violations of common sense and common decency.*—H.L. Mencken

At 16, Paul Boone writes articles reviewing new computer games for *Mac Home Journal* and aspires to launch a game development company of his own. Such ambitions are not that uncommon in his hometown of San Jose, California, the heart of Silicon Valley. What is unusual is how easily he has been able to incorporate his interest in computers into his education—and why.

Paul, his sister Cristie, 17, and brother Curtis, 12, have been educated at home, by parents who are convinced that children learn best when they are free to explore areas of interest in an independent, self-directed way. When the kids were younger, their mother, Jill, spent a great deal of time reading with them and actively encouraging their learning. Now, she explains, they all engage in independent learning activities. Cristie is most interested in the study of literature and takes courses at a local community college. Curtis is interested in ancient history and attends a weekly community college class in art history with his mother. Paul has developed his programming skills through books, on-line discussions, and constant experimentation. He recently got press credentials for a game developers' conference, allowing him to rub elbows with people who may someday be his colleagues. "All the companies are looking for 'self-motivated' people," he notes, and his education has developed that quality.

Jill explains that she supports her children's particular interests while creatively encouraging them to study important subjects that don't initially attract them. To get Cristie interested in studying science, for instance, Jill found literary treatments of astronomy for her to read. "I'm more of a guide or facilitator than a teacher," she says. "I help my kids research topics and find materials. I help them find opportunities and ensure that they get a well-balanced education."

Across the country, in the Washington suburb of Waldorf, Maryland, Marilyn and Chesley Rockett's two youngest sons have followed a more structured curriculum—but a similar philosophy. Marilyn argues that children can learn much more effectively when their learning experiences are not confined to textbooks, classrooms, and grade levels. "The emphasis has always been on learning rather than simply moving on," she says of the education she's given Jeremy, 17, and Jonathan, 19, at home. (Jonathan attends Hillsdale College in Michigan; his younger brother will join him there in the fall.) When the boys began to study American history, Marilyn sought out books at the local library exploring the impact of American artists, scientists, and political leaders. She and her husband took the boys on an excursion to Valley Forge, Pennsylvania, and had them write up their experiences. While studying the Civil War, she went with them to Ford's Theater and the house of Samuel Mudd, the doctor who treated John Wilkes Booth after he shot Lincoln. This interdisciplinary approach, she says, has helped her children "see the connections" among the many forces that influenced the nation's development.

The two families certainly have their differences. While the Rocketts are evangelical Christians and consider religious instruction a vital aspect of home learning, the Boones shun organized religion and encourage their children to follow their own spiritual paths. The Rocketts have used various commercially available pre-packaged curricula, which they then tailor to their own situation. The Boones have taken a less-structured approach, largely allowing their children to focus on the subjects they find most inspiring (while gently prodding the kids to ensure a breadth of coverage).

Both families agree, however, that most private and government-run schools are incapable of supporting the individual learning needs of their children. Both contend that the "socialization" that occurs in schools is generally inimical to learning and personal growth. Both consider home schooling a way of strengthening the bonds of the family. And both the Rocketts and the Boones make a distinction between learning—which is ongoing and boundless—and institutional education, which is tied to a specific time and place. "Living is learning," wrote John Holt, the late author of the classic books *How Children Fail* and *How Children Learn* and an early champion of the home schooling movement (which he preferred to call "unschooling"). "It is impossible to be alive and conscious . . . without constantly learning things." Although not all home schoolers are admirers of Holt (some of his more conservative critics consider him a "child worshiper"), most share his belief that learning is something that occurs "all the time."

It is just this sort of thinking—a concern for independent thought, a longing to strengthen the family, and a frustration with the bureaucratic limits of conventional schools—that is leading the home school movement into the mainstream. Home schoolers are a statistically small but rapidly growing and increasingly influential force in America. Their numbers have jumped from 15,000 to 20,000 in the late 1970s to perhaps 600,000 today (some estimates put the number above 1 million). The trend is likely to continue, as new products and institutions develop that make it easier for parents to educate children at home.

Particularly intriguing are the trend's potential ripple effects. While it's difficult to imagine a mass exodus from traditional schools in the near term, the home school movement may help create a future in which families have an extraordinary number of choices to educate their children. The movement has shown that children do not need formal institutions to learn and thrive. While standardized test scores of home schoolers are open to charges of statistical bias (due to the near impossibility of obtaining a random sample), Pat Lines, senior research analyst at the U.S. Department of Education, says surveys of state examinations demonstrate that such children "consistently test above national norms."

Home schoolers also provide an inspiration, and a growing market, for a variety of institutions, products, and services that offer individualized learning. Education still tends to be structured around a basic economy of scale: It's a lot cheaper to have one teacher lecture to a large class in a structured way, and at the same time and place, than to tutor students one on one. New technologies allow education to be unbundled. Lectures can be recorded and transmitted to, or videotaped for, anyone, anywhere, any time. Educational software programs allow students to work at their own pace, getting instant feedback on their work. CD-ROMs can make important books compact, inexpensive, and interactive. Internet services and educational networks allow scattered students access to specialized expertise.

Sheldon Richman, author of *Separating School and State*, believes that the growth in home schooling represents "demand-side entrepreneurship," which he argues would flourish if decentralized learning policies were adopted. Instead of depending on schools, Richman says, parents would be encouraged to ask themselves, "What educational opportunities can I take advantage of for the benefit of my child?" The instructional expertise, group interactions, and custodial care schools offer would continue to be valued. But families would no longer rely on such services exclusively, and children would engage in a mix of learning experiences, some at home, some not.

Such unbundling, which allows for both structured and unstructured learning, gets education away from the idea that learning is best provided in a setting that has much in common with a rigidly structured 19th-century factory. "Schooling," notes Howard Gardner of the Harvard Graduate School of Education, is a mass-oriented phenomenon based on a "uniform idea": "You teach the same thing to students in the same way and assess them all in the same way."

The home school movement suggests that educational choices need not be limited to public and private schools. Rather, parents can create far more flexible arrangements, relying on an array of learning services, resources, and technologies that enable their children to learn at home on a part-time or full-time basis. We can begin contemplating a future of learning opportunities analogous to the innovation and decentralization that is currently taking place in traditional workplaces.

"There's been a huge change in the way people think about education," says Diane Ravitch, a senior scholar at New York University and former head of research in the U.S. Department of Education. "Under the old paradigm, there was only one means—the government school system. The ends—well-educated students—varied wildly." Now, she argues the public appears increasingly willing to allow the means to vary if the ends are kept constant. She notes that more than 250 charter schools, which reduce restrictions and red tape, have been created in taxpayer-financed systems throughout the country and points optimistically to school voucher efforts in Milwaukee and other cities.

If Ravitch is right that people are beginning to stress educational ends over means, it is quite possible that the taste for experimentation and innovation in education will embrace more meaningfully the notion of individualized learning. A number of proposals have been put forward that explicitly seek to shift funding from institutions to learning opportunities for individuals. Over $300 billion—that's the amount spent on K–12 education annually—is at stake.

One idea, advocated by David Barulich, a Los Angeles-based education policy consultant, would provide "performance grants" directly to parents. The grants, which would be linked to annual examinations and available to any family whose child or children did not attend public school, would allow the family to actively choose the learning services it finds most suitable. Those might include traditional private schooling, specialized tutoring, on-line services, community college classes, or any other combination of formal and informal education. Lewis Perelman, author of *School's Out*, also argues that families should be directly funded and supports what he calls "microvouchers," based on family income, that can be used to buy educational services. Still another plan, conceived by Sharlene Holt of Middletown, Pennsylvania–based ESANet, champions "educational savings accounts." Like the medical savings accounts now bandied about in Congress, ESAs would provide a series of tax incentives that would enable parents to deduct money from their total tax liability for each child who does not attend a public school.

Such efforts have never been more crucial or, given new technologies, more possible. We are entering a new economic era that stresses entrepreneurship at all levels and places a premium on the ability to continuously upgrade knowledge and skills. If individuals are to prosper in this turbulent era, they must, first and foremost, learn how to learn—how to actively acquire new skills as their existing ones lose value. The new economy rewards passion, agility, creativity, initiative, and independent thinking—qualities that today's schools and classrooms often discourage.

On the surface such sentiments jibe exceedingly well with the proclamations of "reformers" in the educational establishment. The Clinton administration advocates "lifelong learning" and has devoted a great deal of energy to wiring schools to telecommunications networks. The president has vowed to connect every classroom and library in the country to the "information superhighway" by the year 2000, allowing him to pose as an agent of change even as he leaves the fundamental educational structure in place.

But experience suggests no reason to assume government schools will adopt more flexible learning arrangements or implement new technologies any time soon, much less integrate them successfully into the learning process. "It took 30 years to get the overhead projector out of the bowling alley and into the classroom," says Roger Schank, director of the Institute for the Learning Sciences at Northwestern University. "Schools don't change."

While Schank believes it is important to set clear goals and objectives for teachers and students alike, he thinks schools leave too little room for "exploratory" learning. Rather, teachers are urged to "cover" a vast amount of material, and keep the entire class moving in lockstep. Children, as Schank sees it, are on "an intellectual chain gang," sentenced to dull, monotonous labor that does little to encourage enthusiasm for education. Schank doesn't think most parents are up to the demands of home schooling and, in fact, he believes the government should create and fund a national K–12 curriculum. But he embraces technological advances that allow for highly individualized learning. He is, for instance, particularly keen on software programs that allow children to create and explore simulated worlds.

Harvard's Gardner similarly stresses the limitations of traditional notions of education. Because schools tend to treat all students in a uniform manner, they are largely incapable of supporting and enhancing the particular skills, abilities, and talents of individuals. In groundbreaking cognitive research over the past two decades, Gardner posits a theory of "multiple human intelligences": linguistic, logical-mathematical, spatial representation, musical, bodily-kinesthetic, the understanding of other individuals, and the understanding of ourselves. He explains that the central educational implication of his theory is that "different styles and profiles of intelligence" cannot be addressed without individualizing the learning process. "This is a new, indeed revolutionary, idea for most persons," he says.

Gardner sees an ally in new technologies. "Technology makes it possible to individualize education," he says. "If we know that someone is strong in language skills or weak in spatial abilities, we can deliver information to them in appropriate ways and also give them viable means of responding. This is the genius of the new flexible, interactive technologies."

The classroom, strictly speaking, is itself a technology. As currently used, however, it is ill-suited to the needs of the individual student. For the most part, personal tutoring is simply not economically or logistically feasible. New information technologies, however, make it possible for students to learn at their own pace and in their own way, with the teacher serving as a mentor and an intellectual coach—guiding, supporting, and questioning individual learners.

Such opportunities can be expected to proliferate as communication costs fall and network capacity expands. Within the coming decade, desktop videoconferencing technologies will enable students to see and speak with experts all over the country rather than rely on a single teacher. And the volume and quality of resources that are accessible online will continue to grow. Such technologies allow students to venture far beyond the confines of a classroom, escaping the boundaries of geography. They decentralize learning, no longer tying it to the physical infrastructure and administrative overhead of schools. Already, telephone companies, cable operators, satellite communications providers, and other innovative companies are investing heavily to create high-performance communication links throughout the nation and globe.

Even that traditional tool of individualized instruction, the book, is becoming cheaper, more compact, and enhanced by new technologies. Software companies such as Microsoft, Grolier, and Compton's are squeezing voluminous multimedia encyclopedias onto a single disc. Another software firm, Corel, has developed a "classic books" program that incorporates more than 3,500 unabridged literary works, detailed profiles of their authors, video clips, and hundreds of illustrations. Inventive math, science, reading, arts, and foreign language programs are also on the market. Multimedia programs are now available that explore everything from human anatomy to global geography to Renaissance art in compelling detail. Users click on icons to hear stories, view clips, and discover interrelated facts. Many programs are linked to sites on the World Wide Web, which is also proving to be a dynamic medium for new learning resources.

At the same time, the continuing evolution of the Internet has made it possible to offer a range of courses and learning services online. Despite the limitations of the medium, instructors are able to address the individual learning needs of the child in a way that is not possible in classrooms. Clonlara School, a privately run learning program based in Ann Arbor, Michigan, provides support, resources, and evaluation services for more than 5,000 students throughout the United States, Canada, and a few other countries.

Marketed as an alternative to public schools, Clonlara helps parents receive any necessary approvals from local school authorities for home schooling. It also runs a "campus school" for about 50 students in the Ann Arbor area. Founded in 1967, Clonlara went online in 1994 and has recently introduced a program called "adults graduating," designed for people over 20 years old who never graduated high school. The school charges annual tuition of $475 per family (textbooks and supplies are extra), offers a curriculum list that individuals tailor to their needs, and provides report cards, transcripts, and diplomas "where desired and appropriate." Clonlara "mentors" facilitate ongoing discussions and guide students to available materials for K–12 courses in algebra, physics, science, geography, government, and other subjects. The secondary school curriculum requires 300 hours of volunteer community service, and Clonlara boasts graduates who have gone on to "four year universities, community and junior colleges, computer schools, trade schools, apprenticeships," and the Armed Forces.

Another on-line learning service, Scholars' Online Academy, was recently launched from Baton Rouge, Louisiana. Instructors and students, however, are located all over the country. Scholars' Online stresses college prep and offers a core curriculum similar to that of a traditional private school. The course of study is designed to meet the general education prerequisites of Louisiana State University.

Students interact through e-mail, newsgroups, list servers, and chat sessions (instructors hold on-line "office hours," too). Annual tuition is based on the number of courses per family, ranging from $250 for one course to $1,120 for eight courses. Students, says informational material, "are free to integrate our courses with those of other curriculum providers," or take courses to prepare for advanced placement tests. Instructors record grades and expect timely completion of assignments, but much of the course preparation and achievement depends on the self-paced study of the individual student (and much of the actual learning takes place offline). Scholars' Online offers extracurricular activities such as *Hereditas*, a journal designed to give students experience in writing and desktop publishing. It also encourages participation in the Junior Classical League, a worldwide youth group that arranges competition in categories ranging from ancient Greek and Latin to photography and doll making.

Just as new technologies have enhanced the productivity of work, they appear to be doing the same for home schooling. "Learning technologies have made home schooling a lot easier and a lot more fun," says Mary Pride, publisher of *Practical Homeschooling* and *Homeschool PC* magazines. She home schools her nine children (ages 2 to 16) using a mix of high-tech resources, programs, and services.

The new resources "have made a lot of difference in terms of what the children have been exposed to and have had a chance to see and learn," she says, noting that her kids are now taking courses from on-line tutors and using software programs to do everything from creating a newsletter to learning to play the piano. Her family is on the leading edge of an expanding market. Hal Clarke Inc., a publishing and market research firm in Boulder, Colorado, estimates that home schoolers spend about $1,500 a year on books, software, videos, and other educational materials. "What is emerging is a more consumer-oriented home school family that wants more help, more conveniences, more books, and more software, and is willing to purchase what is needed," according to the *Education Industry Report*.

Critics of individualized learning—and home schooling—stress schools' role in developing social skills such as cooperation, collaboration, and communication. "One of the principal functions of school is to teach children how to behave in groups," writes NYU professor Neil Postman in the journal *Technos*. "School has never been about individualizing learning. It has always been about how to learn and how to behave as part of a community."

Such comments are misdirected: No one is arguing that technology be employed to the exclusion of human contact and personal warmth. Individualized learning hardly implies learning in isolation. Communications technologies and networks can enlarge one's set of possible associations and even allow for collaborative learning projects that cannot be replicated in the classroom. In a proper setting, they can help facilitate both individual *and* interpersonal skills.

And the "community" of the traditional school, like the community of the assembly line, is not necessarily something to be celebrated. It often includes bullying, contempt for learning, and rigid conformity. The tedium and monotony of institutionalized education is more than many—

perhaps, most—children can bear. As Tracy Kidder writes in *Among Schoolchildren*, "It is as if a secret committee, now lost to history, has made a study of children and, having figured out what the greatest number were least disposed to do, declared that all of them should do it." Kids enter school bursting with energy and enthusiasm. Such fires, however, are often extinguished by a regimen that offers no real outlet for them.

In fact, recent surveys reveal a staggering amount of apathy and ennui among adolescents. In his new book *Beyond the Classroom*, Temple University psychology professor Laurence Steinberg presents the results of a three-year longitudinal study involving 20,000 students in nine high schools in California and Wisconsin. He found that an enormous number of students are "disengaged"—that is, listless and jaded "toward education and its importance to their future success or personal development." Writes Steinberg, "between one-third and 40 percent of students say that when they are in class, they are neither trying very hard nor paying attention."

It's also worth noting that the number of children given Ritalin treatments in school for alleged cases of attention deficit disorder exceeds 1 million, a 250 percent increase since 1990. One wonders if ADD is not in some way built into traditional school models. While such developments cannot be blamed squarely on the schools, they are no doubt a big part of the problem.

Similarly, the case against learning technologies is weak, especially when all firsthand experience suggests that such technologies can stimulate interest and bring abstract concepts to life in a way that traditional pedagogical techniques cannot. Like critics of individualized learning, opponents of emerging technologies are locked into an either/or mindset. For instance, in *Silicon Snake Oil*, Clifford Stoll, an astronomy professor at the University of California at Berkeley, argues that today's technologies are a poor substitute for real experience. "Every hour that you're behind the keyboard is sixty minutes that you're not doing something else," he says.

Stoll's math is flawless, but his reasoning is off the mark. Current learning technologies certainly have significant limitations, but they also can provide an excellent alternative to classroom lectures and other school activities that fail to enliven young minds. They are powerful tools that can extend our range of experience and enhance our faculties of learning, just as new technologies enhance our work. Most important, one doesn't have to choose between, say, a multimedia software program about ancient forests and, as Stoll prefers, "a quiet meditation among thousand-year-old redwoods": One can do both.

Indeed, this sense of expansive opportunity is something that families involved in home schooling already understand. They are not merely trading in one set of limited options for another. Far from creating antisocial computer geeks, individualized learning has helped make children active, involved members of their communities.

Jeremy and Jonathan Rockett, for instance, both joined the International Thespian Society and have performed in plays under its auspices. They've also participated in sports leagues and tournaments put together by home school support organizations. Volunteer work—tutoring young children in Washington, D.C., and delivering books from the local library to homebound adults—has been an important part of the learning process too. While home school parents often are accused of sheltering their children from cultural diversity, Marilyn Rockett argues that her own family's experiences speak to the contrary. "It's life that's diverse," she says. "Not a closed classroom."

The Boones are similarly engaged in social and community activities. They too are active volunteers at their library. They are also involved in several informal learning groups. Curtis, Paul, and Cristie all participate in a sign language class and a creative writing club held in their home. Such gatherings bring together numerous children—and debunk the myth that one needs a conventional school to learn how to interact with others. "People don't question whether you can get a good education through home schooling," points out Jill Boone. "But they do raise questions about socialization." One thing the Boone children say they are often asked is, "How did you learn to stand in line?" It's a telling question.

The experience of such families underscores an important point: Families do have choices. Whether or not political efforts to encourage taxpayer-funded alternatives to government-run schools ultimately succeed, families already have the option of withdrawing from the educational system. (Many home schoolers oppose tax-funded schemes, which may entail greater regulation.) As leaving or supplementing traditional schooling becomes more attractive and less costly, the egalitarian ideology and assembly-line pedagogy that dictate one-size-fits-all education cannot remain unchanged.

. . . .

"Doing Something" in a Catholic School

Brother Bob Smith

This selection first appeared in *The American Enterprise* magazine's November/December 1995 edition. Brother Bob Smith is principal of Messmer High School in Milwaukee, Wisconsin.

I grew up in Chicago during the early 1960s, and my parents taught my sisters, brothers, and me to appreciate and respect all people. We learned to seek out the common things that make us neighbors, not to focus on minor differences like race, religion, or income. When I am asked why I choose to minister today in the place I do, I always refer back to an incident that happened early in my life.

I remember walking with my mother and another woman on Madison Street in Chicago one afternoon, and standing outside a large public high school. As we waited for the light to change, the school dismissal bell rang, and a door banged loudly open. Our attention was immediately grabbed by a young man as he ran from the school down the middle of the street. I was struck by the fact that he didn't look for oncoming cars. A mob of 100 or so other students seemed to nab the boy in mid-air. They threw him to the ground and then proceeded to "stomp" him with a vengeance. Many of the students literally walked on the young man, and footprints of blood followed people as they completed their senseless deed. As a young child watching the crazed frenzy of the mob and the defenseless boy, the only thought in my mind was "Why doesn't somebody do something?"

Then my mother and her friend pushed me against a building and told me to wait. As I stood watching, they shoved their way through the mob and dragged the boy to the curb. That act of courage by my mother and her friend left a permanent mark on my life. No one honored them for their actions, and some would call them "nuts" for what they did. But they saw an injustice and acted. The fact that the boy being stomped was white and my mother and her friend black did not make a difference. Those two women were Christians, and their Gospel values were being tested. Dante said in *The Inferno* that "the hottest places in hell were reserved for those who remained silent in times of moral crisis."

Three years ago, I decided, in the name of the Catholic school I serve as principal, to try to "do something" to help low-income students in inner-city Milwaukee. The public school system in Milwaukee is poor. The drop-out rate is over 50 percent, and the typical student who does graduate leaves with a D+ average.

When I first got involved, Milwaukee had an experimental voucher program that excluded religious schools. The State Department of Public Instruction fought against having any voucher system, and reluctantly began to administer it only after losing a court challenge it pursued all the way to the State Supreme Court. After the state administrators finally put together their vague list of conditions schools needed to meet in order to accept vouchers, we believed that we were eligible under the criteria. Although we are a Catholic school, over 50 percent of our students are non-Catholic. More than 65 percent live at or below the poverty level. Demographically, Messmer High School is quite similar to Milwaukee's public inner-city schools.

But that is where the comparison ends. The graduation rate at Messmer is 98 percent. Of that number, over 80 percent go on to college. We have virtually no problem with drugs or violent activity, and do not have students bringing weapons into our building.

We felt that our school environment could save a few voucher students from almost certain academic death in the public school system, so we applied, and to our surprise were told that we were eligible. Within a few days the Milwaukee papers got the news and printed a front-page story about the Catholic school becoming eligible for public funds. They invoked the specter of other religious schools enrolling in the program and threatening the public school status quo. What happened in the next year was truly unbelievable.

First, we received from the Wisconsin Department of Public Instruction a request for data stretching to three single-spaced pages. Then two teams of "investigators" descended on us. The state had not investigated any other school that applied to the program, but all of our classrooms, financial records, textbooks, trophy cases, and yearbooks were pored over for three full days. The bookcase in my office was examined when I went out to get coffee. In addition to mentioning in their report a picture of the Last Supper on my office wall, the state investigators counted the number of crucifixes in classrooms, listed any known Catholic donors who contributed to our school, and mentioned sports awards won in the 1960s in the Catholic Athletic Conference.

The bureaucrats did not, however, talk to any teachers, students, or parents about the quality of our educational program. They never noted that although the majority of our students are non-Catholic, the church provides large tuition subsidies to our school.

When our request for equal participation in the state voucher program was eventually denied, I went to Madison for an appeal hearing. It turned out to be frighteningly like a criminal trial. The state's legal counsel interrogated me for $7\frac{1}{2}$ hours! "What is the significance of different colored clerical shirts for your job, as seen in various yearbook pictures?" "Who writes the daily prayers read each day during morning announcements?" Most puzzlingly: "Doesn't the Pope ultimately control our school?"

I found the questioning sometimes amusing, often very sad. Our only intention was to help needy students who voluntarily selected our school to get a high-quality education. The voucher from the state would pay for barely half the cost of educating each student. The rest we were willing to make up ourselves.

As I've observed thousands of our youth either drop out or graduate from public schools with dysfunctional skills, I have felt in many ways like I did when I was a small child watching a man be trampled. I have asked myself again, "Why doesn't someone do something?" The difference here is that it is not a frenzied mob that is doing the damage but educated and well-paid adults working in the public sector.

My story does have a happy ending, though. Over the past two years a number of people have joined together to break the gridlock on educational freedom in Wisconsin. Governor Tommy Thompson, Bradley Foundation head Michael Joyce, Milwaukee Mayor John Norquist, and

State Representative Polly Williams have gotten passed through the state legislature the first school choice voucher program that places religious schools on equal footing with others. In late July, the governor came to Messmer High School to sign the bill.

Great forces will be marshaled in an attempt to derail this new law in the courts. But we have powers on our side too. In addition to some brave political leaders, we have the greatest authority of them all—God Almighty.

Index

About the Editors

WILLIAMSON M. EVERS is a research fellow at the Hoover Institution and a member of its Koret Task Force on K–12 Education. He is a specialist on curriculum, instruction, standards, testing, and accountability. Evers was an education policy adviser to George W. Bush during the 2000 campaign and served as a member of the education advisory committee for the transition. In 2001, President Bush appointed Evers to the White House Commission on Presidential Scholars, and U.S. Secretary of Education Rod Paige named Evers to the National Educational Research Policy and Priorities Board. He served on the California State Standards Commission (1996–98) and also serves as a member of the California state testing system's question-writing panels for history and mathematics and its grading-standards panel for history. Evers is a member of the policy board of the California History Project, which provides training to K–12 teachers of history. Evers has also served since 1997 on the board of directors of the East Palo Alto Charter School. He edited and was a contributor to *What's Gone Wrong in America's Classrooms* (Hoover Institution Press, 1998) and was a contributor to *A Primer on America's Schools* (Hoover Institution Press, 2001), edited by Terry M. Moe. Evers has also written articles on education policy that have appeared in such newspapers as the *New York Times*, *Los Angeles Times*, and *Education Week*.

LANCE T. IZUMI is a senior fellow in California Studies and director of the Center for School Reform at the Pacific Research Institute (PRI). He is the author of several major PRI studies, including *Facing the Classroom Challenge: Teacher Quality and Teacher Training in California's Schools of Education, California Index of Leading Education Indicators* (1997 and 2000 editions), and *Developing and Implementing Academic Standards*. He serves as a member of the California Postsecondary Education Commission and of the Professional Development Working Group of the California Legislature's Joint Committee to Develop a Master Plan for K–12 Education. His articles have been widely published, appearing in *Notre Dame Journal of Law, Ethics and Public Policy, Harvard Asian American Policy*

Review, *National Review*, *Wall Street Journal Europe*, *Sunday Times* (London), *Los Angeles Times*, *Investor's Business Daily*, *San Francisco Chronicle*, *Orange County Register*, *Sacramento Bee*, and many other outlets. Izumi is a regular contributor to the *Perspectives* opinion series on KQED-FM, the National Public Radio affiliate in San Francisco.

PAMELA A. RILEY speaks and writes frequently on school choice, charter schools, and other education reforms. She is the coauthor (with Lloyd Billingsley) of *Expanding the Charter Idea: A Template for Legislative and Policy Reform* and *Parents, Teachers and Principals Speak Out: A Survey of California's Charter Schools.* She has served as a consultant on charter schools to the California Department of Education and to the Charter Schools Institute of the State University of New York. She is chair of the board of directors of the Towers Preparatory School, an inner-city school chartered by the West Contra Costa Unified School District and scheduled to start in Richmond, California, in fall 2001. Riley founded and administers the San Francisco Independent Scholars program, a $2.4 million scholarship program for students who are attending independent and parochial high schools or pursuing independent or home study programs leading to a high school degree. She is a founding board member of the California Network of Educational Charters, a member of the national Charter School Friends Network, and a longtime member of the Association of Educators in Private Practice, an organization of for-profit and not-for-profit private sector education providers.